W9-CDL-568

This is
AUSTRALIA

Koala Books of Canada Ltd.
Importers & Distributors
14327 - 95A Avenue
Edmonton, Alta. T5N 0B6

This is
AUSTRALIA

Lansdowne Press
Sydney Auckland London New York

PUBLISHER'S NOTE

Australia settled comfortably into the good life in the quarter century following World War II. International political and ideological waves were, for the most part, mere ripples by the time they reached our shores; and the irony of the 'lucky country' tag was missed or ignored by a nation bent on pleasure.

But as the seventies began there were signs that Australia was stirring awake after its long and relatively undisturbed doze in the sun. A mood of challenge and change could be felt, and it seemed that the early years of the new decade were ushering in an exciting and significant period in the nation's history. The time was ripe for an honest, authoritative assessment of Australia — its heritage, its new values, its place in the world, its expectations.

That was the genesis of *This is Australia*. It is, we believe, a necessary book. With the onset of the eighties it became obvious that *This Is Australia* demanded, and indeed deserved, a major revision. The photographic content has been extended and updated. Yet we have retained many of Reg Morrison's original photographs which in the intervening years have become classics.

We do not always share the views of our contributors, nor do we expect that all Australians will agree with every view expressed; however, we do share the general mood of optimism.

Designed by Mark Newman

Published by Lansdowne Press
a division of RPLA Pty Ltd
176 South Creek Road, Dee Why West, NSW,
Australia 2099
First published 1975
2nd edition 1977
3rd edition 1978
2nd Impression 1979
4th edition 1982
© Copyright RPLA Pty Ltd 1975
Produced in Australia by the Publisher
Typeset in Australia by Savage and Co. Pty Ltd,
Brisbane
Printed in Hong Kong by Leefung-Asco Printers Ltd

National Library of Australia Cataloguing-in-Publication Data

This is Australia.

Rev. ed.
Previous ed.: Sydney: Summit, 1977.
Includes index.
ISBN 0 7018 1559 0.
1. Australia — Addresses, essays, lectures. I. Ruhen,
Olaf, 1911–.

994

All rights reserved. No part of this publication may be reproduced, stored in a retrieval system, or transmitted in any form, or by any means, electronic, mechanical, photocopying, recording, or otherwise, without the prior written permission of the publisher.

ACKNOWLEDGEMENTS

The publishers would also like to acknowledge the assistance of Dorothy Braxton, CSIRO, Canberra; Alan Foley Pty Ltd; George Higgs, Mining and Geological Museum, Sydney; the staff of the Photo Library, News Ltd; the Rural Department, ABC; Julie Vint, Taronga Park Zoo; and Sally White and Peter McLaughlin, *The Age*.

PHOTOGRAPHIC CREDITS

The publishers would like to gratefully acknowledge the photographic contribution of the following individuals and organisations: Bruce Adams, pages 20, 21; *The Age,* Melbourne 259, 262-3; Art Gallery of New South Wales 232-3; Australian Museum, Sydney 219; Australian Picture Library 44, 330-1, 347; Russell Bauer, Tasmanian Wilderness Society 223; BHP 74, 75 (above), 78, 102; Alan Birtles, *Herald Sun* 167; Bob Burton, Tasmanian Wilderness Society 223; Dr David Cohen 296, 302, 309, 311; Department of Education, Macquarie University 292-3; Trevern Dawes 133; Neil Duncan, *The Australian* 344; Rennie Ellis, Scoopix 342-3; John Fields 211; Ron Gordon 121, 122 (above), 123 (above); Roderick Hulsbergen 252 (below right); Ray Joyce 30, 103, 114 (below), 118; Vic Joyce, Exposure 116; Gary Lewis 213 (below); David Malin 268-9; Roger Marchant 205, 228, 241, 286; David McCarthy 129, 199; Don McMurdo 237, 248, 249 (below); Harry Miller, Taronga Park Zoo 219 (below left and right); Mining and Geological Museum, Sydney 104-105; Michael Morcombe 27, 38-9, 212 (above), 213; Mt Isa Mines 75 (below); Mark Newman 110 (below); News Ltd 20, 68, 73, 77, 85, 89, 100, 101, 109, 112, 152, 156, 159, 164, 170, 172, 173, 184, 186, 192, 206, 214, 234, 246, 247, 254, 255, 297, 299, 301, 313, 320, 325, 328, 337; Nimrod Theatre 249 (above); Bob Maccoll, A.I.S. (courtesy CSIRO) 265, 275 (above), 278, 279; PBL Marketing 339 (below left and right); Alan Power 224-5; Bill Russell *The Australian* 350; Ken Stepnell 121 (below), 122 (below), 125; Rick Stevens, *Sydney Morning Herald* 168; Richard Woldendorp 26, 97, 134, 137, 138-9.

CONTENTS

CONTRIBUTORS

Olaf Ruhen, a freelance writer, divides his interests between outback Australia and the South Pacific. Born in New Zealand in 1911, he started writing after early experience in outdoor occupations, particularly deep-sea fishing. After four years as an R.N.Z.A.F. pilot during World War II he moved to Australia, where he worked for eight years as a journalist with the Sydney *Daily Telegraph*, the Associated Newspapers organisation and the *Sydney Morning Herald* before turning to full-time freelancing and contributing to the *Saturday Evening Post*, the *Encyclopaedia Britannica* and publications of the National Geographic Society. His work, both fiction and non-fiction titles, has been published in the U.S.A., the U.K., Australia, New Zealand, Germany and Scandinavia and he reviews books for several periodicals, including *The Age*, Melbourne.

Peter Ellery has watched Australia's vigorous post-war economic development as a juvenile participant working after school and during school holidays on the family farm in Western Australia, and as an adult observer. As a cadet journalist he reported on agricultural matters during the period when Western Australians were turning bush into farmland at the rate of half a million hectares a year. He subsequently specialised in political reporting in Melbourne and Canberra, returning to Western Australia to report on the mineral boom, from the second half of the 1960s. He has also worked in the Sydney newspaper world and has been a contributor to leading overseas financial newspapers, including the *Financial Times* and the *Economist*, specialising in natural resource development and political/economic matters in Australia. He now works in public relations in the natural resource development field, working in Perth but travelling extensively throughout Australia.

Patrick Tennison's journalism has appeared in every major Australian newspaper and magazine, from *The Australian* to *Penthouse*, the Melbourne *Sun* to *The Bulletin* and *National Times*. He has also written for overseas newspapers, including Britain's *Daily Express* and *The Guardian* and the newsagency *Agence France Presse*. As a radio and TV producer and broadcaster he has conducted interview and comment programmes for the ABC, Radio Australia, and Voice of America, and broadcasting services in Britain, Ireland, Canada and New Zealand have commissioned his work. Since 1967 he has lectured in journalism to adult education classes and been involved in cadet journalist training programmes. His first book, *Meet the Gallery*, was published in 1968, followed in 1972 by the very successful study of 'suburban neurosis' among housewives, *The Marriage Wilderness*, and by *Defence Counsel*, 1975, *The Lucky Country Reborn*, 1976, and *Heyday or Doomsday? Australia 2000*, in 1977. He has also contributed sections to books about Australian industry, crime and sport.

Malcolm Mackerras, born in 1939, is currently a lecturer in government at the Royal Military College, Duntroon, but is better known as Australia's leading analyst of election results. He is a regular election commentator on television and radio and in the newspapers, and is noted for the publication of his 'electoral pendulum' which shows seats according to their vulnerability. In addition to his many academic and journalistic articles he has published five books, including *Australian General Elections* which reached the best-selling list before the 1972 federal election.

Rabbi Brasch, chief minister of Sydney's Temple Emanuel for thirty years (1949–79), has pioneered Reform Judaism in four countries. He has doctorates of Philosophy and Divinity. Life Vice-president of the Australian and New Zealand Union for Progressive Judaism, he served as a member of the governing body of the World Union for Progressive Judaism, he has been president of the Australian Jewish Library Association and guest professor in Hebrew at St Andrew's College at Sydney University and visiting professor at numerous American Universities and Colleges. In recognition of his services to the community, he was awarded both the Order of Australia and the O.B.E. After one year's assignment (in 1980) in the 'deep south' of the United States, Rabbi Brasch was appointed by the Governor of Alabama an Honorary Lieutenant-Colonel of the Militia. The foremost Jewish lecturer, broadcaster, telecaster and scriptwriter in Australia, Rabbi Brasch has written many best-selling books including: *The Star of David; The Judaic Heritage; The Unknown Sanctuary; How Did It Begin?; How Did Sports Begin?; How Did Sex Begin?; The Supernatural and You!* and *Australian Jews of Today*. He writes a regular column on 'Religion and Life' for the Sydney *Sun-Herald*, and for four years has had a weekly television programme. The Australian Association of the United Nations awarded him the Media Peace Prize for his literary and broadcasting work to promote good will.

Peter Cowan worked in various city and country jobs before taking an arts degree at the University of Western Australia. He became a teacher, and was senior tutor in the Department of English at the University of Western Australia. He has published five books of short stories: *Drift* (1944) *The Unploughed Land* (1959) *The Empty Street* (1965) *The Tins and other Stories* (1973) *Mobiles* (1979). His two published novels are *Summer* (1964) and *Seed* (1966). He has contributed to and edited a number of anthologies of short stories, and wrote a newspaper column on conservation. He has travelled abroad and in Australia, and is particularly interested in Asia. He is at present working on historical studies, having published three books concerned with biography and history in Western Australia.

Don Dunstan was born in Fiji and educated there at an establishment school and later at University College in Adelaide, South Australia. Always a rebel, he became a Socialist and member of the Labor Party at University. After practising Law in Fiji he returned to South Australia and was secretary of Actors Equity as well as a lawyer when at the age of 26 he was elected to the State Parliament. When Labor won office in 1965 he became Attorney General and Minister for Social Welfare and Aboriginal Affairs. On the retirement of the Premier, he was elected Premier in 1967 but his party was defeated in 1968. After two years as Leader of the Opposition, he led his party to victory in 1970, and was consistently re-elected Premier until ill-health forced his retirement from active politics in 1979. As Premier, he took responsibility for the arts and took South Australia to the highest per capita expenditure on the arts in Australia. He was, as Minister, responsible for the creation of the statutory companies in drama, dance and opera, the final form of the Festival Centre, and the creation of the South Australian Film Corporation.

Peter Pockley graduated from Melbourne University and gained his D.Phil. at Oxford. His early efforts as a 'communicator of science' were in teaching, and in writing a standard text on physical chemistry for British schools. He returned to Australia in 1964 and became the first scientist employed full-time by the local media to communicate science to the general public. He was the ABC's Director of Science Programmes for nine years, and the first satellite TV shows for Australia and the Apollo space broadcasts were among his major credits. While with the ABC he was elected to the Science and Industry Forum of the Australian Academy of Science. In 1973, Pockley became the University of N.S.W.'s first Adviser, Public Affairs. He has been Australian correspondent for the international journal *Nature* and was a member of the Film, Radio and TV Board of the Australian Council.

David Cohen is associate professor of education at Macquarie University in New South Wales. In 1980 he was Director of Studies in the New South Wales Department of Education. He has special interests in curriculum development, implementation and evaluation, alternative education and progressive schools, teacher education, science education and creativity. After obtaining degrees in science and in education from the University of Melbourne and his Ph.D. from Michigan State University, he taught for several years in Victorian schools and also lectured at the State Colleges of Victoria — Toorak and Hawthorn. He has also worked as consultant to several parent groups in establishing primary schools, and his international activities have taken him to the United States, the United Kingdom, France, New Zealand, the Philippines, Israel and Poland. His publications include several books and numerous articles on education and science education. Professor Cohen received the G. S. Browne Prize for Educational Practice (1962) and the Australian Industries Development Association's Science Education Award (1966).

Ian Moffitt is the author of *The U-Jack Society; An Experience of Being Australian* (which was acclaimed as one of the finest books ever written about Australia after it appeared in 1972) and *The Australian Outback*, in Time-Life Books' World's Wide Places series, based on a light plane journey into the Simpson Desert and Central Australia. He has also contributed to many books on Australia, and is now writing fiction. He worked as a newspaper reporter, sub-editor, feature writer and foreign correspondent for many years in Australia, Asia and the United States, where he spent three years as New York Editor for News Ltd of Australia to join *The Australian* newspaper and later *The Bulletin*. He left *The Bulletin* to write a novel based around the Chinese Civil War.

Jim Shepherd has worked as a feature sporting journalist and columnist for two Australian newspaper chains. In a life almost totally devoted to the observation and recording of sport he has written for more than 84 Australian and overseas newspapers and magazines, besides handling every imaginable commentary task as sporting director for the Sydney television channel, TEN-10, and for years before that for a Sydney radio station. He has written four books on Australian sport and established his own book and magazine publishing company.

Alan Renouf trained originally in the field of law. During World War II he served with the A.I.F., which he left in 1943 to join the Department of Foreign Affairs in Canberra. Except for three years, when he was a Legal Counsellor in the United Nations Secretariat, he remained an Australian diplomat until 1979 when he chose to retire.

Most of these 36 years as a diplomat were spent abroad — in London, New York, Cairo, Washington (three occasions), Paris (twice), Brussels, Lagos, Belgrade and Lisbon. Alan Renouf held eight appointments as head-of-mission. At the start of 1973, he was appointed Secretary of the Department of Foreign Affairs. His subsequent and final assignment was Ambassador to the United States.

Since retiring, Alan Renouf has been a Visiting Fellow at the University of Sydney and a commentator and lecturer on international relations. He has published two books — *The Frightened Country* in 1979 and *The Champagne Trail* in 1980.

Reg Morrison is one of Australia's foremost photographers. At the age of twelve, he was a keen amateur photographer and carried out his own developing and printing. He moved into serious professional photography in 1958, after spending four years as a journalist with West Australian Newspapers. Since then, he has worked with many different kinds of cameras and covered an impressive variety of assignments. He has won Australian and international awards, including the coveted International Nikon Photo Contest.

His major published works include *Australians Exposed* (a widely acclaimed photo-essay), *This Is Australia, Australia — The Greatest Island*, and most recently, *Australia — A Timeless Grandeur*, which portrays the unique beauty and diversity of this country's natural landscape.

THE LAND

Olaf Ruhen

'By the time a second generation grew...they had come to love the country...'

The First Fleet to Australia could well have been the most haphazard and ill-prepared expansionary move any major power ever launched. It seeded a growth that remained weakly for generations. The new arrivals failed to recognise the island continent's great riches and this failure set a pattern. Almost every form of wealth and power lay latent there, awaiting a discovery which, until the last two or three decades, came typically by chance.

Admittedly the First Fleet's task was difficult. The voyage took eight strength-sapping months and terminated in a land not known at all. As a comparison, the plantation of Virginia two centuries earlier brought settlers to a land where the fauna and flora were related to those of the homeland and their properties known, where the original inhabitants were expert in agriculture and the exploitation of metals and an export trade (for example in sassafras root at £1 a pound) was established before the Colony. That Colony had its difficulties but the link with England took little more than a month, settlement had been preceded by many explorations, and Richard Hakluyt had published lengthy histories of contact which cleared away much of such mystery as the land possessed.

The early settlers ... dreams and reality

For the First Fleeters in Australia nothing seemed to go right. They settled in one of the less fertile of the coastal regions. Their tools could barely cope with the harsh and heavy timbers that impeded clearance, or indeed with the virgin soils beneath. The original inhabitants had not the slightest intention of trading with them, or any desire for any possessions the newcomers could offer in trade or as incentive to employment. The forests and shores afforded little vegetable food, native animals were scarce and small and most of the people unarmed, and a Government restriction forbade the use of boats to harvest the sea's bountiful supplies of food. Half the available labour was wasted, being employed in guarding the other half, and their accomplishments were pitiful. In nearly six months, as Surgeon John White recorded, they had built only four huts for officers, these from cabbage-tree trunks.

'I have known twelve men engaged for five days in grubbing up one tree; and, when this has been effected the timber has been only fit for firewood.'

Left: **Simpson Desert. McDouall Stuart passed among these sandstone battlements in 1860.**

11

He found the Colony's prospects less than pleasing in view of the weak state of the people, the great labour of clearing the ground and the scarcity of tools, most of what they had being worn out by the hard timber or lost in the grass by convicts who otherwise had to wield them.

The worst failure of the expedition was the lack of a power source. Human muscle, most of it ill-nourished and under-developed, was the only force they could apply towards the construction of a whole new national economy. The few cattle they had landed could have assisted but careless supervision let them escape into the bush. Attempts to replace them by imports were hounded by ill-fortune: more than eight years passed before a bullock team was working efficiently. In the same year a mill was erected.

Adoption of such new methods dawdled, for the workforce was conditioned to the hoe and the handcart. But its members dreamed of a better life, a life of ease possibly to be found in some other district of the new land. The first exploration beyond the immediate environs of Sydney, undertaken ten years after settlement, was intended to demonstrate the falsity of such beliefs held very strongly at that time by convicts newly arrived from Ireland.

Above: **Dispossessed of their tribal hunting grounds, their water holes soiled by white man's stock, the Aborigines gravitated to the tiny slums of wood, wire and corrugated iron that grew up on the fringes of towns.**

Overleaf: **Towering above the shadowy dunes of the Simpson Desert, these two sandstone buttes catch the first rays of the rising sun. These hard-capped relics are typical remnants of an older plateau.**

But little enthusiasm backed the desultory probing of the wilderness for the first 20 years, after which the promise of the wool trade indicated a desirability of developing land beyond the very limited and slowly increasing hectarage necessary for the Colony's sustenance.

In this period the promise of the land lay all in grass, the source of all energy, the prime essential for progress. Grass provided the power for land transport, through horses and oxen. Even the ships could not be built without the animals to haul the timbers and the fuel, to draw water and activate mills. In grass lay the potential for overseas trade; the promise of grass in the unpopulated spaces supplied the enticement for the inhabitants the country needed.

Above: **Living alone on her denuded plot on the outskirts of Perth, in Western Australia, this old woman typifies the fierce independence of the pioneer landholders.**

Right: **Carranya station, at the edge of the Tanami Desert. Burgeoning technology has finally breached the old barriers of isolation, heat and aridity.**

While the first adventurous men went out, the stay-at-homes attempted to make the new land as much like the old as possible. Besides the plants they introduced for economic value, they stocked their gardens with hollyhocks and cosmos, their stable-yards with oak and elm and poplar, their boundaries with hedges of hawthorn and sloe, their creek banks with iris and willow. And by accident or design brought, too, a host of introduced weeds. Goats and pigs ran free about their cottages; treasured rabbits crouched in backyard hutches; hens, ducks and geese made the suburbs clamorous with familiar Old Country sounds.

Most of the officers who controlled the early settlement had shared West Indian experience, and perhaps because of this the houses were built to designs more suited to the climate than the English cottage; but all other standards were those of the Old Country. Householders sought to make little use of Australian flowers or vegetables.

The introductions permitted farmyards to approximate the homeland models but the results of husbandry were disappointing. When unremitting work had cleared the mainly useless trees in the settled area, the grey podzolic soils remaining proved of low fertility. Flood plains provided a few sites where a rich tilth gave a better return but on these Commissioner Bigge, reporting to England on more than 30 years of settlement, made a scathing comment, surely not altogether without foundation:

'In these tracts I observed some decent habitations that had been established by the emancipated convicts, but there were also a great many that were within reach of the inundations of the river, the owners of which persisted in exposing themselves and their property to its ravages that they might indolently reap the benefits of the fertility that is left behind. The tracts on the shore of the river Hawkesbury have thus afforded support to many of the most worthless and indolent

cultivators, and the produce has been diminished in quantity as well as quality by the successive cultivation of the same grain and by the admixture with it of rank weeds and wild vetches.'

For the independent Australian much more profit derived from trading, from shipping ventures, from timbers such as cedar, and from harvesting the rich produce of the virgin seas and their islands: sandalwood and sealskins for China, pearl and tortoiseshell for London and Paris and whale oil for the lamps of the world. On the land, development and establishment costs, in energy more than in cash, made pastoral enterprises much more rewarding than agricultural enterprises, in spite of high prices for locally consumed maize and vegetables of inferior quality. But the increase in flocks and herds made the exploitation of new land essential, and sent the explorers out.

The explorers

Following the lead of Blaxland, Lawson and Wentworth, Evans completed the conquest of the Blue Mountains in 1813, opening the fertile plains beyond, and within six months Governor Macquarie, who had greatly disturbed the general lethargy, ordered a road constructed, a task William Cox completed in another half year. Now the explorers concentrated on the development of the interior, discovering the westward-flowing rivers, the Lachlan and the Macquarie.

Oxley, having followed the Lachlan almost to its junction with the Murrumbidgee, went north the following year, cutting back to the coast at Port Macquarie and discovering country of excellent promise. John Howe made the first overland contact with Newcastle through difficult country, assisting to open the fertile Hunter Valley, previously approached only by sea.

John Kennedy, Hamilton Hume, Charles Throsby and others seeking land for cattle found it in the Southern Tablelands, and once cattle were established in these remoter areas, service ports were opened along the coast and exploration became automatic and unceasing. From about 1817, the outward movement from the Port Jackson centre, almost static for three decades, resembled the action of oil on crumpled cloth, filling the valleys and flats as the liquid fills the veined hollows of the fabric. The herds followed hard on the explorers' heels.

By 1826, the year before Cunningham climbed Mount Dumaresq and sighted the million and a quarter hectares of the rich Darling Downs, the Governor decided to establish 'limits of location', beyond which land was neither sold nor let. Soon these enclosed 19 counties, comprising about 90 000 square kilometres. Commissioners appointed in 1825 divided the land into counties and parishes but by 1830 their work devolved upon the Surveyor-General, Major Mitchell. The boundary of the limits followed the Manning River in the north, then the Mount Royal and Liverpool ranges to Wellington, linked Molong, Orange, Cowra and Yass and then turned eastward, approximately following the courses of the Murrumbidgee and Moruya rivers.

But planning ever lagged behind necessity, and something like a population explosion among domestic sheep and cattle was at this time forcing acceleration of the outward movement. Moreover, since publication of the Bigge report, free Englishmen were becoming more conscious of the possibilities latent in the Colony, and a vast world-wide improvement in shipping enabled them to put migration plans into action with greater ease. Not yet the ocean-going steamship, but the iron-hulled carrier with a more modern sail plan cheapened sea transport.

Right: **Owner of the Nullarbor property, Koonalda, Cyril Gurney is a survivor of the hardy breed of pastoralist who successfully pushed white settlement to the most desolate fringe areas of semi-desert.**

Opposite: **Australia's arid heartland exacted a heavy price in its early white intruders. The initials on this tree near Mataranka, N.S.W., on the eastern edge of the Simpson Desert, are those of one of the explorer Charles Sturt's party who died in 1845.**

Above and right: **Bullock drivers or 'bullockies' at rest. Teams of bullocks provided a means of heavy transport from the early days of Australia's settlement until the 1920s. They were particularly active in the timber industry, hauling logs out of the dense rainforest along the eastern seaboard. Australian folklore has been enriched by this special breed of men noted for their colourful vocabularies and bushcraft.**

People in dozens and scores poured across the artificial frontiers. In the Port Phillip district in the south, men like the Hentys, with ambitions as wide as the horizons they challenged, thrust inland from the coast. The better pastures of the south enticed Tasmanian adventurers. Still other explorers, eyes searching always for signs of good land (dominant tree types, matted grasses, a burgeoning wildlife) linked the settlements with their tracks.

There were always those who hoped that in addition to discovering good grass, and good land where descendants might establish a continuity of influence, they might discover a hidden Paradise. Theirs was a continuation of the vision that

dreamers had cherished long before the continent was discovered, the dream of discovering a culture that matched or transcended their own; the dream that persists today as the probes go out to other planets. Scientists as well as fiction writers postulate the existence of other communities as advanced as ours or more so; they have sent them messages and listened for their signals. As far as the written word goes back, the minds of men have detailed the beauty and the balm of the Hesperides, the Fortunate Isles, the Islands of the Blest. Plato's legend of Atlantis is so acceptable to the human mind that people have always believed it, in whole or in part.

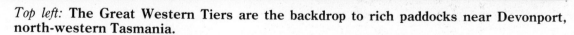

Top left: **The Great Western Tiers are the backdrop to rich paddocks near Devonport, north-western Tasmania.**

Above: **Evening idyll near Bermagui on the south coast of N.S.W.**

Right: **A poetic landscape near Wagga Wagga, in the Western Slopes region of N.S.W. along the Murrumbidgee River.**

Nearly half a century after the movement of population began, Ernest Favenc, explorer and writer, discovered fine country in Queensland below the Gulf of Carpentaria and on over the Barkly Tableland to Darwin; but all the time he entertained an unlikely hope that he might encounter a nucleus of civilisation or the traces of a vanished one. In an appendix to a novel he wrote on the subject, he canvassed the idea publicly:

'The absence of ruins of any sort can easily be accounted for by the fact that they built their houses of mud which, after being abandoned to the mercy of successive tropical wet seasons, would soon disappear.'

It was proving much more difficult to see that the empty land contained all the

elements necessary to build a highly developed society of the future. Australians in this era fell into categories; the most of them perhaps, as elsewhere and always, into that which comprised all those who sought a subsistence or at most a competence from their surroundings as they found them. At the other end of the scale were the dreamers, alert to seize upon such opportunities as offered. They were greatly outnumbered: at least 20 years before the announced discoveries of gold indicated a real road to fortune and brought migrants in their thousands, individuals had made occasional discoveries of the metal and kept their finds as curios.

Mitchell was one of the dreamers who looked into the future. Not only did he envisage a river 'its course analogous to that of the Amazon's' and giving entry

Left: **A stark beauty rises out of the desolation. Decades of overstocking conspired with the uncertain rains of central and north-western Australia to reduce many areas of former savannah to semi-desert.**

Above: **Byron Nathan was born in 1885 to a young lubra and an English adventurer. Working cattle until he was 68, he then became his own boss with a small pastoral property near Boulia which he worked for almost 20 years.**

and communication to the interior, but he hoped to be the one to find it and was impatient to put behind him the boundary of settlement, which then extended 500 kilometres from Sydney.

'I felt the ardour of my early youth when I first sought distinction in the crowded camp and battlefield revive as I gave loose to my reflections... It seemed that even war and victory, with all their glory, were far less alluring than the pursuit of researches such as these; the objects of which were to spread the light of civilisation over a portion of the globe yet unknown, though rich, perhaps, in the luxuriance of uncultivated nature and where science might accomplish new and unthought-of discoveries; while intelligent man would find a region teeming with useful vegetation, abounding with rivers, hill and vallies, and waiting only for his enterprising spirit and improving hand.'

When supplies failed to reach him, Mitchell had to abandon this probe which opened up new country towards what became the Queensland border. The extraordinary pressure of survey work postponed for four years resumption of the exploration work he loved. On the second of two expeditions to the south-west he discovered rich grasslands he named 'Australia Felix' and encountered the Henty family ensconced in a growing establishment on the coast, ready to move inland.

Britain now moved to approve settlements in South Australia, Western Australia and New Zealand, having shown little interest in the Australian area for 60 years, apart from settling Tasmania. But encouragement for the individual was scant. Even while Mitchell was at the Henty household, an Act of Council in New South Wales attempted to curb the squatting boom by issuing annual licences at a cost of £10 each. The system discouraged any sound development of new holdings, for

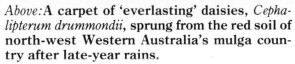

Above: A carpet of 'everlasting' daisies, *Cephalipterum drummondii*, sprung from the red soil of north-west Western Australia's mulga country after late-year rains.

Top right: Everlastings near Lake Moore, Western Australia.

Right: Coreopsis lanceolata, a naturalised exotic, butters railway and road verges in western New South Wales at springtime.

Left: A climate of harsh extremes demands evolutionary specialisation. These baobab or bottle trees, native to the drought-prone northern areas of Australia, are so named for their ability to store water in their trunks.

licences had no guarantee of tenure. So settlers erected flimsy buildings, usually no more than a framework clad with bark. Their fences were non-existent and no surveys established exact location had fencing been possible. But the boom in the wool industry ensured large profits.

Intrusions on native hunting grounds led inevitably to hostilities in which the natives had no chance at all. Their easy conquest by small parties of white settlers demonstrated that they would not cause a permanent or difficult problem; authorities thereafter displayed no interest in securing any rights for tribal occupiers. But the small annoyances and complaints arising from the spearing of sheep did lead to the establishment of a Border Patrol of the Police Force and in 1839 to the levy of a tax on cattle pastured beyond the boundaries. While settlement on Crown Lands could be discouraged or controlled, there was no way in which the Government could stop the pasturing of stock in those unfenced wilds.

In Tasmania a highway, which from 1818 linked the northern and southern settlements, encouraged the spread of land exploitation. Land grants and access to cheap convict labour gave additional impetus, and once the wool export began in the same year — 1818 — a rural prosperity emerged. Wheat for New South Wales and cattle

Joe Talbot, one time proprietor of the hotel in Hammond, S.A., takes his evening stroll through the crumbling hamlet. Situated in what used to be a thriving pastoral area at the southern end of the Flinders Ranges, Hammond finally died in 1972 when the old hotel was refused a renewal licence after 95 years of trading.

for Mauritius swelled the exports, and by 1825, when the Colony of Van Diemen's Land was separated from New South Wales, prosperous farmers were building substantial homes in the English style.

The excitement of establishing a splinter settlement at Port Phillip in 1836 created another Tasmanian boom. During the previous year most of the best land south of Bass Strait had been claimed. Indeed when Governor Arthur in 1831 abolished free grants in favour of an auction system, the land remaining was not of that potential liable to raise excitement. Yet not much of the alienated land had been cultivated. Most of the best tracts, in the broad valley which lay between Hobart and Launceston, were held by a few individuals who saw their best returns in the breeding and marketing of stock.

On the mainland so far the explorers had been barely ahead of the settlers, and sometimes behind them. In 1839 Angus McMillan struck south from Goulburn to find new pastures in what is now Victoria. From a station on the Tambo River, which the Omeo Highway largely follows today, he established a route to Corner Inlet, after repeated attempts on the heavily timbered country. This gave a Victorian outlet to the pasture production of the Monaro. He named many Victorian features, including the Mitchell River which runs into the Tambo.

In both Western Australia and South Australia a confusion over land tenure arose for a variety of reasons, one being that land contracted for or bought in Great Britain was not surveyed. When bankruptcy of the State ended the period of systematic colonisation in South Australia in the early forties, it was put on the same footing as the other Australian colonies. Western Australia made such little progress, from an apparent lack of labour, that in the mid-century settlers petitioned the British Government to make it a convict settlement.

In 1842, under the pressure of migrations from the southern States, a ban on free settlers in the Moreton Bay district was removed. Settlement spread north, south and west.

Self–reliance

Life for pioneers was harsh, but not unduly so. Typically masters of improvisation, they lived in huts wrested from the materials at hand. A sturdy framework of poles, pegged and morticed, carried a cladding of bark or slab walls; the large bark sheets stripped readily from river gums and a few other eucalypt varieties represented almost the only labour-saving innovation Australia had to offer. A more permanent building had walls of timber, split and slabbed rather than pitsawn; the stubborn hardwoods were most easily handled thus. The workmanship which raised the buildings was excellent; at least it proved so in those which are still preserved today, and they are not truly rare, with only the roofs several times renewed.

These were primarily of bark, fastened down by small logs slung over the ridge, or thatched with rushes when these were available, or sometimes with the more unsatisfactory mountain grasses. Floors were the natural earth, fireplaces stone or timber plastered with clay. In warmer districts fireplaces were set outside. Where settlers feared native attacks, holes in the wall that served as windows could be closed with heavy shutters. Fear was more prevalent than was justified, yet the earliest of the pioneers, those furthest out, were an intrepid lot.

Peter Cunningham in 1827 listed the normal ration for convict farm workers and one cannot imagine that the free-ranging settler fared much better: 'Their usual allowance: a peck of wheat [two gallons or six kilograms], seven pounds of beef or four and a half of pork; two ounces of tea; two ounces of tobacco; and a pound of sugar — weekly, the majority of settlers permitting them to raise vegetables in little gardens allotted to their use, or supplying them occasionally from their own gardens'. Not many natural products of the land supplemented such fare, and orchards and vegetable gardens took time to establish.

Rachel Henning, writing from the Rockhampton district of Queensland in 1864 described the weekly rations as eight pounds of flour, two pounds of sugar, a quarter pound of tea and a nominal 16 pounds of beef, though actually this latter was unlimited. People could also pay for pickles, vinegar, currants, sardines and jam, items brought by wagon and ship from Sydney. The store also carried tapioca, rice and sago. Beef not used immediately after killing was salted down or smoked.

The Hennings, proprietors of a well-financed enterprise, established themselves in 'a long low building built of dark-coloured slabs of wood with a verandah in front and the doors and windows opening into it. It contains five rooms: the first is our bedroom, the next the store and the next the parlour. At the back of ours is Biddulph's and Mr Hedgeland's room and at the back of the parlour is another bedroom wherein reside any other members of the "staff" who happen to be at home — more than half are always at the outstations. The kitchen is next-door to the house and behind are the men's huts, sheds and gunyahs, etc.

'The house stands on a low hill at the foot of which runs the creek which supplies us with water, and a very pretty creek it is, with deep banks covered with trees and shrubs. We have a piece of ground fenced and dug for a garden at the foot of the hill, but at present it only contains some pines and pumpkins, and some petunia cuttings...'

She described the verandah chairs: two straight poles held together by cross-pieces and leant against the wall. A strip of strong canvas of the sort then used for wool-bagging formed the seat and back. 'The most comfortable kind of easy chair I know,' endorsed Miss Henning.

Australians do not share the passion of Americans for saving samples of pioneer furnishings. Seldom did the weather keep pioneers housebound to work at their crafts. Such items as they contrived were frequently thought too rough for future generations to treasure; the white ant and the timber borer usually assisted in the decision to discard. In the gunyahs the furniture was often stabilised by being tamped into holes in the dirt floor.

For the men on outstations, amenities generally were fewer. Normally they waited until relief: the weekly rations carried out to them on horseback. They were remote from any company except the stock they guarded and the birds and animals of the wild. Natives constituted their chief enemy in some areas at least, but even without these their lives were constantly at hazard. A broken leg sustained some days before the rations were due could mean death. Even a toothache could be afforded no relief.

Small wonder that on the first day of temporary freedom most of them turned

European furniture proved highly unsuitable for the tropical and sub-tropical climatic conditions which prevailed in many parts of Australia. Early settlers displayed considerable ingenuity in constructing lightweight, comfortable furniture such as this squatter's chair.

Above: **Heavy with winter wool, a flock of Merino sheep heads for the shearing sheds in the picturesque hills west of Gundagai.**

Left: **Shearing on Koonalda station, Nullarbor, W.A. Strong-backed shearers bend over sheep — a board-boy or shed hand sweeps away the dags while the shearer in the background cleans his comb.**

to the bush shanty and its colonial rum. When company was available conversation and group singing provided the chief amusements; books were rare, though the illiterates numbered less by comparison than in English communities.

The lonely life unhinged the minds of many shepherds so that people called them 'hatters', and for nearly a century the class was recognisable. Edward S. Sorenson, in his *Life in the Australian Backwoods,* described one Jack the Rager:

'Only the flies by day and the mosquitoes by night disturb the peace, only the cries of the birds and the rustling of leaves break the quietude. To the hatter by temperament this is an ideal state of existence, and a man who loves to talk, but likes to do all the talking himself is suited by a dog listener as well as any...

'It was election time and Jack was putting up for No Man's Land. Standing beside a gidgee-stump on which stood a quart-pot of water and a pannikin, he orated with

great *empressement*, punctuating with hand-clapping and "hear hears", interjecting and making sarcactic remarks and wheeling this way and that in reply thereto. Now and again he would point his thumb at the wilga-bush on his left and tell the mulga-tree on his right that a gentleman wanted to know what he was going to do about his deceased wife's sister . . . He had closed a successful meeting when he was suddenly semi-paralysed by hearing a real clap and a real "hear hear" in the darkness beyond. It was the boss.

'Sometimes, as cranks of the bush often do, he amused himself for hours at a time trying to match the spiral columns on the lids and bottoms of [cylindrical]

DAME MARY DURACK — pioneering Western Australian

For many Australians, particularly those who live in the western third, the person of Dame Mary Durack Miller incarnates the otherwise intangible gifts of the best of the pioneers, the men and women who transmuted dreams and visions to a robust reality, fortified by their love of Australia and their faith in its future. Her best-loved book, the classic *Kings in Grass Castles*, tells the story of her family's two and a half year trek across the continent, and the part it played in the development of the Kimberleys.

Her husband, the pioneer airman Horrie Miller, established an airline that countered problems of lonely distance for the Outback families. Her daughter, Robin Miller Dicks, a pilot like her father, an author like her mother, in a life far too short worked unselfishly for the Flying Doctor Service. The dark people knew her as 'the Sugarbird Lady' after her tremendous fight against the spread of polio in the Outback by her widespread distribution of Sabin vaccine disguised in sugar lumps.

Dame Mary herself, at first working with her sister Elizabeth, established well-springs of understanding in lifelong efforts to assist the Aboriginal people. She has always devoted some of her singular strength to the benefit of the Catholic Church and to the vigorous creative community in Western Australia. In short she has given her whole life in tribute to her land. She writes, in an account she has titled 'A State of Surprise':

'What can be told in a few paragraphs of the sprawling State which holds my heart and is my home? To begin with it might be said that she has kept her white inhabitants in a state of surprise from the time of their arrival to the present day.

'Looking back a century and a half we find the new arrivals confronted with the disconcerting discovery of their unique isolation. The sheer size of the colony — one third of the Australian continent, half as big as Europe — was then seen not as an asset but as a major impediment.

'Expansion was slow from the temperate south to the arid 'marginal' regions and slower still to the sub-tropical north, while most of the interior extending to the eastern boundary was habitable only to the tribal Aborigines.

'The pioneers, originally so proud of their free settlement, were soon clamouring for convict labour. Eighteen years of transportation helped the staggering colony to its feet and it struggled hopefully along until the 1890s when prospects were dramatically transformed by the discovery of gold on its desert fringes.

'The more recent discovery of other minerals including iron ore, bauxite/alumina, tantalum, uranium and silver lead zinc, as well as natural gas on the North-West Shelf and diamonds in the Kimberley district have launched the State on a new and exciting era of development.

'The city of Perth which has claimed some 896 500 of Western Australia's 1 262 900 inhabitants, presents an increasingly impressive skyline. Its borders, however, are still in a sense as wide as the State itself for the people's interests remain closely tied to the land, the seasons and the primary markets.

'By and large Westerners are as materialistic as the average Australian and every bit as hedonistic. "The land of sin, sand, sorrow and sore eyes", as the colony was dubbed in bygone days, might be better described today as one of "sun, surf, sail, swimming pools and Swan Lager". Nonetheless, while naturally delighted at the upgrading of their State from the 'Cinderella' of the Commonwealth, her people tend to look askance at brashly money-based values. They are increasingly wary of the threats posed by unrestricted "progress" to their priceless heritage of unique plant and animal life and are well aware of the advantages they enjoy in inhabiting one of the last frontiers of peaceful existence in a troubled world.

'For myself, I feel at home anywhere within the boundaries of this still surprisingly easygoing State, from towering forests of the south to the vast plains and rugged ranges of the north. I am happy also that I feel at home with her inhabitants — be they descendants of early colonists from the British Isles, comparative new-comers from many other parts of the world or the original people of the land who claimed my affection in the first impressionable years of my life.'

Left: Gelding (at Hidden Valley station, N.T.) is a common practice and improves the tractability of stock-horse teams.

Above: **Mick Hayes of Caltowie, in South Australia, was for 60 years a drover in the northern reaches of the State.**

Right: **This early watercolour depicts with some warmth the domestic side of life at the gold diggings, Forest Creek.**

wax-match boxes, by playing peg-knife and other silly games. If you came quietly on his camp at night it was not unusual to hear a heated discussion going on between him and the fat-lamp. As he tersely put it when surprised, "Just a little argyment between me and Slushy". Sometimes they had a row and an imaginary fight and Slushy was kicked out of the tent. At other times he sulked as a result of the pig-headedness of the other fellow and wouldn't speak to the fat-lamp for a week. He would even "see him further" before he would light him.'

Hope, more than anything else, led the colonists into the wilderness where there seemed a very good prospect indeed for even the penniless to establish a family fortune. Hope faded in the early forties when trade languished in the Mother Country, still so called, and the expanding production of Australian pastures met with little buyer interest.

Then Henry O'Brien of Yass recommended the export of beef tallow and this proved a resounding success. Almost immediately the wool market improved. In

April 1845 the *Sydney Morning Herald* proclaimed that 'sheep-farming, which two years ago was pronounced on all hands a losing concern, is now the most profitable investment in the country. What with the high character of our tallow and the remunerative price of our fleece, our pastoral interest — the ruling interest in Australia — was never in a more auspicious position than at the present moment'.

In his *Sydney in 1848* Joseph Fowles reported 'our denizens of the pasture-plains boiling down into tallow sufficient meat, per annum, to feed nearly half a million of persons because we have not mouths to eat it; and our denizens of the city luxuriating in all the delicacies which the well-appointed hotels and restaurants of Sydney provide on the most princely scale'.

The spectacular gold discoveries of the fifties not only changed the face of settled Australia but increased the cultural differences developing between her and the Old Country. In part, at least, this followed an intensification of the American influence, implanted in the first instance by the whaling fleets. American captains keen to survey new oceans had reached Australia with the Second Fleet and were to outnumber the British vessels. The population increase organised by the golden magnet was drawn from the whole wide world; those who came with practical experience, not only of gold recovery but also of the subsidiary trades it engendered, came from California or by way of that State. They brought with them a New World methodology in land clearance, stock handling, business management and the like, and though American problems differed somewhat from the Australian, they were much more closely related than those of Great Britain. Those who numbered their stock in thousands and their employees on the fingers of one hand could not be expected to attend the birth of each lamb in the hurdled pen, or remove the fleece by the ancient British methods.

The goldfields gave enormous impetus to transport, because of the great fluid population planted at seeming random, usually remote from any supplies. The independent bullock-driver became one of the more solid citizens, typically in business for himself or, if not, paid at a rate considerably higher than that earned by more settled labourers. The roads followed their tracks, and the efficiency of the cattle in getting their loads over ditches, rock shelves, marsh and running water was such that for a long time little attention was paid to road improvement.

On the more heavily travelled routes the governments of the various States erected railroads, to which the teams acted as feeders. The fear of Victoria and New South Wales, that a river trade might rob their city merchants of commodity handling by channeling produce to South Australia by way of the Murray, Murrumbidgee and Darling, speeded rail construction. With competitive rates they diverted nearly all to Sydney and Melbourne, a centralisation process that can be judged now as having progressed too far, particularly when, in the next century, union troubles and government policies induced a decadence in the smaller ports.

But in the Victorian age an established transport helped the inland towns and the richer land-owners. Some of the larger homesteads were small villages. Though the housing of stock was not necessary in the Australian climate, large woolsheds were, with ample accommodation for the transient as well as the regularly employed workers.

By the time a second generation occupied the holdings the cultural break with the Old Countries was beginning to show. The settlers had come to love the country

TOM HARE — Outback administrator

As the decade of the seventies closed, Tom Hare, OBE retired as executive officer of the Northern Territory Reserves Board, a position which had fitted him admirably because of his concern for the country and its wildlife, and his appreciation of its beauty. The scene he left differed greatly from that on which he entered. He writes:

'The vastly improved communications have made administration much easier: telex, vocadex, computers and mini-jets have simplified the problems of vast distances and remoteness. At the opening of the CSIRO Wildlife Laboratory in Darwin in July 1972 the Division Chief Harry Frith said, "People tend to regard the Northern Territory and the Kimberleys as the Great Outback. I suggest there is no longer a Great Outback — improved communications have seen to that." The day of the Outback administrator has passed. But improved communications have endangered the wildlife which depended on inaccessibility for protection, so maybe solving one problem has created others.'

Hare first saw the parched and dusty township that was Alice Springs as one of 29 signallers sent to man stations in Darwin and Ambon in December 1941, on Japan's entry into the war. He was to endure arduous conditions there, but after he had lost a quarter of his trim body weight he was posted to a teleprinter station in Alice Springs for six months. In 1949, after three years in the New South Wales Public Service he returned to make his life there.

'I'm really no city person and the Public Service seemed dull. I wouldn't see anything but routine advancement and I never had the feeling of doing anything really important.

'I'd served under the late Colonel Lionel Rose when he'd been District Veterinary Officer in Cootamundra, so when he came to me in Sydney and told me he was going to start an Animal Industry branch in the Northern Territory, that it would be the first organisation of its kind and that he wanted me to take the senior administrative job with him, I thought the prospects exciting. I'd be able to do something for the pastoral industry.

'In 14 very happy and useful years these prospects were realised. Colonel Rose was almost a double of Field Marshal Montgomery in appearance, quick-witted, even-tempered, and never suffered fools gladly; unnecessarily rude at times, but an excellent administrator and a veteran of two wars. He worked hard and played hard; he built up a great organisation.

'The difficulties of the pastoral industry when he came included the lines of communication; cattle were walked out, often over 50 to 60 kilometre dry stages. He set about with a great deal of vigour to reduce the distance between watering points to 24 kilometres and doubled stock route bores from 70 to 140 or 150; then when truck transport came in, built trucking yards. In the early sixties I accepted the position with the Reserves Board.

'Alice Springs has changed tremendously from a population of 1 500 when I went there to something more than 15 000 today. Now it's a very modern town and has lost a lot of its atmosphere. Once we knew everyone, and parties were on at the drop of a hat.

'The outstanding developments have been in the transport and tourist trades, and these are interlinked. The standard gauge railway from the south was completed in October 1980. People were slow to realise its effect: 19 hours from Adelaide to Alice year round, drive your car on to a flat-top and travel in comfort. Fast cattle transport. The road-rail transfer at Alice promotes the transport service trades and tourist requirements have given building a boost. Alice Springs used to be a cattle town with a bit of mining. Mining has fallen to nothing and the cattle industry has reached a peak, for there's a limit to the herds you can run under open range conditions.

'The growth of tourism affects the Reserves Board vitally. People are there before the Board is ready for them. Ayers Rock is a classic example of more people than you can handle with the facilities available. It also has problems associated with Aboriginal mythology; it's one of the places best known to overseas tourists and tourist organisations have promoted it vigorously.

'Let's look at development. While problems associated with Aboriginal equity are associated with the Mereenie gas field west of Alice Springs, that should have an effect, especially if by some chance it is kept in the Territory for the industries associated with mining in the north.

and its indigenous products, and no longer planted their gardens with importations. But typically, they still did not understand this tender land. They were inclined to mine its productivity rather than nourish the source of that wealth. When drought brought a scarcity of grass they slashed the scrub so as to bring its leaves within reach of their animals' browsing. To keep life in their breeding-stock they brought the vegetation to the point of hazard. After fences lined their boundaries, their overstocking impoverished a soil that frequently had little stability.

Such effects were not immediately apparent. The first big paddocks might enclose 250 square kilometres or more and the stock concentrated near the waterholes.

'I believe the *Aboriginals' (N.T.) Land Rights Bill* is a disaster, particularly for the Aborigines. The late Prof. T. G. H. Strehlow, acknowledged as Australia's leading authority on Centralian Aborigines, claimed to have positive proof that land would not necessarily go back to traditional owners, and I agree. Anyway, it's separatist legislation — why single out the Northern Territory? I would describe the legislation as a federal government attempt to salve the national conscience at the expense of the people of the Northern Territory, both black and white.

'People tend to overlook the birthrate; primitive people couldn't support large families, but now the Pitjantjatjara people west of Ayers Rock and on the Docker River have families of six or eight, and they're typical. So the problem is escalating. Employment opportunities are not there even if they wanted to work. I'm not being critical. It seems to me they might have the right idea. They lived and live for today and we live for tomorrow.

'The same problem of displaced people must have been faced elsewhere, and probably even solved. But it was one of the reasons that sent me to live elsewhere on my retirement. In addition my work was finished — time to give someone else a go. And the long hot summers begin to tell; evaporative coolers don't totally overcome them. I was not sure that I wanted my girls to grow up in the atmosphere of aggressiveness which quite possibly will erupt in physical violence, and I think they will be better being brought up here in South Australia where the Teutonic work ethic still predominates.

'Because of the large uninhabited areas of the Territory people tend to think we don't have much need for conservation even in this fragile country where the desert areas are very sensitive to the impact of people. This is shown by pastoral leases being granted in very marginal country which stretches out into the Simpson Desert. Eventually all this will do is bring the desert areas closer and closer. I know one property of which the owners were on drought relief the second or third year it was occupied. This indicates a lack of appreciation for conservation not only by people here but by higher authority.

'In the Top End, which is better able to withstand the onslaught of people, you have the same lack of appreciation. The classic example is the Kakadu National Park. We asked for it from 1955, then it was alienated for pastoral purposes. When we almost got to the stage of getting the inferior country that was left uranium was discovered. Now the Park has been proclaimed. But though the Territory has self-government with responsibility for conservation, the Park is federal, administered from Canberra by an English professor.

'We didn't miss any of the so-called blessings of city life. People have said, "You must regret that you can't go to good entertainment, to symphony concerts, to art shows, things that enrich your cultural outlook". When I ask how often they've been in the past year they'll say, "Oh, I haven't been at all, but I just like to know I can go if I want to". So probably people from remote areas see more of these events than people who live among them, because when they go on leave they are hungry for them and seek them out.

'I'm more interested in natural culture. In the city any section of the community can hold others to ransom and this offends my sense of independence. The rights and wrongs of a situation don't come into it at all. You're subjected to blackmail day by day. I have my birds, and if I went to a city the conditions would not be good for them. I keep these beautiful Gouldian finches, among many others — and I want to be able to see them in large numbers in conditions as natural as I can contrive for them — for example with living trees in the aviaries where they can nest, and where they spend their lives.

'People in the Outback do look to the fleshpots more than they used to. You can't really call Alice the Outback. People there enjoy the things people enjoy in cities. But when you get a little bit away from that town you're on your own, and if you don't carry what you need to sustain you, you could be in trouble. People seem frightened of this, but when they are involved with it they enjoy it. I know that when people are bogged there two or three days on a bus tour something really unusual happens. This becomes the highlight of the tour for them, rather than what they paid for when they left home. Those who live here take it as something that can happen any time. It's a challenge.'

When rain provided surface water they fed out into the less-used growth at a distance, allowing the scrub and grass near the waterhole to regenerate. But when fences subdivided the area, heavier stocking saw each section eaten bare. Hot sun converted the exposed soil to dust; blistering winds carried it out over the horizons. Efficiency was seldom tempered with the wisdom of restraint.

More characteristic were the battlers, the people hoping to wrest a fortune from the soil but settling for a living. Typically they inhabited a remoter district and lived harder, their family and personal expenses cut to a minimum, their operating costs higher for each unit produced because of their distance from the transport streams and their dependence on primitive facilities and makeshift. Ruthless in their dealings with the land, they fired the bush to clear it and fired the grasses each

On the sands of the coastal fringe, as well as on the desert floors, wind and water create their ever shifting patterns. Australia's coastline has altered continuously during its long geological history and began to assume its final shape only about 25 million years ago. Wide, white sand beaches are a notable feature of the north-west coast of Western Australia and may sweep almost unbroken for up to a hundred kilometres and more.

Above: Extreme tidal fluctuations along the north-west coast leave their tortuous mark on the mud flats of bays and estuaries.

Opposite: A coastal lagoon in Western Australia, banked by sculpted dunes.

year for the sake of the succulent new shoots on which their animals thrived. And typically, after years of progress when good seasons favoured them until their confidence was high, a brace of drought years would destroy their equity.

When the ploughs went in to the low-rainfall areas nearer the continent's centre the topsoil blew away in dust clouds that harassed their existence and reddened sunsets across the Tasman in New Zealand.

The search for new land, good land, developed a new kind of person. The early pioneers, with short stages in front of them, moved with heavily laden wagons as, even at that time, the narrow-bodied conestogas moved across the American prairies. The later adventurers stripped down to essentials. In Australia they needed little or no protection; no wild beasts menaced either the people or their herds; the natives

Above: **Libanangu settlement, Wattie Creek, N.T., was established in 1965 by Gurindji pastoral workers who walked off a nearby station in protest against exploitation. In 1975 they finally won their right to the land.**

Overleaf: **Yarding the mob at sundown.**

were harmless in most districts and indeed could be enlisted as helpers. The men moved out with what they could carry on horseback; half a dozen men with half a hundred horses could move swiftly and lightly over the country.

Cattle running free in the enormous unfenced holdings were controlled because of the scarcity of surface water over much of the country. On the huge quondam sea-beds the sparse rainfall drained swiftly away through the limestone that had once been caved coral, and many kilometres separated the watercourses. Cattle usually grazed no more than eight kilometres or so from the waters, and therefore a few men could control six or seven thousand square kilometres. Right from the start the pastoralists learned to make use of the trained ability of Aborigines to read signs. For the black man's survival this skill was essential; the white man learned to turn it to economic advantage. If cattle had not drunk at a waterhole they were not, in normal seasons, in the hills beyond. Simple deductive ability enabled the mustering teams to scour in a few days holdings larger than many an English county.

A droving team of six men could and often did convoy in safety herds that would have required the attention of more than 30 American trail-herd hands, and take them over tougher country, the packhorses maintaining mobility in terrain that would stall American chuck-wagons, light and adaptable as they were. Over the whole of the Australian continent a man could travel in safety, his only hazard the snake, his only essential personal gear a blanket and groundsheet besides what he wore, though in seasons of rain the mobile team might stretch a tent-fly over a sapling.

A man who travelled with cattle rejected even such elemental furniture as a sleeping-bag — the constriction it imposed could be a fatal handicap in the event of cattle rushing. He made most of his gear himself, usually from rawhide, sometimes from tanned hides he bought. A man with pride might plait his own stockwhips, or plait a bridle from the superior, glossy kangaroo hide. Handiwork of this nature filled the otherwise unused evening hours: every good stockman could pad his own saddles, riding or pack, sew his own packbags and belt and saddle pouches, shoe his own horses and make their hobbles, or lay up a rawhide rope. For hobbles the ubiquitous rawhide was found to be unsuitable — horses with the cunning of Satan would soak them in surface water until the rawhide loosened, and they could work the hobbles off.

Nat Buchanan, who came to Australia as a six-year-old, joined the gold-rush to California in his early twenties and returned unsuccessful to find that mismanagement had lost him the station he owned with his brothers in the New England district. He became an overlander, moving stock and sleeping by his saddle, and then worked a station near Longreach in Queensland. Poor prices broke him and at the end of 1877 in search of new country he explored the Barkly Tableland between Rankine River near the Queensland border, and the Overland Telegraph line, more or less on the route of the main road north to Darwin today.

He thus opened up some of the very rich country of the north. He pioneered the Murranji track, with its seasonal dry stage of 180 kilometres which invariably took a toll of cattle lives and endangered men. The jeopardy in this 180 kilometres between waterholes is best measured against the 13 to 16 kilometres which grazing herds, unpressed, took a day to cover. Buchanan won stockman renown when he took Australia's largest travelling herd, reputed to be 20 000 cattle, from the south-west corner of Queensland to Glencoe and Daly River in the Northern Territory.

In 1883 the Durack family, having held outback stations on Thylungra Creek, took 8 000 cattle in four mobs right across the top of Australia to found a Western Australian dynasty. They lived two and a half years on the trek in the wilds.

The Jardine brothers, when their father was appointed Superintendent at Somerset, farthest north on the Australian mainland, went on the road with 42 horses and 250 cattle from Rockhampton. In his magistracy, Jardine Senior was expected to keep a supervisory eye on the troublesome sea traffic from a completely lawless New Guinea. Ten months on the track, the sons lost 30 horses and 50 cattle from plant poisoning and a number of the survivors weaved in crazed and agonised pain from eating the macrozamia cycad, which today is still a hazard on that route.

Such losses were not high compared with some in the waterless Centre. In 1901 a good drover, Jack Clarke, took 500 bullocks out of Queensland along the Birdsville Track for millionaire owner Kidman, and reached Marree in South Australia with 72 survivors.

Among the worst sort, independence of action fostered some crime. Probably the most famous episode was Harry Redford's theft of a thousand cattle from Bowen Downs in Queensland in 1870. He pioneered the stock route along the Thomson, Barcoo, and Strzelecki rivers by which he took them to South Australia. Unknown cattle duffers ten years later lifted a smaller mob from Queensland for sale in Adelaide. The owner, from Bullee Downs, tracked them and reached Adelaide just in time to claim the proceeds of their sale at auction, but the cattle had changed hands at least once, and the duffers had disappeared.

Roughriders, strongly reminiscent of their American counterparts, regularly gather throughout Australia for rodeo events — calf roping, bull riding, saddle and bareback bronc riding; injuries are worn like medals. The standard time for staying on the beast is eight seconds, although some have lasted as long as 90 minutes. One of the most popular rodeos in Australia is held annually at Mareeba, in northern Queensland.

Right: Laconic stockmen intently observe proceedings in the main ring at the Royal Easter Show, Sydney.

The foundations of not a few fortunes were laid in stolen cattle. The lifting of branded mobs had its dangers, but many a herd was augmented with musterings of cleanskins. And I knew one station owner in the Northern Territory whose proud boast it was that, though he owned 16 000 cattle he had never bought a beast.

Tough and amoral, callous of the rights of others, some of these men abused the Aborigines in remoter districts to a scarcely believeable degree.

In March 1919 the Reverend James Watson, ex-chairman of the Methodist Aborigines Mission in the Northern Territory, was reported by the Melbourne *Argus* as saying: 'If there be such a thing as conscience then there are white men in

Right: **George Kulka has worked for over 20 years in the cane fields around Mossman, on the north coast of Queensland.**

Opposite: **The dramatic burning of sugar cane near Cairns takes place once a year during winter, the dry season. In this way, snakes, insects and dry leaves are eliminated, making the cane easier to cut. Harvesting takes place within 48 hours — otherwise the cane loses its sugar content.**

Australia whose consciences must have the lash of scorpions. I have stood in a compound where the blacks have been driven, and men, women and children shot down. We speak of the atrocities of the Hun with horror but there are men with the same instincts in northern Australia. Scattered and raided with musketry by these devils, whole communities wiped out.'

The smaller holdings of the dairy farmers, the cane farmers, the orchardists, the vintners, the market gardeners hugged the towns and cities, their markets. The prospects of stock raising seemed unlimited until the great droughts of the last years of the century. After one slashing bad year in 1888 the weather ameliorated, but in the cities the boom was breaking and markets dropped, more because of manipulative excesses than any inherent weakness in the country. From 1895 the dry years began again, and in 1902 all the southern States experienced their worst year on record.

Overstocking, induced by holding stock against the poor markets of the early part of the decade, undoubtedly contributed. Thirst and weakness slashed the tally of Australian sheep by half. A compensation was the subsequent more careful husbandry which brought about a greater weight in fleece and meat for the average marketed animal thereafter.

But neither in the far Outback nor in the closer settlements did Australia have time to develop in significant proportions a yeomanry, an establishment over several generations of families wedded to familiar land. The short history of the rural development was itself unsettling. Not only did the development of ever larger herds on larger holdings tend to move the young country worker to new locations, but the large areas worked by skeleton staffs encouraged the formation of a large nomadic grouping of seasonal workers with no tradition of stability. Then three-quarters of a century of significant gold strikes, not only in Australia but also in California, New Zealand and several Pacific islands, but especially New Guinea, tended to promote a general restlessness. Not only gold, but other more or less temporary excitements supported this influence. The Australian, unlike the European, regarded the cutting of domiciliary ties as a normal precursor to a life in the country.

This became almost a tradition when, beginning with the Boer War, a series of overseas conflicts exerted powerful recruiting influences over young Australian men. The response was strong in the Outback, and Australians, used to living on horseback, relaxed for days in the saddle, established a reputation for cavalry dash and a kind of rebellious efficiency. In the Boer War and later in World War I their horsemanship ensured them a place in the spectacular front of major engagements.

BARNEY ROBERTS — poet, publisher and pig-farmer

Barney Roberts, poet, publisher and pig-farmer, seems to have become all of these things simply because of the love he has for Tasmania. His farm straddles gentle rolling country at Flowerdale, on the north-west corner, near Bass Strait, and here he revels in the Apple Island's unique beauty, travelling frequently on camping trips to favoured bush locations, or the Great Western Tiers, which provides the locale for his novel *The Penalty of Adam,* or the incomparable south-west. He is a man of the land, though he might well have returned to bank-clerking after the Second World War except for four years in which he was a prisoner of war in Austria. Here he spent most of the winters at forestry work, felling trees or snigging logs and carting them to the sawmill, and when he returned, attuned to the outdoor life, he settled to dairying on the property he holds today. The love that identifies him with his natural surroundings is based on a knowledge of his island's fauna and flora so detailed it is an entertainment of privilege to accompany him on a Tasmanian ramble. He writes:

'Tasmania, originally known as Van Diemen's Land, was founded in 1803 as a penal settlement and administered from New South Wales as a part of the British Colony.

'The original inhabitants of the island were distinct both physically and culturally from the Australian Aborigines. Their tribal lifestyle was simple and primitive. They lived in caves and rough bark shelters, inhabiting the coastal, or climatically more desirable areas and consequently came in contact and conflict with the white settlers who usurped their lands. It is a sad commentary of the times and something Tasmanians have to live with that their beautiful island was settled at the cost of a complete race of gentle people. Within 40 years the tribes had been dispersed and only a handful of broken, dispirited wrecks remained, at first incarcerated on Flinders Island and later at Hobart Town to wait for death, and with Truganini's, the total elimination of the full-blooded Tasmanian Aborigines.

'Contrary to popular belief, Captain James Kelly, in his narrative describing his journey around Tasmania in 1815, several times remarks on the physique of the Aborigines as tall and well-formed. Once he was accosted by — "six huge men, black natives, each of them above six feet high, and very stout made —". Another time he refers to — "an old man about six feet seven inches high —".

'Today only a few mutilated middens and some artifacts remain of an ancient and extinct race of people.

'One of the reasons England sent convicts to Tasmania at the beginning of the 19th century was the remoteness of the island. From nostalgia the first settlers grew hawthorn hedges, planted English trees in gardens and parks and climbing roses to adorn porches and verandahs. Blackberries and rabbits thrived in their new environment in a climate not dissimilar to that which prevailed in the land from where they came.

'For some time settlement was confined to the lower altitude, fertile areas in the east and north of the colony and along the banks of the Derwent and the Tamar rivers. Only the most intrepid explorers adventured into the hostile, rugged Central Highlands and the wild south-west.

禪師倉藏之墓

One of the most lucrative of the Outback industries, pearling was also by far the most dangerous. Cemeteries at Darwin, Thursday Island, and the main pearling centre, Broome, W.A., bear grim witness to the risks involved. Most of the divers who worked out of Broome in its heyday around the turn of the century were Japanese, as these gravestones attest.

'In those first few decades, apart from the Aborigines, the escaped convicts, known as bushrangers, posed a constant threat to the farmers and settlers who ventured into the more remote areas. After the Black War, the Governor directed the 'cleaning up' of bush rangers and gradually settlements and roads reached outwards, extending into areas of little or no use for agriculture to capitalise on the mineral and forest wealth and later for hydro-electric purposes; roads that were to allow tourists, fishermen, skiers, and bushwalkers to enter more and more of the island's isolated regions.

'Still today Tasmania remains remote from the civilised world; Hobart, the gateway to the Antarctic; the western coast as ever in the path of the Roaring Forties; the Central Highlands in the winter months claiming still occasional lives of the unwary and those who would dare to underestimate the moods of the mountains.

'Yes, Tasmania remains remote. It contains one of the world's last wilderness areas; rainforests which include the tallest hardwood trees in the world (*Eucalyptus regnans* up to 100 metres tall), the unique Tasmanian 'Pines' (King Billy, Huon, Celery Top and Pencil Pines), impenetrable Bauera or Native Rose and the notorious Horizontal Scrub the trunks of which, in the deep rainforest gullies bend horizontally and shoot up a mass of new branches which in turn bend over, until a maze of twisted trunks remain, as forbidding as its name, *Anodopetalum biglandulosum*. They are low-altitude mountains — only a little over 5 000 feet (1 600m.) but nevertheless extraordinarily beautiful and affording some of the world's best mountain trails, scenery and rock-climbing; thousands of lakes on the Central Plateau — second only to Finland in number.

'But the charm of the island lies in the variety of its offerings. Regular summer rains, bountiful water supplies in rivers and creeks for irrigation, and rich volcanic soil have made Tasmania the garden State, ideal for dairying, orcharding and sheep, cattle, and vegetable growing; and the northern and eastern beaches attract thousands of tourists annually.

'From the sophistication of the casino and world-class hotels, from the peace and beauty of Devonport on the Mersey, Launceston on the Tamar and the capital city Hobart on the Derwent with Mount Wellington towering above the city's southern suburbs, to the weird uniqueness of the surrounding mountains of the mining town of Queenstown, to the wildest and toughest of wilderness areas, where only the fittest may go, Tasmania has something for everyone.

'One thing above all else which must be preserved for the nation, for the world, is Tasmania's wilderness. Few people seem to appreciate the world crisis that has developed as wilderness areas in all countries are being destroyed. Slowly but constantly Tasmania's wilderness is being eroded by the flooding of magnificent wild rivers, and mining and forestry interests, all of which allow easy access for vandals and incendiaries, and if not stopped will inevitably, slowly but certainly destroy the State's greatest, irreplaceable asset.

'In Tasmania today, because of its isolation, its remoteness, the traveller will find an honesty, a cleanness, a friendly, quiet welcome from its people.'

The twentieth century . . . change accelerates

Home again, their experience in and out of hostilities increased a rural dissatis-
faction with the lack of amenities in the Outback. In a parallel development they
brought a modernisation programme to the farms and stations. From World War
I many learned the use of machinery and on their return introduced it to their
work and adapted it. Even aircraft: in 1922 P. J. McGinness and W. Hudson Fysh
inaugurated the first civilian service in eastern Australia with the first flight of
Qantas. The feat stirred imagination with its spectacular solution to some of the
Outback's problems of isolation. The growth of such services and also the introduction of other machinery brought new skills to country centres, and so diversified the
population. At the same time the openings which they provided in the urban world
seduced many country youngsters to city opportunities — far more than in previous
generations.

Left: The tiny, lonely, moving speck of tractor and farmer patterns its way across the field at Crystal Brook, S.A., in preparation for the spring sowing.

Top: Tall, majestic poplars in the Matchwood Forest, near Echuca, Victoria. They are parti-cularly suited to flood-prone, fertile areas, and their roots can tolerate wet conditions.

Above: The dark chocolate earth of Table Cape once formed the neck of a volcano. Volcanic debris has weathered into some of the richest farming land in Australia.

Among the effects of the struggle for amelioration of country conditions came the birth of the Country Party. The fiscal protection which smoothed the way for urban workers was to some extent paid for by farmers: their product sold on world markets at open prices; their needs had to be procured at the high Australian price brought about by imposts on imports to protect the local manufacturers and their employed workers. The Labor Party introduced a federal land tax designed to break up the big estates, and that seemed another urban raid on the farmer. Accustomed to the paternalism that supplied most material wants and only minimum wages, some farm workers supported farmers in their opposition to less than moderately successful Labor attempts to increase farm wages.

So farmers' associations generally recognised the desirability of separate political representation. The first move had come in Western Australia in 1914 when a newly formed Country Party secured direct representation in the State Parliament and gave some effective voice to wheat-grower interests. At war's end other groups were established in Queensland, Victoria and New South Wales, and a federal organisation was formed which adopted a programme in 1919. Today its strength still lies in an independent trading ability whereby it gains concessions in payment for support, and it has not indulged in dreams of dominating government.

Some of these concessions may have seemed to threaten ideals of private ownership and control of land, which remain dominant. But the promise of better financial returns has wedded these to the establishment of a variety of government marketing boards and co-operatives, and government-strengthened rural credit.

Between the wars, a severe recession in the early twenties and the world's worst depression in the thirties smudged the economic picture, a process assisted materially over most of the continent by the hungry drought years of 1919 and 1927.

World War II, more than any other single event in history, instituted changes in the rhythm and tempo of country life. Perhaps the most spectacular was in the field of aviation. During the war the Empire Air Training Scheme trained 38 000 aircrew, 10 000 of them overseas. Some at least adapted the new techniques to their peacetime existence. Need for capitalisation slowed the introduction, but dozens, then hundreds of aircraft were employed in top-dressing, seeding, crop-spraying and vermin destruction. In 1956–57, the first year for which figures are available, the areas so treated totalled nearly half a million hectares. In the next decade this area increased more than tenfold. On hundreds of Outback stations pastoralists could inspect the condition of stock and pastures from small aircraft, and direct and supply mustering teams. The station aircraft also had a social function, carrying the pastoralist to country race meetings and other leisure functions, cutting down the time spent on travel.

Australia continued her involvement in overseas wars, particularly in Asia, and after the helicopter demonstrated its versatility in the Vietnam affair it rapidly became a necessity in peaceful operations back home.

These wars and the corresponding internal growth had utterly demolished the ringbark mentality that cleared a tree at a time. Huge areas scheduled for improvement were brought to agricultural readiness in swift, efficient operations made possible by heavy machinery. Among the earliest of these operations was the clearance in Central Queensland of the acacia known as brigalow, with its attendant imported pest, the prickly pear. Where these operations pursued their natural development and were transmuted into the clear-felling of forests for the woodchip industry and the total clearance of large coastal areas in the process of sandmining for rutile and other elements, a brushfire of public consternation arose in protest, difficult not to justify, at least in part.

Left: **Morning tea for a cane field labourer near Innisfail, northern Queensland.**

Overleaf: **The Family Hotel at Tibooburra, a remote and desolate corner of north-western New South Wales, is a unique kind of pub; it boasts work by two of Australia's most famous** painters. Patrons, like station manager Jack Williams, may take their choice of this mural by Clifton Pugh in the front bar, or a delicate felt pen sketch by Sir Russell Drysdale on the other side of the wall in the lounge.

The large-scale operations were ruthless in their wholesale blanketing of extensive areas; many of the minor plants and animals threatened had significant functions in the ecology and perhaps in the future of science. Other threats to the land's primeval cover come from the drowning of huge areas under water dammed for power or irrigation; in Tasmania, considering future plans as well as those brought to fruition, fears are expressed for the survival of the Huon Pine, one of Australia's most valuable softwoods. It is not impossible that the massive operations presenting a new top-cover have already begun to influence climate.

The introduced disease of myxomatosis reduced the rabbit population dramatically, bringing huge barren tracts back into production, or permitting their redevelopment. In nearly all instances where introduced animals have thrived at all they have thrived too well, and even the useful beasts of burden, the horse, the donkey and the camel have become pests in country where they were allowed to run feral.

Machinery has replaced them all. The motor-cycle has superseded the horse in sheep country furthest out, the helicopter under specialist hands performs miracles on cattle musters as it works in conjunction with teams of small four-wheel drive vehicles, stripped to utilitarian bareness. The same combination musters the valuable buffaloes of Northern Territory plains, the wheeled vehicle actually capturing solitary animals with an iron arm. The beach buggy has replaced the camel in some of his functions and, used without restraint, is certain to do irreparable harm to the fragile ecology of the sandy deserts.

Heavy machinery has been brought to the development of open-cut mining on an unprecedented scale and, almost as an afterthought, been diverted to the creation of instant ports, instant towns and thousand-kilometre lengths of road. Such installations have promoted new intensive uses for nearby country. The accountant in his office, able to order change from computerised data geared to financial considerations, wields a tremendous power, usually for good though sometimes not. On Cape York Peninsula wholesale clearances of rainforest do not promise any permanent profit from the thin coating of soil exposed; the animals and the plants have disappeared and the first exuberant crops have proved to have been the best. Weeds flourish better, and science with its chemicals is sometimes of temporary and questionable help.

Chemicals even spread from the air seem to have been inefficient against the locust plagues. These seem to have increased, and perhaps the countryman who for generations has eaten the locust-eating bustard, a gastronomic prize, is most at fault. Other of his operations have discouraged other agencies that could have kept plagues in check: the foxes, cats and pigs his predecessors introduced have created a rarity of ground-nesting birds. Imported mice have appeared in plagues of unbelievable numbers. In 1917, 550 tonnes of mice were destroyed near one South Australian town. Seven tonnes of mice were poisoned against a single fence at Sheep Hills, in the Victorian mallee country.

With awareness, the battle against the plagues of the land is conducted with aids ever more specialised. Aerial bushfire patrols, pesticides employed against threatened crops, water control by dam for flood and drought, hormone sprays for introduced plant plagues of lantana and blackberry. Scientists have brought the scarab beetle to control the fly, and keep searching for a control for the giant toad — introduced to control cane-beetle, but inefficient there and a menace elsewhere. Most effective in the long run will probably be the educative programmes instituted to meet continually altering challenges of nature.

Education, direct or indirect, has made the biggest change in country life. Cooma, a small country town, had one hotel and a 'greasy spoon' cafe until it became the headquarters for the Snowy River hydro-electric and irrigation scheme and attracted thousands of workers from all over the world. Overnight these workers, on high wages and danger money, effected a metamorphosis and locals quickly developed a taste for sophisticated entertainment and diversified meals.

Today people adjust ever more easily to the immigration influx, though some resent it. Horizons are broadened by travelling theatrical companies and art exhibitions. New systems of recording, wider coverage of radio and television have given the Outback higher standards of music.

Milling sheep await Geoff Houston who hand feeds his ewes on his property, Kelvington station, in the Boomi district of northern New South Wales. Hand feeding is carried out as an inexpensive and often desperate measure in order to maintain stock during drought — or to improve the condition of sheep before lambing or showing.

Two Australian innovations, years ahead of the rest of the world but arising mainly from urgent problems, began in the twenties to reduce the handicaps of remoteness. The Flying Doctor Service, linked with a huge amateur radio network that covered the whole interior, ensured that medical advice was available on the instant and that doctors could be flown to the more serious emergencies. The associated School of the Air utilised the same network to bring erudition to the homestead children. Housewives used the network in the afternoons once or twice a week in regularly organised sessions. Often a member of this club might dress for the occasion and describe her apparel over the air waves.

Post-war availability of heavy machinery improved the road system out of sight. As late as the mid-fifties the main road along the Queensland coast, Australia's Number One Highway, was in places no more than twin ruts stretching shakily across wallows where vehicles bogged on any rainy day. Towns like Bowen were cut off on their land approaches for weeks of every wet season. But in the sixties

Above: Once the mainstay of long distance travel in the remoter regions of Australia, the camel was first introduced in any number by the Victorian Government for use by the Burke and Wills expedition across the continent in 1860. Working camel teams, like this one on Anna Creek station near Lake Eyre, S.A., are rare now; camels remain mostly as wild herds in semi-desert areas or in tourist-oriented camel farms.

Right: The immensity of this road train, at Marlabore, S.A., is attested to by the fact that it may tow as many as eight dog-trailers, each up to 60 metres long. A network of beef roads was constructed between 1961 and 1974 to replace the costly and time-consuming cattle droves.

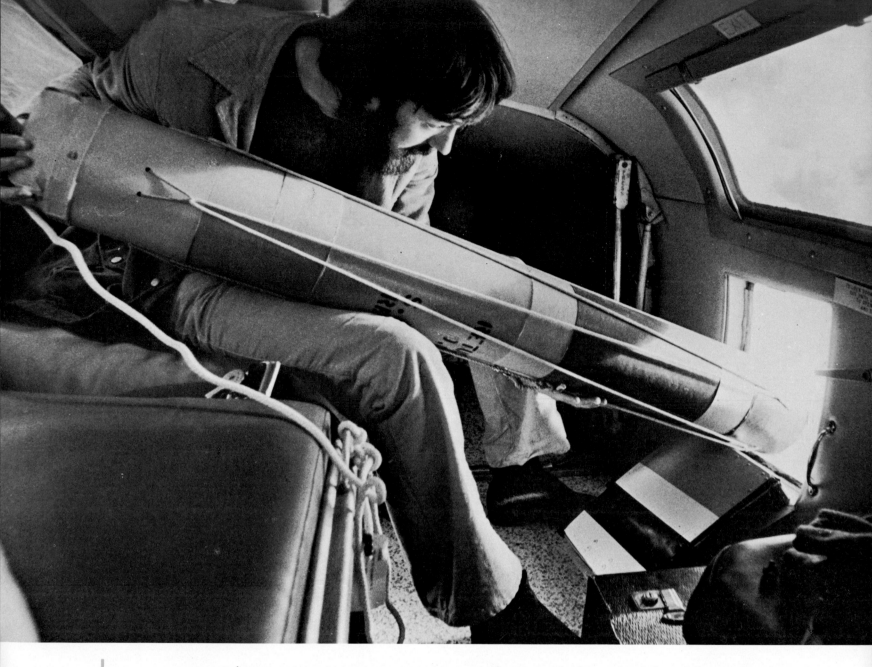

a vast improvement was apparent everywhere, and the principle of Long Service leave crowded the roads with Australians, some of them able for the first time in their lives to realise the dream of seeing their own country. Catering to them implanted pleasant motels in every community, and increased that community's functions. Travel became more comfortable and acceptable.

The principle of Long Service leave was set out in a decision of the Commonwealth Conciliation and Arbitration Commission in September 1959. Prior to this, on a road linking Alice Springs with South Australia, the traveller might meet three cars on a lucky day. Immediately after the principle was established I passed 150 cars on an ordinary day on that same road, and found cars and caravans on minor roads in remote territories. Among them were tourist buses, equipped sometimes with camping gear.

Communities seized on the benefits of this flow. Historical societies flourished, and towns promoted festivals. Grafton celebrated its jacaranda flowering, Bowral its tulips, the Barossa Valley its vintage, Innisfail its sugar, Ballarat its begonias and townships in the Adelaide Hills their autumn leaves.

Beef roads extended into the most remote cattle country, greatly enlarging its carrying capacity because the road-trains that replaced the drovers could bring to meatworks and markets the younger animals that would have succumbed to the long hard drives, and deliver all animals in prime station condition. In addition, road-train delivery eliminated the 'rush' or stampede, with its heavy stock losses and danger to man. The tourist industry has also benefited from beef road access to beauty spots previously hard to reach.

The century's halfway mark was the dividing line between complacent Australia, satisfied with her lot, and the thrusting community that is seeking the utmost exploitation of her resources. Machinery, more than any other factor, has brought

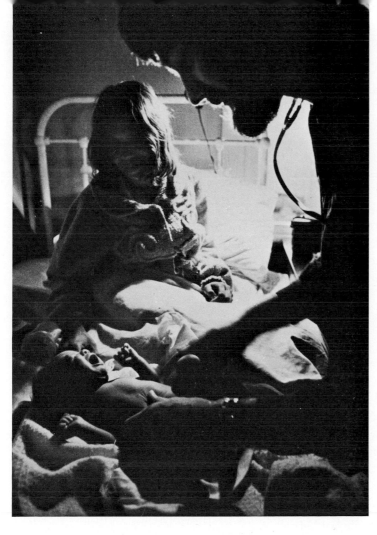

Opposite: **Broken Hill Flying Doctor, Jeffrey Harrild, launches a supply-filled aerial torpedo, part of a relief air drop to the flood-isolated inhabitants of White Cliffs, an opal mining town in western N.S.W.**

Left: **Tibooburra, in the north-west of the State was also flood-bound. During ward rounds at Tibooburra Hospital, Dr Harrild examines a premature baby he delivered two weeks earlier.**

country living to an approximation of suburbia. A horse teamster, working with his team for seven hours 'tight chains', that is, effectively moving farm implements for that time, could expect to start work at 4 a.m. bringing his team in to feed and groom them, and could perhaps expect to perform his last chore 17 hours later. He spent his weekends, at least in part, seeing to his resting team and their harness. Today the tractor driver finishes when he stops the engine, and he gets paid extra for overtime.

Heavy investment in plant was one of the pressures towards larger holdings in the sixties. Smaller farms were amalgamated and some complained of their elimination — but the trend towards specialisation preserved some. On holdings large or small the trend will continue to accelerate, especially with such prospects in view as on-farm production of alternative fuels. The pig and poultry markets are responding to local demand made more urgent by the world-wide increases in beef, mutton and lamb consumption. Wineries have flourished, and many new ventures started. Sugar and cotton production is on the increase. The trend to specialisation continued through the seventies, encompassing the individual worker as well as the management of the several properties he might serve.

Some new skills and tendencies appeared in rural areas through communes of one sort or another, established by a more rebellious generation seeking alternative life-styles, or sometimes by splinter religious groups. Such communes have attracted men, women and families with urban skills and tastes, as full-time or part-time residents, and some have flourished, though others not unexpectedly have died on the vine.

Diamonds, aluminium, natural gas, uranium, oil shale — every new development even before fruition attracts a proliferation of service industry units, to their enrichment and the country's. New processes aid exploitation of other valuables such as coal. But sometimes one wonders about that First Fleet's failure to recognise potential, and the *laissez-faire* of the generations that followed. Is it still operative? Are there great rewards we still ignore, as our great-grandfathers overlooked the neglected gold? Have we analysed the potential of what we hold?

There is, at hand, the example of Antarctica. We claim a large area, a claim not really endorsed by any significant powers. To give it body we have established a few scientific outposts there, and encouraged our scientists to add their contributions to the body of human knowledge.

Is this enough? Along that coastline are enormous fishing grounds, and perhaps we have a duty to exploit them in view of world hunger. If we solved union troubles we could develop the capacity to build, say, one or two hundred large modern fishing vessels annually, fleets capable of packaging the unconsidered wealth of the Antarctic Ocean, and not by any means too great a drain on those extensive seas. At least such developments would be cogent arguments supporting our claim to the region.

Again the efficient exploitation of our own bordering seas was not attempted until the sixties and seventies, in spite of a wealth of sea-produce that has lured large fleets from the other side of the world. Again problems associated with organised labour have prevented Australian use of material and energy to create an efficient productivity.

Though conditions of country living approach closer and closer to those in the city's better suburbs, the dust, the flies and the distances remain. Against these, the open-air life and the absence of weary commuting hours made compensation. The television programmes the countrymen watch, the radio they listen to, offer the same entertainment as their city cousins enjoy; their late-model cars transport them to any other entertainment they fancy.

No longer valid are the chief rewards of the pioneer: the fierce joy of self-sufficiency proved, the prime satisfaction of wresting a living and sometimes a fortune directly from the soil, of demonstrating from the well-tried resources of the inner person an ability to cope with the land and the seasons, of establishing homestead and holding where the generations unborn can grow and develop, of celebrating inwardly the small quiet triumphs of improvisation.

Independence is no longer possible, and the individual on the land is no more than the firing chamber in a machine largely beyond his control. The tightening constriction of communities striving to adapt their form to the necessities of the global village is unwelcome always, but over and above its influence there remains a freedom to taste the great delights of life beyond the haze of city smoke.

In the Outback, men and women enter upon an inheritance from generations for whom the realisation of dreams lay always just over the lip of the horizon. It was for their dreams that Australia's ancestors left their native lands only to find that, like the foot of the rainbow, the dream will move ahead of them, forever in sight, and forever just out of reach.

Above: **In the tiny hamlets, like this one at Reid, W.A., which lie scattered across the Nullarbor beside the railway, consumerism comes but once a week with the arrival of the Tea and Sugar train — a mobile town, complete with shops, doctor, dentist, library and social worker.**

Right: **On either side of Reid, the steel threads of the railway wobble away into the heat haze, part of the longest straight stretch of line in the southern hemisphere.**
Overleaf: **A lone runaway provides a few moments sport at Anna Creek station S.A.**

THE ECONOMY

Peter Ellery

'...to become one of the richest nations on earth...'

Viewed from any angle, Australia's economy looks set to become one of the strongest as the world spins its way towards the turn of the century. The basic structure is sound, if in need of some fine tuning to reduce unemployment and curtail inflation which are also endemic in virtually every other so-called Western nation.

Australia's farmers, among the most efficient in the world, produce enough to ensure self-sufficiency in most foodstuffs with substantial surpluses to provide a healthy export trade. The country is rich in vital mineral resources such as iron ore, bauxite, nickel, copper, lead, zinc, mineral sands and other ingredients necessary for the sustenance of an industrial society. And the 14.6 million Australian people have demonstrated in their two centuries of growth from a society of convict exiles that they have the innovative and technical skills and political stability to maintain a strong economy.

But the icing on the cake, setting Australia ahead of virtually every other Western nation, is a rich endowment of energy resources.

The development of vast deposits of black coal, natural gas, uranium and shale oil during the next few decades is expected to insulate Australia from the effects of manipulations and instability in world oil markets while establishing an export trade which will provide Japan, Europe and the United States with vital energy supplies.

In the process, these developments are expected to catapult Australia into the ranks of the top half-dozen energy exporting nations. It is this prospect, and the stable political climate, which has led economists to coin the expression 'lifeboat Australia', reflecting the image of a secure, well-stocked lifeboat riding serenely through tempestuous economic and political seas.

Australia's energy resources

The inventory of energy resource projects under way, or soon to get under way, is staggering. In 1981, the Commonwealth Department of Industry and Commerce estimated that at least $35 000 million had been committed, or was about to be committed to the development of mining and manufacturing projects. The bulk

67

Left: **An isolated floating oil rig on the North-West Shelf near Dampier, W.A.**

Open cut mining at Mary Kathleen, Queensland. Although the mine reopened in 1976, a combination of low prices and the high cost of processing the relatively low-grade yellowcake into uranium oxide has led to the projected closure of the mine.

of the sum was taken up by investments in energy, and energy-related activities — $10 390 million for coal, $8 300 million for oil and gas, $4 030 million for aluminium, alumina and bauxite and $1 200 million for uranium. The ANZ Bank, using different criteria, put the total higher at $38 000 million while the Australian Industries Development Association, casting its net still wider in an equally authoritative estimate, put the figure at $80 000 million.

On past form the impact of this expenditure should spread throughout the community, with something like 70–85 per cent of the total spent on Australian manufactured materials, goods and services — notably steel and manpower. The developments, many of them occurring in remote areas, will also require very heavy investment on public utilities such as power generation, telecommunications and water supply, and on infrastructure items such as roads and airports.

Fortuitous geology ensures that Australia is self-sufficient in almost every mineral of economic importance in the modern world, with the exception of crude oil, and much more than self-sufficient in some of the most vital energy commodities including coal and uranium. Minerals with reserves capable of sustaining large export industries include black coal, natural gas, and uranium, all sources of energy, and non-energy minerals such as iron ore, bauxite, nickel, copper, gold, lead, salt, beach sands, silver, tin, tungsten and zinc.

Of these, coal and all of the other non-energy minerals named, are already being exported in significant volumes, contributing to very healthy trading figures. But it is the growth potential for virtually every one of the resources named and particularly the energy resources, which is focusing world attention on Australia, and which makes its economic future look so bright.

With supply on hand in the form of minerals in the ground, it only required the forces of demand to unlock it. These forces are operating now on a greater scale than ever. Just about every move that the Organisation of Petroleum Exporting Countries (OPEC) has made in recent years, has made Australia's energy resources more competitive in terms of price and more desirable in terms of the security offered by a supplier which is a long way from the world's trouble spots.

Coal is by far the most important reserve of primary energy in Australia. The remaining discovered reserves, which occur mainly in the Sydney Basin of New South Wales and in central-east Queensland, are estimated to be equivalent in energy content to about 170 billion barrels of oil, of which only three billion will be required within Australia by 1990. By way of comparison, Saudi Arabia's reserves of approximately 200 billion barrels of oil are the largest in the world.

Energy experts see coal as the world's major immediate alternative source of energy to oil. They estimate that international coal production will expand by two and a half to three times and provide at least half the increase in the world's energy needs over the next 20 years. International trade in steaming coal, which is used to generate electricity, will have to grow by up to 15 times to satisfy the likely demand, and Japan in particular is going to need to increase its steaming coal imports by up to 50 times by the end of the century.

These forecasts by the World Coal Study explain why investors propose to pour at least $10 000 million, and perhaps much more, into developing new coal mining facilities in Australia. The study predicted that the bulk of the enormous growth could come from four countries — the United States, Australia, South Africa, and Canada, with the United States and Australia by far the most important.

Australia exported 38 million tonnes of coal in 1977. The annual total is expected to rise to 160 million tonnes by the end of the century, by which time plant and equipment will have been installed to lift actual producing capacity to 200 million tonnes.

Even before the price of oil doubled in 1979, Australian steaming coal was competitive in many national and regional markets. Since the oil price rise its attractions for generating electricity have become compelling. As well as the price advantage, consumers have found good reason to diversify their source of energy supply and Australia's political stability is seen as a major bonus. Because of these advantages, Australia is the preferred source of supply of steaming coal for 25 per cent of the European market. Japanese projections indicate that Australia and the United States will each share about one third of its market for steaming coal. With these projections in mind the Australian coal mining industry is gearing up for the biggest development phase in its history.

Though coal, with exports even now valued at some $2 000 million a year, will continue to be the major export industry during the 1980s, the biggest surge in development expenditure will be in the oil and gas industry.

Australia is already approximately 70 per cent self-sufficient in crude oil production, and as such is better off than any other Western nation except Norway, Britain and Canada. But the vast distances and sparse population of the continent make Australia more dependent on oil-fired forms of transport than any other nation on earth and 70 per cent self-sufficiency, with a production decline forecast by the end of the 1980s, is regarded as being far from satisfactory.

Known recoverable oil reserves now stand at 2.1 billion barrels against the nation's expected requirement of 3.4 billion barrels during the 1980s. A massive exploration effort is under way both offshore and onshore to make up the shortfall. Expenditure on petroleum exploration rose to approximately $200 million in 1980 as exploration companies responded to the incentive of a world parity pricing system and some promising new discoveries onshore. At the same time spending on development rose to about $300 million.

These figures are 'peanuts', however, compared to the vast expenditure planned throughout the decade to tap the natural gas reserves of the North-West Shelf.

The presence of big reserves of natural gas discovered during the search for oil, is an especially bright aspect of the energy picture in Australia. Reserves are estimated at 4.2 billion barrels of oil equivalent. Each of the mainland State capital cities is reticulated with pipeline gas but current plans are for only about 25 per cent of the reserves to be consumed internally, leaving a large surplus for export. Some 50 per cent of the reserves lie beneath deep water off the north-west coast, and a consortium led by the Australian company, Woodside Petroleum, is preparing to produce some of this to supply natural gas and gas liquids to Australian markets and liquefied natural gas for export. Construction has already begun on the $5 000 million project which is Australia's biggest natural resource development to date. When production reaches a plateau later this decade, 50 per cent of the output in the form of pipeline gas and gas liquids will be available to Australian markets — representing a boost in energy production equivalent to a quarter of the current production of crude oil from the Bass Strait. The other 50 per cent of production will be exported, establishing a new export trade comparable in magnitude to the coal industry.

But developments such as the North-West Shelf, and others planned for South Australia's Cooper Basin area, will not solve the oil deficiency. Projections indicate that even the current level of self-sufficiency will fall off after seven or eight years unless new discoveries are made or substitute liquid fuels developed.

Vast sums and much technical ingenuity are being expended to achieve both objectives. The number of exploration permits being issued, the amount of seismic shot, the number of wells being drilled and the general level of activity in oil exploration is reaching higher levels each year and there are reasonable prospects that more oil will be discovered.

However, the most spectacular efforts to achieve self-sufficiency, and perhaps

Opposite: **Port Kembla, N.S.W., steelworks and loading wharves. Originally developed in 1883 as a harbour for shipping coal from the nearby Mount Kembla mine in the Illawarra Range, Port Kembla has grown into Australia's largest steel-making centre.**

Above: **Newcastle harbour today contains 5400 metres of commercial wharfage, serving as an economic and trade centre for the Hunter Valley. Newcastle's prosperity is based on coal and steel. Coal exports in 1981 reached 13.2 million tonnes and are expected to reach 18 million in 1982.**

Left: **A bauxite refinery at Gove, Northern Territory. Large deposits of bauxite, the raw material for aluminium, have been found on the Gove Peninsula at the north-eastern tip of Arnhem Land.**

SIR CHARLES COURT — Western Australian Premier

If Australia is identified by people abroad as the land of natural resources, Sir Charles Court, Premier of Western Australia until his retirement in January 1982, is identified by Australians as the man of natural resources.

Since his election to the Western Australian Parliament in 1953, he has worked tirelessly to promote the development of Australia's natural resources generally and Western Australia's natural resources in particular.

It is no coincidence that, of at least $35 000 million estimated to be spent on mining and manufacturing projects in Australia, the lion's share of it will be spent in Western Australia.

Charles Walter Michael Court was born in Crawley, England, in 1911 and migrated to Western Australia with his parents when still only a few weeks old. His father, a plumber, could not get regular work in Western Australia for a long time and the frugal, Nonconformist Courts had a tough introduction to the State of which their son was to become Premier.

He attended State primary and secondary schools, leaving at 15 to become an office-boy to a legal firm before being articled to a chartered accountant at the equivalent of 75c a week.

While at school, he developed a love for music and played the cornet as a one-man band for the Salvation Army.

On completing his accounting degree at the age of 21, he set up business in his own practice at the height of the Great Depression in 1932. The dining table and chairs from his parents home served as his first office furniture and he supplemented the meagre income from his practice by playing the cornet with local bands, going on to become a musician with Australia-wide recognition.

In 1940 Charles Court enlisted in the army as a private. He was commissioned soon after and rose rapidly through the ranks to become a Lieutenant-Colonel.

He was awarded the Order of the British Empire for distinguished service on Bougainville Island during the war. Those who served with him during those days recall a dedicated worker who seldom had time to join in the revelries which relieved the tension and boredom of camp life.

With the war over he returned to his accountancy practice and from this time developed a keen interest in the remote north of Western Australia through his contact with clients in the mining and pastoral industries in that region.

Elected to Parliament as the Liberal member for the prosperous suburban seat of Nedlands in 1953, he quickly made his mark as a public figure. When the party was elected to office in 1959 he became its Deputy Leader and the Minister for Industrial Development, the North-West and Railways in the new government which went on to serve a record term of 12 years.

During that time Minister Court played a leading role as the catalyst and focal point for enormous mineral developments, mainly iron ore, which transformed Western Australia from an economic backwater to the strongest growth State in the Commonwealth. He also developed a reputation as a vigorous opponent of excessive control emanating from Canberra.

The Liberal Government was defeated in 1971 and Court succeeded the late Sir David Brand as party leader during the period in Opposition.

In 1973 he led the party into office again, becoming Premier of a government which he pledged to further resource development in Western Australia.

A tireless and articulate exponent of resource development and the virtues of private enterprise, he is eagerly sought as a speaker at business gatherings in Europe, Japan and the United States. He continues to joust with the Commonwealth policies on resource development matters.

Not unexpectedly, many of his policies were strongly opposed by extreme conservationists who regarded him as a blind and authoritarian proponent of big business.

He works long hours, rising before dawn and rarely getting to bed before midnight. Taciturn on personal matters, it is difficult to judge what has driven Sir Charles Court in his enormously successful bid to open his State's resources to the world.

Perhaps it stems from his spartan upbringing in a strict Nonconformist household and the difficulties his own father had in finding work.

Married with five sons and many grandchildren, he will admit that he wants Australia to be a prosperous and secure place for his grandchildren. Despite the predictable opposition his policies incurred, there are many Australians who share his belief that Australia will be a more prosperous and secure place if it develops its resources to serve the world.

more, in oil are in the field of shale oil development and oil from coal technology. Oil shale is a fine grained sedimentary rock containing organic matter which when heated yields substantial amounts of a complex oily liquid from which synthetic crude oil can be derived. Australia has vast deposits of oil shale in the Toolebuc marine formation which underlies about 700 000 square kilometres of the north central part of the continent, and smaller but more accessible deposits in old lake beds along Queensland's eastern coastal strip. One of these deposits at Rundle in

Queensland is being evaluated for possible development by a consortium which is led by Esso Australia and also includes the project initiators, the small Australian entrepreneurial companies, Southern Pacific Petroleum and Central Pacific Minerals.

The developers face many challenges, but the potential is great. At full production the Rundle project could produce about 200 000 barrels of oil a day — equivalent to about 30 per cent of Australia's requirements in the early 1980s. During the

This twin-strand continuous slab caster at Port Kembla — the largest works of BHP's steel division — has an annual capacity of one million tonnes of steel.

construction period it could employ 6 000 to 7 000 people and the total cost of development could be of the order of $10 000 million. At its ultimate production level the project could mine about 165 million tonnes of oil shale and 195 million tonnes of waste and overburden each year, making it one of the largest open-cut mines in the world.

Above: **The art of longwall mining, Newcastle. Over the last decade, considerable technical advance has refined this technique which is capable of producing large volumes of coal in a variety of conditions.**

Left: **Underground mining has also been transformed at Mt Isa, in western Queensland. Heavy machinery makes cavernous drives in place of the mole-like burrows of older methods.**

If the Rundle project proceeds there are other oil shale projects to follow. Half a dozen other promising oil shale deposits are currently being explored with a view to development to further increase the production of oil in Australia.

Further down the line, a number of groups are examining the prospect of producing synthetic oil from both black and brown coal in Australia. Since the raw material is present and the technology for producing synthetic crude from both shale and coal is well established, it will be the economics of the projects under review which will be the key to their success. Given better than a 50:50 chance of success in the search for conventional rock oil, and fair prospects for developing synthetic oils on a commercial scale, there is some hope that Australia will develop an exportable surplus of oil after 1995.

If coal, oil and gas and synthetic oils dominate the immediate future for energy resources, uranium appears to be the resource of the future.

Australia's proven reserves of uranium amount to almost 300 000 tonnes which represents 18 per cent of the Western world's reasonably assured low-cost deposits, or 26 billion barrels of oil equivalent. This estimate does not include the giant Roxby Downs copper-uranium deposit in South Australia, which has not yet been fully evaluated. None of the known reserves will be required for consumption within Australia in the next decade. Moreover the estimated reserves could be increased up to 50 times with the development of fast breeder reactors in which case they would become vastly more valuable than all of Australia's other energy resources together.

Production of uranium in Australia first started at the Mary Kathleen deposit in the 1950s, but the mine was closed down after a few years. Now Mary Kathleen has been re-commissioned and three other projects — Ranger and Nabarlek in the Northern Territory and Yeelirrie in Western Australia — are operating or close to development. There are at least five other potential mines including Roxby Downs. Production from Mary Kathleen, Ranger, Nabarlek and Yeelirrie is expected to total about 6 500 tonnes by the middle of the decade. With an eye to the longer term a group of mining companies is examining the possibility of a commercial uranium enrichment industry while the Commonwealth Government is seeking access to enrichment technology from France, Japan and the United States.

Given the proposed development in coal, gas and uranium, and excluding the long-term hopes for synthetic oil, the Department of Trade and Resources has forecast that Australian energy exports will increase from around 25 million tonnes of oil equivalent in 1980 to 180 million tonnes by 1986. This will represent an annual increase of over 24 per cent. For 1991 the figure is put at 290 million tonnes of oil equivalent, implying a ten per cent annual growth rate for the second half of the 1980s.

If this output is achieved, Australia will rank along with some of its OPEC benefactors among the leading five or six energy exporters in the world. But the prospect of exporting very large amounts of primary energy resources is only half of the opportunity presented by OPEC activities. Opportunities for utilising energy resources within the country to process abundant resources of non-energy minerals have also been vastly enhanced. For example, higher energy costs are bringing major changes to the world's aluminium industry.

Australia's bauxite reserves, the raw material of aluminium, are estimated at more than 4 900 million tonnes, representing a third of the world's commercially extractable bauxite. Bauxite is being mined at remote Gove in the Northern Territory, at Weipa in North Queensland and in the Darling Ranges near Perth, Western Australia. Despite the enormous resources and its leading role as a producer of both bauxite and alumina, Australia's output of finished aluminium has been small by world standards. Less than a tenth of the annual alumina production has been processed into primary metal.

Now all that is changing. In Japan the incremental cost of base load electricity supplied to heavy industry has been estimated at roughly eight Australian cents a kilowatt hour. The indicated figure in Europe is four cents, for the United States three cents and for Australia with its vast low-cost coal resources, just 1.5 cents. Aluminium smelting is an energy intensive process — some people call the light metal 'congealed electricity'.

Doug Anthony, Leader of the National Country Party, talks here with Sheik Yamani, Minister for Petroleum and Mineral Resources for Saudi Arabia (one of the principal members of the Organisation of Petroleum Exporting Countries). Between 1973 and 1975, OPEC was instrumental in quintupling the price of crude oil.

The result is that while 30 per cent of Japan's smelting capacity is now idle, Australia's capacity is expected to increase from 280 000 tonnes to more than one million tonnes by the middle 1980s. This will represent almost one-tenth of the Western world's capacity, and make the aluminium business larger than the iron and steel industry in terms of dollar output in Australia. At that output, the value of foreign earnings at current prices from overseas sales of aluminium metal could approach $2 000 million a year, putting this industry also in a class approaching coal.

The upsurge in smelting capacity will also create a need for big increases in electricity generating capacity. This is expected to be almost double, from 21 000 megawatts to 41 000 megawatts by 1990, at a cost of about $10 000 million.

As the oil price revolution continues, opportunities are being recognised for processing in Australia other mineral resources such as mineral sands and magnesite, which also require large amounts of energy. And so the country enters the final years of the twentieth century, buoyed up by the market forces unleashed by OPEC, to become one of the richest nations on earth and a major force in sustaining the beleaguered Western economies.

Most of the resource developments referred to will take place in a part of Australia which is virtually unknown to most Australians — the great Outback of Western

Above: **The gas flare from a Goodwyn well, North-West Shelf, where exploration continues under the combined partnership of BHP and Shell. Gas is one of the most sought after resources.**

Right: **The vehicle manufacturing industry is one of the biggest employers of factory labour in Australia. The Australian Government is adopting an increasingly protectionist stance.**

Australia, Queensland and adjoining areas — which occupies more than three-quarters of the continent.

Despite the image it represents to the world of a nation of limitless resources and vast open spaces, Australia is essentially a typical urbanised, industrialised Western economy, differing mainly in that it draws riches from its Outback appendage. While the mining industry employs a mere 90 000 people, 1.2 million in the workforce of 6.5 million people are employed in the manufacturing industry. The value of factory production has more than doubled in the past five years and now exceeds $20 000 million a year.

Manufacturing industry

A drive through or flight over the approaches to the great cities of the south-eastern seaboard, or Perth, the western capital, is evidence of this industrialisation which had its beginnings before the turn of the century in the need to turn out special machinery for the peculiarities of Australian agriculture, and which gained a broader base in two world wars. Thousands of hectares are devoted to factory buildings — dun coloured structures with serrated roofs generally set in a splash of green lawn amidst an olive-dun Australian landscape of gum trees, security fences and bitumen paving.

Modern industrial Australia has largely escaped the gloomy, polluted environments of the industrial nations of the northern hemisphere — except for the older (pre-1940) industrial suburbs of Sydney and Melbourne.

To the predominantly young population — the great majority of which has grown up with the era of industrialisation — it may seem that factories have always been part of the Australian scene. But manufacturing has not come easily and does not fit naturally into the economic life of a nation which owes its prosperity and ascendancy in trade to vast primary resources which respond, sometimes with lavish rewards, to the application of relatively little labour and a great concentration of capital and technology.

Before the Federation of the Australian States in 1901, the relatively few factories operating produced goods mainly for local consumption — stump-jump ploughs, crop strippers, shearing appliances, pickles, ham, furniture, bricks, and clothing made from imported fabrics. Facilities existed for the repair of imported machines rather than their manufacture, and considerable energy was devoted to the preliminary processing, such as wool scouring and saw milling, of staple primary products.

Federation removed interstate trade barriers and introduced a uniform protective tariff, creating an umbrella of artificial protection under which manufacturing industries flourished. This growth quickened with World War I which curtailed the availability of manufactured goods from abroad and boosted local demands.

Australia's industrial giant, the Broken Hill Proprietary Co. Ltd, took the momentous step from mining and smelting lead ores to making steel during the war, and the orders flooded in, commencing an extraordinary saga of growth by a company which has always paralleled and sometimes outstripped the greater national move to industrialisation. The burgeoning new steel-maker generated the establishment of a host of related and subsidiary industries. Extensive manufacture of machinery was also begun and a wide range of products such as textiles, metal and electrical goods were added to Australia's previously modest output of manufactures.

The end of the war saw the creation, in 1921, of the Tariff Board which further assisted new manufacturing industries by means of protective tariffs against overseas competition. Expansion of manufacturing continued unchecked until the Depression of 1929–33, which caused many factories to close their doors and put one Australian worker in every three on the dole.

A slow return to prosperity from 1933 onwards, together with tougher import restrictions and a depreciation of the Australian currency, brought renewed activity and when World War II broke out in September, 1939, Australia had a well-established industrial base from which to supply the Allied cause in the South Pacific and east of the Suez Canal. Once again, fired by the furnaces of war, Australian factories went to work to supply the Australian people and their allies with goods which had previously been imported from Britain and Europe. And once again, the wartime expansion brought on-going benefits.

With peace came a steady flow of migrants to Australia from the war-torn Old World — more than 3.5 million since 1947 — bringing new skills to the factory floor and rapidly expanding the home markets for Australian produced goods.

The inflow of new settlers, coinciding with a period of unprecedented prosperity and growth for the basic rural and mining industries, created the climate for rapid industrial expansion in terms of both volume and production and diversity of products.

The Australian motor vehicle industry was born in the early post-war period and grew to become one of the biggest employers of factory workers. Today it produces some half a million new vehicles a year, of which nearly a fifth are exported to more than 70 countries.

The domestic appliance industry also flourished in the post-war era to supply the demands of the newly prosperous Australian housewife. The demands of ebullient consumerism in turn created new opportunities for the heavy industries.

Overseas capital flowed in a steady stream during the fifties and sixties to increase petroleum refinery capacity, establish new fertiliser plants and chemical complexes and turn out an increasing range of pharmaceutical products, machine tools and electronic equipment. Breweries, strongly Australian owned and always healthily productive and profitable in the thirst-forming climate, flourished as never before.

Australian mechanical ingenuity, originally born of a need to improvise in the Outback, produced a range of products for local markets which became competitive abroad. Though only a sixth of all factory output is exported, it makes up almost a fifth of all exports. Australian-made photographic equipment sells in West Germany, Australian light aircraft for agricultural purposes sell in the Pacific and Asia and Australian foundry equipment sells in Canada, the United States, Japan, and Sweden. Australian-made cranes were used in the construction of the world's tallest building in New York.

As a generalisation, the State capitals are the centres of labour-intensive light and medium manufacturing. Heavy industries such as steel making, metal refining and shipbuilding are concentrated in Newcastle and Wollongong, which together with Sydney form the great urban concentration of central New South Wales, at Geelong in Victoria, Whyalla in South Australia and Kwinana in Western Australia. The half dozen or so new aluminium smelters which will be established during the eighties will also be located in and around these sorts of areas.

Coal, from the vast alluvial beds beneath and around the city, fires the blast furnaces and hot strip mills of Newcastle, oldest and smokiest of the Australian industrial centres. But its surf beaches, and the Hunter River which links it to the vineyards upstream, distinguish it as a typically Australian city.

Wollongong, sprawling untidily beneath the Illawarra escarpment, populated by one of the heaviest concentrations of migrants in Australia, was the fastest growing urban centre during the expansion of its steelworks in the fifties and early sixties.

Geelong, on the western side of Victoria's Port Phillip Bay, is the centre for a major alumina smelter with petrochemical plants superimposed on the solid structure of an old pastoral port and service centre.

Whyalla, set on the dry western shore of Eyre Peninsula, near the head of Spencer Gulf and in sight of Iron Knob, the great mountain of iron that is the reason for the city's existence, is also heavily peopled by migrant factory workers from the Old World. Australia's third steel making city, it has also become the centre of the government-subsidised shipbuilding industry.

Kwinana, 40 kilometres from Perth on the flat sandy coast of Cockburn Sound, is the best planned of the heavy industrial centres. Hundreds of unoccupied hectares of sparse scrubland separate its giant metal refineries and the oil refinery which is its source of energy. Ships discharging cargoes of crude oil and fertiliser feedstock, or loading metals for overseas destinations, anchor out from sandy beaches, many kilometres of which remain accessible to the public.

Beyond the heavily populated south-east coastal crescent stretching from Brisbane to Whyalla, and the concentration of people around Perth in Western Australia, there is little manufacturing industry of consequence.

The decentralists dream of — and plan for — great industrial complexes based on the richness of Western Australia's Pilbara iron ore and natural gas deposits, and the vast coal reserves of Queensland's Bowen Basin. Less ambitious plans to establish light and medium industry at Albury-Wodonga on the New South Wales-Victorian border, at Bathurst-Orange in New South Wales and in other large provincial towns are being implemented, but not without difficulty. Queensland, with its resources evenly spread along its coastal strip, has shown a natural tendency towards decentralisation of industry to a greater degree than the southern States.

But by and large, in the most spacious land on earth, the dream of decentralised industry has many philosophical adherents and few practical activists. Government ministries for decentralisation have been set up, but withered away from time to time with little to show for their efforts. Urban Australians may curse the spread of their manufacturing complexes which are swelling the growth of and breeding future pollution problems for their traffic-choked cities, but few are willing to establish new factories and new industry in the Outback.

But if decentralisation of manufacturing poses a socio-economic challenge for Australia in the last quarter of this century, it is nothing compared to the challenge of structural re-adjustment and tariff reform in manufacturing industries.

Eight decades of uninterrupted protectionism in Australia have spawned and nurtured a major industrial civilisation beneath the clear sky of the southern hemisphere. In many ways it is more admirable than the industrial civilisations of Europe, America and Japan. Australian factories are newer and cleaner, working conditions are generally better and aggressive trade unionism, combined with predominantly favourable economic conditions since World War II, ensures that Australian factory workers are well paid. Industrial development has fulfilled a national aspiration which pre-dates the formation of the Australian nation from a group of pastoral colonies — the desire for economic independence and a wider range of job opportunities than could be provided by a rural based economy.

But since the mid-1970s, Australian manufacturing has been suffering from similar malaises to those which have affected industry in Europe, the United States and Japan and which are basically the manifestations of deep-seated changes in the structure and aspirations of society at home and competition from vigorous new industrial powers abroad.

The motor vehicle industry, the textile industry and many others have been confronted with the problems of competition and high wages, high inflation, high social costs and diminishing protection and productivity.

While many economists and politicians argue that a surfeit of protectionism has nurtured many industries which are inefficient and an unnecessary drain on the economy, others contend that unemployment would rise and the social choices open to Australians decline dramatically if protection were abandoned.

The Tariff Board has been replaced by the Industries Assistance Commission which has the monumental task of instituting significant tariff reforms. The challenge is to remove undesirable forms of protection without disrupting the economy, and in particular without further reducing the level of employment. Judging by initial performances, and considering the broad spectrum of the vested interests opposed to tariff reform — from employers to employees — it will not be easily achieved.

Australia's increasingly sophisticated communications network (connecting far-flung urban and country centres) is essential to the functioning of commerce and industry; and as an island, Australia enjoys the advantage of many ports along its vast coastline, providing efficient links with the outside world.

The financial institutions

If the blue-overalled factory hand driving to his work in an outer suburb in a small late-model car is the prototype of the modern Australian, the grey-suited office worker is the archetype. By occupation, seven out of every 100 Australians are administrative, executive or managerial workers — the serious denizens of the sombre concrete and glass towers of downtown capital Australia.

These are the business decision makers, the cautious, conservative, wheeling-dealing, money-spinning doers, who in three decades have transformed Australia from a sylvan backwater, albeit an urbanised one, to a voice to be heeded in the world's trading circles. Supported by an army of clerks — out of every 100 Australians employed, 16 are clerical workers — the Australian archetype runs the manufacturing companies, the mining houses, the uniquely Australian stock firms, which dispose the products and supply the requirements of the rural community, the retail establishments and the capital raising financial institutions, which occupy the central city areas.

As the nation has grown fat on the success of the capitalist system, Australians have tended to take for granted or find fault with the vital role played by the private sector financial institutions in their daily lives. The banks, insurance companies, stock exchanges, building societies, merchant banks and finance companies have gone about their daily business unheralded and largely ignored except when some weakness or aberration in the system has thrust them unfavourably into the headlines and public notice. Yet they have played and will continue to play an increasingly important part in the formation and mobilisation of massive amounts of new capital that is essential to the development of the nation's resources.

During the previous period of high growth in the 1950s and 1960s, some 90 per cent of all new capital invested was drawn from domestic savings. This was largely overlooked because of the publicity devoted to a chauvinistic concern about the role of foreign capital. Investment from overseas has accounted for a mere ten per cent of total capital. But it attracted a disproportionate share of unfavourable attention because it was channelled into areas of high risk and high profit return.

If the relatively modest role of overseas capital in financing the economic expansion of the 1960s and the 1970s was a cause for some concern, then financing the resources boom of the 1980s is likely to provoke controversy of major proportions. From whichever way it is viewed, the task of financing development, costing somewhere between $30 000 million and $80 000 million, appears to be beyond the capacity of Australian money supply.

With a total annual income (Gross Domestic Product) running at slightly in excess of $100 000 million, Australia's private capital spending is amounting to just over $10 000 million a year. This puts into perspective the capital cost of such developments as the North-West Shelf project, which is put at $5 000 million in 1980 dollars, and Rundle, which (if it proceeds) may turn out to be about $10 000 million. The national savings run at about 20 per cent of total income, and an increasing proportion of household savings is being channelled into short term deposits in institutions such as the building societies, savings banks, finance companies and credit unions.

The growth of the building societies in particular has been spectacular, with total assets rising at an annual compound rate of over 30 per cent during the past decade. The societies have always existed in Australia but they have been achieving high levels of growth only since the middle sixties. To a large degree this mirrors the increased prosperity of the lower income Australians, arriving at a situation where for the first time in their lives they can consider putting their savings into something more rewarding than an old sock or local post office branch of the savings bank. It is also testimony to the techniques used by the societies to capture the small investor's dollar, techniques which have raised some disapproving eyebrows in the competing savings banks.

But, whatever the savings banks may think, there are many hundreds of thousands of Australian home-owners who would not be home-owners if it were not for the hard-sell, investment-winning ways of the building societies. Though they have performed well, their image over many years has been tarnished by the history

Brokers eagerly place their bids at the Melbourne Stock Exchange.

of the building society collapses which occurred during the crash of the 1890s. They depend for their borrowings on the prosperity of the small investor. Drawing on the least sophisticated end of the lending market, they are far more susceptible than the other financial institutions to volatile movements in their deposits.

The peak hour traffic crawls out of the city. A mounted policeman provides a pre-industrial solution to a post-industrial problem.

By comparison with the building societies, the assets of the trading banks grew by an annual compound rate of only 13.6 per cent from 1967 to 1978, while the growth rates of the pension funds and life assurance offices have been even lower.

Australia's banks have the reputation of being a pretty conservative bunch, and only for this reason they are not always revered national institutions. Bastions of security and discretion, they are tightly regulated and protected by government and their own collective desire to avoid unseemly competition, and they are vital to the stability of the national economy.

This has not always been so. Australian banks closed their doors during the great financial crash of the 1890s and some were severely shaken again during the Depression of 1929–33. Today, by virtue of the government's long established central banking policies which proscribe a statutory reserve deposit and closely regulate every facet of traditional banking activity, they appear impervious to all but the most calamitous of economic shocks (but not necessarily up to the challenges now confronting them).

Structurally the banking system is organised into the Reserve Bank, the Australian Government's central bank which administers banking policy and regulates reserves, the Commonwealth Banking Corporation with its trading and savings banks, 13 trading banks including the six privately owned major banks, and government and privately owned savings banks. In addition the Commonwealth Banking Corporation administers a Development Bank with special functions to assist primary and secondary industry development, and the major trading banks have

established the Australian Resources Development Bank with the main objective of assisting Australian enterprises to participate more fully in the development of the nation's natural resources.

The banking scene has been remarkable in the 1960s and 1970s for the rapid development of merchant banks and finance companies which are challenging the deposit banks in some areas of their traditional business. But an examination of this development reveals that all the major trading banks have extensive interests in these quasi-banking organisations. Their existence is to a large extent an indication of the growing sophistication of the Australian financial system, and of the economy which is creating demands for new services and specialisations within that system.

But add all the trading banks together and they would still not represent a giant by international standards. Even if their conservative attitudes towards investing in resource developments relax, as they appear to be doing, they will not have the capacity to contribute the vast funds required for the resources boom.

On the other hand, the long-term savings institutions, the life offices and the pension funds, are clearly shaking off their previous reluctance to become directly involved in mineral resource ventures. Until challenged by the building societies the life offices, which straddle the country like a medieval colossus, were traditionally the main vehicle for private savings in Australia.

From behind the discreet facades of their functional steel, glass and concrete head office blocks, they dominate the Australian property market and the markets in ordinary and fixed interest securities and government bonds. In terms of assets they tower over all but a handful of the more visible industrial and mining companies, and in the late sixties and early seventies their rate of growth exceeded the rate of growth in national income.

Most of the assurance companies are mutual societies, owned by the policy holders. Some are of foreign parentage, particularly British, but their associations with Australia generally began in the old colonial days. Until recently they enjoyed a privileged existence in comparison to other financial institutions, pampered by government tax incentives but obliged by law to invest at least 30 per cent of their life office funds in government and other securities. Before the 1960s they generally confined their non-government investments to the safe and secure property market, loans on mortgages and to a lesser extent the share market.

Criticism of this conservative approach, and the obvious advantages of investment in resource projects has led to a gradual change from this policy. In the 1960s and 1970s, the life houses began investing significant sums in mining and large-scale pastoral developments. Now the National Mutual is reported to be putting up to $50 million into resource projects during the first year of operations of a new venture sector, while the giant Australian Mutual Provident Society is talking of directing around a tenth of its cash flow for equities into a newly established resources unit.

Then there is the share market and the company sector itself.

After operating for many years virtually as a closed club for the initiated, the share market became a conversational set piece for every social gathering during the spectacular boom and crash of 1969–71 as Australians talked of those they knew who had made fortunes overnight, and later of those who lost them. The aftermath of that boom has seen a continuation and intensification of the debate on the role of the markets in the economy, and the need for more self-imposed and government controls. It also saw a sharp decline in the value of new share issues from a peak of $1 000 million in 1969–70 when the tiny speculative mining company, Poseidon NL rocketed to overnight fame, and later infamy, on the hopes generated by its discovery of a rich nickel deposit at remote Mt Windarra in Western Australia's parched eastern goldfields.

The market has moved slowly but surely to reform itself and subsequent bull markets have been more soundly based, and less prone to scandal, than the Poseidon boom. But the stock market is an erratic and strictly limited source of new capital for mining companies. In the five years before 1980, when the market was generally quiet, mining companies raised less than $350 million in new money. During the booming market of 1980 the sums raised increased substantially, but Australia can-

RUPERT MURDOCH — publishing magnate

As the Australian economy has become increasingly significant to the rest of the world, so Australia's businessmen have gained increasing prominence in world business. None is better known, however, than Rupert Murdoch, controversial publisher of Sydney, London, New York and places in between.

The son of the late Sir Keith Murdoch, the revered Chief Executive of Australia's giant Herald and Weekly Times publishing group, Murdoch graduated as a Bachelor of Economics from Oxford University and had his first introduction to practical journalism as a sub editor in Fleet Street.

He was on his way home from England in 1953 to start work from the bottom in his father's personally owned newspaper, the *Adelaide News,* when his father died. At the age of 22 years Murdoch suddenly found himself the proprietor of the paper.

He admits to a competitive and acquisitive nature and it soon began to manifest itself when he acquired first the *Horsham Times* newspaper in provincial Victoria, followed by the *Sunday Times* in Perth. The next step was a momentous move into the hurly burly of publishing in Sydney, then and still one of the most competitive newspaper cities in the world.

In an interview in Perth in 1963 the publishing whizz-kid could see no further prospects for expansion: 'We don't want to expand much further,' he said. 'We are at the stage where we have the assets we went after. Now we want to improve them.' A year later he plunged the Australian newspaper world into turmoil by launching the national daily newspaper the *Australian*.

In 1968 he burst onto the world scene by outmanoeuvring the leading British publisher Robert Maxwell for control of the mass circulation *News of the World,* a weekly with the biggest circulation of any English-language newspaper. Fleet Street, then as now, was bedevilled by soaring costs, falling revenues and debilitating battles with powerful Labour unions. This however did not deter Rupert Murdoch. Other acquisitions including the *Sun,* the biggest circulation daily newspaper in Britain, followed.

His technique of using sensational journalism to boost flagging circulation and fall-

ing revenue was highly successful but brought controversy down on Murdoch. In one sensational incident he was shouted down by the studio audience in an interview with television celebrity, David Frost.

Controversy did not deter Murdoch however and he later launched himself into newspaper publishing in the United States, using the same colourful and controversial formulas. His major New York acquisition, the *New York Post,* devoted sensational coverage to both the Sky-lab re-entry into the earth's atmosphere and the 'Son of Sam' murders, prompting one critical analysis of the Murdoch methods headed 'Sky-Lab misses Son of Sam'. It might appear that he had reached the peak of his career with the acquisition of the revered *Times* and *Sunday Times* of London in early 1981. It should be remembered that 18 years previously he had himself forecast an end to further acquisitions.

Now in his early fifties, Murdoch heads News Corporation Limited, a media conglomerate with interests in Australia, New Zealand, Britain, the United States and Hong Kong, and encompassing all facets of newspaper, magazine and book publishing, television and radio broadcasting, paper making and recording. In Australia he is also Joint Chief Executive of Ansett Transport Industries, having acquired a significant interest in that company which also has television interests.

An ardent nationalist, his Australian publications are vigorous proponents of expansionary economic policies. In January 1973, soon after the election of Australia's first Labor Government for more than 20 years, he told an Australia Day dinner in London: 'We are no longer content that Australia will go on being inevitably, irreversibly or without protest a metal quarry for Japan, pastoral lease for distant investors, factory for Detroit, distant province for Madison Avenue or a South Pacific windbreak for French nuclear scientists'.

At home in Australia, Britain or the United States, Murdoch is courted by political leaders because of the influence he controls. But beneath the internationalist is a chauvinistic Australian, determined to see Australia win a strong place in keeping with its economic importance to the world.

not rely on such an erratic performer to underwrite development which will see many bull and bear markets during the next two decades. (The term 'bull market' refers to strong buying demand and upward price movements. A 'bear market' is the term for a depressed market.)

As for the ability of companies to generate investment capital from their own internal resources, this is directly related to profitability which can be as erratic as the share market. In any case, the size of individual resource projects these days is such that even the biggest companies find it necessary to restrict their financial exposure by joint venturing with other companies and by borrowing heavily from the Australian and overseas capital markets.

If the finance available for resource developments from the banks and quasi-banking organisations, the life houses and pension funds, the share market and

Rupert Murdoch (*right*) with Australia's Prime Minister, **Malcolm Fraser** (*left*),
on Mr Murdoch's sheep property. Both are large landholders and divide their
interests between town and country.

internal company funds are all lumped together, they might amount to something
like $1 000 million a year. This falls far short of the needs of resource developments,
and clearly Australia will be seeking enormous sums from abroad to underwrite
the developments proposed.

There is no doubt that overseas financiers will have both equity funds and loan
funds available to invest in 'lifeboat' Australia. The question for Australians will
be at what price in terms of selling off the farm. Based on past attitudes and given
the degree of government intervention in issues such as overseas control, it is unlikely that foreign companies will substantially increase their ratio of control.

Home ownership

Although funds are far more readily available for home building than corporate expansion, the free-wheeling building societies and their competitors have failed to sustain the high rate of home ownership which has been a source of Australian pride since 1901. Of almost five million private houses and flats in Australia, some 67 per cent are owned, or are in the process of being purchased, by their occupiers. This is the highest rate of home ownership in the world, but represents a reduction of a few per cent over a decade. That it is occurring is a source of some concern — but the reasons are almost certainly related more to the increasing congestion of the big cities and the pressures toward higher density living than to economic circumstances alone.

With few exceptions, every young Australian couple desiring to own a home can do so today, though it may require the sacrifice of the young wife working for a few years. The homes are being built bigger and better than ever before and with the munificence of the building societies there are mortgages to match for those who can afford the interest. If proof of this is needed, it is in the statistics. The proportion of homes built in the high class materials of brick, brick veneer, concrete and stone has increased by 250 per cent since 1950 while the proportion built from humble timber has fallen by 90 per cent. Built-in amenities and appliances have become a standard feature of the Australian home of the 1980s, a contrast with the spartan square three-bedroom cottage without trimmings of any sort which was the norm in pre-war times. The other refinements include more than one car in every garage (one vehicle for every three persons), and a telephone, television set, refrigerator, and a range of other appliances in almost every home.

Like the troubled securities industry, the home building industry is a super-sensitive barometer to the national economy. Though it has been prosperous more often than not in the post-war years, it has had its share of downs as well as ups. Since 1960, shifts in government fiscal and monetary policies have severely reduced the rate of home building on several occasions, sometimes by accident and more often than not by design.

Though home ownership is within the reach of every Australian who cares to strive for it, the striving is becoming more arduous as land costs increase along with the cost of materials and labour. Provision for low-cost housing for the lower income groups, traditionally an area for government concern, lags well behind requirements for the same reasons.

Despite the many problems, the home building industry has kept up a staggering pace, almost trebling the number of homes in existence since the end of the war in 1945. In doing so, it has covered the broad hectares surrounding the old pre-war cities with vast landscapes of three-bedroom brick and tile cottages within each of which resides a small segment of the Australian dream.

If the home builders have managed a cracking pace, the builders of commercial and high rise buildings have in their own way been equally staggering. Australians, aided often by overseas investors, began to reshape the centres of their major cities in a big way in the 1960s. For more than a decade the skylines of all the State capitals were distinguished by a fretwork of partly built office towers and lean, busy cranes. The downtown areas were brutishly gutted of their medium-rise pre-war buildings, subjected to the incessant din and dust of demolition and construction and remodelled in standardised concrete and glass to resemble every other big city in the Western world.

There is evidence that the office building boom peaked before the mid-seventies when it was realised that it was creating a king-sized glut in office space. Now, although the rush to redevelopment is more sedate, and the inner city noise levels more tolerable, the work still goes on.

Increasingly though, the developers have been turning their attention to the opportunities for value-increased land utilisation and construction offering beyond the central city. Tourism and recreation, which now employ some 400 000 people, have provided lucrative openings. So too has a revolution in retailing which has seen the development of American-styled enclosed shopping centres which fit like a glove into Australian suburbia with its sprawling residential areas and emphasis

The tightly packed south-eastern suburbs of Melbourne are indicative of the
city's explosive growth since World War II. In that time, the population has
more than doubled.

on the car. The first such centres were built in Sydney and Melbourne in the early
1960s. Since then they have spread and prospered until they cluster around the
middle and outer suburban circumferences of the cities like satellites around a celestial body — each occupied by its own department store branch, variety store,
food supermarket, attendant smaller retailers and a host of local solicitors, dentists,
doctors, travel agents and real estate agents and other services of the inner city.

Australian wholesalers and retailers employ some 1 200 000 people. Annual sales
have increased steadily and occasionally spectacularly and reached $30 billion in
1979–80. It is a highly competitive and almost wholly Australian-owned business.
Ultra-fine profit margins and the forceful personalities of many of the home grown
and occasionally self-appointed merchant princes are likely to keep it so.

Anomalously, while retailing remains highly competitive it is also increasingly
concentrated into the hands of fewer and fewer big companies which are increasing
their power over manufacturers because of their buying strength. Because of
competition, retail price maintenance among food lines disappeared in the 1960s,
and in all other areas in the early 1970s. The appearance of the discount house
in strength during the early 1970s provided further opportunities for the Australian
housewife to obtain genuine retail bargains.

Rural industry

In the Australian suburbs the housewife shops for her bargains. In the cities, their sprawling industrial fringes and the large provincial towns, more than 12 million Australians go about their daily business very much in the way of the urbanised people throughout the Western world. There is little direct contact for average urbanites with the wider land, rich in resources and opportunity, which begins where the suburbs stop. They see it fleetingly on annual leave, a strip of land at most a few kilometres wide on either side of the bitumen which carries them to a coastal or mountain resort. They may visit or fossick around the ruins of a ghost mining town or 'rubberneck' at Ayers Rock and Alice Springs in the dead heart. The archetypal executive frequently sees it from 9 000 metres as he jets between the capitals sipping a scotch and soda and referring importantly to the notes he carries in his ubiquitous briefcase.

But every day the Outback and the continental shelf impinge indirectly on the life of the urban Australian, like the hot westerlies which blow over Sydney in the summer, or the cool southerly busters which bring change, thunder and rain.

A little over two million people live outside the State capitals and the big provincial centres. They live on the scattered farms and pastoral station homesteads, in the rural townships, the forestry camps and fishermen's shanties and in the transplanted air-conditioned plastic push-button suburbs which have been built to make life livable for the workers at the isolated new mining enterprises of the Outback.

Australia has a population density of fewer than two persons per square kilometre over the whole continent, which makes it as sparsely settled as any land on earth. But if the densely populated coastal regions and their populations are extracted, the figure is considerably less for the Outback area. It is those two million people, and those 6.5 million square kilometres, which distinguish Australia economically and socially from the rest of the world and which give it so much reason for confidence in the crisis which looms for the Western economies in the final years of the twentieth century.

Some 4.7 million square kilometres of Australia's total land surface of 7.5 million square kilometres are taken up by agricultural and pastoral holdings. Much of this is semi-desert, capable of carrying only a few animals to the square kilometre. Though gross farm product makes up a quarter of gross domestic product, it accounts for almost 40 per cent of the nation's exports. Roll the contributions of the other primary producers, the miners, fisheries and foresters, into the export account, and they amount to more than 75 per cent of the annual exports which are now worth more than $18 000 million. Without this contribution the thin blue line of the balance of payments surplus would quickly become the thick red line of a deficit, and the standard of living which Australians have become accustomed to would be impossible to sustain without mortgaging the future against massive borrowings from abroad.

The rural industries have played a key role in the development of Australia since the first settlers erected their tents on the shores of Sydney Cove in 1788. Attempts to produce grain to supplement the rations brought with the First Fleet began almost immediately, but without conspicuous success. Two and a half hectares were planted to wheat and failed. Of the small flock of sheep which landed with the First Fleet, only one animal survived its introduction to the cheerless colony.

From this discouraging start, by a slow process of trial and error, success and disappointment, in a harsh environment totally alien to the plough and the shepherd, have evolved a wide variety of rural industries, rich in production and frequently profitable to their farmer practitioners, though they are sometimes reluctant to admit that their life is not always struggle and adversity. Over the years, and because of the strong and continuing influence of the politically well-organised farming community, governments at both State and federal level have introduced a complicated structure of guaranteed prices, subsidies and controlled marketing to sustain the farmers against adversity, either natural or economic.

Though only one sheep from the First Fleet survived, John Macarthur, an enterprising officer with the soldiers sent to protect and maintain order among the first

At Nyngan shearing shed, 'Wocka' (Warwick Gibson) flings a freshly shorn fleece onto the sorting table — to be skirted and classed before bailing and trucking to market.

settlers, soon imported more. The British market for wool was booming and he decided to breed specifically for wool. The first clip he exported from New South Wales in 1807 attracted a good price and much interest because of its quality. By 1827 the struggling colony, perched precariously on the edge of the unexplored continent, was competing more than successfully with the woolgrowers of Saxony who had dominated the trade for centuries. Within 40 years of Macarthur's first commercial clip, New South Wales was producing more and better wool than any country in the world and settlers were pushing out through the grasslands of the colony's unknown interior to take up more land and to let their flocks multiply.

Multiply they did. Throughout the nineteenth century and far into the twentieth, Australia's economy rode proudly, and sometimes it seemed almost exclusively, on the sheep's back. Not any old sheep mind you, but the Australian Merino offspring of the first Spanish Merinos imported by John Macarthur in 1797, the dumb, diligent producers of the finest quality wool in the world.

Macarthur's Merinos proved to be superbly adapted for life in much of the Australian interior save the most arid of the deserts. Even there they flourish in the occasional wet years. The Merino led the first settlers into what was to become Victoria, and wool quickly became the staple product of the six main Australian colonies.

Superphosphates and small doses of mineral trace elements put new life into the ancient, weather-leached soils of Western Australia's otherwise marginal lands. Fertilisers, and the use of a new wheat strain (one of a thousand developed to suit Australian conditions), produced this harvest near Merredin, east of Perth in Western Australia.

Sheep numbers increased from 20 million in 1861 to 180 million in 1970 when the clip peaked at 923 million kilograms. Australia is by a long way the world's biggest producer of sheep and wool. There has been a decline in sheep numbers and the size of the clip since, partly because of drought which from the earliest days has periodically decimated the flocks, but mainly because of a prolonged downturn in wool prices during the 1960s which reached a trough in 1970–71, causing many wool men to diversify into beef and other more profitable avenues of production.

That downturn in prices appears to have been the inevitable result of competition from synthetic fibres which together with the upsurge in mining, may finally have overtaken wool's pre-eminence in the Australian economy. But it may be premature to write wool off. For nearly 200 years the industry has roller-coasted from boom to recession, subject to all the marketing uncertainties of a staple natural commodity which produces according to the laws of nature and sells according to the whims of man.

Whether it has entered a permanent decline or a temporary eclipse, wool will remain important to the Australian economy for the foreseeable future. Its supremacy as the premier item of export has been overtaken by coal and wheat, and will be further overtaken in the near future by aluminium and natural gas; but there is too much invested in wool growing in Australia and in the manufacture of woollens elsewhere for it to slip quickly into oblivion as a vital industry. And as the promoters of wool are quick to say, its natural fibres have qualities which the synthetics cannot emulate.

In the meantime, it has carried Australia into maturity and the spin-off from its economic impetus over almost two centuries has contributed enormously to the

Left: The table wines of tomorrow ferment in a clinical array of steel tanks at Tolley, Scott and Tolley's modern winery in the Barossa Valley, S.A.

Below left: Shovelling white wine lees from a fermentation vat at Hamilton's Ewell winery, Adelaide, S.A.

Below right: Vineyards at 'The Grange', Magill, S.A. Here, in 1884, Dr Rawson Penfold planted vines 'for medicinal purposes' for his patients. This small project escalated into Penfold Wines which has part of the 7 490 399 litre export wine market.

development of other rural industries. It has also stamped itself indelibly on the Australian character. The lean, laconic, sun-bronzed Australian of the popular image is a sheepman first of all. He may also be a wheatgrower.

Whatever else they may have learned when they lost their first two and a half hectare crop of wheat at Sydney Cove in 1788, the early settlers learned that if they wanted to grow wheat they had to work at it. For many years they laboured with dismal results, spurred on only by the knowledge of the vast distance which separated the tiny colony from a more reliable source of grain.

While the economic successes of first wool, and later gold mining, attracted romantic attention to the bountiful new Australian colonies, a handful of small landholders battled to grow a few miserable hectares of wheat against seemingly insuperable odds. Gradually some breakthroughs were achieved. It was recognised that the varieties of wheat imported from the Old World were largely unsuitable for the Australian climate and experimentation with the breeding of new varieties began. More than 1 000 new varieties of wheat have since been bred to suit Australian conditions, increase yields and also increase resistance to disease.

The soils seemed particularly inhospitable to cereals until it was discovered that there was an almost universal deficiency of phosphates in Australia's ancient weather-leached soils. The introduction of superphosphate fertiliser boosted yields substantially. The advent of the tractor and the development of large sophisticated seeding and harvesting machines and bulk handling equipment overcame another problem — the chronic shortage of labour which had prevented farmers from cropping the broad hectares required to produce reasonable sized crops from the comparatively low yields that were attainable.

On the marketing side of wheat, demand and price fluctuated with disturbing unpredictability, leaving the farmer with large surpluses and low prices when growing conditions were best, and high prices and shortages of grain in times of strong demand. Most of the wheat crop is exported, and is thus dependent on overseas markets which are subject to sudden variations depending on world-wide crop and economic conditions.

The establishment of a wheat stabilisation plan guaranteeing a firm price for all production and the surge in world population and grain demand since the end of World War II encouraged a major increase in wheat growing capacity during the 1950s and 1960s. In Western Australia, the discovery that trace mineral elements would substantially boost crop yields increased agricultural potential enormously. Some eight million hectares of new land were brought into production for wheat and sheep raising in the 20 years from 1949. Not even the Canadian prairies or the Russian steppes have witnessed agricultural land development on such a grand scale.

In 1968–69 wheat farmers delivered some 14 million tonnes of grain to the Australian Wheat Board — a crop record which was not surpassed until 1978–79 when 17 million tonnes were delivered. The enormous volume of 1968–69 strained handling and storage facilities and over-supplied the market to such an extent that a quota was thereafter imposed on production in each State. Since then the market has improved while the farmers, restrained by the temporary quota system and a run of bad seasons until 1978–79, have diversified into other cereal grain production. But the demands of a hungry world and the long struggle of Australian farmers, culminating in their ability to produce satisfactory grain yields in low rainfall areas from land that is naturally infertile, will ensure the continuing strength and vitality of the industry. Australia now ranks third in the world after the United States and Canada as an exporter of wheat. The vast spread of the wheat-growing lands, in all States except Tasmania, gives a fair guarantee against catastrophic crop losses, even in years of fairly widespread drought.

Wool and wheat are the staples of the Australian pastoral and agricultural industries but they are by no means the only primary products of significance. The variety

Right: **Until comparatively recently, sheep sales were the yardstick of the nation's economic health. Today, minerals have the edge over wool as the major export in financial terms.**

of production is expanding rapidly as farmers are pushed by opportunity, economic necessity and increasing confidence in their own mastery of the environment to experiment and diversify.

The coarse grains, barley and oats, have always been grown, but production rose significantly after limitations were imposed on the wheat crop. Sorghum, maize and rice have become important crops in the past decades. More recently oil seeds have become important crops as State energy authorities and private enterprise organisations experiment with crops which might produce an acceptable and renewable alternative to rock oil.

Some 20 million tonnes of sugar cane are produced each year on about 300 000 hectares of fertile soils in the tropical north of New South Wales and in Queensland. The yield of refined sugar is well above two million tonnes a year of which about three-quarters is exported, making Australia one of the major suppliers of the world's sugar markets. Consideration is also being given to the use of sugar cane to produce ethanol, an alcohol fuel which can be used as an alternative to motor spirit, especially from the Ord River region of Western Australia.

Meat, long a traditional product of the agricultural and pastoral areas, has acquired new significance with the world population explosion and the hunger for proteins. Australia's cattle herds have had their own population explosion in the past decade, rising to a total exceeding 30 million animals, mainly destined to become beef. Australia has now replaced Argentina as the biggest meat exporter in the world. The herds are widely distributed through the agricultural and pastoral regions. Cattle graze intensively in the cool pastures of the southern States and with rather less enthusiasm or effect on harsher native pastures of the northern Australian cattle stations (one of which may comprise up to 400 000 hectares of land and run a beast to every 2.5 square kilometres in a good season). Intensive pasture improvements in the southern areas have boosted stock carrying capacity

Above: **One of Australia's newer fruit crops, dates are still in the trial stage; but, as indicated by this healthy young plantation north of Daintree, Queensland, the problems lie in the processing and marketing rather than the production.**

Left: **Leaf from this country's only commercial tea estate, near Innisfail, began to reach the nation's teapots in the early seventies after years of experimental growth and trial harvests.**

for both cattle and sheep. In the north, irrigation feed lotting is being experimented with to boost cattle carrying capacity.

How many Australians now in their forties and fifties recall the popular teaching in the schools of their childhood — that the Australian continent, then supporting six or seven million people, could at best support 20 or 30 million, that its agricultural lands could not support many more, and that some of its vital resources were already in danger of exhaustion if not carefully conserved for future generations?

The population has doubled in the 35 or 40 years since those pessimistic times but the application of science, technology, faith and elbow grease to the often parched and poverty stricken countryside of the post-Depression days has wrought miracles. With wool, wheat, meat and virtually every other rural product the challenge is no longer 'Can enough be produced?' but 'Are the markets big enough?'

The multitude of marketing authorities and statutory bodies which have been established to supervise this delicate end of rural business have been aggressive and successful. Until the 1960s, Australia relied on Britain and to a lesser extent Western Europe to take most of its surplus rural produce. When Britain contemplated entering the European Economic Community during the 1960s, Australian farmers slept less soundly. But Japan and the United States have since become major customers as Britain and Europe have declined in importance. In recent years vigorous selling has established flourishing new markets for Australian primary produce in Japan, Eastern Europe, the Arabian Gulf and Africa.

The Australian rural industries were imposed on an alien and inhospitable continent by the human need to survive, and having survived, to prosper. By virtue of their export strength and long-established institutions they dominate the economy and politics of the country to a greater degree than the newer, larger manufacturing industries and mining.

Left: **Afternoon shadows are cast into the regular furrows of a freshly turned paddock at Narrabri, northern N.S.W., seeming to meet just at the foothills.**

Above: **Crop dusting aircraft are mainly used for economy over large areas of cultivation or where the terrain prohibits conventional means. Superphosphate increases the yield.**

The facts of life, however, are that the 350 000 or so Australians employed in farming and in agricultural services are the lynchpin in the economy. Australia is one of the few nations of the world which combines the ability to feed itself and produce substantial food surpluses with the ability to produce a wealth of mineral resources and a wide range of manufactured goods. Take away the lynchpin of self-sufficiency in food, and it would rank with many other countries which may be rich in either food, minerals or manufacturing ability, or perhaps a combination of two of these staples, but not all three.

The future

The combination of natural wealth, sound economic management and political stability should guarantee a rich future. But that goal will not be achieved without some effort and at some cost.

Above: **Steel is loaded at Newcastle port, 160 kilometres north of Sydney, for shipment to the People's Republic of China. Exports to all countries may account for up to 25 per cent of iron and steel despatches annually.**

Right: **Viewed from central Sydney — Darling Harbour, one of the busiest ports in Australia. The international shipping terminal boasts twelve operating berths and eight layout berths for repair work.**

A world recession could delay some of the resource projects now on the starting blocks. But since most of them are energy-based, they will be less vulnerable than resource projects which are entirely dependent on the strength of economies outside Australia.

There is considerable concern about where the skilled labour will come from to man the resources boom. There are simply not enough tradesmen and technicians in Australia to meet requirements. Just as clearly, the recruitment of large numbers of skilled labour from overseas will be unpalatable to the Australian union movement while there is still a high percentage of structural unemployment in the Australian workforce.

Labour unrest itself is frequently cited as a dire threat to future prosperity and although the number of days lost because of strikes has fallen in the 1970s, Australia is still among the world's most disputatious nations. The figures are well above those of Japan, Scandinavia and most of Western Europe, but about equal with the United States and lower than the rate for Canada, Italy, Spain, Ireland or India. There is a tendency of Australians to beat their breasts excessively about labour problems, perhaps because they have fewer problems of a more serious nature

to be concerned about. The fact is that Australia has lived and prospered with disputatious unions for many generations.

Perhaps the major problem to be faced during the 1980s will be to manage the resources boom so that its benefits are spread reasonably evenly across the population. Development of the magnitude that is being forecast can be expected to create a massive build-up of foreign reserves. This can lead to higher inflation rates unless the government cuts tariffs or hardens up the currency. The first course could cause dislocation and unemployment in the manufacturing industry, and the second would threaten the competitiveness of the rural export industries.

For better or for worse, however, Australia is launched on a course which will bring it face to face with the problems of managing wealth throughout the 1980s and beyond. The vast majority of people are inclined to think that it will be for the better.

Four views of the coal industry: then and now.

Above: Newstan colliery near Newcastle. The continuous miner drum head rips into the coal face; rotating arms gather the coal onto conveyor belts where it is transported by shuttle cars from the mine.

Left: Miners at Northumberland colliery in the early 1900s hand-bored the coal face, filling it with dynamite to blow the face apart. The naked flame lamp used was highly dangerous in a mine with the ever present possibility of methane gas.

Above right: This 30 000 tonne Japanese bulk coal carrier loads, via automatic feed conveyor belt system, at the Maritime Service Board Loader, Newcastle.

Right: From the early 1800s, coal was loaded by wheelbarrows and later by horse powered cranes. Here, in 1905, hydraulic cranes load the ocean sailing vessels at the 'Dyke', Newcastle.

THE CITIES

Patrick Tennison

'A determinedly urban society...'

Australia's 'Outback' myth that seems to get most international attention is exactly that — a myth. Sure, mate, it is a sunburnt country. Or most of it, anyway. And it has certainly got sweeping plains. But who lives on them? Any sunburn felt by Australians is more likely to be of the weekend ration — and a larger dose on annual holidays.

From the earliest times of white settlement Australia has been a determinedly urban society. Today, more than 80 per cent of the 14.6 million population live in cities. And that, despite Henry Lawson, 'Banjo' Paterson and all the other bush pushers, is a world record. Almost a quarter of the population, a group of slightly more than three million, lives in just one city, Sydney.

Sydney

Big, bustling and brusque, Sydney is the birthplace of the Australian nation. A scrambling scrimmage of a city, erupting with life. Like Venice, Rio or Capri, it is a city where water is a vital complement to the land it is built on. Blue tongues of water from Sydney's harbour spread into dozens of craggy bays and coves and inlets.

Also, within 32 kilometres of the city centre there are stretches of more than 30 ocean beaches. Here surf and sun abound in a relaxing climate that gives Sydney an air of physical freedom no other Australian city enjoys quite as much. Nature seems a close neighbour of the air-conditioned purpose that fuels the city's business boilers.

Here, in a calm little bay on the harbour shoreline, on 26 January 1788 landed an unlikely band of people destined to found a new nation. That First Fleet, as history now calls it, comprised 11 small sailing ships, two warships, three storeships and six convict transports. In all, less than 4 000 tonnes of wooden vessels. They had sailed from England, by way of South America, on a voyage of almost 23 000 kilometres that took eight months. In command was Captain Arthur Phillip, appointed by King George III as the first governor of New South Wales. He named the inlet where they landed Sydney Cove, in honour of Britain's Home Secretary, Viscount Sydney.

The settlement that grew from that motley bunch of none too willing pioneers

Left: **The building boom of the bouyant sixties has begun to stabilise.**

took its name from the place where they first came ashore. They numbered just 1 030 'souls', as recorders of those times liked to call people. There were 736 convicts — 188 of them women — 17 convicts' children shipped with them, 211 marines with 27 wives and 19 children, Arthur Phillip and his personal staff of nine, and another group of ten comprising other officials, their wives and two servants. Another 13 men were drafted from the crews of the ships to serve in the new settlement.

During the long voyage from England, 36 men and four women had died. On the same journey, seven children had been born, some of them to the convict women. In the storeships came a variety of grain seeds, plants, horses and cattle. The list included even vine cuttings, to ensure that the new colony could be self-supporting in wine. From their accommodation aboard, the first settlers moved to tents ashore. Then, a few weeks later, they launched Australia's first industry: brick making. And the building programme begun then continues today. Phillip wanted Sydney

Left: **And the urban growth continued. Atop an office tower, a workman overlooks Circular Quay and the western arms of the harbour. Australia has the dubious distinction of being one of the most urbanised nations in the world.**

Above; **Rain, hail or shine, one of the few remaining traditional street sweepers makes his way through Sydney's inner suburbs. Waste disposal and cleansing services are essential operations vulnerable to industrial action.**

to be a well-planned city. Streets, he ordered, should be 200 feet wide. But then, as now, Sydney displayed a wayward attitude to anyone wanting to lay down firm rules. The streets were built where people walked, and the first buildings beside those streets. Today Sydney does have a few avenues '200 feet' wide. But they came long after Arthur Phillip.

Top: Cloaked by ominous skies, North Sydney's mushrooming landscape. Since the opening of Sydney Harbour Bridge in 1932, North Sydney has developed into a city in its own right, vying commercially with the city of Sydney.

Above: Perched on Sydney Harbour, the Opera House provides a stunning focal point as one of the city's many ferries carries commuters across its idyllic waters.

There are large Chinese communities in Sydney and Melbourne and Chinese New Year is celebrated with firecrackers and traditional, acrobatic displays — a perennial source of wonderment to the young (*far left*).

Harry Seidler, sporting his characteristic bow tie. Harry Seidler & Associates were first stage prize-winners in the Parliament House design competition.

Now, almost two centuries later, Sydney has matured into a worldly-wise city of wealth, poise and agreeable disposition. Nature ensured its basic handsomeness. Sydney's profile is a dramatic skyline of tall modern buildings that give it lines that seem, at times, more rigid than graceful. To compensate, the city has acquired

HARRY SEIDLER — transforming suburbia

Visionary. Missionary. Pragmatist. In little more than 20 years, Harry Seidler's architectural expertise has re-shaped the physical profile of Sydney. To a lesser extent, it has also added some useful plastic surgery in other capital cities.

Back in 1955, when Seidler was just beginning to enrich Australian architecture with his work, Robin Boyd wrote of him with typical Boyd reservation: 'Harry Seidler is primarily an artist rather than a technician'.

But the respected Boyd could already describe Seidler's work as 'architecture of excitement'. And it has been that quality that has most underlined his achievements to that time, and since.

Sydney is Seidler's base and his monuments there surround him: the circular Australia Square building, the MLC tower, the flat block at Blues Point that was Australia's highest residential structure when it was built. In the Sydney suburbs, his house designs still stand out for their originality. Interstate, his new office block for the Conzinc Rio Tinto company enriches the Melbourne skyline. Overseas, he is represented by buildings in Washington, Singapore, Mexico and, in Paris, the new Australian embassy building.

Slim, crinkle-haired, his calm personality neatly contained behind mod gold-rimmed glasses and a selection from his bow tie collection, Seidler came to Australia by way of Vienna, England, Canada, the United States and Brazil: 'There aren't many countries where a 25-year-old architect who is new to the place would have been given a chance as I was.'

His father, a Viennese shirt maker, took the family to England in 1938 as Nazism began to infect Europe. Harry Seidler had just begun studying architecture in England when war broke out and he was interned, first on the Isle of Man and then in Canada. There he was able to get a security clearance, continued his studies at the University of Manitoba and graduated in 1944. He worked briefly for a Toronto architect before winning a scholarship to Harvard where he studied under Walter Gropius. Other influences in this expanding period were Marcel Breuer and the artist Josef Albers: 'Albers taught me visual fundamentals. He showed me why our eyes react to visual phenomena, why certain things are beautiful'.

After a few months in Brazil and more study with Walter Niemeyer, Seidler moved to Australia on the urging of his parents who had migrated after the war.

His first look at a Sydney suburb produced a shock reaction: 'My God, what have I done?'

But his first commission, a home for his parents in suburban Turramurra, began a transformation of suburbia he believed could happen. His design astonished the conservative suburbanites, disturbed other Sydney architects, and resulted in litigation with the local council before it could be carried out in the clean lined way he wanted. He won not only his fight with the council but that year's Sulman Prize for domestic architecture as well.

From 1952, when he arrived, his battles with civic authorities drew as much attention to his revolutionary styles as the designs themselves won him more commissions. But as no other architect before him, he was able to give to Sydney home design the clean, modern outlook he saw as most fitting for the rugged and outdoor nature of the city itself. From houses to apartment blocks to office blocks to town houses, always fresh and innovative designs have whooshed from the Seidler drawing board as the Sydney parameters have moved outward and upward.

Today the Sydney he first viewed with distaste has become his operational base. True to his concept that architects should not just design buildings but re-shape the cities that house them, on any day he can look around Sydney and observe the re-shaping his own amazing mind has produced.

a number of architectural gems, most outstanding of which is the $100 million Opera House, its white billowing roofs stretching out over the harbour waters. Close by too, spans the bridge of grey steel, arching high into the sky, an earlier symbol of the city's adventurousness.

Office complexes, insurance companies, banks and government buildings vie in a dramatic steel and concrete thrusting for the skies. Topping them all, the crown on the Sydney skyline, is the soaring Centrepoint Tower erupting 305 metres from ground level. At its peak, diners eat and sip wine in a revolving restaurant that offers a high-level panoramic view of ocean, city, harbour and mountains to rival any in the world.

In the bitumen and concrete canyons of the commercial heart thrums the beat of people, cash registers and computers; Hilton and David Jones, AMP and IBM, consulates and protest groups. At night the streets become neon glitterways. Below ground, high above ground, people gather, work, travel, dine. Like an ant's nest, a giant circling cave has been dug out beneath the city to cope with transport pressures. Into it, day and night, the red and blue electric trains burrow through the eternal subterranean darkness with their human cargoes.

Right: **In a tantalising blue haze, a stripper weaves her spell over the audience in a Kings Cross nightclub.**

Below left: **Quite by accident, Sammy Lee formed his All Male Revue 'Les Girls' when he recruited three effeminate male members of his staff to fill his chorus line. They were so popular he launched 'Les Girls'; and they continue to confuse and astound audiences.**

Below right: **Carlotta, 'Les Girls' shining star, artfully cosmeticised and fluffed up with bright feathers, awaits her/his cue to take centre stage — and dazzle a packed audience.**

Opposite: **'Boobs, Broads, Bright Lights and Bawdy Bars'. Kings Cross lures tourists and locals alike to seek its many questionable pleasures.**

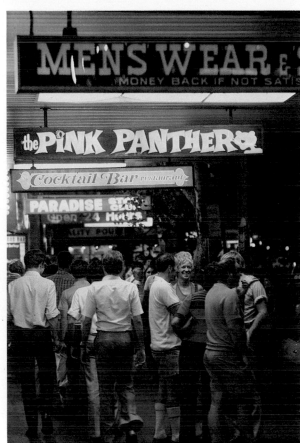

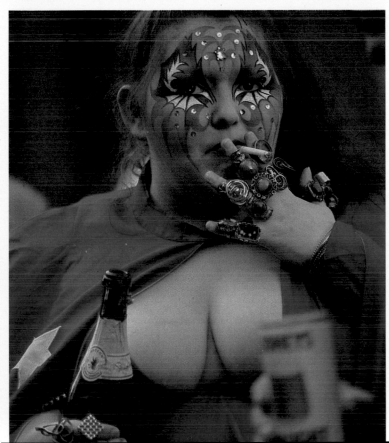

Sydney presents always a frenzy of movement, colour and shapes. Its big buildings are usually grey, white or black, though one, rising tall on the north side of the harbour, is a glowing pink. Fed by the vitamins of ambition, enriched by the protein of success, each year they grow taller. Ingenuity is stretched to find for them new, different shapes: square, round, curved, triangular. In Park Street towers the highest residential building in the southern hemisphere: the Park Regis. In its basement, six metres below street level, diners sip their drinks as they watch the steaks sizzling on the iron grill. High above their heads, separated by 44 floors of steel and concrete, swimmers play in the rooftop swimming pool.

In just recent years Sydney, always innovative, has been adding more centre-city apartment blocks to this thriving cityscape. While transient visitors stay briefly

LILY MADDEN — Aboriginal community worker

For Lily Madden 'It's not where you live, but how you live — and bring up your children'. Lily Madden, her husband Chicka, and their four children, live in the inner-city area of Sydney, the nucleus of a large percentage of the urban Aboriginal population. 'You've got to live in the city — for the kids' sake. You can't get away from the fact that there are more opportunities here.'

The Madden household is a comfortable, warm and friendly place, with smiling kids and neighbours constantly ducking in and out. Family has always played a dominant role in Lily Madden's life. Lily, whose maiden name was Gordon, was the third youngest of a family of ten. She spent most of her childhood in Baryugil in northern New South Wales. Here, her father, five brothers and seven uncles worked in the asbestos mines.

The first major upheaval in her life occurred at 14 when her mother died. The most important thing was that the family stay together and, with her father, brothers and sisters, Lily Madden moved eventually to Brisbane. Her education was interrupted and she went to work to help keep the family together. She worked as a machinist in Brisbane before moving to Sydney, experimenting with a variety of jobs ('seeing what I could do') . . . and married Chicka Madden. Her family is still close to her — 'a brother up the road and four sisters within half a mile'.

For the past seven years, either on a full-time or a part-time basis, Lily Madden has worked at the Aboriginal Medical Service. The Medical Service, run by an admirably determined Naomi Myers, is one of a number of services *for* Aboriginals, run largely *by* Aboriginals (such as the Aboriginal Legal Service and the Aboriginal Children's Service). These organisations have become a focus of self-help for the Aboriginal community, a vehicle for determining Aboriginal identity in New South Wales. However, what are seen as constant 'hassles' with federal government departments, have hindered the expansion of services which many Aboriginals would like to have seen develop.

Lily Madden has worked mainly in the field of nutrition. She, and other Aboriginal women, have developed a variety of programmes at the Medical Service, including cooking and sewing classes, deportment classes and programmes for pensioners (which have become so popular that many of the women will travel from outer western suburbs for the companionship and the lunch devised and prepared by the participants themselves).

Despite the fact that many Aboriginal families have settled in the outer suburbs, Redfern (home of the 'Rabbitohs', the South Sydney Rugby League team which has traditionally boasted a number of Aboriginal players) is still seen as the place 'where it's all happening' — and the classes serve the important social function of keeping people informed.

The supplementary food package programme has proved an immensely practical and successful experiment. The package, at a cost of $2, consists of a fortnight's daily nutritional needs for expectant and breast-feeding mothers and children who are considered by the doctors to be 'at risk'. The fruit and vegetable programme, at a cost of $1, consists of a weekly delivery of fresh fruit and vegetables (bought at bargain prices by members of the staff) to 'at risk' families. 'It's successful,' Lily Madden emphasises, 'because we're doing things ourselves.'

Yet Lily Madden worries about the kids. Her own children are notable successes. Lee, 19, was in 1981 school captain at Cleveland Street Boys High (an inner-city school with a commitment to happy relations among the various ethnic groups in attendance at the school). There is something of a tradition of leadership in the family (Craig, in sixth class, was also a school captain). Lily attributes the leadership qualities to Chicka Madden's calm strength and stability.

Sporting prowess also runs in the family and the Madden's living room is dominated by trophies. In 1982, the Aboriginal community raised $3000 to send both Lee and his sister Deidre to the United States to pursue their promising tennis careers.

Lily Madden sums up the task which she and other Aboriginal community workers see ahead of them: 'It's taking time but it's always good to see how the kids are going. There's a bit more fighting and hard work to be done — we've still got a long way to go'.

Amelia Hart

Three views of Sydney's Martin Place, in the heart of the city. The State Parliament House lies at the eastern end, and the General Post Office and banking area at its western extreme. The plaza, the largest area of its kind in the city, dissects six of Sydney's busiest streets and boasts an amphitheatre (*below*) where daily lunchtime concerts are staged, a controversial sculpture (*above left*), and shaded seating areas. The G.P.O. (*above*) was built between 1866 and 1886. A major Classical Revival building, it features a long colonnaded arcade and central tower.

Opposite: A panoramic view across the harbour of the city of Sydney. The Royal Botanic Gardens, to the left of the Opera House, stretch for 29 hectares and are the principal botanic gardens in Australia.

at its various hotels — including the luxuries of the esteemed Hilton, Wentworth or Boulevard — more of her permanent residents are returning to live in new apartment units overlooking the streets where the city and the nation as we know it today began life. Once traffic-choked, her central Martin Place has been converted to a gardened pedestrian mall.

Fanning out from the city, spreading north and south beside the beaches, and creeping westward to the mountain range rising 45 kilometres from the sea, Sydney's suburbia sprawls determinedly. Again, variety. Discreet Wahroonga on the upper class North Shore ignores the challenge of trendy Woollahra, just east of the city. Redfern looks old and tired from struggle. Mt Druitt, way to the west, appears younger and better equipped. Balmain, old but in the process of rejuvenation, clings to its own little corner of the harbour. Paddington, its terrace houses rediscovered after a century of disinterest, demonstrates the arts of the investor, the decorator and the promoter of that 'something new and different' that always excites Sydney.

But close to the hub jostles the ever-lively Kings Cross. Here the street spruikers and wayside amplifiers chorus the siren song of Sydney's permissiveness. Here strippers strip, gamblers gamble, dawdlers dawdle in a brassy orchestration with counter-pointing flesh and fantasy. Yet here too, as everywhere, change intrudes. Now it is new tunnels and rock channels for rail and road extensions. Bitter conflict flares between developers whose money is on high rise and the 'antis' who want no change in the status quo. Struggles like this are embedded into Sydney's history.

Approaching its 200th year, Sydney is enjoying the peak of good health and survival despite an often chaotic past. Today the city handles the chaos of modern change and the burden of people and traffic congestion as it has handled past political, industrial and economic disturbances.

In 1788, when it was all just beginning, Arthur Phillip wrote enthusiastically of his selected site as having 'the finest harbour in the world, in which a thousand ships of the line may ride in the most perfect security'. To the shores of that harbour have gathered more people than Phillip ever imagined, to live in life-styles far different from those of his time. This is the curious plot of the drama of Sydney, that two centuries later it is fulfilling the original plan Phillip had in mind for it. He sought to make a settlement that was viable, secure and eventually prosperous. Sydney today stands proud and high in the list of the world's big cities that are agreeable to live in.

119

Melbourne

Between Sydney and Melbourne there is a bitumen ribbon 900 kilometres long called the Hume Highway, a railway system converted to a standard gauge only in 1961 — and a certain rivalry. But it is a rivalry discussed more in Sydney than in Melbourne. 'Surely,' Melbourne is inclined to say, 'everyone can see for themselves . . .'

Melbourne is 57 years younger, born in 1835. And less populous with 2.8 million people. But Melbourne considers itself somewhat better mannered. And it is wealthier, having inherited much of the lush legacy of the gold discoveries in its provinces last century. Most of the gold, naturally, flowed through Melbourne and a lot somehow stayed. It sparked a boom in population, development and business energy. Except for brief Depression lulls in the last century and during the worldwide 1930s slump, that boom has continued unrelentingly.

Melbourne always wanted to be big, but without the hectic bustle. Melbourne yearned to be great, but also gracious, and the remaining older architecture still murmurs that attitude. This is proclaimed by the stately State Parliament building in Spring Street; by the older churches in Collins and Bourke; by the domed vastness of the Exhibition Building, erected with equal measures of haste and care for an international show-off in 1880. Even the city's older banks remain, appropriately, the most ornate in the country. Melbourne has always been circumspect, never grabbing too quickly at new-fangled fads that might later go out of acceptable fashion.

Melbourne had Australia's first steam railway, which opened for business between the city and Port Melbourne on 12 September 1854. But it was more than 100 years later that, unlike most of the other capitals, it sanctioned a State lottery. It also approved more permissive (by Australian standards) liquor laws. Bless Melbourne's conservative heart, the city has even retained its tramways . . . and come to be glad of it. Today and for many years ahead Melbourne's citizens will be riding these great green juggernauts. Long before anti-pollution became a cause, Melbourne decided trams were preferable to buses. Like the city itself, these ancient but steady conveyances follow their pre-set route. Both, too, seem to have acquired the steady knack of keeping to timetables.

Melbourne's most jealously protected endowment is the vast spreads of parkland, both in and right around the central city area. For every 1 000 citizens it has been estimated that the city has 2.5 hectares of parkland. At South Yarra, the Royal Botanic Gardens retain, in an era of motor freeways and soaring concrete offices, the rare delights of large sweeping lawns, leafy trees, multicoloured gardens and a lakes complex populated with swans, ducklings and myriad species of visiting wildlife.

You could say that civilisation was so keen to extend itself to Melbourne that not one but two founders rushed in and vied with each other for the honour of launching the project. First, but not quite legally, came the noble-minded John Batman. On 8 June 1835, with an adventurous little band of settlers from Tasmania, he rowed up the Yarra River and stepped ashore to proclaim his immortal line: 'This will be the place for a village'. Batman spearheaded an imaginative immigration approach on behalf of a conservative and rigorously right-minded group that called itself the Port Phillip Association. They had studied various earlier explorations, including a brief landing by Matthew Flinders, of the Port Phillip Bay area which Melbourne now straddles. They reasoned that land beside the river feeding into the bay would make an ideal settlement site. Their aim was 'free' settlement, as distinct from the earlier convict-based inaugurations of Sydney and Hobart.

It was arranged that Batman would 'buy' the site from its traditional Aboriginal holders. And so was drawn up a formal Deed of Sale for 600 000 acres. The Aborigines were paid in goods reckoned as more useful to them than the whites' paper currency: tomahawks, flour, blankets. It was all as formal as it was later deemed illegal. The British Crown had already proclaimed itself title holder to the land and a transaction like that could have no official recognition.

Hardly had the ink dried on Batman's quaint document when along came a sec-

Above: **The Melbourne Cricket Ground, capable of holding in excess of 110 000 spectators, was once host to the 1956 Olympic Games. Ranged behind the cricket ground, from right to left, are the new Olympic Pool, sprinting track and velo-drome respectively.**

Right: **Melbourne's Sidney Myer Music Bowl seems to loom over the large audience like a bat. The aluminium sheet and steel cable structure provides superb acoustics for outdoor entertainment. It is the venue for free concerts, 'Music for the People', and a variety of cultural activities.**

ond founding party, this one led by the more prosaic John Pascoe Fawkner. He arrived on 29 August 1835, with a squad of craftsmen eager to get down to the job of establishment without any of the frills of negotiations. The two founders brought with them different notions of settlement. Fawkner brought journeymen ready to begin at once the hard work of construction, a different approach from

121

Above left: Australia's second largest city, Melbourne, where the Yarra River flows without haste under Princes Bridge. The dome of Flinders Street Station, home of the first Australian rail service in 1854, and the spires of St Paul's Cathedral are dwarfed by the immensity of modern skyscrapers.

Left: The Westgate Bridge (to the fanciful eye, like an enormous prehistoric lizard) spans the lower Yarra and links Melbourne with its western suburbs. Scene of a tragic collapse in 1970, its construction took 37 lives and cost over $200 million.

Above: Melbourne's City Square Cafe, adjacent to St Paul's Cathedral, recreates something of the atmosphere of Europe.

Right: Antique street lamps elegantly adorn the steps of Victoria's State Parliament House in Spring Street and royally proclaim Melbourne's eminence as Australia's capital before the construction of the National Capital in Canberra.

Batman, who represented the softer-handed investors interested in financial speculation. A steely confrontation between the two parties existed until the Law sorted out the legalities. But for the building of Melbourne to proceed, speculative finance and trade skills were both needed.

Throughout its history, the development of Melbourne reflects the positive union of both skills. By May 1836, 13 homes had been built. But the place still had no definite name. Among several suggestions was one, Batmania, which citizens since are grateful was never adopted. Instead, in 1837, the settlement beside the Yarra River was officially named Melbourne, in honour of England's Prime Minister, Lord Melbourne. That same year, on 1 June, Melbourne planned its first legally authorised land sale, but first the Assistant Surveyor-General of Sydney, Robert Hoddle, arrived to lay out a street plan for the city. From the street muddle already evident in Sydney, the authorities had accepted the lesson that only advance planning would ensure a more orderly growth in Melbourne. Hoddle is scarcely remembered today, but the generously wide streets and open space areas he drew on his first maps remain a silent monument to his farsightedness.

At that first land sale in 1837, small central city properties fetched prices as high as 150 pounds. Only two years later some were changing hands for 10 000 pounds. Melbourne had started early on its course of becoming the wealth capital of the nation. Gold, discovered a few years later, accelerated the inrush of money and people. It became a favourite site for the headquarters of mushrooming new companies. Being the most centrally situated settlement in Australia was another factor. That was important, too, in the choice of Melbourne as the first national capital from 1901 until a fledgling Canberra opened for the business of politics in 1927.

Melbourne has somehow always managed to accept the inevitable historical changes with serenity. Like the River Yarra which flows unhurriedly right through the city and suburbs, Melbourne prefers the stable and the functional to the hasty and spectacular. The tourist showplace, the National Gallery in St Kilda Road, was completed on schedule for its opening on 20 August 1968. It cost $13 million, exactly what it had been budgeted to cost. Australia's finest art gallery, it faces the country's finest avenue sweeping straight and curved in a wide, tree-lined swathe from the city almost to the sea at St Kilda. On this route, 100 years before the builders began erecting the gallery, bushrangers bailed up travellers making the journey by night. On a hot evening 50 years later Dame Nellie Melba, a name she took in salute to the city of her birth, took rides in an open carriage in the cool evening air while her patient Town Hall audience would wait for her to return and continue her concert.

Melbourne has also given Australia more political leaders than any other city: men as diverse in their views as Bruce and Scullin, Menzies and Calwell, Deakin and Holt. Here a lad named Peter Thomson, later to become Australia's most famous golfer, first played golf on the Royal Park course. Here, at Fisherman's Bend, was born a car they called the Holden. Any listing of national figures produced by Melbourne would be almost as diverse as it would necessarily be long: tennis player Frank Sedgman; satirist Barry Humphries; TV 'king' Graham Kennedy ... Gough Whitlam, former Labor Prime Minister, was born in suburban Kew. Liberal Prime Minister, Malcolm Fraser, was educated at Melbourne Grammar School. On 9 October 1964, a 16-year-old Aboriginal boy won a bout at Melbourne Stadium that was the first rung of a climb in boxing that would see him ascend nearly four years later to a world title. His name ... Lionel Rose. Three years before Rose's fight there, another 16-year-old who had migrated to Australia from France had his first professional fight. He was Johnny Famechon, who also went on to be a world title holder after making his boxing debut in Melbourne Stadium.

Since the late 1940s, Melbourne's atmosphere has undergone a dramatic change as a result of a major influx of migrants. It has become home to more migrants than any other Australian city; its Greek ethnic population alone exceeds 125 000. Prahran High School's enrolment of 1 100 comprises 90 per cent of students with a migrant background. A Housing Commission high rise block of flats in Fitzroy houses 3 600 people who speak a total of 24 different languages.

Flemington racecourse which, since 1860, has staged the Melbourne Cup on the first Tuesday in November. Horse-racing, with its attendant gambling, is a truly national sport with a rich heritage of feats and folklore.

With traditional understatement in its operations, Melbourne continues to fulfil the City Council's motto 'We gather strength as we grow'. Here are headquartered most of Australia's biggest business corporations: BHP, CRA, ANZ, ICI. Spanning the Yarra near its mouth, the West Gate Bridge soars and curves in a gracious understatement of the fact that it is the nation's longest and tallest bridge structure. Soberly adventurous in its own circumspect way, Melbourne is the world's only city to declare itself a public holiday each year for a horse race, the Melbourne Cup.

But it sees nothing unusual in that.

To compensate for its recent rush of tall building development, it converted the heart of its Bourke Street retail area into a gaily paved and pot-planted mall. It demolished a row of shops and a faded hotel to create a City Square — complete to tumbling waterfall — that provides a walkway link between its solemn Town Hall and lawn-lined St Paul's Cathedral a block away. In the Wentworth Hotel, fifty floors above Collins Street, guests sleep, dine, gaze spellbound at views of Port Phillip Bay and the hamlets huddling its shores. Just across the Yarra, 40 feet below ground, an ant's nest of engineers, designers and workmen are busy with details of the Arts Centre theatre complex, a complementary structure to the still new National Gallery.

Melbourne still gathers strength, still grows yet.

125

Brisbane

In Brisbane the mixing of parts old and new is, well, different. It is, first, the nation's most tropical State capital, basking the year through in an average of nearly eight hours of daily sunshine. So its goes about its various businesses in a more casual way than most cities its size.

Brisbane, at many points, has installed its new buildings and features right beside the old. Today and Yesterday are often neighbours in a sometimes surprising mixture of different generations. This can startle at first. But then, like a newly-discovered cocktail, the recipe can be most stimulating. On Wickham Terrace, beside the original Observatory built by convicts in 1829, stand modern office blocks, motels and smart restaurants. In suburban Bardon, set amid today's homes, schools and nearby shopping centres, the historic 1865 mansion Fernberg sits, where State governors have resided since 1910.

Australia's great post-war building boom reached Brisbane later than it swept through most other capital cities. Until the mid-sixties the city had changed little from the preceding 20 years. Then very swiftly, as usually happens, in just one decade, the Brisbane skyline changed utterly and dramatically. Now the city took on the true late twentieth century look. As new buildings soared, freeways snaked out from the city on major traffic routes. As part of the new look, the city also got more open space. A stack of dreary old buildings in front of the imposing City Hall were ripped down to make the enlarged King George Square one of the outstanding city squares in Australia. Beneath the square is tucked a car park, a modern solution to the internationally modern parking problem. In this same recent period, some of Brisbane's older theatres were renovated. New ones sprang to life. A wide range of new restaurants suddenly appeared, to give appropriately flattering treatment to the local sea food and fresh fruit that still rank as expensive delicacies in other cities. Brisbane began attracting tourists who were not merely transients on their way to the nearby beach resorts of the Gold Coast or to more tropical parts further north.

Left: **The Albert Street Methodist Church contributes impressively to the townscape. Completed in 1889, the Victorian Gothic Revival church was constructed in red brick and white Omaru sandstone.**

Above: **A worker's cottage in the inner-city suburb of Spring Hill. Noteworthy features are the semi-circular vault at the entrance and the delicate cast iron tracery of the balustrades.**

Right: **The AMP building looms impressively over neglected warehouses.**

Brisbane City Council's municipality is a duchy of almost 1 000 square kilometres, a State within a State, that employs a staff of 10 000 to supervise the city's public road transport, electricity supply, roads, water, all development.

One advantage that Brisbane inherited was a city centre rail system, conveniently underground. Brisbane was Australia's first capital to tunnel rail routes below the city, more than 60 years ago. With a population of 900 000, city and sun-blessed suburbs have spread themselves generously over a series of low hills that offer endless and ever changing variety in their views.

Through it all lumbers majestically the broad Brisbane River. Five traffic bridges cross the river. All are modern in design. All are different. Each has its own special strength and beauty to complement the impressive power of the forever twisting and turning river. One of these vital arteries, the William Jolly Bridge near the city centre, is built in a 'through arch' design unique in the southern hemisphere. Brisbane's multi-columned City Hall, site of municipal power, commands attention and affection as the city's outstanding major building. Its clock tower looms proudly 100 metres above the street. An observation platform near the pinnacle offers visitors a 360 degree panorama view of the city. Inside the building, the city's main concert hall commands attention too for its unusual circular design.

Brisbane is still moonlit river cruises and backyard profusions of tropical fruit delights: papaw, mango, passionfruit. To these have been added the brightly glazed AMP building, a spectacular landmark in the business area, the tall and slope-fronted new Lennons-Plaza Hotel, brisk shopping arcades.

Befitting its welcoming sub-tropical setting, Brisbane has set aside 50 square kilometres of its land for parks, gardens, recreation areas and forest reserves. Outstanding among these is Mt Coot-tha, rising more than 300 metres in its own reserve just eight kilometres from the city centre. Especially at night, its summit offers breath-taking views of the city spread below. Closer to the city and on the river bank, New Farm Park displays 12 000 rose trees, as well as avenues of jacaranda and poinciana trees which bloom each spring making a profusion of colour. Typical of the mixing of different eras, the State Parliament House, a fine example of French Renaissance architecture built in 1868, is sited in its own garden of tall trees facing the splendid Botanic Gardens set on the curving river bank. Behind the Parliament building, the new Riverside Expressway links with the Captain Cook Bridge to speed cars between the river's north and south banks.

It was close to where that expressway now begins, at North Quay, that the New South Wales Surveyor-General, John Oxley, stepped from a rowing boat on 28 September 1824, and decided to establish a settlement. A convict settlement had already been set up that year on the coast 45 kilometres away at a place called Humpybong, now, thankfully, named Redcliffe. But conditions there were less than ideal and so, on 24 December 1824, the grim little colony within a colony moved to Oxley's new site.

At first it was named Edinglassie, before it was given a new name in honour of the Governor of New South Wales, Sir Thomas Brisbane. Among the first stone buildings erected was the Colonial Stores. It was later enlarged, but the original ground floor walls still remain near the river bank. In unrelenting heat the convicts sometimes suffered barbarous treatment. Free settlers were forbidden by law to come closer than 80 kilometres to this area where strict military rule operated unchallenged. In the circular mill, now the Observatory, men were forced to walk a treadmill as many as 14 hours a day as the mill ground hominy, a kind of maize used to make porridge that was an important part of an inadequate diet. A century later, in 1929, Australia's first experimental television signals were beamed from this same building.

In 1839 the Sydney authorities decided to abandon the penal settlement and by 1842 free settlers, who had been moving into nearby districts in growing numbers, began establishing homes in Brisbane. But the city's early growth was very slow. At the first land sale on 9 August 1843, centrally sited allotments could be bought at up to 250 pounds an acre. By 1846 Brisbane's population was still only 829. But other areas in what is now the State of Queensland were developing more quickly. And on 10 December 1859, the State was proclaimed a colony separate from New South Wales. At the time of that proclamation, the population of

Above: The sandstone-faced City Hall, facing King George Square, was completed in 1930, its 91 metre Italian Renaissance clock tower an impressive landmark. The imposing facade features Ionic colonnades which flank the Corinthian columns of the central portico. The pediment contains a sculpture by Daphne Mayo. Development of King George Square (with its underground car park) has created a popular forum area and pleasant lunchtime meeting place.

Right: The Mt Coot-tha Botanic Gardens, six kilometres from the city centre, cover 57 hectares at the foot of the mountain. The dazzling variety of flowers and shrubs (the plant collection already includes 90 species of palms and 140 varieties of the pineapple family) is a testimony to the sub-tropical climate. Indoor displays are housed in glass domes.

Brisbane was 5 000, in Queensland it was only 25 320, and the State Treasury held exactly two pence.

But Brisbane grew as population and industries expanded throughout the State. Thanks to its wide, deep river, Brisbane held its position as the major port as beef and dairy herds flourished on inland pastures. Coal was discovered in abundant quantities 40 kilometres to the west at Ipswich. The vast wheat lands of the Darling Downs, farther west, opened up. And then the sugar industry to the north. Later came the gold discoveries at Gympie, 150 kilometres north, and later in the State's far north.

As the capital of an essentially agricultural State, Brisbane remains a commercial metropolis with a vital agricultural background. Texans boast of the size of their State; Brisbane is the capital of a State more than twice as big. Where once bare-bodied convicts sweated to carve a colony from the wilderness, today air-conditioned offices stand amid smartly displayed shops.

With its historical links with yesterday, and a kindly, balmy climate, Brisbane stands uniquely among Australia's capitals as a cross-section of all the major factors that are themselves uniquely Australian.

Opposite: The Breakfast Creek Hotel, built in 1889, is a popular subject for local artists. Explorer John Oxley is reputed to have breakfasted on this spot.

Above: The Queen Victoria Bridge arches gracefully over the Brisbane River, linking south Brisbane to the central business district which is silhouetted in the background.

Left: The South-Eastern Expressway snakes its way along the Brisbane River, connecting the city of Brisbane to the Gold Coast, only 45 minutes away by freeway.

Adelaide

Adelaide ranks as Australia's most remote capital — in terms of temperament, not kilometres. It has been neat, trim, almost obsessively proper and quite passionately work-oriented from the day of its birth. That is the way Adelaide appears to most visitors. Neighbouring Melbourne gets into an escapist mood every autumn for the fun get-together called Moomba. That curious word just happens to translate from the Aboriginal as 'backside'. More demure Adelaide in the same season stages a higher-browed Festival of the Arts. But only once every two years.

And the 800 000 residents who live close by the gentle River Torrens like Adelaide for that. And for its cultural achievements and its innovative social legislation which today is often well ahead of other State's statutes.

This is the city where, as a child, Judith Anderson roamed the hills of its eastern border picking wild blackberries and stuffing them in her newly laundered bloomers. She later went on from there to become an internationally acclaimed actress, collecting stage and screen honours and being made a Dame on the way. As she was doing all that, a young man was stunning the cricketing world with his batsmanship, becoming Sir Donald Bradman before turning to the more sober career of stockbroker. Two of Australia's most prestigious scientists were launched: Sir Howard Florey and Sir Marcus Oliphant.

Millions of Australians have lived in homes or bought properties probably not knowing a debt they owe to Sir Robert Torrens. It was he, as South Australia's Premier in 1857, who introduced a Bill in the State Parliament to simplify the laws of land transfer. Torrens Title has since been nationally adopted as a system to simplify and safeguard land sale transactions. Like its talented sons and daughters — and the list of sons should properly include also the great vaudeville comedian Roy Rene — Adelaide's own story is one of diverse talent used with unswerving dedication to score deserved success.

World authorities rank Adelaide with Washington and Edinburgh for the successful thoroughness of its planning. King William Street, 40 metres from side to side, is the widest main street in any Australian capital. Four broad terraces, named for the points of the compass, provide a perimeter for the city proper. They in turn are girdled by a green belt, with industrial and residential areas beyond. Whether the facility is old or new, a town plan or a cultural festival, Adelaide has always striven for excellence. St Peter's Anglican Cathedral in Pennington Terrace summons worshippers with a peal of its eight bells that are classed as the finest in Australia. Over at West Beach, sea lions and seals, dolphins and sharks, as well as other varieties of sea creatures, are on view or perform daily at Marineland, which is the largest completely enclosed aquatic complex of this type in the southern hemisphere.

One of Australia's early explorers, Captain Charles Sturt, first conceived the idea of settling this particular region. In 1828 he accepted a commission from Governor Darling in Sydney to lead an expedition to trace the courses of the Murrumbidgee and Darling rivers. This journey of more than 6 500 kilometres led him inevitably to the Murray River, which he followed to its mouth. He later published a detailed account of his expedition. It contained some thoughtful suggestions for a new colony somewhere near the Murray's mouth. As early as 1801 the ubiquitous Matthew Flinders had surveyed that part of the coast. Thirty years later Captain Collet Barker and a party trekked inland from the sea and decided this area between the hills and the coast would be ideal for settling. Sturt's writings clinched the whole concept.

In 1835 a committee was set up in London to foster a migration scheme to the new area. One of its patrons was the Duke of Wellington, no less. And the name chosen for the new settlement was Adelaide, in honour of the wife of the ruling King William IV. As first governor, the King appointed the distinguished naval officer and veteran of Nelson's battles of the Nile and Trafalgar, Sir John Hindmarsh. It was to be a free settlement — no convicts — and one where the most welcome would be hard-working, God-fearing people, prepared to invest their physical energies as well as any money they had into the venture.

Adelaide's first settlers were the nearest Australia had to the Puritans who had

Rundle Mall, which crosses one of Adelaide's busiest thoroughfares. Increasingly, city planners and pedestrians are acknowledging the benefits accrued by closing congested inner-city streets to motor traffic.

sailed to America in the *Mayflower* 216 years earlier, except that they were not fleeing from religious persecution. In July 1836 the ambitious band landed at what is now the Adelaide beach suburb of Glenelg. Despite all the careful organisation, a bitter dispute soon erupted among them. Hindmarsh and the settlement's planning surveyor Colonel William Light, both very determined men, fought vigorously over the issue of exactly where the new settlement would be sited. Light won. A grid plan he set out was finally adopted and put into practice. Hindmarsh was recalled to England. Following the ideal of keeping rigorously to systems, a municipal body was inaugurated in 1840 to provide local government in the area, becoming the first civic body of this type in Australia.

With the settlement well established, the colonists turned to the education of its future leaders. In 1847 the Collegiate School of St Peter opened with that purpose largely in mind. It continues the same task today. Among the nation's capitals, Adelaide has always enjoyed some status as being slightly different, even insular. The reputation as 'the city of churches', a commodity with which Adelaide has always been well endowed, has perhaps enlarged this image. But what is often overlooked is that the creation of Adelaide presented some special difficulties that made stern demands on early inhabitants. In many ways the climate is less kind than other capitals enjoy. Summers are long, hot and dry. The annual rainfall is the least of all capitals.

From the beginning, too, home-builders were unable to obtain adequate local supplies of quality timber to build their homes, and Adelaide today has a higher proportion of brick and stone homes than other major cities. But it does have the luxury of more than 30 kilometres of wide and sandy beaches less than half an hour's travelling time from the city centre. From Outer Harbour in the north to Seacliff in the south, these are a prominent suburban feature. Also, to the east, are the famed Adelaide Hills, a splendid Natureland and vast green oasis beside the busy metropolis.

Over the last 20 years, new building developments have almost completely transformed the city's skyline. In one year alone — 1968 — a record 44 500 square metres of new office space was added to Adelaide's commercial stage. Each year has seen fresh expansions. Originally the city planners had imposed a building height limit of 40 metres to restrict high rise development. That, however, became pushed away under the thrust of commercial and industrial expansion.

Post-war years brought an inrush of industrial development to balance the State's essentially primary production of the pre-war era. Expansions in the motor car industry have proved especially valuable, making Adelaide today one of the nation's strategic car manufacturing centres. More recent discoveries of uranium and natural gas are now giving fresh impetus to the economic and industrial growth of this diverse city. For here, amid bustling commerce, unobtrusively sits the South Australian Museum, containing the world's largest collection of Aboriginal artifacts — plus items from Papua New Guinea and Melanesia in a range not duplicated anywhere else in Australia.

Above: **Adelaide's Festival Centre, home of the biennial Festival of Arts. The building's fine acoustic design and striking appearance have merited international acclaim.**

Right: **The grand porch of Parliament House, Adelaide, with its carved marble capitals and entablatures, is the finest of its kind in Australia.**

With the calmly idle River Torrens and its complex of lakes forming a picturesque centre-piece, Adelaide's well-planned beauty comes from a neat mixing of its buildings, old and new. Outstanding among the new is the $6.5 million Festival Theatre, opened in 1973. Behind an eye-catching modern exterior, it contains a 2 000 seat auditorium that has won high critical acclaim as a concert hall, opera house or to whatever other purpose it has been put.

But the old buildings are cared for too. That list includes the Holy Trinity Church of England built in 1838 and the oldest church in the State. In its tower, still working, is the original clock made by the clockmaker to King William IV. Still preserved, too, is Grange, the home of Charles Sturt built in 1840. In it still are some of the furnishings Sturt's family brought from their original home in Cheltenham, England. On North Terrace the National Trust now cares for Ayers House, helping it earn its keep as a restaurant and reception centre. The land this house stands on was bought in 1837 for 12 shillings. In 1846 a chemist, William Paxton, built on it a two storey stone cottage. Nine years later it was bought by a prominent politician-businessman, Henry Ayers, who commissioned architect George Kingston to plan a series of extensions. Among additions made over the next six years was a ballroom ranked in its time as the best in the State and still preserved today.

Whether in a sparkling new theatre or a nineteenth century mansion, Adelaide demonstrates special qualities of purpose, stability and durability. They remain a continuing reflection of the people of dedication who dreamed of a city here and insisted it must be a good one. People like Sturt, Barker and Colonel Light, whose original plan remains a remarkable national, as well as local, achievement.

134

Perth

In the family of Australian capital cities, Perth displays an open freshness, a sense of freedom and youth that none of the others can quite match. Perth is, to many, what San Francisco is to Americans. Visitors invariably proclaim Perth the friendliest and most welcoming of the major Australian cities. The city is unsophisticated, nurtured in a gentle climate, living a life that is less hurried, less worried. Some of Perth's most famous sons demonstrate its special qualities in their public performances: the direct but often humoured frankness of Bob Hawke, former ACTU President and now a Member of Parliament . . . the fierce determination of Sir Charles Court . . . the irreverence and flair of publisher Max Newton . . . business-sportsman Alan Bond . . . high-flying industrialist Lang Hancock.

Since 1961, when Perth citizens burned their lights all night to guide American astronaut Colonel John Glenn on one of his high and perilous earth orbits, Perth has been known as the City of Light . . . but it equally deserves titles like City of Air, City of Sun, or City of Grace. Graceful in name and reality is the Swan River which curves through the metropolis. Graceful are the major streets such as wide, tree-lined St George's Terrace, one of the country's outstanding boulevards. Graceful are the green-lawned and uncluttered suburbs, their spaciousness underlined by the 1 200 square kilometres of parks, sports reserves and open land areas that spread about the city.

Enjoying a climate similar to but drier than Sydney's, Perth radiates a similar outdoors style of life, a sun-drenched expressiveness that has come to be recognised internationally as a genuinely Australian life-style. Being smaller than Sydney has produced benefits. Perth has been able to cope more smoothly and retain more natural heritage in the transformations of recent decades.

In the early 1950s the city adopted a Metropolitan Regional Plan to handle the expected growth rate. Developments have been bigger than the plan's designers imagined. But the plan has always been able to adapt to handle them. Over recent years, more than $30 million has been spent annually on new city buildings. And interspersed with them are still the plazas and shopping malls that make Perth a pedestrian's delight. No matter how much it grows, Perth is determined to remain the broad-spaced, airy, sunny city it has always been.

The history of Perth, too, is different from the story of other Australian cities. In 1827 the British Colonial authorities in London suspected that the French were contemplating a colony on the Australian west coast, to rival those the British had already established on the eastern seaboard. To study possible new sites in the west came Captain James Stirling. He saw the river that was named after the black swans that glided on it and was immediately ecstatic at the prospect of a settlement here. So enthusiastic were his official reports that he created what became known as Swan River Mania in London.

'The climate,' he wrote, 'appears to be delightful and must be highly favourable to vegetation, which was accordingly observed to be most luxuriant'. And sure enough, on 12 August 1829, the first white settlers arrived to begin the building of a town at the site Stirling recommended about 16 kilometres up river from the mouth of the Swan. By the end of 1829, the settlement boasted 300 residents. Stirling came too, first as Lieutenant-Governor and later, in 1831, as Governor of the new colony. He proved as popular with the new settlers as he was enterprising. Eventually he was knighted for his services and is remembered in Stirling Gardens in the city and the Stirling Range not far outside it.

But the 'mania' generated by his early reports diminished. Perth's early development was slow. One deterrent was isolation from the other Australian settlements; it was 4 000 kilometres from Sydney to the east, for instance. British authorities also used the opening up of this section of the continent to unload some of their surplus convict numbers. By 1837, only 350 houses had been built in Perth. In 1848, the population was still only 1 148. And another 1 400 people were living in Fremantle and other nearby settlements. By 1858 Perth's population had struggled to 3 000 and Perth City Council was inaugurated. But residents' numbers still lagged: 5 000 in 1871 . . . 8 400 in 1890. Then . . . gold! Major discoveries were made in the harsh desert areas east of the city. By the end of the nineteenth century, the population of Perth had jumped to 27 000 — and kept going.

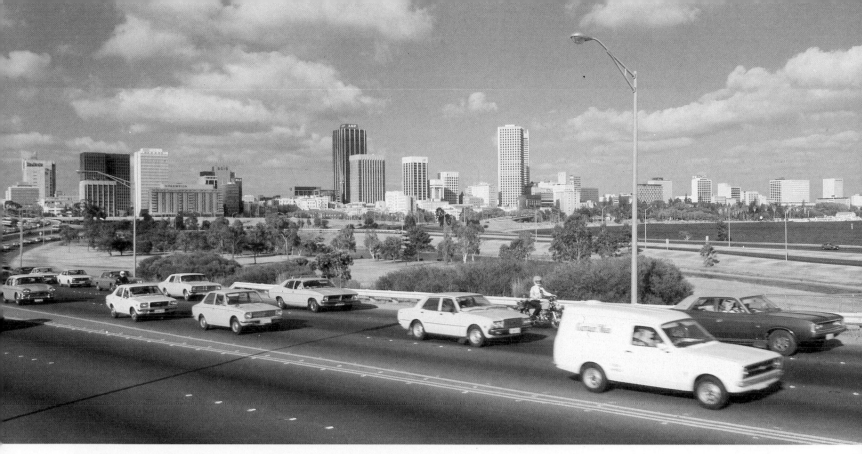

Perth, viewed from Narrows Bridge, overlooking the waters of the Swan River. In order to build this smooth approach to the city, much of the river shallows was reclaimed.

Already by that time the awesome problems of distance and isolation were fading. Shipping services, the main transport and communication link, improved with every year. A telegraph service to the east coast opened in 1877. Ten years later Perth's telephone service began operating. But it was not until 1917 that a rail link with the east was made.

This century has witnessed Perth's most spectacular population leaps: 200 000 in 1930 doubling to 400 000 by 1960, then more than doubling again to 850 000 today. Civic authorities estimate that by the year 2000 the population will reach 1.5 million. Although 'the eastern States', as they are known, are only a few hours away now by modern aircraft, a sense of isolation, of being a little away from it all, remains a major part of the city's special charm. It has given Perth an independent spirit that was displayed, for instance, in a popular vote taken in the whole State in 1932 to secede from the rest of Australia. That vote, fortunately for the nation, was never acted on. But similar sentiments continue to exist today.

Australia's first free university was in Perth. This, too, was one of the first capitals to stage a civic festival of art, music and drama that attracts international artists and attention. With care, Perth has preserved much of its past as it forges into the future. A mill built in the 1830s to grind wheat remains as a museum. The earlier Town Hall, built in the style of an English Jacobean market hall, is kept intact and only the tulip fields of Holland can rival the riotous colour of Perth's flower displays every spring.

Almost unbelievably vast discoveries of iron ore and a range of other minerals — even, more recently, diamonds — in the State's hinterland have reflected much of their glowing new affluence towards Perth. A world facing an energy crisis has looked anew at the astonishing geological riches being unearthed in this State. One earlier major industry, whaling, is now discontinued by Australian Government command. Meanwhile others have burgeoned. Since 1955 the Kwinana oil refinery, with its $400 million worth of ancillary industrial complexes, has operated only 32 kilometres from the city's centre. A modern day 'boom town', Perth is fittingly furnished with Australia's largest Entertainment Centre: an indoor auditorium with seating for 8 000. Each February, the Perth Festival celebrates with music, art and theatre the splendours and personal talents of this remote but special piece of civilisation that is, in so many ways, unique — not just to Australia, but to the world.

137

Above left: **Western Australia's Government House, vaguely reminiscent of the Tower of London, was built by Governor Hampton in the 1860s with the help of convict labour.**

Far left: **Lifesavers on Mullaboo Beach, which is one of many beautiful beaches easily accessible from Perth and renowned for fine surf and a relative scarcity of sharks.**

Left: **Sailing on the Swan River (named after the profusion of black swans which inhabit its reaches). This broad, calm expanse, with its convenient central location, is a popular spot for all forms of aquatic indulgence.**

Above: **Perth by night, viewed from King's Park — a profusion of lights almost as dazzling as a candlelight parade. With a population of 850 000 citizens, this increasingly sophisticated city boasts the largest entertainment centre in Australia.**

Right: **King's Park covers 405 hectares and rates as one of Perth's major attractions. Within its perimeter lie a superb botanic garden, a huge floral clock and a delightful restaurant.**

Hobart

Hobart is a city that is a very special blend of riverscape and mountain vistas, a mixture of the old and the new settlement, chilled in winter but bathed in clear sunlight for most of the year. Although it is the State capital farthest from the tropics, Hobart enjoys a daily average of six hours of sunlight throughout the year. The mountain backdrop and riverside setting give Hobart a European alpine atmosphere that seems almost unreal in this antipodean latitude. It could almost be a busy market town on the Rhine or Danube.

Like Perth, Hobart enjoys its isolation from the nation's main population centres. Citizens will call the Australian mainland 'the other island' while conceding only a partnership of equality between the two.

Hobart is pleased to retain, and display, its genuine links with the past: streets named Byron, Nelson, Gladstone and Waterloo in the days when those names were contemporary. Then, from the past commemorated in those streets, Sandy Bay Road snakes its curved route out of the city and into the suburbia of modern homes huddled along the shores of the majestic Derwent River.

No other capital city waterway is as blue as the Derwent. None is so unspoiled. On both banks, sudden land rises provide memorable vantage points to watch this glistening waterway; whether its business at the time be the commerce of big ships, the weekend display of pleasure craft, or the spectacular fleet of yachts each year finishing the Sydney-Hobart ocean race. Straddling the Derwent is the humpback Tasman Bridge, broken by a shipping disaster in 1975, now mended, and again the major artery link joining the two sides of the city. On the river's east bank, the suburbs of Lindisfarne and Bellerive with their flower-splashed avenues provide spacious suburban relief from the narrow streets of the city proper.

Among Australia's major cities, only Sydney is older than Hobart. Here, on the Derwent, the first attempt at a settlement was made in September 1803 at Risdon, about eight kilometres upstream from the present site of Hobart. From Sydney, Governor King had despatched Lieutenant John Bowen with a founding party of 35 convicts and ten officers to establish a penal post on the island that was at that time called Van Diemen's Land. But the original Risdon site proved unsuitable, so the settlement moved downstream in February 1804 to the present site of Hobart. Named after Lord Hobart, the Secretary of State for the British Colonies, Hobart began its life that year with a total of 433 residents, 281 of them convicts.

Sited at the farthermost point of the globe from the British authorities, the early history of Hobart Town, which it was called officially until 1881, abounded with confusion and conflict. Being so far away, it seemed an ideal dumping ground for unwanted convicts. At nearby Port Arthur, massive ruins of cell blocks four storeys high demonstrate the large numbers shipped in.

In 1811 Governor Macquarie voyaged from Sydney to inspect the bristling penal outpost, was horrified at the confusion he saw, and promptly sat down and drew up an orderly town plan for the settlement. But it soon drew upon itself the undistinguished description of 'the Gaol of the Empire'. Between 1817 and 1830, more than 13 000 convicts were shipped in to eke out misery-filled lives in the struggling town. As a balance, the authorities also sought to encourage free settlement in the colony's rich pasture lands. Farmers were enticed with offers of free land grants, generous loans and a plentiful supply of cheap convict labour.

Fertile pastures, so similar to England's own, were soon producing high quality wool fleeces to be shipped out from the busy Hobart wharves. From the seas around came harvests of sealskins and whale oil. To collect them, ships from all over the world sailed up the Derwent. Prosperity from all this trading produced a new civic awareness among Hobart's civilian population. As this grew, public feeling increased against the continued transportation of convicts. This reached a peak by 1852 when the city established its first municipal council. A year later transportation ended. Hobart was launched as a completely free enterprise society.

Today it is a city of 167 000 people. And the Derwent, one of the nation's noblest rivers, remains its focal point. In its upper reaches, on the city's outskirts, it meanders narrowly through smoothly sloping farmlands. No other place in Australia looks so much like a piece of England transplanted; Devon, perhaps, or some of the gentler terrain of Sussex. After flowing through the city, it broadens

These old warehouses at historic Salamanca Place, Hobart, serviced a team of thriving merchants in the days when timber ships and whalers were a common sight.

dramatically. In some places it becomes more than three kilometres wide. Here, as in the city, it is also usefully deep. At the city docks its depth is more than 20 metres. Towering behind the city, the great bulk of Mt Wellington looms to a height of 1 400 metres. Beside it, Mt Nelson contributes another 400 metres. Capped, as they often are, in cloud or snow, they contribute picturesque strength to the mixed cityscape below. Twisting up and around the body of Mt Wellington are 20 kilometres of sealed roadway. All around the Olympian edifice are forests, preserved as they always were. Close by the river's edge, beside the white pillars of the Tasman Bridge, Queen's Domain provides another 2.5 square kilometres of parkland to the city. Here, around the imposing Government House are public playgrounds: swimming pools, tennis courts, the Hobart cricket oval.

National Trust 'A' classifications, to be preserved at all costs, have been awarded to 77 historic Hobart buildings. Most are in the earliest settled area around Battery Point. They include a cluster of dockland warehouses in Salamanca Place built in the 1830s. Modern history nudges the early nineteenth century in the upper city sections. Here the ubiquitous AMP building, banks and office blocks have become new neighbours to grey stone constructions more than a century older.

But the most sweeping contrast is visible in the entertainment sector. Hobart is home to Australia's oldest surviving legitimate theatre: the Royal in Campbell Street. And just a short distance south towers the circular Las Vegas style casino opened for business at Wrest Point in 1973. Its theatre is the sumptuously appointed Cabaret Room, which is just part of the $10 million complex of gambling areas, restaurants and 195 self-contained guest rooms.

A settlement founded on the despair of some of the world's most wretched convicts has evolved into a commercial and tourist centre. Some of the old buildings provide the tangible links in the chain of years reaching back to the past. Like the new edifices close by, they are part of the story of this now tranquil and aesthetically moving city.

Above: **A bird's eye view of Hobart, the second oldest capital city in Australia. Located on the Derwent River, with its fine deep-water access for shipping, the city has benefited greatly from the construction of the Tasman Bridge in 1964 which encouraged the growth of new suburbs.**

Left: **Hobart, viewed across the tree covered slopes of Mt Wellington, at whose foot it lies. In winter, the mountain is capped with snow.**

Above: **The many attractions of the Salamanca Place street markets.**

Above right: **The nearby penal settlement at Port Arthur was established in 1830 and held 30 000 convicts during its existence. Today, the cell blocks, prison yards and watchtowers, and the ruins of the fine church (built in 1837) are major tourist attractions.**

Below: **Constitution Dock, Hobart, where whaling ships of old laid anchor. Today, it comes into national focus, as the destination of the Sydney to Hobart Yacht Race.**

Canberra

Canberra, from its beginnings, has always been the Pastoral Symphony among the various rhythms of different Australian cities. As the national capital, it carries the distinguished title of the nation's first city although it was, in fact, the last of them to be built. But being last built has meant also that it was more carefully planned than some of the others. Here good fortune and successive paternal governments have combined to treat the residents generously. Canberra is also a living monument to a dream that has recurred more regularly in this century: that people should be able to fashion for themselves living quarters that suitably complement the natural setting.

To this serene inland site, people transported all the paraphernalia they needed for modern living: the bitumen and glass, street signs and air conditioning, steel and concrete. With them they fashioned a modern city that rests easily in its environment. Here and there, they even helped Nature where they thought it useful. A string of lakes was created to provide an easier balance between scenery and buildings. Perhaps in the narcissism of politics they sought also to add a reflection to what had been done.

In some ways Canberra is a modern miracle. Strict civic codes have ensured that even hotels and emporiums be clean-lined and non-garish. Here even the buses purr softly as they grope through their often confusing routes. Here banks and office blocks must share space with gum trees in an unexpected arrangement that is ideal to the point of being bizarre, simply because it is so rare. Lucky Canberra was built on a giant meadow. Low mountains shelter it. A lazy little stream, the Molonglo, carelessly passes through. As a city, it belongs to this country as much as it belongs to the whole nation.

On 7 December 1820, a settler at nearby Moss Vale, John Wild, set out on a small expedition to discover what sort of land lay around where he lived. He came, before long, to the site where Canberra stands today. In his diary he described it: 'a beautiful clear plain ... fine rich soil, plenty of grass, beautiful river'. By 1823 free settlers were fanning out from the restlessness of Sydney, pushing their sheep and cattle herds the 300 kilometres to the new pasture Wild had written about. In 1838 a sheep herder named Joshua John Moore bought 1 000 acres of the land. He paid five shillings an acre for it. A few months later he added another 742 acres to his holding. Of course he was not to know, but he had actually bought the land where one day would stand the Australian National University, Canberra Community Hospital, the city's Civic Centre, a Roman Catholic cathedral and a racecourse.

For the next 70 years the area cruised peacefully through its almost unnoticed pastoral existence. It went under different spellings of the name local Aborigines gave it: Canbury, Kembery, Camberry, Caamberra, Kamberra, and finally, Canberra. But according to the Aborigines, they all meant the one thing. Meeting place.

Australia's six States federated in 1901, an event that was of course known to the residents of this natural amphitheatre beside the daydreaming Molonglo. They could not have known the sweeping change that event would have on their district. The decision to federate was made before plans were initiated to establish a site for a national capital. Temporarily, the Federal Parliament met in Melbourne while studies got under way to choose a place suitable for the headquarters of the new federal administration. In the first nine years, more than 40 sites were considered. Eventually it was decided that a spot placed somewhere between Sydney and Melbourne would be preferable. And because of the potential Canberra's setting offered, it was agreed that here would be built a showplace capital.

In October 1909, the Australian Government reached agreement with New South Wales on the transfer of land within the State that would become the Australian Capital Territory with Canberra its heart. That spelling was decided on, after it was also decided to retain the name.

Now the government had to decide what sort of city would be built in this placid meadow. An international competition was launched for a design. It drew 137 entries from all parts of the world. It was eventually won by an already well-respected architect and designer in Chicago, Walter Burley Griffin. He drafted a design of

Despite the meticulous planning of American architect Walter Burley Griffin, in which major areas are linked by concentric circles, some visitors to Canberra find it difficult to determine where they are.

wide circles and contoured curves, with occasional long straight vistas in front of prominent buildings such as Parliament House. Anticipating the automobile age then just barely gaining momentum, he mapped out wide streets. Most important of all, his plan retained the bushland green.

In 1911 the federal authorities resumed the land Joshua John Moore had bought so cheaply in 1838 and the job of building the new city began. Work was interrupted by World War I, but resumed in 1921. On 9 May 1927, the new city was formally launched with a ceremonial opening of the national Parliament in its new quarters by the Duke and Duchess of York, later to become King George VI and Queen Elizabeth. While that was all very spectacular and historic, for the next 30 years Canberra slumbered as a city.

By the early 1950s its population was only 34 000. Even politicians generally stayed only when parliament was in session. Public servants posted there found off-duty Canberra life something to be endured more than enjoyed.

Canberra began changing in the late 1950s when the government of Sir Robert Menzies decided it should play its proper role as the nation's governmental and administrative centre. Departments with administrative headquarters in Sydney and Melbourne were moved, with suitable protests from the public servants, to Canberra. In less than 20 years the population quadrupled. Then it went on growing, growing, to the 240 000 who live there today. New schools, shops and other facilities were provided. One thing Canberra has become noted for is the highest-rating education system in the country. New suburbs fanned out over surrounding hills and valleys. A little less suddenly, Canberra became one of the nation's major tourist centres. People actually came to see their national government in action ... well, in debate anyway. And the city transformed from a dull bush town to a glamorous 'happening' place offering tourist accommodation equal to any in Australia.

Parliament House itself has become a major centre of interest where 'real live' politicians, who often appear on television, can be seen in the flesh. In 1979, the

Top: **Viewed in the foreground at the termination of Anzac Parade — the Australian War Memorial, a stylised Byzantine structure.**

Above: **The Carillon on Lake Burley Griffin, a musical instrument, was built in 1963.**

Left: **The new High Court building, Canberra, was opened in May 1980 by Her Majesty Queen Elizabeth II.**

search for a new Parliament House was launched by way of an international design competition. The winning design, submitted by the world renowned architectural firm of Mitchell, Giurgola and Thorpe, is brilliant in its simplicity and in its respect for the symbolic concepts of Walter Burley Griffin. The new Parliament House is expected to be completed in 1988, in time for the Bicentenary celebrations.

About 50 overseas countries maintain diplomatic missions in the city, their buildings often reflecting their home country's traditional or representative architecture. But the variety of building covers a wide range: from the classical National Library on the lake shore, to the igloo-shaped Academy of Science, to the newest architectural wonder and conceit — the High Court building that, from a little distance, looks like a transported castle from Disneyland.

But always the essentially rural setting lingers. This is still the typical Australia, the bush, that no architectural style has yet managed to replace. But Canberra's cleanness, openness and modernity blend with the bushland setting like an artful piece of jewellery.

The Papua New Guinea embassy, like many others in Canberra, is an architectural statement reflecting the culture of its people. This one is called a 'Haus Tambaran' or spirit house and the carved post is intended to ward off evil spirits. The first foreign mission in Canberra was established by the United States Government; in 1942 they built their Williamsburg Colonial compound on one of the best sites in Yarralumla. Since then, the number of exotic diplomatic residences has proliferated — and they have become a popular tourist attraction.

147

And the rest . . .

Australia's capitals, different as each one is, have a talented back-up group of provincial cities interspersed between them. Each, like the capitals, has its own qualities and character. No two are quite alike, even those industrial twins near Sydney, Newcastle and Wollongong. Each of these has its high chimneys, blazing furnaces and the people who operate them. Each has fine sand beaches and surrounding belts of bushland. But the flavours differ, as their histories differ. The open-neck way of life that was Darwin before it was devastated by the Christmas cyclone of 1974, has returned with the post-cyclone rebuilding of this ultra-relaxed Northern Territory capital.

Distinctive in its mixing of styles is Geelong. Here Shell, Ford, Alcoa and International Harvester make their products, which are shipped out from the harbour along with the wool and wheat that are trucked in from the nearby Victorian Western District. This busy and historic industrial and commercial centre just happens to lie on slopes easing down to the broad sweep of Corio Bay, with its circle of calm beaches and lawned embankments.

Unique again is South Australia's Elizabeth, a brave new post-war experiment in satellite city building, where a transplanted community lives out a novel concept. Queensland's Townsville of the tropical north could be almost in another country from the wheat city of Toowoomba high up on the Darling Downs in the south of the State. And on the New South Wales-Victoria border yet another plan develops: the rivalrous twins Albury and Wodonga are being merged, with government help, into a larger development.

Cities large and small, all different, help form the patchwork pattern that is Australian life. Pioneers, bushrangers, epic moments in history are remembered. As tomorrows are planned and moved towards.

Opposite page; above left: **A new city has grown out of the wreckage left by Cyclone Tracy in 1974. Perhaps more than any other building in Darwin, the casino symbolises the new city — affluent and brashly aggressive.**

Above right: **Complete with minarets and iron lace, the Central Hotel, Cairns, exhibits the ostentatious optimism that came with the swift success of the sugar industry around the turn of the century.**

Above: **The mineral and pastoral wealth of Queensland's central north shows in the decorous affluence of its business capital, Townsville, (a city which gave little hint of future prosperity in its inauspicious birth with a carcass-melting works).**

Right: **Gold discoveries near Charters Towers in the 1870s prompted the construction of an artificial harbour at Townsville at the mouth of the Ross River. The estuary remains as a sheltered marina for fishing boats and pleasure craft.**

149

POLITICS

Malcolm Mackerras

**'The frequency of elections has one beneficial effect.
It reduces the amount of ballyhoo.'**

The governmental system of Australia may best be described as a cross between those of the United Kingdom and the United States, leavened by some features unique to Australia.

The basic conventions by which the ministry is chosen from the party (or coalition) enjoying the confidence of the lower house are derived from the British model. However, the United Kingdom has a unitary system with all other levels of government subject to the will of Westminster, whereas Australia is a federation in which a written constitution lists the powers of the Commonwealth Parliament but leaves other, or residual, powers in the hands of the six 'sovereign' States. This model is more like that of the United States. Indeed, in some respects the Australian Constitution is based on the Constitution of the United States.

This cross-breed was the result of historical development. The settlement of Australia took place in a number of separate colonies. By the end of the nineteenth century there were six such colonies, each with its own two-chamber parliament, but 'Australia' remained a geographic expression like 'Europe', with no political entity.

In the last decade of the nineteenth century public opinion increasingly favoured one Australian nation. As Edmund Barton, later to become Australia's first Prime Minister, proclaimed it: 'For the first time in history, we have a nation for a continent, and a continent for a nation'.

After a series of Convention Debates in the 1890s the colonial politicians thrashed out the Constitution which came into force in 1901. 'The Commonwealth of Australia' was thus created and the six colonies became the 'Original States'. Though the politicians who wrote the Constitution were in many ways far-sighted, there were many contentious questions which could only be settled by compromise. It is also a conservative document that has become an anti-socialist device — and the bane of Labor governments. Where the post-war British Labour Government met no legal or constitutional difficulties in nationalising a number of key industries, the Australian Labor Government found that its nationalisation plans were declared invalid by the High Court. Where British and New Zealand Labour governments had no difficulties in introducing their universal health schemes, Australian Labor had much difficulty.

151

Left: **This piece of ambiguous symbolism is a typical Northern Territory gesture.**

A particular way in which the Constitution has become conservative has been in its formal amendment. The Constitution can be amended if most voters in a majority of States agree to an amendment proposed by the Federal Parliament. Although 36 proposals to alter the Constitution have been put to the electors at referendums since Federation, only eight have been approved. But although the people have refused federal governments extra powers there has been a substantial *de facto* increase in federal power. This has been caused mainly by the financial dominance which the Commonwealth enjoys over the States, and has been assisted by the changing legal climate in the High Court which has interpreted the Constitution in a manner more favourable to the Commonwealth.

At the time of Federation the main political dispute was over 'free trade' or 'protection', but by 1910 the free traders and protectionists had united against a new enemy, the Australian Labor Party (ALP), which won the election that year for the first time with a majority in both houses of the Federal Parliament. Since 1910 the contest at all elections, federal and State, has been fundamentally between the ALP and various conservative parties which may be lumped together under the title 'anti-Labor'.

Australian Prime Minister, Malcolm Fraser, enjoys a drink and meets the people.

The success of the parties, federally and in each State, is set out in Table 1.

TABLE 1
Years of Party Control
of Australian Governments 1910-1980

	Years of Labor Rule	Years of Non-Labor Rule
Federal	18	52
New South Wales	40	30
Victoria	9	61
Queensland	39	31
South Australia	23	47
Western Australia	34	36
Tasmania	50	20

The Federal Parliament

Under the Constitution there are two houses of the Federal Parliament, both of which are elected directly by the people by universal adult franchise.

The upper house is known as the Senate and represents the six States equally, regardless of population. Since the 1949 election there have been ten senators from each of the six States of whom five are elected every three years for six-year terms in a rotational system. Since the 1975 election there are also two senators for each mainland territory. There are 64 senators in all.

The lower house is known as the House of Representatives and is elected for a term not exceeding three years. According to the Constitution: 'the number of such members shall be, as nearly as practicable, twice the number of the senators' and 'the number of members chosen in the several States shall be in proportion to the respective numbers of their people'.

Whereas senators for each State are elected with each State as a single electorate, members of the House of Representatives are elected from single-member districts, the boundaries of which change at each redistribution. The present boundaries were drawn in 1977 and (with a minor adjustment giving Western Australia an extra seat in 1980) have applied for the elections of December 1977 and October 1980.

TABLE 2
The General Election 18 October 1980

State/Territory	Electors	Senators*	Members
New South Wales	3 183 091	10	43
Victoria	2 413 273	10	33
Queensland	1 355 374	10	19
South Australia	849 302	10	11
Western Australia	749 286	10	11
Tasmania	273 477	10	5
Australian Capital Territory	135 957	2	2
Northern Territory	55 160	2	1
TOTAL	9 014 920	64	125

* To give the full numbers I have shown ten senators per State. Actually only five per State were elected in 1980 as the other five had been elected in 1977.

At the general election for the House of Representatives held on 2 December 1972, the ALP was returned for the first time in 23 years. Its period in office was marked by clashes with the Senate which resulted in two double dissolutions (with both houses dissolving) followed by general elections in May 1974 and December 1975. Table 3 sets out the percentage of votes polled by each party, and the numerical strength of each party in the House of Representatives, after the general elections of 1972, 1974, 1975, 1977 and 1980.

TABLE 3

Party	1972 %	1972 Seats	1974 %	1974 Seats	1975 %	1975 Seats	1977 %	1977 Seats	1980 %	1980 Seats
Australian Labor Party	49.6	67	49.3	66	42.8	36	39.6	38	45.1	51
Liberal Party	32.1	38	34.9	40	41.8	68	38.1	67	37.4	54
National Country Party	9.4	20	10.8	21	11.3	23	10.0	19	8.9	20
Democratic Labor Party	5.2	—	1.4	—	1.3	—	1.4	—	0.3	—
Australia Party/ Democrats	2.4	—	2.3	—	0.4	—	9.4	—	6.6	—
Other	1.3	—	1.2	—	2.4	—	1.5	—	1.7	—
TOTAL	100.0	125	100.0	127	100.0	127	100.0	124	100.0	125

These were the five most recent general elections at the time of writing, and serve as a basis for a discussion for the various parties and their sources of strength and weakness. The next few years may see yet another change of government and some changes in the shape of the conservative parties, but the basic choice between Labor and 'anti-Labor' is not likely to change.

Parties and the electoral system

Australia, like the United Kingdom and New Zealand, has a party system based on social class. However, it differs in having more than one anti-Labor party. Where the United Kingdom has the Conservative Party and New Zealand the National Party, Australia has a coalition of the Liberal Party (representing the urban middle class) and the National Country Party (representing the rural middle class) — a difference mainly caused by Australia's electoral system.

While the United Kingdom and New Zealand elect their lower houses by the 'first past the post' counting of votes, Australia elects its House of Representatives (and all lower houses of the mainland States) by 'preferential voting'. The geographical nature of the House of Representatives resembles other democracies in that single-member districts return one MP. However, whereas 'first past the post' gives the voter only one choice and the winner is the candidate with the most votes, 'preferential voting' requires voters to place a number, in the order of their choice, against the name of each candidate on the ballot paper. A candidate is not elected unless he or she has more first preference votes than all other candidates combined. Where no candidate has such a number, the candidate with the fewest first preference votes is excluded and the second preferences as nominated on the ballot papers are distributed among the remaining candidates.

Under 'first past the post' voting, the anti-Labor forces are generally organised as one party behind one candidate to avoid fragmenting and wasting the anti-Labor vote. Under the Australian system, however, it is possible for both a Liberal and a National Country Party candidate to oppose a Labor candidate because they can exchange preferences against the ALP.

Table 3 shows that the three main parties are Labor, Liberal and the National Country Party. Labor represents 'the working class' and draws much of its organisational strength from its association with the trade union movement. The Liberal and National Country parties act as a coalition because they hold fundamentally similar views of society.

Political history since 1910 points up the conservatism of the Australian electorate. As can be seen in Table 1 Labor has been in office at the federal level for a total of 18 years, while the total for non-Labor is 52 years. Short periods of Labor government have been typically followed by long periods of non-Labor government. And the ALP has never won more than two consecutive elections, while non-Labor has won as many as nine consecutive elections.

After the 'free traders' and 'protectionists' merged in 1908, the dominant non-Labor party was known variously as the 'Liberal Party' (1908-16), 'National Party' (1916-31), and 'United Australia Party' (1931-44). When, in 1944, Robert Gordon Menzies founded a new LIBERAL PARTY from the ruins of the defeated United Australia Party, he put together an organisation which was to lead the longest-lived government in federal history. After an initial defeat in 1946 it went on to victory in 1949 (in coalition with the Country Party) and remained in office until 1972. It regained office in 1975.

The party was formed, in Menzies' words, 'to produce unity of organisation among those who do not support socialism as a solution to Australia's political and economic problems'. The Liberals, holding the reins of federal government for 28 of their 36 years, have been the most successful party in Australian history. And yet, except in the Victorian and South Australian State Parliaments, they have always needed the support of a coalition with the Country Party.

The Liberal Party claims to be the only true 'national' party. In its view the Labor Party is a 'class' party, the Country Party is 'sectional' and only the Liberal Party stands for the nation as a whole and 'the freedom and importance of the individual'.

Above: The Senate Chamber during the formal opening of Parliament by the Governor-General, Sir Zelman Cowen. In his Opening Speech, the Governor-General addresses members of both Houses of Parliament. At the conclusion of the speech members of the House of Representatives return to their own Chamber. *(Published with permission of the President of the Senate.)*

Right: Seated in the ornate Speaker's Chair, Sir Billy Snedden presides over the House of Representatives. The Speaker's Chair was presented to the House by the United Kingdom Branch of the Empire Parliamentary Association in 1926 and is a replica of the Speaker's Chair which stood in the House of Commons at Westminster. The Royal Arms over the canopy are carved out of the original oak from the roof of Westminster Hall. The hinged flaps are fashioned in oak from Lord Nelson's flagship HMS *Victory. (Published with permission of the Speaker of the House of Representatives.)*

In reality the Liberal Party's representation in parliament is largely from urban middle class districts. This has been a source of great disappointment to many who would like to see the Liberals win a substantial number of country seats — to promote their status as a national party and rid themselves of dependence on the Country Party. In the 1949 election, the Liberal Party won as many country seats as the Country Party, though not enough for outright victory, and has steadily lost country seats ever since despite the steady growth of the urban middle class community and a thinning out in country areas. In 1975 and in 1977 the Liberals did win an outright majority in the House of Representatives but still needed the support of the National Country Party for a Senate majority. Liberal dreams of government in their own right now seem further than ever from reality.

'City-based' is the Country Party view of both the Liberal and Labor parties.

Looking well satisfied, with an election victory behind them, a meeting of the leaders of the Liberal-Country Party coalition. From left to right, Doug Anthony, Prime Minister Fraser, and Sir Phillip Lynch who resigned from his position as Deputy Leader in 1982.

In Labor's eyes the Liberal Party is the party of 'the vested interests of wealth'. Whatever the claims, this much can be said: in all Australian cities support for Liberal and Labor varies directly according to the affluence of the suburb. Wealthy suburbs such as Vaucluse in Sydney and Toorak in Melbourne can be relied upon to provide a voting preference for Liberal over Labor in the ratio 5:1. Conversely, very poor suburbs such as Redfern in Sydney and Richmond in Melbourne give similarly strong support to Labor. It is the suburbs in the middle of the scale, such as Bondi in Sydney and Ringwood in Melbourne, which are finely balanced and determine the fates of governments.

There were, I believe, four reasons for the Liberals' success in maintaining office for 23 unbroken years. They were: divisions within the Labor Party; the political skill of Sir Robert Menzies; fairly successful economic management; the ability to maintain reasonably harmonious relations with the Country Party and thus preserve the image of a united government.

It is still too early to say how long the present Liberal Government will last. At the time of writing (November 1981) it has been in office for exactly six years. The strength of Malcolm Fraser's leadership seems to be its major asset. Certainly Fraser's electoral record is impressive so far. On 13 December 1975, he won the largest-ever majority in the House of Representatives (55 seats). On 10 December 1977, he won the second-largest-ever majority (48 seats), while on 18 October 1980 he won a substantial majority (23 seats) which was about the same size as the majority Menzies first won in 1949.

The COUNTRY PARTY was formed in 1919. Its growth was made easy because of the introduction in 1918 of preferential voting which meant that supporters could afford to vote for the Country Party without letting Labor win.

There is no doubt that the Country Party has been very successful in gaining concessions for Australia's rural communities, especially farmers. The problem for the Country Party has been that although rural Australia continues to contribute nearly half of Australia's export earnings its share of the total population is shrinking. Keeping pace with this fact has been the Country Party's greatest challenge — and so far it has succeeded.

In the first place it has taken some seats from Liberal and Labor. The CP can obviously hold or even improve its position if it can gain seats from other parties at a faster rate than its own seats are eliminated in redistributions.

Second, it has persuaded the Liberal Party (and, therefore, the Parliament) to agree to changes in the Electoral Act permitting a 'rural bias' to the seats. For many years it has been the practice of Australian mainland State parliaments to have fewer electors in country constituencies than in city constituencies, a practice which did not exist in the Federal Parliament until relatively recently. When the Liberal-CP coalition came to office in 1949 it did so on a set of electoral boundaries in which there were practically equal numbers of electors in all seats. But as a result of amendments to the Electoral Act in 1965 and in 1977, electoral boundaries now contain a 'rural bias' of ten per cent (ie. for every 100 electors in urban seats there are 90 in rural seats). Hence, over a 30-year period of urbanisation the CP has kept its redistribution losses to only two seats.

Third, the Country Party has tried to 'broaden its base' in a number of ways. The principal of these has been the promotion of tariffs for manufacturing industry to win city support. In Labor's eyes the CP has changed from 'the party of wealthy graziers' to 'the party of wealthy graziers and manufacturers'. In its own eyes the CP is 'the party which represents the productive people in the community' and 'those who live outside the capital cities'. In 1975 the party changed its name to the National Country Party.

Ranged against this Liberal-CP coalition at every election is the AUSTRALIAN LABOR PARTY. Its party policy is to contest every seat at every election. The coalition parties generally offer the voter either a Liberal or a CP opponent to Labor — few seats are contested by both Liberal and CP candidates.

Labor, the oldest of the three parties, was formed in the 1890s when the unions realised that industrial action had to be supplemented by political action. Since its first victory in 1910, its history has been one of splits and recoveries depending on the phases of the electoral cycle.

The Labor Party is nominally a socialist party. As long ago as 1921, the Federal Conference of the ALP adopted the 'socialisation objective' which stated as policy the 'socialisation of industry, production, distribution and exchange'. However, to accommodate every shade of opinion the same conference adopted the 'Blackburn amendment' which made exceptions of all industries that were socially useful and not exploitive. With the notable exception of the Chifley Government (1945-49) which attempted, unsuccessfully, to nationalise Australia's banks, ALP governments generally have shown little enthusiasm for the nationalisation of industry.

Labor's problems in the period since World War II have attracted a great deal of notice, but they must be seen in the context of Labor being out of office for most of the period.

Though Labor is predominantly an urban working class party, it does win a few country seats in constituencies with mining communities or large railway towns, or where it has an unusually good candidate. However, the policies of the Whitlam Government damaged Labor in country areas to the point where there are now no safe Labor seats in the country.

Typical of the setbacks to Labor in the country was the loss of the seat of Riverina in 1980. The inclusion of Broken Hill in Riverina in 1977 made it a Labor seat and Broken Hill had always had a Labor member. No longer. Whereas Broken Hill was continually represented by a Labor member from 1901 to 1980, it now finds itself with a National Country Party member.

Labor cannot win a federal election until it wins a significant share of the country seats. At the moment 40 of the 125 seats in the House of Representatives can be regarded as basically rural. Of these, 20 are held by the NCP, 15 by the Liberals and only five are held by Labor.

On a more general level the barriers to the electoral success of the Australian Labor Party have been:

.. Australia as 'a land of opportunity and prosperity' does not provide fertile soil even for mild forms of socialism. It is widely believed that differences in wealth are due not to privilege but to hard work.

.. Labor's opponents have had some success in portraying Labor as being subject to undue communist influence.

.. The electoral boundaries are mildly gerrymandered against Labor.

.. Internal divisions, sometimes resulting in splits. Since 1910 three major splits (the first two occurring while Labor was in power) have kept the party out of office for long periods: the 1916 'conscription split' which brought it down and kept it out until 1929; the 1931 'Depression split' which toppled Labor and kept it out until 1941; the 1955 'communism split' which kept it out until 1972.

The damage caused by the first two splits has long since been repaired. The effect of the 1955 split, however, was the establishment of the Democratic Labor Party which polled between five per cent and ten per cent of the vote at each election it contested between 1955 and 1972.

This, in essence, is what happened. From the mid-forties onward the fear of communism was such that an organisation led by Mr B. A. Santamaria, indirectly associated with the Catholic Church, attempted to infiltrate the trade unions and the Labor Party with anti-communist members. The organisation, popularly known as 'The Movement', was so successful that some of the party's more left-wing members became afraid of its power.

Late in 1954 the Leader of the Labor Party, Dr H. V. Evatt, attacked Santamaria and the Movement, and in 1955 the entire Victorian Branch was suspended because it was regarded as being under Movement domination. The 'old' Victorian executive and anti-communist members in other States (not all of them, incidentally, members of the Movement) then left the Labor Party and formed the DEMOCRATIC LABOR PARTY.

The DLP believed that the Labor Party was dominated by communists and the 'pro-communist left', and recommended that its voters should give their preferences to the Liberal-CP coalition and not to Labor unless Labor abandoned its left wing. Since Labor has refused to oblige, DLP preferences have been a critical source of support for the Liberal-CP coalition.

Two prominent Labor Party identities at the federal level — Bob Hawke, Shadow Minister for Industrial Relations and former President of the ACTU, and Bill Hayden, formerly Treasurer in the Whitlam Government and now Leader of the Opposition.

Formed in anti-communism, and with religious overtones, the DLP has tended to move further and further to the right and is generally regarded as the most right wing party in the political spectrum. The retention of the word 'Labor' in its title is a misnomer, but serves as a reminder that some of its present members were in the Labor Party 25 years ago.

Since the primary objective of the DLP was to keep Labor out of office until it came to terms on the left wing question, the election of a Labor Government in 1972 was, for Labor, a recovery from the 1955 split, and for the DLP, ultimate defeat. It had to look for a new home and proposed a merger with the Country Party. The proposal was given a trial run in Western Australia at the 1974 election as the 'National Alliance', but proved disastrous for both parties in that State.

At the 1980 federal election, the DLP contested a few Victorian seats in the House of Representatives and put up a Senate team in Victoria. The party's vote was so low that we can, to all intents and purposes, certify the DLP as dead.

In its day the DLP wielded great power through its preference votes to Liberal candidates and through its senators who held the balance of power in the upper house from 1965 until 1974. From 1970 to 1974 there were no fewer than five DLP senators but they lost their seats at the 1974 double dissolution election. From then on the road has been all downhill.

A fifth political grouping, the AUSTRALIA PARTY, had its origins in the Vietnam War. In 1966 a Sydney businessman, Mr Gordon Barton, inserted in Australian newspapers an advertisement calling for opposition to the war. Within weeks he had formed the 'Liberal Reform Group' and was running anti-war candidates in Liberal seats at the 1966 federal election. After its first electoral foray, Barton's group changed its name to the 'Australian Reform Movement' before becoming the Australia Party in 1969.

During the three years of the Labor Government the AP vote declined from 2.4 per cent to 0.4 per cent. The result was that its activists decided in 1977 to wind up the AP and join a new, more broadly based group, known as the Australian Democrats.

Australia's newest political party, the AUSTRALIAN DEMOCRATS, emerged as a result of the decision by Prime Minister Malcolm Fraser to exclude former Liberal minister and MP since 1960, Don Chipp, from the full ministry which Fraser formed on 18 December 1975. Fraser and Chipp had been as far apart as the Liberal spectrum would allow, Fraser being conservative and Chipp liberal. Chipp's exclusion was not a surprise but it left a bad taste.

It took Chipp another 15 months to break with the Liberal Party. He resigned in a speech to the House of Representatives on 24 March 1977, in which he criticised a number of the government's policies. He attacked the established parties as being beholden to pressure groups and vested interests — Labor to the trade unions, the National Country Party to the rural sector, and the Liberals to big business.

When Chipp resigned a large number of people contacted him, suggesting he form a new party. Suddenly the Democrats were formed, led by Chipp and composed of new members, some from the Australia Party and some from the former Liberal Movement in South Australia (a breakaway party in that State). Opinion polls showed a growing vote for them at both federal and State levels. As a middle-of-the-road party the Democrats decided not to recommend preferences to any major party.

At the election on 10 December 1977, the Democrats won two seats in the Senate and at the election on 18 October 1980 they won a further three. In other words they now have five senators and play an important part in the politics of the upper house, where they now hold the balance of power between the Liberal Government and the Labor Opposition.

The effect of the Democrats holding the balance of power is now being felt. In the 1981 Budget the government brought in new sales taxes on a wide range of goods. the Democrats and the ALP have used their numbers to delay the introduction of these new taxes.

The Australian electoral system

With the exceptions of the Federal Senate, the New South Wales Legislative Council, the South Australian Legislative Council and the Tasmanian House of Assembly, all parliaments are elected by preferential voting from single-member constituencies.

To illustrate the preferential system, there is a suitable example in the 1972 election for the Victorian seat of Bendigo in the House of Representatives.

There were four candidates. Thus, each voter was required to number his ballot paper 1, 2, 3, 4 against the candidates' names in his or her (the voter's) order of preference.

Because no candidate received an *absolute* majority on the first preference votes (see Table 4), the lowest polling candidate (Mr Brennan, DLP) was eliminated and his second preferences were distributed *as full votes* among the remaining candidates, with 3 417 votes going to the Country Party, 592 to the Liberal Party and 258 to the Labor Party. Once again there was no absolute majority. The lowest poller of the three (Mr Pearce, CP) was eliminated and his second preferences, along with the third preferences of the 3 417 votes he had received from Brennan, were distributed between the two remaining candidates — with 11 375 votes going to the Liberal Party and only 855 to Labor. The Liberal candidate, Mr Bourchier, squeezed home with a majority of 165 over Labor's Mr Kennedy.

SIR ROBERT MENZIES — Australia's longest-serving Prime Minister

Robert Gordon Menzies (1894-1978) was the most famous son of the little Victorian town of Jeparit in the Wimmera wheatgrowing district. His father, James Menzies, owned a general store there and served as Liberal member for the district in the Victorian Legislative Assembly from 1909 to 1919.

Young Robert had a good intellect and educated himself through winning scholarships. At no stage was the Menzies family considered to be part of the Establishment and his upbringing was never a privileged one.

In 1910 Menzies went to Wesley College in Melbourne on a scholarship where he studied well, took no part in sport and never became a prefect or a class leader, except in the academic sense. In 1914 he went to Melbourne University to study Law on an exhibition and graduated in 1916 with First Class Honours and several prizes.

He was a lieutenant in the University Rifles but never enlisted in the First World War. This caused later accusations of cowardice which were to haunt him until the end of his political career. He said it was a family decision to keep him home. Two of his brothers had volunteered to serve overseas.

After graduating, Menzies was a barrister and became a King's Counsel in 1929. In 1928 he was elected to the Victorian Legislative Council but transferred to the Legislative Assembly in 1929. He was a senior minister in Victorian State governments for much of this period and from 1932 to 1934 was Deputy Premier.

An important day for Menzies was 15 September 1934. On that day at the age of 39, he was elected Member for Kooyong, a safe seat he held continuously until his retirement in 1966. He went straight into the Lyons Cabinet as Attorney-General and in December, 1935 became Deputy Leader of the United Australia Party — the predecessor of the Liberal Party.

In April 1939 Lyons died and, after a brief period when Dr Earle Page was Prime Minister — a period marked by a bitter clash with Menzies — the Prime Ministership passed to Menzies, then only 44.

Menzies proved to be an unsuccessful Prime Minister at his first attempt (April 1939-August 1941). He seemed to be incapable of handling the problems of the war and was eventually disowned by his own party. The greatest election debacle for Australia's conservative forces occurred in August 1943, when they were decimated by Labor under the triumphant leadership of John Curtin (who died in office during his term). Menzies became Leader of the Opposition immediately after the 1943 disaster, improved the Liberal vote but failed to win at the next election in September 1946, and went on to victory at the historic election of December 1949.

Perhaps Menzies' greatest achievement was in founding the Liberal Party in 1944. The old UAP had become a shambles and Menzies believed Labor could not be beaten except by a new party — hence the formation of the Liberal Party.

Robert Menzies won seven consecutive elections (1949, 1951, 1954, 1955, 1958, 1961 and 1963) before retiring undefeated in January 1966.

Always a great royalist Menzies was made a Knight of the Thistle by the Queen in 1963.

What judgements are to be made of the man who served longest as our Prime Minister?

It depends, of course, on your viewpoint.

His admirers see him as having set the course for a prosperous Australia in the second half of the twentieth century, a prosperity shared by all Australians.

His detractors see him as having been very lucky, kept there by DLP preferences, enjoying a prosperity shared by other Western countries and getting the praise for presiding over tranquil times.

Always a man of tranquillity, Menzies retired in 1966, the first Prime Minister to retire of his own volition. He died in 1978 at the age of 83.

TABLE 4

Bendigo 1972

	Bourchier (Lib)	Brennan (DLP)	Kennedy (ALP)	Pearce (CP)
First preferences	13 637	4 267	24 326	8 813
Brennan votes transfer	592	–	258	3 417
Total	14 229	excluded	24 584	12 230
Pearce votes transfer	11 375	–	855	–
FINAL TOTAL	25 604	excluded	25 439	excluded

This example shows why Labor so heartily dislikes the present system. Although Labor does receive some preference help from the Australian Democrats, it otherwise relies on 'leakages' (such as the 1 113 votes from Brennan and Pearce) from anti-Labor candidates. It is common for Liberal or CP candidates to come from behind to beat Labor, but the reverse occurs less often.

My view is that Labor somewhat overdoes allegations of unfairness in the preferential voting system. While it is certainly true that Labor's opponents exploit the system it is not clear that the result would be very different under 'first-past-the-post'.

For example, had there been a 'first-past-the-post' contest in Bendigo there would have been only one anti-Labor candidate (presumably Mr Bourchier) competing in a straight fight with Labor. The result, I believe, would still have been a narrow Liberal victory.

Another common objection to preferential voting is that it permits excessive minority pressure, although this view depends largely on whether the voter likes or dislikes the minority in question. There is, however, no doubt that the Liberal Party, by depending on the CP, has had to make concessions to rural interests.

Equally, Liberal dependence on DLP preferences gave the DLP disproportionate influence over Liberal policy in the past. This influence has waned considerably since the disastrous decline in the DLP vote.

Labor has a stronger case in the matter of electoral boundaries which are normally loaded against Labor in three ways.

Since country districts are usually more conservative than city districts, 'rural bias' favours the conservative side of politics. This benefits the National Country Party and, to a lesser extent, the Liberal Party.

Although boundary lines are drawn by supposedly impartial electoral commissioners, it is claimed that some commissioners favour the party in power. In practice this has usually meant the Liberal-NCP axis.

Finally, in some cases the geographical distribution of voters hurts Labor because Labor wastes votes in impregnably safe seats while Liberal strength is spread more economically.

However, before agreeing too wholeheartedly with the Labor proposition that 'the boundaries are crook', two points should be made.

There are degrees of unfairness. For example, the anti-Labor bias of the federal and Victorian boundaries is relatively mild and Labor can win a workable majority of seats when it wins a sufficiently large majority of votes. On the other hand, the boundaries for the Queensland Legislative Assembly and the Western Australian Legislative Council are such that Labor has little chance of achieving a majority of seats no matter how large a majority of votes it might receive.

Also, in my view, Labor's remedy for this situation is in itself of dubious fairness. Labor wants to create federal and State electoral districts that are 'equal in population', with total population rather than enrolled electors as the basis of distribution. It so happens that many non-electors are congregated in working class districts containing large communities of migrants who have not been naturalised and a higher ratio of children than in middle class areas. In practice, if all seats were equal in population Labor seats would have fewer electors. The system would favour Labor.

Some countries have developed bi-partisan agreements on their electoral systems. In the United Kingdom the Conservative and Labour parties (but not the Liberal Party) agree that the system is fair. In New Zealand the process is officially bi-partisan. Unfortunately, however, there seems little possibility of a bi-partisan approach in Australia while the National Country Party demands some rural bias to which Labor is opposed. The prospect for Australia is a continuation of the party struggle over the electoral system, and of gerrymandering in particular.

The Senate, the NSW Legislative Council, the SA Legislative Council and the Tasmanian House of Assembly are exceptions to Australia's prevailing tradition of single-member constituencies. They are elected on the basis of proportional representation from multi-member constituencies, or from States as a whole.

In the case of the Senate each State returns ten senators altogether, with five normally being elected every three years for six-year terms. To be elected, a candidate needs to win a 'quota' (usually one-sixth) of the votes. This produces a party composition in the Senate different from that of the House of Representatives. Whereas the House is composed entirely of members of the geographically concentrated parties (Liberal, NCP and Labor), the Senate offers prospects of election to minor parties or independents whose evenly spread vote can obtain a quota. The most successful of these minor parties had been the DLP which held the balance of power in the Senate from 1965 until 1974. During the last term of the Liberal-CP Government, the DLP was able to use its position in the Senate and the power of its preference votes to press the government to favour DLP policies, especially in foreign affairs, defence and State aid to private schools.

More recently the Democrats have been the main beneficiary of proportional representation, now holding five Senate seats. The details are shown in Table 5.

TABLE 5

Present state of parties in Senate

Liberal	28
NCP	3
ALP	27
Democrats	5
Independent	1
TOTAL	64

Electioneering in Australia

The most distinctive feature of Australian electioneering is the sheer frequency of elections. Australians are compelled to go to the polls on an average of once a year. Voter turnout at these polls is always over 90 per cent — due to voting being compulsory — but there can be no doubt that the frequency of polls causes boredom with the electoral process.

The basic reasons for so many polls are the three year parliament and the some-times separate elections for the House of Representatives and the Senate. Hence the electors of New South Wales have voted for the House of Representatives in 1961, 1963, 1966, 1969, 1972, 1974, 1975, 1977 and 1980; for the Senate in 1961, 1964, 1967, 1970, 1974, 1975, 1977 and 1980, and for the State Legislative Assembly in 1962, 1965, 1968, 1971, 1973, 1976, 1978 and 1981 which has meant that the people of New South Wales have been compelled to vote almost once every year since 1961. In addition there have been separate federal referendums in 1967, 1973 and 1977 and separate State referendums in 1961 and 1978. In the other States the frequency of the elections has been very nearly as great, though, fortunately for them, State upper and lower houses are elected on the same day and there have been no State referendums.

Bob Hawke, former Rhodes Scholar, displays
his talent as a much sought after orator.

One effect of the frequency of elections is that more people now favour a four year
parliament. In September 1981 at a referendum held in conjunction with the general
election, the people of NSW approved an amendment to the NSW constitution
to lengthen the maximum period between general elections in that State from three
years to four years.

Australia has no laws compelling parties to disclose the state of their finances
either in a general sense or in relation to the amount each spends at an election.
Bits of information are published, but nothing more. For example it is known that
Labor's national budget for the 1969 election (which Labor lost) was $50 000 but
was $250 000 in 1972 (when it won). It is commonly believed that party leaders
have their own 'slush funds' existing separately from the party organisation.

There seems no good reason to doubt that the Liberal and National Country
parties are better endowed financially than Labor since they represent the wealthier
part of the community, especially business interests. Undoubtedly these interests
have more money to spend than the trade unions, which are Labor's power base.

The Labor Government attempted to change the law so that parties would be
compelled to disclose their sources of funds, but the proposal was resisted by the
Liberal and National Country parties which clearly wish to protect the interests
of their donors. However, one consequence of the lack of proper laws relating to
party finance is that each party is open to wild accusations by its opponents.

In 1981 the NSW Labor Government introduced a new scheme of public funding
of election campaigns. This should correct abuses, at least in that State.

Organisation of parties

Australian parties are organised on a federal basis. Even the ALP, which is dedicated to a unitary system of government and the abolition of the Senate, organises itself on an essentially federal basis. Each State has a branch of the ALP and each is equally represented at the National Conference (the party's supreme policy-making and governing authority) and on the executive.

The National Conference normally meets every two years and consists of: six delegates from each of the six State branches; the Leader and Deputy Leader of the ALP in the House of Representatives and the Senate; the six State ALP parliamentary leaders; a representative from the ACT; a representative from the Northern Territory; and a representative from the Young Labor organisation, a total of 49. It last met in July 1981 at Melbourne.

Although equality for each State delegation has been the norm in the past, future conferences of the ALP will provide a 'weighting' in favour of the more populous States.

The Liberal Party's Federal Council is similarly organised on the basis of State equality. It meets annually and does not bind the parliamentary party.

Each of the three main parties is made up of separate State branches or divisions which run their own State affairs — including the selection of candidates. There are wide variations in the procedures through which candidates are chosen by the parties in the various States. Each main party also maintains a Federal Secretariat in Canberra to carry out research and co-ordination between the States, together with a fair amount of public relations work and the servicing of members of the Federal Parliament, but the bulk of organisational work is carried out at State divisional offices.

The government of the day exists by maintaining the confidence of the House of Representatives through total party discipline, and each vote is virtually a foregone conclusion in favour of the government majority. Political bargaining is thus at a discount in the House.

The situation is more interesting when the governing party does not control the Senate — and this was the case, in an acute form, during the period of office of the Whitlam Labor Government. During the first term of the Whitlam Government the numbers in the Senate were as follows: ALP, 26; Liberal, 21; CP, 5; DLP 5; Independent, 3.

Although the combined Liberal-CP-DLP numbers constituted a majority, the numbers of any one group added to Labor's gave Labor a majority. Most proposed legislation was either passed without opposition or blocked by the combined Opposition, but there were a few cases of wheeling and dealing between the Labor Government and individual Opposition parties.

For example, in November 1973, the Opposition parties were threatening to hold up the *States Grants (Schools) Bill* because the government was proposing to abolish grants to certain well-to-do schools, contrary to a promise given by Whitlam when he was in Opposition. The impasse was broken only when the Leader of the Country Party, Mr Anthony, arranged with Labor a compromise solution which seemed to meet some of the objections. Thus the bill was passed with CP and DLP senators voting with Labor against the Liberals.

A similar incident had occurred in September, 1973, when the government brought in legislation to amend the Constitution to give the Commonwealth Parliament powers over prices and incomes. The Labor Caucus (the Parliamentary Labor Party) had resolved to gain power over prices, but it would have taken six months to present the matter to the people at a referendum unless legislation was passed by the Senate. Accordingly, a deal was made with the DLP by which the five DLP senators would support the legislation if power over incomes was also sought.

The 1974 and 1975 double dissolutions

It had been speculated almost from the first day of the Whitlam Government that a double dissolution would inevitably result if, as expected, clashes between the houses occurred; the double dissolution in 1974 came as no surprise.

In essence, the Senate can cause a double dissolution by *twice* rejecting, refusing to pass, or passing with amendments unacceptable to the House of Representatives, any proposed law which has been passed by the House.

By August, 1973, Mr Whitlam had the technical grounds for a double dissolution when the Senate, for the second time, rejected the *Commonwealth Electoral Bill* (No. 2), 1973. He did not, however, seek an immediate double dissolution: there was too much evidence of the government's unpopularity, and many felt that Whitlam would be defeated at the election following such a dissolution.

The Opposition parties, at the same time, began discussing whether they should force a double dissolution through the Senate's power to refuse 'Supply'. (The term 'Supply' refers to the passage of money to keep the government running.) This power of the Senate can be used to force a double dissolution by withholding Supply until the Prime Minister agrees to face an election.

MALCOLM FRASER — Australia's second longest-serving Prime Minister?

John Malcolm Fraser (1930-   ) would have to be regarded as the most controversial of Australia's conservative Prime Ministers. At the rate he is going he will, after Menzies, rank as the second longest-serving.

Like Menzies, Fraser was a third generation Australian and descended from Scottish emigrants. Menzies' father and Fraser's grandfather had both been members of the Victorian Parliament, and Menzies knew Fraser's father through the Melbourne Club and Victorian upper class society. But there was a difference. The Frasers were now rich landowners, and young Malcolm had been to Oxford. By contrast Menzies had little in common with the squattocracy. Both, however, were educated at private schools in Melbourne.

Menzies and Fraser had in common the fact that both represented Victorian seats in the House of Representatives. The difference is that Menzies represented a metropolitan Melbourne seat where Fraser represents a Western District grazing seat.

There are some similarities. Both men once attacked their own Prime Minister and resigned from the government (Menzies in 1939 from the Lyons Government, Fraser in 1971 from the Gorton Government). Both spent some time on the backbench rejected by their parties. Both held the office of Leader of the Opposition immediately before becoming Prime Minister.

Malcolm Fraser first contested Wannon in 1954 when he was only 24. He narrowly failed to defeat the sitting Labor member. In December 1955 he won Wannon and has held it ever since with large majorities.

In December 1956 he married, and Malcolm and Tamie Fraser now have two sons and two daughters.

Considering that Menzies and Fraser are so often compared it is strange that Fraser never made it into a Menzies Ministry. Promotion came to him in January 1966 to the Holt Ministry, the first formed after the retirement of Menzies. He became Minister for the Army.

When Harold Holt disappeared into the sea off Portsea (Victoria) in December 1967, Fraser was one of those Liberal members who backed John Gorton to be Prime Minister. As a result of Gorton's elevation, Fraser was promoted to the Cabinet as Minister for Education (1968-69) and, after the 1969 election, as Minister for Defence (1969-71).

In March 1971 Fraser and Gorton fell out.

A series of newspaper articles culminated in a refusal by Gorton to deny a story, submitted to him before publication, to the effect that Gorton had told a senior Army officer that, in the event of a dispute between the Army and Defence Minister Malcolm Fraser, Gorton would support the Army rather than the Minister. Fraser, resenting what he saw as 'significant disloyalty to a senior Minister' resigned his portfolio. When, at a subsequent party meeting, half the party opposed a confidence motion moved in him, Gorton accepted the inevitable and relinquished the leadership. William McMahon, the Deputy Leader since 1966, won the leadership.

Fraser was out of the Government from March until August of 1971, sitting lonely on the backbenches. In August of 1971 he returned as Minister for Education under McMahon, a position he held until the defeat of the McMahon Government in December 1972.

On Friday, 21 March 1975, Malcolm Fraser walked out of a Liberal Party meeting as the new Leader. Eight months later he was Prime Minister.

In October 1975, after a series of stumbles by the Whitlam Labor Government, Fraser decided to block Supply in the Senate to force an election. Whitlam refused to advise the Governor-General to dissolve so, on Tuesday, 11 November, Remembrance Day, Sir John Kerr dismissed Whitlam, installed Fraser and dissolved both houses of Parliament.

So far Fraser has not looked back. Having won three elections with record or large majorities he seems set to become Australia's second longest-serving Prime Minister.

A Labor devotee pays homage to party leader Gough Whitlam during a pre-election rally at Blacktown, Sydney, in 1972.

EDWARD GOUGH WHITLAM — Labor Prime Minister

For a large number of young to middle-aged Australians Gough Whitlam (1916-   ) was the only Labor Prime Minister in their memory. Yet in many ways he was not typical of Labor Prime Ministers. Where Ben Chifley, Labor Prime Minister from 1945 to 1949, had been an engine driver, Whitlam had been a lawyer.

Whitlam was born in the Melbourne upper middle class suburb of Kew (in the heart of the Kooyong electorate, incidentally) on 11 July 1916. Both his parents were Australian-born, as were three of his grandparents. All were from Victoria. His father joined the Victorian Public Service in 1901, transferred to the Commonwealth Crown Solicitor's office, and eventually became Crown Solicitor himself.

There was a stand-off period during which neither side took action to force the situation, and it was announced that a normal election for half the Senate would be held on 18 May 1974. But there was an unexpected development. Senator V. C. Gair, former leader of the DLP, was appointed Ambassador to Ireland — a move designed to enable Labor to take his seat at the normal Senate election.

Whitlam, therefore, was the only Prime Minister to grow up in Canberra, where he lived from 1928 until 1935. Fred Whitlam, his father, was a very senior and well-paid public servant and the family lived comfortably, even during the years of the Great Depression.

Like Menzies, Whitlam was a very good student but had little interest in sport. Like Menzies he studied law, going to Sydney University early in 1935 at the age of 18. He graduated in both Arts and Law.

During the war, Whitlam served in the Air Force and became interested in politics only towards the end of the war. He joined the Labor Party during August 1945 at the age of 29 — a late start.

In 1942 he married Margaret Dovey, the daughter of a prominent Sydney lawyer who later became a judge of the New South Wales Supreme Court. Gough and Margaret Whitlam have three sons and one daughter.

In 1950 he contested (unsuccessfully) a seat in the New South Wales State Parliament and entered the Federal House of Representatives as member for Werriwa in November 1952, at a by-election caused by the death of the former Labor member.

The young Whitlam was regarded coldly by most members of the Labor Caucus. He was a 'silvertail' where they were working class. He was an 'academic' where some of them had only a primary school education. Nevertheless, he worked hard and by 1958 was a member of the Labor front bench.

In 1960 the Labor Leader, Dr H. V. Evatt, resigned to become Chief Justice of New South Wales. His Deputy, Arthur Calwell, became Leader and Whitlam was elected Deputy Leader.

Calwell fought and lost three elections — those of 1961, 1963 and 1966. After his third loss he stood down and, on 8 February 1967, Gough Whitlam became Labor Leader and Leader of the Opposition. He was the eleventh Leader of the Federal Parliamentary Labor Party.

The next six years of Whitlam's career were a bit like the equivalent period of Menzies' career.

Both men spent similar periods (approximately six years) as Leader of the Opposition before achieving victory. The greatest election debacle for Australia's conservative forces occurred in August 1943, when they were decimated by Labor under the triumphant leadership of John Curtin (who died in office during his term). Menzies became Leader of the Opposition immediately after the 1943 disaster, improved the Liberal vote but failed to win at the next election in September, 1946, and went on to victory at the

historic election of December 1949. Labor's greatest election setback took place in November 1966 when Harold Holt triumphed (only to die in office). Whitlam took the Opposition helm shortly afterwards, in February 1967, improved Labor's standing but failed to win at the October 1969 election, and gained a memorable victory at the election of December 1972.

In each case, six years as Leader of the Opposition involved rebuilding the party. For Menzies it meant transforming the outmoded United Australia Party into a modern and more representative Liberal Party. For Whitlam there was no change of name, but there were fairly important changes in the party's structure and image. It is perhaps interesting to note that during the election campaigns which preceded their own elections as Opposition Leaders, both men were accused of disloyalty: Menzies to his Leader, Fadden, in 1943; Whitlam to his Leader, Calwell, in 1966.

In December, 1972, after receiving a telegram from Sir Robert congratulating him on his election victory, Whitlam sent a reply which said: 'You would, I think, be surprised to know how much I feel indebted to your example, despite the great differences in our philosophies. In particular, your remarkable achievement in rebuilding your own party and bringing it so triumphantly to power within six years has been an abiding inspiration to me'.

But if Whitlam modelled himself on Menzies in Opposition the opposite was the case in Government.

Where the December 1949 election ushered in 23 years of the Liberals, the December 1972 election produced only three years of Labor. Where Menzies retired undefeated in January 1966, Whitlam was dismissed by the Governor-General on 11 November 1975 and rejected by the electorate on 13 December 1975.

Following his defeat Whitlam resumed as Leader of the Opposition, a position he carried on rather listlessly throughout 1976 and 1977.

The year 1977 was the last effective year of Whitlam's political career. During that year he —
: completed ten years as Leader of the ALP
: became the longest-serving Leader of the party and
: dismally failed at the election which was held on 10 December 1977.

On election night he announced he would stand down as Leader and in 1978 he retired from Parliament altogether to become an academic.

An informal moment for Labor Party MPs (from left to right) Elaine Darling (Queensland), Joan Child (Victoria), and Rosemary Kelly (Canberra). Although the first woman member of the House of Representatives — Dame Enid Lyons — was elected in 1943, Australian woman politicians still have to battle for pre-selection.

Pandemonium resulted, and the Opposition senators forced the double dissolution. Thus Mr Whitlam became the third Prime Minister to fight a double dissolution election, the second (after Menzies) to win such an election and the first to be forced to the polls by a hostile Senate.

For Whitlam, however, the trouble was that he continued in a minority in the new Senate. The election for the whole new Senate returned 29 Labor senators, 29 Opposition and two Independent Liberals. Labor legislation blocked by the Senate in the previous Parliament was passed at a joint sitting of the two houses in August, 1974 but the new Senate was as determined as the old to frustrate the will of the Labor Government. One major piece of legislation passed at the joint sitting was declared invalid by the High Court.

Towards the end of 1974 there was a serious deterioration in the economy. Unemployment rose and Whitlam's popularity fell dramatically. Pressure grew on the Opposition to force a further double dissolution. To do so was made all the more easy when anti-Labor State governments in New South Wales and Queensland abandoned a long-standing practice. In 1975 Labor senators who died or resigned were replaced by anti-Labor senators. (Under the Constitution, State parliaments fill vacancies in the Senate. There had been a gentlemen's agreement that the person chosen would belong to the same party. In 1977 the Constitution was amended to ensure that successor senators would belong to the same party.)

On 16 October 1975 the Senate decided to withhold Supply to the Labor Government. A crisis developed when Whitlam refused to advise the double dissolution of Parliament and the Senate persisted in its course. On 11 November 1975 the Governor-General, Sir John Kerr, in a rare use of vice-regal powers, dismissed Whitlam and commissioned the Leader of the Opposition, Malcolm Fraser, as caretaker Prime Minister until elections could be held. The elections on 13 December 1975 produced a landslide to Fraser's Liberal Party.

During the three years of the Whitlam Government the Senate used its powers as never before. It rejected more bills than had been rejected in the entire period from 1901 to 1972. For the first time the Senate showed that it could use its powers to break a government.

The current political outlook

Table 6 sets out the present party control of the various governments showing the date of their original election.

TABLE 6

Present Party Control

Federal	Lib-NCP	(since 1975)
New South Wales	ALP	(since 1976)
Victoria	Lib	(since 1955)
Queensland	NCP-Lib	(since 1957)
South Australia	Lib	(since 1979)
Western Australia	Lib-NCP	(since 1974)
Tasmania	ALP	(since 1972)

WILLIAM GEORGE HAYDEN — present Labor Leader

On 22 December 1977 Bill Hayden (1933-   ) became the twelfth Leader of the Federal Parliamentary Labor Party. He did so largely because the post was thrust upon him, not through any sense of ambition.

Of Hayden's eleven predecessors seven had become Prime Minister (Watson, Fisher, Hughes, Scullin, Curtin, Chifley and Whitlam) while four had never become Prime Minister (Tudor, Charlton, Evatt and Calwell). Time alone will tell whether Hayden joins the seven or the four.

Hayden's admirers often compare him to Curtin and Chifley and in one way he is like them. He comes from a low income background. Unlike Menzies, Fraser and Whitlam he never went to an exclusive private school.

Although Hayden is sometimes now seen as 'an academic' his background was quite different. Being from a poor family, he had little chance to learn (although he did quite well at high school).

At the age of 17 he took a job as a clerk in the Queensland Public Service. At 20 he joined the police force.

In 1957 he joined the Labor Party and in 1958 became Secretary of the Ipswich East electoral executive committee.

The next few years were important for Hayden. He enrolled for adult matriculation studies, married a miner's daughter, Dallas, and in 1961 became Labor candidate for the federal seat of Oxley, then held by Dr Donald Cameron, Minister for Health in the Menzies Government. He was not expected to win the seat which, though including the Labor centre of Ipswich, also included a large and conservative rural area.

However, something unexpected happened. There was a landslide swing of nine per cent to Labor in Queensland at the election of December 1961 and in Oxley it was ten per cent. Labor gained eight seats, including Oxley, so he became an MP at the age of 28.

Hayden has held the seat ever since, partly through hard work and partly because subsequent redistributions have turned it into a natural Labor seat. It is now the only safe Labor seat in Queensland.

In 1963 Hayden began a University degree course from the University of Queensland. He graduated Bachelor of Economics in 1967.

Hayden's hard electoral work paid off in 1963 and 1966. At both elections Labor went backwards generally, but Hayden increased his own majority.

Hayden became Shadow Minister for Social Security in 1969, and, on Labor's election in 1972, became Minister for Social Security. At 39 he was the youngest Minister in the Whitlam Government though he ranked fourth in a ministry of 27, thus indicating his high standing with his peers.

Undoubtedly the introduction of Medibank was Hayden's greatest achievement as Minister for Social Security.

On 6 June 1975, Hayden became Treasurer, a position he held until the dismissal of the Whitlam Government.

At the 1975 election Labor lost 30 seats throughout Australia. Hayden's seat of Oxley was the only Labor seat left in Queensland.

After the 1975 defeat Hayden considered giving up politics but he decided to stay on and, after becoming Opposition Leader in 1977, seems to be now a committed politician.

Neville Wran, Premier of N.S.W., has held office since 1976. His popularity has led to considerable Press speculation as to ambitions he might have to enter federal politics.

At the time of writing (November 1981) the Federal Liberal-NCP Government of Malcolm Fraser has won three elections and another election will not be needed until the end of 1983. Mr Fraser has a comfortable majority and is the only Liberal Leader, apart from Menzies, to win three successive victories. When he completes his present term he will be the second longest-serving Prime Minister in Australian history, next to Menzies. So he looks very secure for the time being.

Although the government does not have a majority in the Senate, developments seem to be working in its favour there. The Democrats have been very restrained in using their balance of power. Furthermore, they seem determined not to provoke a double dissolution.

A popular venue for protestors, peaceful and otherwise, the New South Wales State Parliament House, Macquarie Street, Sydney. Imposition of considerable cost restraints, including staff ceilings, in the public service area has led to industrial action by more militant public servants.

The State governments in four States look secure for the moment — in New South Wales (under Neville Wran), Queensland (under Joh Bjelke-Petersen), South Australia (under David Tonkin), Western Australia (under Ray O'Connor).

In Victoria the present government looks like being defeated next time round. Victoria's Liberal Government is now the oldest in Australia — over 25 years of age. In June, 1955 it entered office under Sir Henry Bolte and he was Premier until August 1972 when Rupert (Dick) Hamer took over. Thus two men, Bolte and Hamer, held the office of Premier between them for a quarter of a century. This was made possible by the fact that the Liberal Party in Victoria won nine consecutive elections.

In June 1981 Mr Hamer stepped down as Premier and was succeeded by his Deputy, Lindsay Thompson. The next election is due by June, 1982 and, if the current opinion polls are right, it will result in a change of government in Victoria. Most pundits now think Labor will win that election.

The political situation in Tasmania is very uncertain at the moment. The future there looks most unpredictable.

Sir Charles Court led the Western Australian Liberals to three successive victories, in 1974, 1977 and 1980. The government of his successor next faces the people about February 1983 — a loss to Labor is possible.

RELIGION

Dr Rudolph Brasch

'It could have become a most powerful force from the beginning.'

From the beginning, religion in Australia was neglected and ignored and, at most, used and abused by the Establishment for its own advantage.

The colony was established without a prayer and the first service on Australian soil seems to have been an afterthought. It did not take place until the second Sunday, eight days after the first landing.

Australia also has the distinction of having been the only 'Christian' country whose earliest parliaments had no divine invocations. Attempts in 1843 and 1844 to change the situation were defeated. Indeed, when in 1851 a renewed effort to put God into the Victorian Parliament, as it were, was again rejected, W. Westgarth praised this defeat of religion as a victory for the spirit of progress. It was a fortunate sign of Australian maturity, he said, to confine religion to 'its proper place' and refuse the obsolete tradition, the 'old remnant', of the British House of Commons.

It took another 11 years, until 1862, for the New South Wales Legislative Assembly to open its session with a prayer. It was the first Australian Parliament to do so but the action was not welcomed unanimously. Far from it—members resented the intrusion of religion and some left the Chamber in protest. Eventually, the government was forced to change the text of the invocation and reword it in a form more innocuously 'neutral'. Religion could have become a most forceful power in Australia from the beginning. Leaving behind its divisiveness elsewhere, it could have, from the outset, proved a uniting, dynamic spirit in the building of a nation.

The very newness of the colony, even taking into account the disadvantage of its penal start, offered infinite opportunities. Merely to transplant institutions and inapplicable traditions from the 'old country' showed lack of understanding and imagination.

But despite everything that was against it, religion made its presence felt and through the initiative of individual ministers, it pioneered significant features which have contributed greatly to the life of the nation, and indeed the world.

It was from Australia that missionaries went out to Christianise islands of the Pacific. Moreover, they did so unsupported by the authorities, neither following the flag nor linked with aspirations of trade, but urged on solely by their consciences.

175

Left: **Faith in Australia is essentially a private matter, rarely vigorously debated.**

Another factor gave Australian religion a unique aspect. Although certainly Protestants were fostered for many years, they were never given the status of an established church. Gradually but inevitably, every denomination, as it was imported into the country, received equal rights to exist and even to ask for financial support from the government.

Anglicans

The Church of England has always been the largest denomination in Australia. At the 1921 census it constituted 44 per cent of the population, in 1954, 31 per cent, and in 1966, 33.6 per cent. However, by 1976 it had dramatically declined to 27.7 per cent. As distinct from the Church of England in Britain, the Church of England in Australia, in spite of some attempt at the beginning to achieve such supremacy, never became an 'established' church.

In a letter Governor Bourke warned the Home Government that in this 'new country, to which persons of all religious persuasions are invited to resort, it would be impossible to establish a dominant and endowed church without much hostility'.

Certainly, in the early days, the authorities fostered the Anglican Church. Yet, slowly and inevitably, it had to take its place within the Australian community of religions without ever gaining the power it had in Britain. It took a long time, however, to become indigenously Australian. To start with, Australia was regarded as so insignificant that it was attached to the diocese of Calcutta, thousands of kilometres away. Not until 1835 was a first 'Bishop of Australia', William Grant Broughton, with his newly established See of Australia, nominated.

For many years, strong links with the home church continued to influence and determine Anglicanism in Australia. The first Australian-born Archbishop, the Most Reverend Marcus Loane, was installed only as recently as 1966. It was then realised that Australia no longer needed (or even appreciated) an imported hierarchy and to confirm the new independence the 27 dioceses of Australia agreed to replace the old name 'Church of England' with 'The Anglican Church of Australia'. Its head was not the Queen but the Primate of Australia. Significantly, it had taken more than 60 years after Federation to reach this historical moment.

The decision was taken after much deliberation and against the wishes and advice of the Archbishop of Sydney who saw the change of name as a most regrettable break with history. But his being overruled was indicative of the democratic government of the church in Australia. That Australian Anglicanism has never produced an historically eminent figure, might well be explained by its synodal government. With its strong lay representation it greatly reduced the possibilities of individual initiative and excellency.

As in almost all denominations, emphases of belief and practice differ within the Anglican Church. As in England, there is a distinct division between Anglo-Catholics (also known as the High Church) and the conservative Evangelicals most strongly represented in the Sydney diocese. The ultra-orthodoxy of the latter led critics to describe it as 'so low' that it was almost 'underground'.

In order to stress its new Australian orientation, the Anglican Church, in conjunction with Presbyterians, Methodists and Congregationalists, published in 1977 a new, interdenominational hymn book. Significantly, this hymnal eliminates metaphors and expressions that make sense in the northern hemisphere, especially Britain, but have little meaning to Australians. No hymn refers to a snowy Christmas! The language used is clear, contemporary, and of literary merit; even the tunes suggested seek to replace the traditional chants.

The publication of *An Australian Prayer-book* followed within a year. It was to be used in conjunction with, but soon largely displaced, the *Book of Common Prayer* of 1662 which had been the model and standard of worship for three centuries. It was a remarkable development, leading towards new liturgies and soon proving so popular that in a short time more than a quarter of a million copies were sold.

Taking up the modern trend of women's lib, the Church also found no theological reason to deny women an office in the Anglican ministry. However, so far, because of constitutional difficulties, it has not gone beyond the verbal declaration. Yet in a lesser field Australia has been the first in the world, so it is claimed, to appoint (at St David's Cathedral, Hobart) a female verger. St Paul's Cathedral, Melbourne, has a female organist and a Mistress of Choristers.

No church can survive this modern age if it disregards its social duty. The Anglican Church in Australia, well aware of this, has been instrumental in not only fostering but actually pioneering essential social welfare and caring activities of many kinds. In 1960, it was among the first, with the Salvation Army, Methodists and an independent group, to establish a hostel exclusively caring for unmarried mothers. Until then, any work of that type was looked upon as so delicate that it was conducted, if at all, clandestinely.

In a youth-oriented and youth-worshipping age, the Psalmist's petition 'cast me not off in the time of old age' has acquired an almost tragic connotation. That is why the Anglican Church inaugurated retirement villages. Substantially financed by the Commonwealth and administered by the Church, they provide comfort, dignity and a meaningful life for many thousands of senior citizens.

Equal in importance and need is the work done for the chronically sick among the aged, those most neglected and least regarded of people. Within the Sydney diocese alone ten geriatric hospitals, with more than 400 beds, attend to their welfare. Hardly ever understood, but symbolic, is their name: Chesalon. It is the name of a site from the Book of Joshua meaning 'Hope'.

Inevitably, however, these tasks will be reduced as more are surrendered to the government. Meanwhile, the Anglican Church has resumed yet another, and the most ancient, religious duty: to act as the conscience of the community, to make its voice heard on issues of national and international importance and, no matter what the cost, speak up. In the words of Marcus Loane, the Anglicans are trying to fulfil a contemporary role by making Australians 'wake up and grow up'.

Catholics

Roman Catholicism has always played a prominent role in Australian life and many factors and prejudices combined to create militant antagonism, intense animosity and distrust.

At first there was the fight for its very existence and for the right to worship 'the Catholic way'. Then came the drawn-out battle for an independent State-supported education. Additional causes of conflict through the years were the ethnic background of priests and people, the inferior social position of Catholics and their resulting association with a specific political party and particular circumstances of the administration of their church. No wonder extremists claimed that Australia's two major religions were Catholicism and anti-Catholicism.

Some challenges for Catholicism in Australia were almost inevitable. The Irish origin of its early majority caused a vocal and active sympathy with their oppressed brethren in the Emerald Isle. Its implicit antagonism against the Protestant British, in turn, immediately aroused further anti-Catholic feeling. Suspicions of disloyalty were increased by the fact that most of the priesthood came from Ireland and were Rome-trained. In a request to the Colonial Office in 1826, Governor Darling said that if, against his wishes, more priests were to be sent to the colony, they should be Englishmen as, regrettably, 'the Catholics here being, I believe, nearly all Irish'. Catholic leaders themselves argued at the time that you could never make a good priest out of convicts. And so grew the accusations of a Papal plot to create a hegemony in Australia to control people's minds and the entire national life.

Even Catholics began to resent the alien influence of their hierarchy and the battle for the 'Australianisation' of the church was not easy. Indicative was the establishment of the theological seminary at Manly, St Patrick's College.

Not least it was meant to break the monopoly of the Irish and to train an indigenous priesthood, eventually to replace imported bishops by an Australian hierarchy. Yet significantly, the first two bishops there were given positions in the distant and minor dioceses of Townsville and Geraldton! Equally telling was the choice of the name for the Catholic students' university societies. Very pointedly they honoured (first so in Melbourne in 1910) the English intellectual Newman, a choice hardly welcomed by Irish priests!

Catholics, who had started in Australia as convicts, for a long time continued to belong in great number to the labouring class. It was not surprising, therefore, that they also played an eminent role in the growth of the Labor Party. This, Catholics maintain, was the only reason why at times a majority of Catholics filled the main Cabinet positions in State governments.

When Australia stopped its financial support of the Church, and its schools, Catholics took it as an outright attack on their faith. Their fight for subsidy of their own educational system became a rallying point. On the other hand, non-Catholics viewed Catholic schools with much suspicion. Wild allegations were made (and strongly denied) that these schools encouraged pupils to enter the public service to gain further influence in Australian politics . . . another Papal plot!

But even the Catholic-dominated Labor Party eventually suffered from the influence of non-believers and communists. Two schools of thought split the Catholic community. One was adamant that Catholics should 'stay in and fight' and thereby continue to exert their Christian influence from within. The other faction, fostered by Mannix-inspired Santamaria, regarded such a policy as futile. Abandoning 'a hopeless situation', they separated to form a new Catholic party that would stress Roman Catholic social principles.

The heated battle for government funds for church education fanned anti-Catholic antagonism and then the great paradox! Political vote-catching caused, not a Catholic-dominated Labor government, but a Protestant Liberal Cabinet to give Catholics their wish. It instituted State support for *all* non-government schools, and a fight that had raged from the 1830s suddenly was at an end.

The world-wide decline of religion has made its inroads into Australian Catholicism as well, but compared with other countries, fewer priests have resigned their office. Within the congregations incidents of disturbance are comparatively rare. This may not so much be the result of deeper religious feeling among Australian Catholics as the Australian temperament which, not reacting precipitously, is not disposed to crisis situations. Its cause might also be found in Australia's remoteness from the ferment of European and American thought and a general apathy towards things spiritual which in this instance would strangely work to the advantage of Roman Catholicism.

A small but significant characteristic of Australian Catholicism concerns the relationship between priests and the people, which lacks the traditional aura of awe and fear. Although not over-familiar, the relationship nevertheless reflects the typical Australian tendency towards mateship.

Australia has been one of the first countries to follow Papal directions for further education of its ordained priesthood. Australia thus became one of the first countries to introduce a pastoral year of practical training for newly graduated priests as well as refresher courses for those having served congregations for some time. Since its inauguration, this process of updating has been further developed and intensified.

Catholicism used to be the major Australian religion to show a considerable increase in numbers in proportion to the rest of the population. This was due to immigration. According to the 1971 census Catholics had grown to more than a quarter (27 per cent) of the people. This compares with 22.6 per cent in 1901; 17.5 per cent in 1935; 20.7 per cent in 1947 and 26.29 per cent in 1966. In fact some authorities suggested that the Catholic Church might eventually overtake the Anglican. However, the census of 1976 showed a notable reversal, a decline to 25.7 per cent. Catholicism thus now shares the disturbing aspects of current trends. Not only did the Catholic proportion in the population fall and do so for the first time since 1933, but Catholicism — between 1971 and 1976 — showed its lowest percentage growth ever.

Right: **Roman Catholic congregations, alone among the major Christian churches, have benefited from the influx of southern European migrants.**

Methodists

It could be said that a snake was responsible for the foundation of Methodism in Australia. After his discharge from the New South Wales Corps, John Lee had settled in Castlereagh on a grant of land he received in 1804. Religion meant nothing to him. Like so many others in the colony, he much preferred gambling and drinking.

One day, so the story goes, while collecting firewood, he grabbed a poisonous snake which instantly bit him. Terrified he might die, he vowed that should he be saved he would mend his ways. More so, he would do everything in his power to turn others from debauchery to a Christian life. Lee survived, and kept his promise. At the back of his home, he built a timber slab church—Methodism had started in the antipodes.

Mere chance again gave the young church its first minister. The small group of Methodists into which Mr Lee's venture grew, felt the need of a spiritual leader. Far from ministering merely to their own needs, he would be of great benefit to the 'thousands of souls perishing for lack of knowledge, both in high and low life'.

They requested the Wesleyan Missionary Society in London to send such a man and wisely stipulated that he should be broad-minded enough to serve 'not in hostility against the [Anglican] Church but rather in unison with it'. Only a man not 'radically a Dissenter' would do.

At that time the Reverend Samuel Leigh was waiting in London to take up duties in North America. But just before he was due to sail, his appointment was cancelled because of the 'disturbed state' of that part of the world and immediately the Society asked Leigh to switch his destination—to Australia.

Economics and politics played a part in the new appointment. Aware that government approval had to be obtained, the Society cleverly pointed out that Leigh's erudition would in fact enable him to serve in a dual capacity and thereby save the government money. He could act both as a minister and a schoolmaster. And that consideration decided the issue. Leigh, who was a man of principle, however, made it clear that he would never stoop to act 'as the hired agent of the colonists'. And when on his arrival in Sydney in 1815, the Governor offered him a much more lucrative position 'under the government' with the promise of a comfortable living and future wealth, Leigh reiterated his determination to stay independent.

That is how he set to work, sparing no effort. He did not wait for people to find him but sought them out. His circuit at times extended to 240 kilometres, and there were times when he got lost in the bush. Within ten days he might preach at 15 different places. In 1820 ill health forced him to return to England. He could, however, do so knowing that Methodism was firmly grounded in the new country.

Well aware of the estrangement of modern society from established religion, the Methodist Church embarked in the 1970s on what it termed 'para-church' activities. Meant to attract those who find it difficult to join in worship, they offer a 'half-way house'. They provide for those still unattached 'in-groups' in which they can mix with church people, but do so without having to participate in any formal religious ritual.

Many developments, indeed, took place in the area of caring, extending to every age group and need. Starting with pre-school centres and kindergartens, Methodists opened day-care centres for children.

The 'Single Society' extends friendship and fellowship to all those who are single, whether by their own choice or through circumstances. This type of group has proved so successful that from Australia it has spread to South Africa and to the west coast of the United States.

The Church became equally heavily involved in looking after the physically handicapped, opening hostels for them and sheltered workshops.

The 'Schools for Seniors' which had grown to 12 branches by 1977, offer the senior citizens of the community a meeting ground and a new sense of belonging. Instead of experiencing rejection in an age that worships youth, they are given a new goal and meaning of life by opportunities for constructive thinking and educational advancement.

Presbyterians

Presbyterians came to Australia in 1802, not as convicts or gaolers. They were Scots among the first 'assisted' free immigrants who were offered attractive grants of 40 hectares of rich alluvial land. Theirs was the first church to be built in the colony—at Ebenezer on the Hawkesbury River in NSW in 1809—solely by voluntary contributions. It still stands today.

Perhaps the greatest gift the Presbyterian Church made to Australia was that of one of its most outstanding clergymen: fiery, freedom-loving, undaunted John Dunmore Lang. He arrived in 1823 to found 'Scots' in Sydney, Australia's first Presbyterian congregation which, with some interruptions and controversies, he served for 55 years. Early during his ministry, he also preached at Ebenezer Church, holding its first Communion service.

Lang took a prominent part in the political life of the country. Representing Port Phillip, he became a member of the Legislative Council. This caused much stir, as some objected to a clergyman meddling in politics. But to Lang's mind a churchman's vital duties included affairs of State.

Numerous indeed were his contributions to Australian life. He agitated for the creation of Victoria as a separate colony. Equally enthusiastically he supported the separation of Queensland from New South Wales. When W. C. Wentworth tried his hardest to introduce an Australian peerage, his scheme was defeated not least by Lang's vehement opposition which he expressed with biting sarcasm.

Above all, Lang was convinced that Australia's future depended on the right type of settlers. In numerous visits to the 'old country' he fostered and popularised migration, pioneering family settlement as a totally new endeavour. In pamphlets and books he expounded his thoughts of a greater Australia. Using the American model but improving on it, he outlined his dream of a 'golden land', no longer tied to Britain but totally free and independent, the United States of Australia.

His is the typical example of the role of religion in Australia—how it never played a significant role as 'the Church', but left its important mark on the life of the nation by the zeal and dedication of individuals. And not the least of them was John Dunmore Lang.

In more modern times, the Reverend John Flynn played his part, in a different yet equally significant sphere of national life. Known as 'Flynn of the Inland', his pioneering work led (in 1912) to the formation of the Australian Inland Mission; to the promotion of hospitals and education in remote areas of the Outback and, most of all (in 1928), to the establishment of the world-famous Flying Doctor Service.

Lutherans

If Australia had its own Pilgrim Fathers, they were Lutherans who came from Prussia seeking freedom of worship. The Prussian government at the time tried to force the Lutheran Church to toe the national line and those refusing to do so were mercilessly persecuted.

One of the leaders of the ostracised Church was Pastor August Kavel, of a Prussian village, Klemzig. He realised that his congregation's only hope for survival was emigration and resolved to lead his flock, just as Moses had once done, out of this modern 'Egypt'.

In 1838 they settled in South Australia and, sentimentally, called their first village Klemzig. From there they proceeded to the Barossa Valley, and out of the small seed grew the Lutheran Church of Australia.

That same year Lutherans also arrived, hundreds of kilometres away, in what is now Queensland. Yet they came there for an entirely different reason. John Dunmore Lang, the famous Presbyterian leader, was responsible for their migration. It was not because of any interest in the Lutheran Church on his part, but out of concern for the Aborigines!

In 1836-37, Dr Lang took up the cause of the Australian Aborigines during a London visit. His agitation resulted in a government grant to subsidise the posting of three Presbyterian missionaries. But no volunteers came forward.

Having failed with his own people, Lang contacted a Lutheran friend in Berlin, Pastor Gossner, who gladly agreed to supply the men. However, there was one condition. To send individual missionaries to pagan people, he was convinced, was futile. The only effective method of conversion was by the example of an entire community. Their way of life would prove the supremacy of their faith and thus win converts.

If Dr Lang would submit to this condition, Gossner promised an entire colony of Lutherans. It was an unprecedented type of selected migration with a spiritual purpose.

Dr Lang accepted and the German Lutheran contingent settled at Moreton Bay. Their missionary reserve covered an area of 260 hectares on both sides of a creek which, biblically, they called Kedron Brook. Their purpose, however, was never achieved and the colony soon petered out. But the story of their settlement, like that of their South Australian brothers, added a colourful note to the pattern of religion in Australia.

Unfortunately, early on — in 1846 — doctrinal differences split up the Lutheran Church. The schism was to last 120 years. In 1966 the two separate Churches — the Evangelical Lutheran Church of Australia and the United Evangelical Church of Australia — amalgamated.

Baptists

A church which was to take a leading part in the fight against drink in Australia held its first service at a hotel: the Rose and Crown Inn in Castlereagh Street, Sydney, in 1831. The Reverend John McKaegh, the Baptist Church's foundation minister, did not stay long with his congregation. Discarding the 'cloth', he became a tobacconist and eventually settled in Tasmania.

Without a spiritual leader, the young community felt completely lost. An urgent appeal they sent to their Missionary Society in London remained unheeded. Its charter, the desperate Sydney Baptists were told, specifically restricted its work (and ministers) 'to the heathens of the world'. And, after all, Australia was not considered a pagan country.

But all was not lost. One member of the committee approached the Reverend John Saunders, a fervent young man, who was anxious to spread the Gospel, no matter where. His first impressions of Sydney were predictably discouraging: 'It appeared as if we had landed among a set of the most degraded and uncomfortable beings we had ever thought of,' he wrote. To top it, many of the men were 'so drunk'.

Undaunted, however, he took up his task. Soon he realised yet another regrettable feature of the colony's religious life. Constant bickering among the various denominations did not contribute either to its status or stature. Above all, Saunders felt the need for Christian unity and, more than a century before modern ecumenism, he spoke up for 'Christian fellowship'. Thus he can be considered a pioneer of interfaith work in Australia.

When poor health forced him to resign in 1847, he had made his mark not only in his own church but in Australian religious life. Son of a London alderman, he had lived up to the inscription of his family crest, 'Nothing without God'. He is remembered as the first Baptist missionary to Australia, 'the Apostle of Temperance', and as a dauntless fighter against transportation.

Congregationalists

Congregationalism was responsible for the first boarding school on Australian soil. It was opened by the Reverend William Pascoe Crook who, with four other men, organised the first Congregational community in 1810. The fact that he, a Congregationalist and not an ordained minister of the Anglican Church, administered the sacrament, led to a clash with Governor Macquarie. Crook was threatened with expulsion from the colony, should he continue to celebrate what was the privilege and prerogative of the Anglican Church alone. His reply was typical of the courage and independence of many of Australia's early churchmen. Even if he had to suffer death, he stated, he would go on holding Communion services the way he had done.

Only towards the end of the 1840s did Congregationalism begin to play a role in Australian life. Its pioneers then, among them David Jones and John Fairfax, have their prominent place in Australian culture and commerce.

The Orthodox Church

Greek sailors, who first visited Australia around the 1850s, told their folks at home of the great country in the antipodes. No doubt, their story started the first migration of Greeks, and towards the end of the nineteenth century their number had grown to form the first Greek Orthodox communities, in Sydney and Melbourne.

However, the Orthodox congregation did not form a local diocese but placed themselves under the ecclesiastical jurisdiction of the Church of Greece. But in 1923, now strong in numbers, the Orthodox Church of Australia was established to become—with New Zealand and all Oceania—a 'Holy Metropolis'—under the Ecumenical Patriarch of Constantinople in Istanbul.

By 1927, with new refugee migrants from Asia Minor, the number of members of the Greek Orthodox Church had grown to 10 000 with communities extending to Brisbane, Innisfail, Perth, Port Pirie and Darwin.

A further influx of migrants from the Mediterranean region and other countries in which the Orthodox Church prevailed, vastly increased its members (and diversity) in Australia. Though sharing the identical spiritual outlook, doctrinal tenets and major ritual, the various groups established churches which reflected their ethnic and cultural background. They included the Greek, Russian, Ukranian, Rumanian, Lebanese (Antioch) and Serbian Churches.

Strong family life has always been one of the distinguishing marks of the Orthodox community. This was linked with a deep pride in their ethnic tradition, which has enriched Australian national life. That only marriages solemnised in the Orthodox Church were recognised in Greece, enabled the religious community to maintain a special link with all its adherents.

However, throughout the years Orthodoxy has gravely suffered from factionalism which gave the Orthodox community extraordinary publicity—not for its religious message but political squabbles. At their very basis is the peculiar organisation of the Orthodox Church in Australia. Legally, its various houses of worship are not recognised as religious communities but as 'limited companies' with, as it were, their boards of directors. This opened the doors of the Church and its administration to political interests which could overrule spiritual endeavour.

Australia experienced an unprecedented immigration of members of the Orthodox Church after World War II. It now occupies the fourth place among the country's major religious groups. It continues in its growth: both in the number of adherents (increased by 33 000 between 1971 and 1976) and the establishment of new parishes. *The Voice of Orthodoxy* resumed publication in 1980 as the bilingual mouthpiece of the Greek Orthodox community.

The Church of Jesus Christ of Latter-Day Saints

Mormon missionaries first reached Australia in 1851. For a hundred years however, the growth of their faith in Australia was very small, in fact, minimal, reaching a total membership of less than 3 000 by 1950. Since then the Church of Latter-Day Saints has experienced an extraordinary growth, within 30 years multiplying its membership twentyfold to almost 60 000.

Several factors were responsible. Mormons, previously decried and shunned, had become socially acceptable. People were attracted by their strong emphasis on family life. Not least, the zeal and dedication of their missionaries had its inevitable impact. Always in twos and travelling the world at their own expense, they developed into a force. By 1980, 800 full-time missionaries worked in Australia, 15 per

Meeting outside their State Centre Chapel at Mortdale, Sydney, brother missionaries of the Mormon Church who have come to Australia to inspire Sydney-siders with Joseph Smith's teachings. They hope to build the first Australian Mormon Temple in Baulkham Hills in 1982.

cent of whom were Australians themselves. Australian missionaries now travel overseas, some even going to Salt Lake City, the very centre of their faith. More than 100 purpose-built chapels extend all over Australia, typifying the spread of a faith which, not so long ago, had to use rented premises and meet in churches erected by other denominations.

The Uniting Church in Australia

Inaugurated in June 1977, the Uniting Church in Australia joined together the entire Methodist Church, 85 per cent of the Congregational and 60 per cent of the Presbyterian communities which, for the sake of unity, abandoned their separate existence. It was the culmination of a development that had started in Australia long before the ecumenical movement had been heard of as far back as 1902. Christian missionaries of various denominations then had combined in their work among the people of the Pacific islands. The United Church of North Australia was another significant step taken in the early 1950s.

The choice of the term 'Uniting' Church is probably unique to Australia. It is meant to indicate that the present union is merely a stage in an on-going process, with the aim of joining together ever more communities who share a deep commitment both historically and theologically to the Christian tradition.

184

Faithful to the ecumenic spirit, the Uniting Church, nevertheless, guards against the danger of achieving its aim at too great a cost by focusing on the lowest common denominator, at the sacrifice of treasured beliefs. Whilst seeking an organic unity, however welcome, it almost equally endeavours to discover ever more areas in which all Churches, even those still unaffiliated, are of one mind and, hence, can act together.

Jews

Many significant features have distinguished the Jews' place in Australia, almost from the very beginning. Contact between Jew and Christian has largely been one of mutual trust and friendship. Until recently, anti-Semitism as an organised force had been unknown and alien to the Australian people. With few exceptions, widely exaggerated through the publicity they received, Australia has practised little discrimination against the Jew.

Typical is the fact that many synagogues throughout the country were built with financial help from Christian friends. Certainly unique in the world was the occasion when the New South Wales Parliament adjourned for Yom Kippur in deference to its Jewish Speaker! Jews have belonged to all parties and sections of the community and at no time have they tried to act as a pressure group or a political force.

Religiously the average Jew, like Christian neighbours, has become increasingly indifferent and apathetic towards faith. Affiliations to the synagogue and active participation in religious life are diminishing. The influence of spiritual leaders has been minimal. In spite of the Jews' presence in Australia ever since the establishment of the colony, only a small number of the rabbis serving the community are Australian-born. And even these had to go overseas to complete their rabbinical studies.

Communities once flourishing in country centres have died out, their former synagogues empty shells, some being used as a furniture store or a garage. Almost 90 per cent of Australian Jewry now live in Sydney and Melbourne. Mixed marriages are increasing with at least 35 per cent of young Jews said to 'marry out'. Although the majority of non-Jewish partners used to seek conversion to Judaism, now many couples no longer care.

The opening of Jewish denominational day schools (of which Mount Scopus in Melbourne is regarded as the largest and best of its kind in the world) is proving most popular and successful in the inculcation of Jewish values and consciousness.

Liberal Judaism, the progressive interpretation of Judaism, was established in Australia, first in Melbourne, in 1936. Since then it has spread to the other capital cities. Its synagogues are known as 'Temples'. Although Temple affiliations are still in the minority, this is attributable for the most part to a lack of available ministers. Orthodoxy's membership majority is only nominal since most members no longer observe the Orthodox Jewish traditions. In fact, many an 'innovation' of Liberal Judaism is now practised by Orthodoxy, most conspicuously the confirmation of girls, known as Bat Mitzvah.

In very recent times, Liberal Judaism has been going through a state of change. Whilst on the one hand reviving some discarded Orthodox traditions, on the other hand it is seeking to introduce a greater role for women, even in the very ritual of the synagogue, causing some concern to those accustomed to the more 'classical' Reform. Historical was the appointment of the first woman rabbi in Melbourne in 1981.

Perturbing for the future of the Australian Jewish community are the figures of the 1976 census. This showed an actual decline of the number of Jews in Australia from just over 63 000 in 1966 to 53 000. In relationship to the total population this further lowered an already small percentage—from 0.5 per cent in 1966 to a mere 0.4 per cent. Nevertheless, of late some spiritual leaders have noted a significant return of youth to their Jewish heritage. Often coming from religiously indifferent and assimilated circles, they are attracted by the very extremes of Orthodoxy.

Muslims

Camel drivers from South Asia were the first Muslims to come to Australia in the 1880s. Deeply religious, one of their first actions was to build themselves houses of worship. Eventually there were 20 mosques. Since then, and particularly so in recent years, a strong migration from many Arab and Asian countries has increased the number of Muslims in Australia to almost 300 000 by 1981. More than 20 Islamic Centres, nine Islamic Councils and approximately 25 Islamic Societies united in 1974 under the Australian Federation of Islamic Councils, which restructured the previous—1954-founded—Australian Federation of Islamic Societies.

Worshippers at one of 26 mosques in Australia bow in prayer. In Islamic countries this ritual is carried out five times a day; here, the two largest mosques, at Lakemba in Sydney and Preston in Melbourne, remain permanently open for the convenience of worshippers.

Constant contact is being maintained with other Muslim centres throughout the world, particularly so Indonesia, India, Pakistan and Saudi Arabia. Visiting teachers from those areas call on the Australian communities. On the other hand, Australian Muslims make it possible by providing the necessary supervision and expertise to have ritually slaughtered meat sent overseas.

Bahais

Bahais, proclaiming the brotherhood of all people in their universalistic system of faith, established themselves in Australia in 1920. Their nine-sided domed temple on the outskirts of Sydney is one of their only five houses of worship in the world. Followers of their faith can be found in more than 300 Australian localities.

The Bahai Temple at Ingleside, Sydney, stands majestically above the northern beaches. It is one of only five such temples in the world, with two more projected for the near future. The nine sides symbolise unity.

Aborigines

Aborigines have an indigenous place in the history of Australian religion. In their pristine state, unsullied by manipulation and exploitation, religion was their very basis of life and the cement that held together their social structure. Their various myths, and particularly their belief in a 'dream time', endowed them with values they cherished and served as the very foundation of their existence. They closely linked individual Aborigines with their ancestors' past, their own totem group and the territory they occupied. But going far beyond, into the spiritual sphere, they also accepted the existence of an immortal soul. This not only survived the death of the body (returning to its ancestral home) but pre-existed their birth. A system of kinship taught the Aborigines a social gospel: to share possessions and to take care 'religiously' of the orphan and the aged.

There was also, to be sure, much in their pattern of beliefs that was primitive, fearful and repulsive to the Western mind. But to them it gave deep satisfaction and a meaningful way of life. The Aboriginal faith imbued their life with beauty, affection and profound belief. Their initiation rites gave each individual a permanent feeling of belonging and an awareness of social obligation.

Much controversy has raged as to the merits or crimes of Christian missionaries. No one can deny that among them were the most dedicated and selfless people and that they gave the hungry blacks nourishment and some sort of home in their mission stations. On the other hand, they destroyed much of the indigenous Australians' proud heritage and social integration. No wonder that thinking members of their race could ask white people, in the words of their poet Kath Walker, what difference it truly had made to 'change our sacred myths for your sacred myths'.

Aboriginal Sir Douglas Nicholls who, through one of the mission stations, became a Christian pastor himself, once confessed that 'perhaps our people—our great people—were really close to God'. In most cases when their tribal beliefs were taken from the Aborigines nothing was put in their place, with the resulting deterioration, degradation and loss of self-respect. And for this Sir Douglas (who from 1976 to 1977 was Governor of South Australia) bitterly accused white people and the Church.

At times there was an invidious competition between the various mission stations in the conquest of souls. Almost possessively, some tried to enforce their specific brand of Christianity on their charges. The effect was not greater happiness but confusion. Anxious not to go hungry, the natives adopted the new faith, not for the sake of their souls but that of their body. What they really needed was a knowledge of a loving God and its application in everyday life. But they became the victim of an atomised Church with divisive dogmas and doctrines.

Nevertheless, in the present mood of putting all blame on 'the Church', it should be remembered, and acknowledged, how, from the earliest days, some of its institutions and representatives showed great concern for the original Australian and went out of their way to help. In great loneliness they carried on their little appreciated work. They were undaunted by the small response of the Aborigine and even less encouragement on the part of the authorities. They were further handicapped by their rudimentary knowledge of Aboriginal values, beliefs and languages.

It is interesting to note that Richard Johnson, first in line of all Australian clergy, was already greatly worried about the Aborigines' spiritual welfare and morality—for a very specific reason. He was afraid that the white settlers' debauchery would act as a bad example and that all chances of conversion would be spoilt by so-called Christians showing hardness of heart, obscene living, and an altogether blasphemous existence.

And that is why in one of his early sermons, he implored the inhabitants of the colony, especially for the sake of the natives, those 'poor unenlightened savages', to change their own way of life. Because if they became 'more and more acquainted with our language and manners, hear you, many of you, curse, swear, lie, abound in every kind of obscene and profane conversation; and if they observe that it is common with you to steal, to break the Sabbath, to be guilty of uncleanliness, drunkenness and other abominations; how must their minds become prejudiced and their hearts hardened against that pure and holy religion which we profess? Oh beware of laying stumbling-blocks in the way of these blind people, lest the blood of their souls be one day be required at your hands'.

His words, spoken so long ago, seem almost prophetic and certainly are most apposite in our time. With the general sense of guilt caused by the injustices done to the Australian native, the present-day church in Australia is trying hard to remedy the dismal neglect of the Aborigine. It does so, however, not by its spiritual teaching but mostly by fighting for their fundamental rights.

Creeds and cults

Australia certainly has been, and still is, the target of numerous old and new cults, philosophies and religious faiths, brought to this country either by migrants or special emissaries. The Salvation Army began its march into Australia with a conspicuous open air meeting in the Adelaide Botanic Gardens in September 1818. Its two founders, Saunders and Gore, had been trained under William Booth himself. To begin with, their operations met tumultuous opposition. Larrikin gangs joined their meetings to cause disturbances, often pelting the 'soldiers' with all types of unpleasant missiles.

Quakers quietly started their work and way of life as long ago as 1832, when two English Friends, James Backhouse, a botanist, and his companion George Washington Walker, came to Tasmania specially to meet other Friends already settled there and to join them 'under concern' to aid convicts and Aborigines. Their efforts went much further. Quakers, in fact, established in 1887 Australia's first co-educational boarding school in Hobart, more than half of its pupils being non-Quakers.

The only connection of the Liberal Catholic Church with Roman Catholicism is historical. It was founded in Holland, in 1870, when it severed its link with Rome, refusing to recognise Papal infallibility. In Australia since 1916, its clergy serve in an honorary capacity and, receiving no stipend, must earn their living outside the church.

Shaven-headed and robed, members of the Hare Krishna sect are a common sight now in Australia's capitals, chanting and dancing among the more mundanely dressed, bemused, lunchtime crowds.

189

Two Americans started the Hare Krishna cult in Australia, at Kings Cross in Sydney, in 1970. Its yellow-robed, shaven-headed followers, as elsewhere, roam the cities or stand on street corners. With odd chants, cymbals and drums, they add their own colour and sound to city life. Few people, however, know or ever care to find out, what it is all about. They are not aware of the devotees' totally dedicated life which demands the sharing of everything (with no private possessions), complete abstention from alcohol, coffee and tea, and the restriction of sex to marriage, and then only for the purpose of procreation.

Scientologists, on the other hand, would probably have gone on unnoticed had their group not been declared illegal as inimical to society. However, again legalised since 1973, they are now recognised as constituting a 'proper' religious denomination with authorised marriage celebrants.

Jehovah's Witnesses, Pentecostalists, the Radio Church of Christ, Christian Scientists, Seventh Day Adventists and since 1850 at least, the Unitarian Church, all have a place in Australian religion, battling for minds and souls.

Religion in action

Never interested in the speculative, Australians were, and are, concerned with the practical aspect of religion alone. However, its social task has been greatly restricted by the modern welfare State. Many of the former vital functions of the church have now been appropriated by the government. On the other hand, the impersonality of bureaucracies gave religion a new and important meaning. Well aware of the opportunity, imaginative and enterprising ministers discovered a new lease of life for an otherwise dying faith. If they did not actually invent them, they ingeniously applied innovations from overseas and adapted them to the Australian scene.

The Lifeline

Today the Lifeline has become not only an accepted Australian institution but has been adopted, though sometimes under different names, in many parts of the world. It all began in the mind of one man.

In 1958 the Reverend (now Sir) Alan Walker of the Central Methodist Mission, Sydney, was well known through radio and television programmes. Countless men and women in distress thought of him first, and his telephone rang day and night. It became impossible to be on call for 24 hours each day, yet to have a silent number in these circumstances was out of the question.

One of the calls Alan Walker received, on a Saturday night, came from a man who identified himself as Roy, who said he was going to take his life. In fact, he had written Mr Walker a letter, and by the time it reached him Roy would be dead. Alan pleaded with him. If only they could meet face to face he might still change his mind. Eventually the man seemed to give in. They made an appointment. But before the time came the police found the body of a man, identified as Roy Brown. A letter attached to his chest was addressed to the Reverend...

The experience prompted Mr Walker to start the project. Aware of a similar effort made in England by the 'Samaritans', he convened a meeting of 30 members of his congregation. On explaining to them his plan to save by telephone people from despair and death, a committee was formed and after three years of deliberations Lifeline was established in 1963. It was to be served by voluntary, but thoroughly trained, Christian men and women. It assured everyone, of whichever denomination (or none), that help was as close as the nearest telephone at any time.

Within the first ten years of its existence, Lifeline received 157 000 calls. Other Australian capitals took up Mr Walker's venture. International *Time* magazine gave it world renown and from Australia the idea spread first to New Zealand, and then to more than 200 cities in the United States, Latin America and South-East Asia. On the average 12 new centres are being opened annually throughout the world.

In 1966 Lifeline became an officially recognised international institution, and by 1980 the calls for help exceeded two million. In acknowledgment of his pioneering work, Alan Walker was both knighted and received an award from the Institute de la Vie, Paris, the total amount of which he donated to establish a Lifeline Foundation. Meanwhile, the scope of Lifeline is further expanding. In its concern with developing countries, it is opening 'Drop-in' Centres, inviting and welcoming people to discuss their anxieties and problems 'face to face'.

The Wayside Chapel

The Wayside Chapel began in a dilapidated four room house in one of the side lanes of Sydney's Kings Cross red light area. Ted Noffs, nominally a Methodist clergyman, had totally rejected what he regarded as antiquated and valueless ritual. He refused to abide by the parochialism of an institutionalised faith in the face of humanity's life and death struggle.

'Let us not talk but act,' Noffs said. People were right to despise meaningless 'verbal Christianity'. They longed for basic, unembellished truth.

Noffs embarked on his ambitious project, the Wayside Chapel, which was to be a vital and dynamic centre of religion, but with a difference. The building was comparatively tiny, but its smallness, far from being a disadvantage, bestows a special intimacy. In this 'church' a minister can never 'preach' or talk 'at' people. He must speak 'with' them and is closely involved with each and every one.

But the very pivot of the Wayside 'Chapel' became its round-the-clock coffee house. It welcomes anyone who, in the solitude of modern life, is yearning for company; who, in the perplexity of present-day problems, is anxious to meet someone to talk to.

The Wayside Chapel became a crises centre and a 'watchtower' for the many, and ever-changing, social issues that confused the community. Certainly, it did not cater for orthodox religion. Experimental in kind, it tried to act as a catalyst to every problem of the moment, to the deepest need of the hour. No social issue was ignored as too dangerous or too political. The Wayside Chapel led the first anti-apartheid action. It was the first to protest against the French nuclear tests in the Pacific when the rest of Australia still showed no concern.

The Wayside Chapel, among the first to take up the question of Aboriginal rights, was responsible for the establishment of the Foundation for Aboriginal Affairs. Paradoxically, it was this Methodist minister who demanded that the New South Wales Government abolish the law which banned the black race from drinking in hotels. Aware of the attitude of his Church towards drink, Noffs took the action for the sake of attaining absolutely equal rights for the Aborigines. Similarly, the Chapel initiated a systematic fight against drug abuse leading, in May 1967, to the creation of Australia's first Drug Referral Centre. And the Chapel is certainly youth oriented. It inaugurated the world's first employment bureau for long-haired youths!

Noffs felt that in crisis situations it was not enough to give advice over the telephone or on the air. A person to person encounter, an eyeball to eyeball confrontation, was essential.

The Wayside Chapel has no members in the traditional sense. Its funds come from outside supporters. Within the first four years of its existence, one million people passed through its ever-open doors. Ten thousand couples were married at the Chapel during the first ten years. Children are not baptised there or christened but 'named'. Debates and discussions are held regularly in the Wayside theatre. Only a dialogue between people, Noffs is convinced, will elicit truth. No opinion is barred, no speaker excluded.

Yet another problem, perhaps the greatest of all in present-day society, haunted Ted Noffs. Parents were at a loss how to prevent their children from becoming involved in the drug scene. Threats of divine punishment, of police prosecution or the devastating effects of drugs on their bodies and minds, he knew only too well, were useless. Somehow, he felt, the problem had to be attacked positively. Instead of reiterating futile negative admonitions, a positive, inspiring message was needed

Above: **Ted Noffs supports the needy and teaches drug restraint at his Wayside Chapel, which began in Kings Cross, Sydney.**

Overleaf: **The Easter observance of the Stations of the Cross, a major event in the Roman Catholic calendar, at Campbelltown, near Sydney.**

which would capture the imagination of the young: 'You are so beautiful, don't destroy yourself!'.

With this aim in mind, in 1980, as its latest venture, the Wayside Chapel opened The Life Education Centre. It provided what Noffs refers to as 'a Children's University'. Using every modern teaching aid, with electronic models and puppets, it impresses on youth the beauty of life. With its unique 'classroom of the 21st century', the Life Education Centre, so Noffs claims, presents the first preventative drug programme in the world. Its success, no doubt, prompted the N.S.W. Government to make a grant of 25 acres of land near Colyton, near St Marys, to provide further facilities of this very type.

Many people continue to frown on the work and worship practised in the small Wayside Chapel at the Cross. But it might well prove a pathfinder in modern faith. By its very nature, the Chapel does not claim to have all the answers. However, as Noffs explains, it is merely 'experimental religion', a first rung of the ladder.

World Council of Churches

The 1980 International Conference of the World Council of Churches held in Melbourne was an historical event, as the first major World Council gathering to be held in Australia. Some churchmen, in fact, went so far as to regard it as the most important religious conference ever to have taken place in Australia, particularly so because of its concern for social justice. No doubt, the this-worldly interpretation of the conference theme, 'Your Kingdom Come', highlighted the controversial position of the Council. Critics resented its implication that salvation was gained almost exclusively on *this* earth, at the detriment of spiritual values.

The majority of its participants came from overseas, from altogether 85 countries. Both the choice of speakers and their subjects revealed a strong Third World emphasis. Telling was 'the people's creed', contained in a booklet published prior to the conference and entitled 'The Gospel according to the Ghetto'. Its commencing words affirmed, 'I believe in a colourblind God, Maker of technicolour people, Who created the Universe and provided abundant resources for equitable distribution among all His people'.

A crisis situation

The latest available census showed an alarming and still accelerating decline of organised religion throughout Australia. With very few exceptions, it concerns every denomination.

There was no legal obligation on the part of Australians to indicate their religious affiliation. In fact, the questionnaire explicitly stated that 'there is no penalty for not answering this question'. The result was a frightening increase in the figure of those who did not care to register their faith. Within five years (from 1971 to 1976), their number had more than doubled: from 781 000 to 1 593 000. This constitutes 11.8 per cent of the total population, as compared with 6.1 per cent in 1971. On the other hand, the poll showed a phenomenal increase of those who actually professed their 'unbelief', as having 'no religion'. Their number had grown from 856 000 in 1971 to 1 130 000 in 1976, i.e. from 6.7 per cent of the population to 8.3 per cent.

In the 1976 census those categorised as 'Indefinite', 'No Religion' and religion 'Not Stated' had become the third largest 'religious' group in Australia, constituting 20.5 per cent of the total population, as compared with 27.7 per cent of Anglicans and 25.7 per cent of Catholics.

In his study of all available statistics relating to 'The State of Christian Belief in Australia', (Rev. Br.) James M. FitzPatrick revealed how since World War II and the 1947 census, whilst the total population had risen by 50.76 per cent, non-Christians had increased by 135.45 per cent and the 'Un-Churched' (a term FitzPatrick introduced to combine the three rather loosely defined categories) by 208.98 per cent! This trend is gaining further momentum and according to the latest available figures the 'Un-Churched' showed a growth of 66.51 per cent, whilst Christians registered a decline of 0.03 per cent.

At the same time, the influence of the philosophy of humanism is making itself felt in ever increasing measure. Secularisation of family life proceeds at a frightening degree. In 1977, 32.4 per cent of marriages were performed by Civil Celebrants, and between 1975 and 1976 the percentage growth rate of divorces mounted to 160.6 per cent.

Never before has Australian religion experienced a more threatening crisis situation. This, however, need not spell decay and catastrophe. Regarded as a challenge and given the right response, it may offer an opportunity of revival and renewal and prove a mere phase of transition.

THE ENVIRONMENT

Peter Cowan

'...a land under threat.'

Australia has always been a land under threat. Fires had scarred its scrub and trees, floods carved away its river banks and inundated its lowlands, its interior reflected drought and the glare of salt. Yet the land held these things in a fragile, ancient balance, adapting its plants and animals to the very factors that threatened it, changing and renewing. The first Aboriginal inhabitants enhanced the threat of fire, and their needs affected the native fauna, but in living from the land they evolved a pattern that most notably held the old balance.

With European settlement all this changed, and only in very recent years have we come to understand, and appreciate, this balance which was lost, and just how fragile it was. It was a balance damaged, perhaps destroyed, before it was understood. In Australia today we look at overcleared and overstocked land turning to desert and to salt, to drying river systems and saline water, to vanishing forests, and wildlife pushed for survival or driven to extinction, increasingly polluted air, and denuded sea coasts. It is clear we have savagely damaged a natural ecological balance we did not understand and perhaps did not care about.

Australia in the 1980s has a valuable fund of scientific knowledge in agriculture, forestry, water conservation, and ecological studies. Departments concerned with conservation and environment have been set up in universities and within government departments. As we enter the last two decades of the twentieth century we can say that we understand our environment reasonably well, and what we are doing with it — and to it. We do not have the excuse of ignorance. The eighties can be seen as a decade in which we make deliberate decisions about our environment, and make them with knowledge of what we are doing.

A country of city people

Increasingly, Australia has become a country of city people. Legends of an earlier colonial era may still linger, in literature, song, television, even Outback agricultural

Left: **More than other continents, Australia has been shaped by the sun. Environmentally, the proof is etched into its arid plains, vegetation and fauna. In this multiple-exposure photograph of the 1976 eclipse, the moon's silhouette obscures 93 per cent of the sun's disc.**

197

Left and above: While Australians have increasingly become alienated from the immense natural beauty and mystery of their ancient land, they continue to despoil their urban environment — here, through unchecked visual pollution, ignorance and carelessness.

Right: Canal estates, Noosa, Queensland. The delicate and intricate ecological balance of mangrove swamps has been damaged irrevocably as suburbia is imposed on what was hitherto a small, informal and relaxed resort of great natural beauty.

shows, but they are distant, and, in this latter part of the century, perhaps increasingly inaccessible to a new tide of immigrants who are establishing cultures which, at least in the immediate future, seem to have little to do with an older Australia; cultures themselves predominantly urban.

Over 80 per cent of the present population find security in urban areas, safe from, or indifferent to, the strange wilderness beyond, the great silence, from what is sometimes still called the real Australia. If home, for most Australians, is the sight of increasing numbers of streets and buildings, kilometres of freeways, blocks of car-parks, the noise of traffic, then it may seem that any consideration of Australia's environment should be limited to the cities; limited to the suburb, the car, the beach, those prerequisites of the Australian dream. And if the dream were to see Sydney stretch from Wollongong to Newcastle, to see Perth stretch from Bunbury to Geraldton, to see instant prototype suburbia spring from the red soil and rocks of the northern mining areas, and a Surfers Paradise slowly encircle the coast — would it really matter?

After all, is there any longer a 'real' Australia where the land retains its natural ancient shapes, its intricate vegetation, its animals and birds, its strangeness and beauty? We publicise these things in our tourist brochures, in some of our immigration material, yet any newcomer must form a first impression of expanding cities and an urban tide engulfing more and more of the coastal plains of the continent.

And for those who move inland, perhaps on some safely conducted holiday tour, that first impression of a future belonging to the cities might well be strengthened by a landscape scarred from a series of rural expansions and retreats, denuded by exploitation — the treeless hectares of the wheatbelt, the sparse shade of dairy and cattle country, the often despoiled and drying tracts of pastoral leases. A landscape familiar and often beautiful in its way, but as controlled, and essentially artificial as any city landscape. Tourist or visitor, even journeying into what was once seen as the untouched centre, the desert land with its own strong beauty, might conclude that little of an original landscape was any longer to be found, that 'real' Australia was change.. The choices and the decisions about change lie in the cities. What else matters?

The earlier answer was, unhappily, that very little else mattered. If for a time that was a pleasant state of ignorance for our cities — and countryside — to develop in, it is one no longer possible. The totality of our environment can no longer be denied, or evaded in the comfort of our cities, though the concept may still have to be argued for.

The past two decades saw this concept emerge to something like respectability, and gain more than lip service from governments and planners, rural and urban. A real public concern and a growing enlightenment have forced governments at State and federal level to consider something better than a piecemeal, sufficient-unto-the-day approach to the effects of industrial, urban, and rural expansion on the environment as a whole. State and federal government began in the sixties and seventies to develop ministries of conservation and environment, to establish environmental protection authorities, and the pressure for this kind of legislation

199

Left: A polluted sunset over an industrial complex at Whyalla in South Australia.

Below left: A strip of commercial jungle in Parramatta, New South Wales. This cityscape could be duplicated in any urban concentration in Australia.

Right: Obsolescence and disposability, built-in sales appeals for many products, are creating a new Frankenstein's monster in the form of waste materials. This automotive graveyard is in a small country town in the far north of Queensland.

Overleaf: In many areas where man has tamed — or raped — the natural environment, the major problems are not those of flood, drought or fire.

Left: **Ellinja Falls on the Atherton Tableland. Although huge areas of Australia are arid, on a per capita basis it is the wettest country in the world. Much of the rain falls on the eastern slopes of the Atherton Tableland on the tropical Queensland coastal strip near Cairns, and nourishes such beauty spots as Ellinja Falls where an abundance of trees and ferns thrives.**

Above: **Beautiful Terania Creek flows through one of the last remaining virgin rainforests of N.S.W. Logging (its more visible effects evident in the photograph, right) was stopped in 1979 as a result of considerable public protest. The State Government is still formulating a policy to accommodate the interests of conservationists and displaced timber workers.**

came directly from expressed public concern, from newly formed conservation organisations, from street marches and protests. People were questioning short-term goals, the wisdom of indiscriminate exploitation of limited resources, the sanity of development at any cost.

None of this was particularly popular with governments, and legislation for environmental planning varied from State to State. Where specific environmental authorities were established, these were to survey and report on the environmental effects of industrial expansion, new industry, forest exploitation, water projects, some aspects of urban development, and the security of national parks and reserves. It was implied the reports would be made public and open to debate. This seemed a major step in the direction of environmental protection, though it was not clear if the reports would be considered as other than advisory, and there was likely to be conflict between State and federal areas which might frustrate many decisions.

This solitary axeman is part of a long tradition which began with the cedar cutters — or 'men of death' — in the early 1800s. They plied their trade in the Big Brush, first in the upper reaches of the Lane Cove River, and later along the Hawkesbury, Clarence and Richmond rivers and the Illawarra coast.

Despite these doubts, there developed a real awakening of the need for environmental policies, and a desire to implement them. There was an admission that the cities were not the isolated clusters of science fiction, independent of an outer world. Indeed the cities might be said to have rediscovered themselves. They became aware they were part of a wider, often unseen, environment, and they discovered their own history. As symbols of a young country, their emphasis had been towards the new, the future. In their drive for expansion there seemed little to value or retain from the past. Concern for human scale, for intimacy and variety, for reminders of other eras and patterns of living, were sacrificed in the trend towards size, uniformity, impersonality. But these very qualities produced a countercurrent, and a realisation that heedless development might destroy the cities as it could the landscape and environment beyond them. Older urban areas listed for destruction became valued because they were old, different, individual, and because, however marred by later fashions, their buildings were often strikingly beautiful.

In the property boom of the sixties, and a generally increasing value for real estate since, the older city buildings too often became victims of the value of their sites. The National Trust, with authority to classify buildings worth preserving, could only parallel the environmental protection authorities in the pointlessness of recommendation without sufficient legislative power. State governments and many major city councils remained reluctant to impede large city development projects, and it was left to a few city councils to work, often against their own State governments, to retain the individuality of the areas under their care.

And though it might be argued that city planning mistakes seem self-perpetuating, the city planners everywhere found themselves under a new scrutiny and faced with a newly concerned public. The effect of city planning on the quality of life, rather than as a tool for economic development, became a major concern.

It would be ironic if the cities fared better in this concern than the country out beyond them, those vast areas which are often seen as the only real focus of environmental issues.

The landscape beyond the cities has seen an immense ebb and flow of humanity. In 1933, 35 per cent of Australians tolerated rural existence, but by the beginning of the seventies only some 14 per cent; indeed by the end of that decade almost 70 per cent of the total population lived in six State capitals and five other major cities — only one of which, Canberra, was away from the coast. If the millions of hectares of farming and grazing country now seem remote to city dwellers their distaste may be reasonable enough. Clearing has been ruthless, often total, deter-

ALCOA — a guide to rehabilitation

Australia ranks with the world's large producers of bauxite, having mines in the Darling Range in Western Australia, at Weipa in Queensland, and Gove in the Northern Territory. There are refineries and smelters in other localities dependent on these mines.

The work done by Alcoa, one of the large producers, in rehabilitating its bauxite leases in the Darling Range has certain aspects peculiar to the locality, but in approach, and what has been achieved, offers a guide for similar work elsewhere, and for open cut mining of other minerals.

In the mining of a selected area, commercial timber is first removed by logging companies. The remaining timber and undergrowth are cleared and burned, exposing the topsoil and overburden which in the Darling Range may be up to a depth of one metre. This overburden and topsoil is removed and stored. The bauxite, some three or four metres of ore, is then mined.

At this stage the result is a barren landscape that would seem to justify the strongest complaints of conservationists.

Rehabilitation begins with the establishment of contour banks, sloping of pit surfaces, and deep ripping to control surface erosion, with the return of the topsoil from the storage piles. With some of Alcoa's leases, the land is then returned to the Forestry Department which may use it for pines or other planting. In the areas which remain Alcoa's concern, regeneration of vegetation is begun. Extensive trials have established the type of tree and shrub cover best adapted, and these include a variety of eucalypts, 14 of which are now commonly used; some, such as marri, wandoo, blackbutt, are local; others, like the Sydney blue gum and red mahogany are eastern States species. Acacia and melaleuca, with native seeds gathered by the Forestry Department and Alcoa, provide a rich understorey, and again considerable experiment has been undertaken to find the successful types and methods of generation. The result of the work since 1966 has to date provided a generally diverse and successful cover of native trees, shrubs, and small plants which has none of the sameness resulting from replanting with pines. Native fauna and bird life is re-entering the areas from the surrounding unmined land.

Another possibility for rehabilitation has been developed in provision of recreational areas, with some tree cover and grasses and ornamental lakes. Experiment with water catchment, water purity, horticulture, agriculture, and urban development of fauna and flora conservation have also been carried out. By 1979 some 1 400 hectares had been completely revegetated, at costs averaging 10 000 dollars a hectare.

Alcoa has applied the same principles to its coal mining areas at Anglesea in Victoria, where there is a predominantly dry heath vegetation.

The rehabilitation and general experimentation has been considerably beyond the letter of the company's requirements under law. The results may not yet be completely assessed. In the Darling Range, areas of unique jarrah forest are lost, and the original vegetation system inevitably altered, but there is a complication here in that sections of forest are under serious threat from the disease of dieback, caused by the fungus *Phytophthora cinnamomi*, estimated to be spreading at possibly 20 000 hectares a year. What is evident is that the result of the rehabilitation after mining offers a reforested area, though one different from the original, the threat to water catchment and soil salinity is minimised, and a habitat is retained for native fauna which is not completely driven from the area.

This kind of land use remains a subject of debate among conservationists, yet it is one that offers no comparison with the total and lasting destruction of an original environment which follows from agriculture.

Left: A Wee Waa family studies the flood level for signs of change. Most country towns are inured to extremes. The hardships imposed are borne with patience, a wry humour and the old 'battler' spirit.

Above: Rich topsoil from the fertile Naomi Valley washes away through the cotton town of Wee Waa, north-west N.S.W., during the summer floods of 1974.

Right: Some houses, built well above the ground, stayed dry. This Wee Waa couple and their friends wade to a tractor waiting to take them to the bowling club for the evening.

mined by short term convenience, large scale machinery operations, overstocking in good and bad rainfall years, perhaps even by a kind of distrust, an emotional fear, of the once surpassingly beautiful natural vegetation, that reminder of an ancient balance.

All this the city might shrug off, as once it did. But the effects of such policies on soil salinity and rainfall are becoming a threat to city water supplies, and drought, like that widespread over Australian rural areas in 1980, results in problems for commerce and industry, employment, and the use of taxpayers money on drought relief. Increasing urban populations discovered the stark limits of water resources not only on further growth but on maintaining their own level of existence; the extensive use of underground water, the limits of which are not yet properly understood, is providing for some cities a short term answer. World history has enough examples of increasingly denuded landscapes that would not regenerate, of desert replacing pasture, but Australia had seemed a fortunate country. That dream, for the city dweller facing water restrictions and high charges, for new industry demanding a high volume of water, began to fade; for the farmer or pastoralist it was not enough to withdraw expenditure, tighten the economic belt, take out an overdraft, and wait for rain. Damage by drought, fire, and erosion, too clearly is becoming irreversible.

Planning for the future

It would be pleasant to think that for Australia all the mistakes had been made, that somehow they had been the result of lack of ecological knowledge back in the bad old days. Yet, just as city planning mistakes often seem to be self-perpetuating, so water catchment areas are still threatened by adjacent farm clearing, by mining, by the new threat of the wood chip industry, and with every rise in the price of wheat comes ruthless clearing of land which can now only be marginal, with low soil fertility and rainfall. Recent newspaper correspondence on the widespread Australian droughts and the effect of clearing has indicated not only a demand for further land releases, but that uncleared land, and unused land, may be still seen as simply unproductive land. The frontier is seen as endless. Very little in fact does seem to have been learned.

Something could still be retained from this increasingly featureless and often increasingly sterile area that takes in most of the inhabited land beyond the cities; but it will have to be done soon. It has been suggested that all farms should retain ten per cent of their natural cover in the interests of rainfall and soil fertility, of birds and native animals — which would in many cases require massive replanting — and that new land should not be totally cleared. While this seems now an obvious and urgent necessity in holding some balance between environmental protection and development, to many farmers and agriculture protection boards, to bushfire boards and shire councils, native fauna is vermin, native plants are a fire hazard, and rainfall just happens. Or it did. The recent drought, a culmination of some four dry years in parts of Australia, has caused a faint doubt that perhaps there is more to it than that, and for the first time some shire councils have come out against overclearing, even warning farmers and suggesting replanting of trees for windbreak and shade areas, and to halt soil drift.

Replanting is possible, and some farms have planted wind and sun breaks and encouraged small areas of regrowth; on trial salt lands there have been experiments with regrowth patterns; and a few farmers have declared their properties fauna reserves.

It can be strongly argued that Australia could now halt any further alienation of Crown Lands. The exploitation of new land now means taking agriculturally marginal land, or reserves. These marginal lands, mainly in the light rainfall mallee and sandplain areas, occurring particularly in New South Wales, South Australia, and Western Australia, have their own beauty and interest. They hold plant species found nowhere else in the world, they are a refuge for rare marsupials and reptiles, and are themselves a factor in rainfall and erosion patterns. Some of these areas are still only partly classified botanically, and their destruction may in fact remove

Like their counterparts all over the world, Australians are concerned at the proliferation of nuclear weapons. At this anti-nuclear march in Sydney in April, 1982, organisers estimated that 50 000 people massed to demand a nuclear free Pacific.

plants we have never known. The clearing of this land produces savage erosion in time of drought, or when the periodic decline of farm prices draws back the frontier. The lesson of South Australia's Goyder Line seems inevitably forgotten.

Because of the unique interest of these areas, and their now limited extent, and because of the hard fact that their conservation may benefit city and country alike in terms of rainfall and soil retention, Australia could say it had cleared enough agricultural land, and would farm what it had more efficiently. Hardly a popular doctrine, and in those political areas where the frontier mentality lies embedded, one which is anathema; yet refusal to face it seems certain to achieve the paradox of losing more land than is gained as established areas are eaten away by increased erosion, aridity, and salt.

Mining

The threat to the land, the changes in environment and balance, have not come only from agriculture. The mineral boom of the 1950s and 1960s saw mining exploration move into areas forgotten or never travelled, and the small claim pegs with their fluttering ribbons of colour seemed to be everywhere. Mining suddenly became the great threat to the natural environment. Yet the fact emerged that most mining

Left; The red kangaroo, *Mega-laia rufa*, is also called the plains kangaroo because it prefers the open grasslands.

Below left: Emancipation came to the female emu a long time ago — the male makes the nest and incubates the eggs for about two months. The brown and white striped chicks grow into Australia's largest birds, flightless, but with vestigial wings held close to the body.

Opposite page, above: The spotted cuscus, *Phalanger maculatus*, is characterised by handsome skewbald markings, hand-like feet and a scaly prehensile tail.

Opposite page, right: The Pygo-pididae family of legless lizards exists only in Australia and New Guinea. They differ from snakes in having ear openings, wide fleshy tongues and, in some cases, vestigial legs. Burton's legless lizard, *Lialis burtonis*, is generally striped and it grows to about 40 centi-metres in length.

Opposite page, below right: A feathertail or pygmy glider, *Acrobates pygmaeus*, hunts for un-plundered blooms among the sweet-nectared blossoms of an erythrina tree in tropical Queensland.

Opposite page, left: The desert goanna, *Varanus eremias*, one of the intrepid dwellers of the dry lands, whose fattened tail con-tains nourishment for particu-larly adverse conditions.

Described by UNESCO as the greatest tragedy since European settlement in Tasmania, the submerging of the natural lake, Lake Pedder, in 1971-72 destroyed at least 18 endemic plant and animal species, a costly sacrifice to hydro-electric power.

caused less damage than farming. Much of the country had been mined before and, in apparently virgin bush, old mine shafts and dumps were sudden reminders of the gold rushes of the previous century. Vast areas of salmon gum, gimlet and mallee in the Kalgoorlie-Coolgardie region were felled for mines using up to 100 tonnes of timber a day for fuel. Today, regeneration has provided stands of new trees easy to mistake for original stands. There are few areas of agricultural land that offer a parallel.

With the 1980s the spectacular rise in the price of gold has forced a new rush of claim pegging, and surface prospecting with metal detectors has flooded old and abandoned gold areas all over Australia. The final effects are uncertain, the land may outlast this invasion as it has those which came earlier, but some species of native animals and the larger birds seem certain to suffer from the increased population in remote areas.

Today's mining is as much above ground as below. Bauxite, iron ore, mineral sands, open cut coal mining, permanently change the face of the land. Top soil and subsoil are removed, and the growth conditions for vegetation altered. Re-establishment may be attempted, but the natural vegetation is rarely replaceable, and the effect on what native fauna survives is yet to be determined. However

OLEGAS TRUCHANAS — a fearless commitment

Conservation in Australia during the 1960s and 1970s was based on growing numbers of people and increasingly well-organised groups. Yet occasionally an individual came to play a part of unusual importance, finding a role and significance that person had perhaps never expected.

Olegas Truchanas arrived as a migrant in Tasmania in 1948. He was born in Lithuania in 1923. Through the war years he was a member of the Lithuanian Resistance Movement, but left his country when it became a part of the USSR in 1945.

In Tasmania he worked first with the Electrolytic Zinc Co. at Risdon. For many European migrants Australia offered a chance to settle in cities which, if different from their own, held patterns of life to which they were accustomed. From the beginning Olegas Truchanas was attracted to something different, he began to discover a Tasmania little known to many of those who had spent their lives in the country. The forested areas of the south-west were in many places a true wilderness, difficult of access, impossible to travel, it was often said. There were deep ravines, heavy timber and mountain vegetation, inaccessible rivers, with storms, heavy rain, and snow to deter the adventurer. It was an area little regarded except for its possible future economic possibilities in timber and mining, and hydro-electricity. Olegas Truchanas began to explore this country, walking, camping, frequently alone, finding places no one else had reached.

In time his reputation as a bushman grew, he made some journeys till then considered impossible, and began to explore the rivers of the region, the Franklin, Serpentine, the Gordon. He made a scarcely believable journey alone down the lower Gordon which had never been attempted before in the history of Tasmania's settlement.

With the physical qualities needed for this often lonely and hazardous work, he possessed great skill as a photographer. He was able to convey to others something of his own artistic vision and deep feeling for a difficult and untouched landscape.

This ability to bring back from these wild and little known places something for others to discover and value, and his ability as a lecturer, became widely known, as did the fact that he was, for all his visionary love of a natural world, also a practical man, who believed conservationists had to come forward with practical solutions. These qualities were perhaps best appreciated in the controversy over Lake Pedder, a central feature of the great wilderness area Truchanas had come to know so well. His illustrated lectures, his constant effort with the authorities determined to open up and utilise this country, notably the lake itself, became a vital factor in the campaign to save Lake Pedder. Through his photographs he could show people something of what they would lose, show them what they had themselves never seen or realised. Though this struggle, which in the end involved so many people, was lost, a new awareness of the beauty and environmental importance of the region had been firmly established.

Olegas Truchanas fought also to save the magnificent Huon pines of the Gordon-Denison River areas. With a companion, Brian Collin, he examined the area in dispute with the Forestry Commission, to report it held 'the only remaining stand of large mature Huon pines in Tasmania, and therefore in the world', and vindicated the need for the area to become a national park. It was established later as a reserve to carry his own name.

When the Lower Gordon Power Development Scheme again threatened the unique beauty of the south-west rivers, Olegas Truchanas returned for a further dangerous journey down the Gordon to replace the photographs he had lost from his home in the disastrous fires of 1967. It was his last journey. He was drowned, near one of the river falls, in the river he had fought to save. By his own vision, his effort, and the beauty of his photographs, he had made not only Tasmanians but all Australians aware of how much there was to value and to save in the south-west wilderness; and to share something of his own love of a fast disappearing Australia.

215

Above: The shallow basin of Smith's Lake, adjoining Myall Lakes, N.S.W., opens to the sea only during high tide and rough seas. Sand dunes on its shores, covered with rich forests of angophora and blackbutt — rare in these conditions — are being destroyed by sand mining.

Left: Public opposition to sand mining began in the late fifties and early sixties as the miners moved inland into the mature forests almost 200 metres above sea level. Mining is to cease in N.S.W. national parks by 1982 — but not before $95 million of mineral sand will have been extracted in five years.

Right: Roads to transport eucalypt trees to the mills for Tasmania's woodchip industry scar the sloping hillside, eroding the naked countryside. The forests may never recover from this devastation.

meticulous the re-establishment, and some companies have been meticulous in their work in this respect, a new landscape is created. Bauxite and sand mining are carried out near population centres and may have a variety of consequences only now appearing. Sand mining, as threatened at Middle Head Beach, or Fraser Island, destroys a unique coastal bushland and alters the dune structure.

Bauxite mining in particular poses a threat to forest resources, to areas where a balance between tree growth and relatively inhospitable soil conditions established unique tree covers such as the jarrah forest of Western Australia. But by the end of the seventies bauxite, though its removal of timber is total, was only one of a number of threats to forests.. Increasing demand for timber forced forest controllers to cut up to and beyond a safe natural replacement level, but a threat now seen as bigger than either of these came with the establishment of wood chip

THE HAGBOOM BROTHERS — lovers of wildlife

Dowerin was an early settled area of the Western Australian wheatbelt. To pass through it is to see land extensively cleared for wheat and sheep, and it is hard to imagine what the country looked like even 50 years ago.

Bill Hagboom's family had been in the district a long time, and when he and his brothers, George and Eddie, took up land in 1939 their properties were among the last selected in the area. They followed the pattern of extensive clearing, but some of the lighter sandy soil was subject to erosion and they decided to let this regrow.

It was an area of york gum and mallee with jams, banksias, ti-tree and wild pear; varied and beautiful sandplain plants had grown all over the light soil country. As this vegetation regenerated and began to reclaim an area of about 200 hectares (some of which still had natural bush on it), the Hagbooms saw possibilities for encouraging animal and bird life.

Animals that had become rare in such a settled district began to reappear. The kangaroos were the most obvious (as many as 50 or 60 grazed in the area), there were signs of the almost forgotten echidna, and the lizards (once a feature of sandplain areas) were returning. A lake began to form, and became a centre for a wealth of bird life. Parrots, crows, magpies, hawks, wrens, rainbow birds and swallows could be seen about the bush land and water; swans, mountain duck, teal, wood duck, water hens, dabchicks, stilts and dotterels were seen on the lake; even cormorants and seagulls have occasionally appeared. With the rapid reclamation of so much swamp and wetland in the coastal plain area of the State, lakes such as this provide refuges for a wide range of bird life — refuges that are likely to become essential if some species of waterfowl are to survive.

The Hagbooms had the area declared a fauna sanctuary. The kangaroos who have adopted it do not damage their crops; they merely eat pasture, which the Hagbooms do not begrudge them. Some of the area extends into adjoining farms, and neighbours such as the McMorran brothers and K. T. Maisey and Sons also encourage areas of natural land which become wildlife reserves.

The work and foresight of Bill Hagboom, his brothers and their neighbours have brought back something of the interest and beauty of the natural countryside to these areas, something to be enjoyed not only by themselves but by many others.

mills. Wood chipping established areas of total clearing which left a bare soil. Scrub and waste timber are burnt on the ground. The cutting licences specified limits and conditions which forest conservationsts claim have already been extended and exceeded. Tasmania, Victoria, New South Wales, Western Australia, have all seen the mills erase scarce forests and extend their threat to new areas, some of great scenic beauty and ecological importance.

In theory the devastated areas will regrow, new forests will emerge; but the mills move faster than the regrowth. Such timber may take more than 50 years to reach an equivalent maturity, the mills will inevitably abandon the areas once heavily and beautifully forested. The results are still being determined, there may be serious erosion on the bare slopes in heavy rainfall areas, there is a loss of scenic beauty, areas once tourist attractions can only be viewed as deserts. Whatever regeneration eventuates there may be permanent loss of many native plants, and native animals and birds, some unique and adapted only to live in the original environment. At best, woodchipping may provide another environment, but it will be unlikely ever to replace the original; at worst it may prove an ecological disaster.

A third factor for change in Australian forests seems at first sight less severe than mining or woodchipping. The use of increasing areas for the planting of pines for timber and pulp replaces one tree with another. But it destroys the environment that sheltered indigenous birds and animals, and which provided the conditions for some of the most unusual and beautiful plants to be found anywhere.

These changes in a natural, older environmental pattern threw greater emphasis on the need for national parks, even if they were to be seen only as the last pockets of an original ecology of great variety and subtlety.

Above right: This unique carnivore, the thylacine or Tasmanian Tiger, is thought to be extinct and was last documented in 1934, (although recent unauthenticated sightings give new hope of its survival). Remains discovered in the Nullarbor area date back 4 000 to 5 000 years.

Below left: The numbat or spiny ant-eater has a long, specialised tongue, adapted for extracting ground-dwelling termites from their mounds.

Below right: The koala is a coastal-dwelling, nocturnal marsupial and feeds entirely on eucalypts. In 1925, two million koala skins were exported from the east coast and, in one year, 600 000 were shot for sport.

Above: **Ayers Rock, after the exceptional rains of 1973-74, seems to float above the 'inland sea' sought in vain by the explorer Charles Sturt in 1844. Rising 335 metres above the plains west-south-west of Alice Springs, the world's largest monolith is the symbol of the 'Dead Heart' for white Australians — and for the black, the symbol of life.**

Right: **Farther west of Ayers Rock are the Olgas, a group of monoliths on the edge of an almost waterless desert extending 1 500 kilometres from the southern Northern Territory across central Western Australia. The haze rose after a day of torrential summer rain.**

National parks

Generous in giving away its land to farmers and graziers, Australia was slow to recognise the need for national parks, and when established they were subject to over-riding claims for mining and grazing. Serious consideration of reserves as areas secure in themselves revealed a confused position, and State legislative attempts to bring some order to the chaos are recent. In 1970, the National Parks and Wildlife Act of Tasmania placed the control of parks and reserves, flora and fauna, under a National Parks and Wildlife Service. South Australia repealed previous Acts to form a National Parks and Wildlife Service, a division of the Department for the Environment, with the Acts of 1972–78. The New South Wales National Parks and

220

Wildlife Act 1967–69 and 1974–76 set aside national parks, State parks, and historic sites reserved under earlier Acts. Victoria set up a National Park Authority from earlier legislation with the Acts of 1958 and 1975–78. Queensland introduced a National Parks and Wildlife Act in 1975–76. Western Australia with an Act of 1976 appointed a National Parks Authority to replace the National Parks Board established earlier.

These years saw significant increases in reserves. By 1979 Western Australia had moved from 130 000 hectares to some 4.5 million; South Australia from 1.2 million to 3.9; New South Wales from 800 000 to over 3 million; Victoria gained something like a threefold increase to 775 000 hectares; Queensland had some 1.25 million and 30 000 hectares of fauna reserves; Tasmania claimed around 623 000 hectares of national parks and about half that in conservation areas.

Clearly, this reflected a change in attitude towards environmental conservation on the part of the States. The increases, however, reflected also the growing pressure of public demand. Over-use threatens the character of most parks near major cities, and as far afield as well known sites like Ayers Rock. For the eighties, the increased cost of fuel may see greater use of near capital city parks, and no one has yet determined the preference of growing migrant communities in this respect, or how they will view national parks at all.

The mining boom which drew attention to the diminishing natural areas of Australia also underlined their insecurity. A declared reserve or established national park could be pegged and an application to mine granted at the discretion of a warden's court. A government environmental protection authority might make recommendations for or against such land use in parks. In many cases the Minister for lands or mines could decide on appeal by the parties. Most States muddled along with a variety of apparent legal safeguards, yet clearly unwilling to retreat too far from their rights in allowing mining proposals. New South Wales did go further in stating that land within a park was exempt from occupation under the Mining Act, and an application for a lease or appropriation of land within a reserve must go before Parliament. But the threat to the parks remained, and government authorities were themselves likely to be contenders for the right to use national parks for their own projects, such as hydro-electricity.

The Lake Pedder controversy highlighted this. Though a central feature in a national park, Lake Pedder was subjected to flooding as part of a hydro-electricity scheme. No other single act within a national park aroused so much controversy. Against all persuasion and argument the Tasmanian Government stood firm, finally rejecting the moratorium offer of the federal government to compensate Tasmania for losses it would incur through a reversal of its decision to proceed.

In the Northern Territory the newly formed Kakadu National Park, likely to become one of the major parks of Australia, is going to have to live with the exploitation of uranium deposits within its boundaries, decisions which this time rest with the federal government.

The concept of marine parks has been slow to evolve, as indeed has the whole idea of conservation of coastal areas. The beaches and the sea have been important features of the Australian way of life, yet industry is still being sited on the coast, industrial effluent is emitted from Botany Bay to Cockburn Sound and the new iron ore towns of the north; heavy population pressures have led to the increasing subdivision of scarce coastal land, and inlet and estuary areas are being sold for housing estates in schemes involving massive ecological changes; the over-use of recreational areas is producing marine deserts along all suburban coastlines. Resulting temperature changes, effluent and mineral dusts, fertilisers and waste, all effect marine growth and sea life; the colours of the weeds and reefs are changing, the very clarity and beauty of the water, so distinctive of Australia, are being dulled.

The Great Barrier Reef itself has been threatened by the surge of interest in oil drilling, and by mining. And before they could be included in any scheme of reserves most of the wetlands of Australia have been drained or filled until those remaining are rare and doubly valuable.

Yet public opinion has proved its effect, and through the sixties and seventies that opinion became increasingly vocal and directed. It had effect in another recent

Above: The great ravine of the Franklin River is threatened with imminent submersion to a depth of some 130 metres should the Tasmanian Hydro-Electric Commission construct a sixth scheme on this the last of the great wilderness rivers.

Right: From the Engineer Range, the Franklin River flows towards the Lower Gordon River. Although it has been classified by the World Heritage and Australia Heritage councils as a world wilderness area (and is thought to contain unstudied relics of Ice Age Aboriginal culture), the concerted efforts of the Save the Franklin campaigners seem doomed to failure.

The Great Barrier Reef runs 1930 kilometres along the north-east coast. Its incomparable variety of marine life is rich and colourful.

Left: Moray eels, *Gymnothorax meleagris*, seldom leave their lairs during the day, preferring to wait in hiding for their prey. Growing up to four metres in length, and the thickness of a man's thigh, moray eels are naturally feared because of their sharp and dangerous teeth but they attack only if disturbed or frightened.

Below left: The harlequin tusk-fish, *Lienardella fasciatus*, is typical of many brilliantly coloured reef fish. Related to the parrot fish and wrasses, the tuskfish are generally pugnacious.

Above right: The delicately fleshed herbivorous green turtle, *Chelonia mydas*, was once harvested for its meat by canneries on several Barrier Reef islands. Now protected, its number are increasing, and it is again a common sight on summer nights to see the females plod ashore to lay their 50 to 200 eggs in the sand. Slow and clumsy on land, they are fast swimming reptiles, and even at a top weight of around 200 kilograms they move through the the water with great speed and grace.

Below right: The long snout of the Raffles butterfly fish, *Chaetodon rafflesi*, probes coral crevices from which its bristle-like teeth extract food particles. Rivalling butterflies in their brilliant colouring, these fish move easily through narrow coral cavities because of their deep, compressed body shape.

controversy in Tasmania in the government deciding against a Hydro Electric Commission plan to flood the Franklin River, instead including it in a Wild Rivers National Park, likely to become an area of great interest and beauty, though the threat is not entirely removed.

Late in the day the Great Barrier Reef has gained some security with the intervention of the federal government, though that government has lessened its own power over coastal areas with recent federal legislation giving the States control over territorial waters.

225

Force of public concern

The Federal Government again, with considerable courage, halted sand mining on Fraser Island, and has stood against threats of legal action from mining companies, and complaints from some municipal authorities. And there is a continuing series of local battles all over Australia by groups dedicated to saving particular areas. Public concern and pressure remains, and has become more efficiently organised.

What kind of environment does this public concern seek? What kind of environment is to emerge in a country as large as Australia, as dedicated to economic growth, to city living, to an increasing population? Can the kind of balance, uneasy though it was, between old and new, natural and man made, that seemed to be emerging from the struggles and reappraisals of the sixties and seventies hold?

This view may need a good deal of optimism if it is to be sustained in the last two decades of the century. Already the eighties states its own clear problems. If the two previous decades gave conservation organisations experience and knowledge, they gave governments a similar insight. However uneasily, government authority then had to give ground and go along with conservation plans and ideas. The eighties poses serious employment problems — problems which may well see a complete reappraisal of living patterns. There are energy problems, high fuel costs, indications of a static or slowly expanding economic consumer demand. Faced with these difficulties it is already clear that government tolerance towards conservation has lessened. Two States have made alterations to their environmental protection Acts, Western Australia in removing the power of its E.P.A. head to vote, and increasing the power of government appointment to the management committee, Tasmania in placing large tracts of its south-west wilderness under Forestry Commission control (and in a decision for a referendum on the damming of the south-west rivers has declined to prohibit interference with the rivers and the Wild Rivers National Park area: the government refused a 'no dams' option in the referendum, voters having to choose between a proposed dam on the Gordon River above the Olga River or below the Franklin River); Victoria delayed power promised for its wildlife division to protect endangered species; public assembly restriction Acts in Queensland and Western Australia aim at least in part at conservation protest demonstration.

It seems inevitable that agreement for the establishment of industry that will provide employment (however briefly and at almost any environmental cost) will be accepted. Shipbuilding in coastal areas of recreational and environmental concern, bauxite smelters in dairying and vineyard country and near water catchment areas, offer evidence from as far apart as the Hunter Valley, Portland in Victoria, Wagerup in Western Australia. The revival of interest in coal will create vast new mining areas, nuclear energy is being canvassed by some States, projects such as the huge North West Shelf Gas will, if they eventuate, create new populations in once remote areas, as iron ore mining already has, with new problems.

Land under threat

Governments will have to make difficult decisions in these years and, by the very nature of the Australian economy, they may make them increasingly in favour of overseas capital and overseas needs. Government concern will, on past evidence, favour the exploitation of scarce and limited resources close to the point of exhaustion; possibly to the point of no return. Conservationists can responsibly point to the vital need of a conservor society for the eighties, but they can hardly expect political endorsement. They can argue the need for an environmental balance that is not mere sentiment or nostalgia, but a concern for a future where the quality of life is not degraded, and if the future of Australia is to lie with its cities and industries, argue that the very existence of these depends on a balance with what lies beyond them; a balance that includes clean air, water, and a soil that will produce food and not waste land. A balance must be struck beyond the short term and it must be held. But at the beginning of the 1980s the shape of that balance is not easy to predict, only that it involves increasing change. Australia remains very much a land under threat.

Although the trade union movement has been instrumental in protecting inner-city areas of historical and social significance from high rise developments, industrial action at sewerage plants contributes frequently to the despoilment of Sydney beaches.

THE ARTS

Don Dunstan

'... a vigour and maturity...'

W hen Australia was hurriedly annexed and settled by Europeans in 1788 there were three apparent motives for the action by Britain — to find a place to which to transport convicts after the loss of her American colonies, to lay a claim to trade in Pacific areas and keep others out, and to find a new source of rope and spars for the navy with the growing difficulty of getting reliable supplies from Scandinavia. The first settlers were convicts and those who guarded them. Free settlement on any large scale did not occur until after 1840. When the settlers came, from the very outset they found a country which to them was so alien and hostile in its climate, vegetation, fauna and the habits of its population, that they tried to alter it to be as like the country they had come from as they could.

The Aborigines, who had inhabited the continent for more than 40 000 years, had a culture particularly adapted to the Australian environment. Not being connected to the European-Asian land mass, they had not acquired the skill of smelting iron. But they had controlled their population growth, and had a rich and varied diet. They were much better off physically than the poor of Europe at the time. They were nomadic, and found it necessary to build only rude shelters rather than permanent housing. But needing to expend much less time and energy than the Europeans on getting food, shelter and clothing, and none on the accumulation of material things (which they regarded as encumbering and foolish), their community life revolved around their music, dance and rich ceremonial. Their history was kept by oral tradition, which regarded all living things as related and of common ancestry. Their visual arts tended to be imprisoned in traditional formalism, but their ceremonial was living artistry. It was spurned and derided by the Europeans, who regarded the Aborigines as the most miserable of savages, to be pushed off their lands and sacred grounds, and hunted down and killed if they resisted. Thereafter, the remnants were to be clothed, Christianised and educated to materialism and the work ethic. The art of the Aborigines was until recent times, neglected, destroyed, or ignored by the European majority in Australia.

And for the art of the settlers early fiction was of little note. Early painters tended to record Australian scenes in a peculiarly English way — the paintings of Gill are charming in their naive view of Australia through an English eye. The artistic life of the Australian community for the last century was provincial, European-derived, what one might expect from a community of antipodean exiles who referred to England as 'home' though most of them had never been there.

Left: **Contemporary ballet has emerged as one of the most exciting and vigorous art forms.**

From the time of the goldrushes Australia rapidly developed as one of the most urban nations in the world. By the latter part of the nineteenth century the majority of Australians lived in large cities. The average Australian lived in a small house on a quarter-acre block. Until the coming of radio and cinema, theatres and vaudeville houses abounded. Apart from melodrama and some operas which had great popularity but have now entirely disappeared from public ken, there was little indigenous theatre — it was all the work of European or sometimes American dramatists.

The first painter to popularise the Australian landscape was Hans Heysen, a son of South Australia's community of German migrants. His most popular works, however, were bathed in Turner-like light and softened and romanticised Australian rural scenes.

The first Australian fiction of note was a crudely written and melodramatic account of the brutality of convict existence — *For The Term of His Natural Life* by Marcus Clarke. It was turned into a successful theatre piece and later a feature film. The only other early work to show any merit was Furphy's *Such is Life*.

The role of the 'Bulletin'

In Sydney a periodical, the *Bulletin,* carried fiction and verse. Its policy was radical, jingoistic, and it proudly displayed 'Australia for the white man' on its masthead. But it did give rise to three major movements in Australian letters which were formative of today's Australia.

The first, through Henry Lawson (verse and short story writer) and versifiers like Banjo Paterson, celebrated the trials and hardships of living in the Australian countryside. They celebrated 'mateship' and wrote in an Australian vernacular clearly cockney-derived. They helped to create the myth of the typical Australian — the sun-bronzed bushman, droving cattle, shearing sheep, humping his swag, drinking black billy tea and downing beer when he could get it. In fact, this was quite untypical of Australians. Henry Lawson himself spent most of his life in Sydney suburbia. But the myth was important in the development of an Australian consciousness, and was illustrated by the painters of the Heidelberg school, who produced a great many paintings of the life of the Outback. Streeton, McCubbin and Roberts came to dominate Australian art in the last two decades of the nineteenth century. One remarkable novel was published which reflects the work of the time though, while Henry Lawson said of it the work was 'Australian — born of the bush', it was probably composed without reference to Australian writing of the time — it is genuine because it is unselfconsciously of the Australian countryside — Miles Franklin's *My Brilliant Career* was published by Blackwood in Edinburgh in 1901.

The second important movement in art and literature related to the *Bulletin* was that of Norman Lindsay and his associates. Lindsay was a cartoonist on the *Bulletin*. He wrote several novels, all of them light-weight, but all of them cocking a snoot at established bourgeois conventions in suburban Australia — they were, for their day, ribald and irreverent. And his art, full of voluptuous and buxom women, and of satyrs and muscular men, often nude and with constant suggestion of sensual licence and enjoyment, was particularly shocking to the prudishness of the time. But those who were in Lindsay's circle were not only iconoclasts, they were little concerned with the popular Outback myth. They reintroduced themes from classical literature to their work and endeavoured to involve themselves in the current mainstream of international intellectual debate.

They tended to be Neitzchean both in their concepts and their undisciplined wordiness — and produced works which for the most part now can be regarded as provincial curiosities, but with the merit of lustiness and gaiety. It is significant that a sense of history in Australia — a sense of Australia's history, that is, is a very recent phenomenon. The Lindsay school were seeking roots in some history — and weren't particularly good historians. But the history they illustrated was their own idea of European and Biblical myth and fairy story: a constant dressing-up (or dressing-down) party.

In music there was no comparable creative work. The one Australian composer of note was Percy Grainger and though he always talked of himself as an Australian composer, his work bore little relationship to Australia. Today he is best known as a collector of (non-Australian) folk tunes, a successful pianist well regarded by his friend Edward Grieg, and the composer of 'Country Gardens' and 'Molly on the Shore'. He spent most of his life abroad and settled in the United States.

Early in the century the theatre deteriorated into an elitist art. Only a small minority was from then on to set foot in an Australian theatre. There were no indigenous dramatists of any importance. Theatrical entrepreneuring was dominated by one company, J. C. Williamson. For the most part they presented the most popular of overseas productions. Significant Australian artists became famous and popular locally — Gladys Moncrieff as the singer of operetta and musical comedy, and Roy Rene, who created an Australian Jewish comic character 'Mo' in vaudeville. But Australia was already exporting its best practitioners in the performing arts. Australia has a climate which seems to produce great singing voices. Nellie Melba led a procession of singers to live overseas, Judith Anderson of actors, and later Robert Helpmann of dancers.

Film, however, developed early in Australia and successful silent feature films were made here before Hollywood. But the American market gave Hollywood an economic base impossible to Australian producers, and by the 1920s the American film interests had bought the theatres, controlled the distribution systems, and could dump into Australia films which had already repaid their costs many times elsewhere. Film-making in Australia became an uneconomic proposition and the film industry died.

The third important movement generated by the *Bulletin* occurred through the influence of Douglas Stewart, a poet of some ability who wrote two successful radio plays in verse — *Fire on the Snow* and *Ned Kelly*, and became the *Bulletin*'s literary editor.

He, though a Lindsay disciple, was nevertheless much more disciplined than the earlier Lindsayites, and encouraged and published poets who have established Australian verse as being worthy of more than local interest, Judith Wright and David Campbell.

Other movements emerged affecting art and literature in the latter years of the 1939-45 war and immediately after it.

The artist who most affected Australian art and the popular conception of the Australian scene was Russell Drysdale. For the first time an Australian artist who was to be popular enough to appear regularly on the walls of motel rooms and suburban living rooms painted a view of Australia in all its starkness, aridity and angularity and did so without compromise. Russell Drysdale taught Australians that the Australian scene was really theirs, and to be at home in. Drysdale's painting was said to be 'the most Australian of all', but it was not aggressive, self-conscious Australianism — it was not the aggressive output of an inferiority complex, a cultural cringe, but a calm and loving celebration of Australian maturity.

But Drysdale's work did not set a pattern inevitably for others, nor was public acceptance of merit in art easily achieved.

William Dobell, a significant artist, entered a portrait of his fellow artist, Joshua Smith, in the competition for the Archibald Prize for portraiture (one of the three major prizes annually in Australian art run at the Art Gallery of New South Wales). He won, and then had to face a court case which sought to deprive him of the prize on the grounds that he had painted a caricature, not a portrait. The evidence against him, and his cross-examination, exhibited the grossest of philistinism. The judge found for him, and a lesson occurred which was educative of the Australian public about artistic criteria.

After the war

Immediately after the war, Australia could be regarded still as something of an artistic desert. In art it was difficult for a painter or sculptor to make a living

Above: **Tom Roberts finished** *Bailed Up* **in 1895, but worked on it again in 1927. Roberts' attention to the atmosphere, and the casual figure arrangement, suggest a typically Australian understatement and even a sense of pride in the event.**

Left: **Australian painting came of age with its Impressionists, notably Arthur Streeton and Tom Roberts, in the late 19th century. Their concern was the catching of a momentary atmospheric effect, an ideal exemplified by Streeton's** *Redfern Station,* **completed in 1893.**

Opposite page: **A rugged, uniquely Australian idiom came to full flower during the 1940s in the work of Sir Russell Drysdale, the father of modern Australian landscape painting.** *A Horsebreaker from the Snowy River* **was completed in 1971.**

by his art. Some other income, whether from teaching or private means, was almost always necessary. Australian composers were unknown and lived through teaching positions. Australian authors and poets could not live from their work. No Australian plays were produced. As for acting — the only actors to get enough work were in a small group in Sydney and Melbourne doing radio plays. Most actors had to get other jobs, and those who displayed outstanding talent — Peter Finch, Zoe Caldwell, Keith Michell — had to go overseas to find adequate work.

There was no permanent work for Australian dancers or choreographers.

Visiting theatrical, opera, or dance companies could get packed theatres if they were of sufficient renown, but they did not present Australian material.

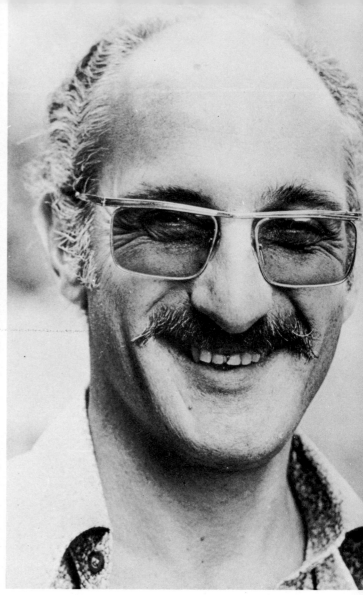

Once it was necessary for artists of all kinds to establish their reputation overseas to gain acceptance in Australia. But the tide at last has turned. The possibility of living and working profitably in one's own country is no longer a dream but a firm reality.

Above left: Novelist Christina Stead has published widely in America and England and is particularly respected for her works *The Salzburg Tale, House of all Nations* and *The Man Who Loved Children.* Following the death of her husband, she returned to the country she had left as a fledgling author, when the Australian National University, Canberra, offered her a fellowship in the creative arts.

Above right: Writer David Malouf spends much of his time in a small village in Italy, returning to Brisbane for the Italian winter — to maintain links with family, friends and homeland. In 1975 he published his first novel, *Johnno*, about growing up in Brisbane. This was followed by *An Imaginary Life*, the story of Ovid's exile among the Scythians.

Left: Nobel Prize winner, Patrick White, is a novelist and playwright. His first novel *Happy Valley* was published in 1939. After graduating from Cambridge University, he wrote sketches and lyrics for the Little Gate Theatre, London. In 1947 he produced his first full length play, *The Ham Funeral.* His recent work, *Flaws in the Glass*, is autobiographical — a controversial and unflinching appraisal of his life and work. He was guest speaker at the anti-nuclear rally in Sydney in April, 1982.

We can now say that this situation has wholly altered. Australia now exhibits a vigour and maturity in the arts which was almost inconceivable in late 1945.

In literature, after a somewhat childish ferment around 1944, Australia has emerged as the possessor of authors who are essentially Australian and whose stature is of world significance. In 1944 a group which had grown from a student association at Adelaide University, pursued through a journal, *Angry Penguins*, a policy of modernity and experiment. Some of the work they published was of worth, some quite meretricious, but it aroused the ire of some more conservative writers, and two of these hoaxed the editor of the magazine by making up some poems and forwarding them to *Angry Penguins* as the work of a young man 'Ern Malley' who had died of Graves disease. *Angry Penguins* published an *Ern Malley Memorial Edition*, the hoax was revealed, and philistines were once again in full cry. But this controversy was really irrelevant to what was to burst upon the Australian literary scene. Two novelists, of immense merit, had been produced by Australia. One of them, Christina Stead, had spent most of her life as an expatriate, though she has returned to Australia. Her books won international acclaim. But the man who has set the seal of great merit on Australian literature is, of course, Patrick White, Nobel Prizewinner for Literature. His novels display an intellectuality, a breadth, a maturity of vision and understanding, which make him one of the greater writers of this century. In the works of both authors, the questions of Australia's identity, of Australian nationalism, of our roots in community feeling, concern about a sense of place or history, are pointless. Like to Drysdale — to them such matters are simply not relevant concerns.

But the procession does not end there. Two other authors — though alas still spending much of their time as expatriates — are clearly writing as the Australians they are, and writing novels of great beauty. David Malouf has written *An Imaginary Life* and Shirley Hazzard her brilliant work *A Transit of Venus*.

In verse, A. D. Hope's verse, though published late in his life, has shown that in Australia's maturity a poet can celebrate Australia in language which is penetrating, exquisitely used, finely disciplined. And a generation of younger poets, among them David Malouf and Chris Wallace-Crabb, are writing with vigour and beauty.

Avenues of support

It is possible now for writers to earn a living by creative work in Australia, and for approved projects in writing to get government-sponsored grants. An Aboriginal Art Foundation is teaching Australians what they have missed of Aboriginal culture.

In the theatre, the creation after the war of the Elizabethan Theatre Trust meant the commencement of a number of permanent theatre companies in Australia and opportunities for actors, producers and authors. At first the amount of presentable drama coming from Australian authors was very small, but Sumner Locke-Elliott's *Rusty Bugles* was put on by a non-commercial theatre in Sydney and then taken up commercially. Then came Ray Lawler's *Summer of the Seventeenth Doll* — which can really be said to mark the beginning of Australia's national theatre. It demonstrated the post-war death of the 'outback-mateship' image of the archetypal Australian, with the steady loss of any high-paying rural employment. It has played successfully overseas, and continues to be revived in Australia. Unfortunately, apart from Alan Seymour's *The One Day of the Year*, and non-commercial productions of Patrick White's plays, little more of Australian drama was to see the stage until the advent of David Williamson and Alex Buzo.

The Elizabethan Theatre Trust, with erratic private funding and some grudging amounts from governments, did not succeed in founding a national theatre company, though it supported a number of companies which led a precarious existence, but it did found a national opera company and a national ballet company.

These have had a great success. The opera is based in Sydney, the ballet in Melbourne, and both tour to other capitals. They are companies of world standard.

The opera has fine singers, and has succeeded in attracting today's greatest diva, Joan Sutherland, and her husband Richard Bonynge, to return to Australia and constantly work with the company.

The ballet, first under Sir Robert Helpmann and Dame Peggy Van Praagh, has produced not only works of the classical repertoire, but ballets choreographed by Sir Robert and by local choreographers, the outstanding being Graeme Murphy. It has toured overseas with acclaim.

After the war, various musical ensembles employed by the Australian Broadcasting Commission were enlarged into symphony orchestras and conductors of renown engaged for them. These now run subscription and other concert series in all the capital cities and tours are made to smaller centres. Chamber music is catered for largely by the Musica Viva Society, which tours Australian and the best of international chamber music ensembles.

Numbers of the States commenced in the early 1970s giving significant support to the establishment and running of State companies in drama, dance and opera. In Adelaide a group of businessmen, together with John Bishop, Professor of Music, established as a privately funded organisation, the Adelaide Festival of Arts, which has since developed into the most prestigious festival in the whole region of the South Pacific and South-East Asia. At first simply a fortnight's gathering of major artists and companies from round the world, it related little to Australia, and was a two weeks' binge of cultural indigestion for a city which then starved for another two years. However, at the urging of Sir Robert Helpmann, who was director of the Festival in 1970, its nature was changed to become the culmination of the local cultural life of South Australia, as that life now goes on all the time — and not only biennially.

What has happened in Adelaide is an example of what is now happening in the rest of Australia. There the State established a State theatre company, of world standard, with its own theatre. A small opera group, also funded by the State, grew into a fine State opera company, for which the old J. C. Williamson theatre in Adelaide was bought and rebuilt into an opera house, which is the company's permanent home. And a small modern dance company, also funded by the State, has its own small theatre and has grown into the Australian Dance Theatre, headed by Jonathan Taylor. The Australian Dance Theatre is shared with the State of Victoria, and has produced brilliant and original works which have gained it great acclaim not only in Australia but at the Edinburgh Festival in Scotland and in the Netherlands and Poland, where it has toured.

In other States, similarly, permanent companies are established and flourishing. In New South Wales the Sydney Dance Company is producing original works of significance, and the theatre company supported by the State has been reconstituted and, under the direction of Richard Wherrett, is packing the audiences in. In the meantime, an independent theatre company of outstanding worth, the Nimrod, continues to present productions of which any city in the world would be proud. In Brisbane, the Queensland Theatre Company is of good standard and is the oldest statutory company in Australia. The Queensland Ballet continues to produce seasons of the classical repertoire. The Opera Company has unfortunately been wound up, though a semi-professional Light Opera Company flourishes.

In Perth, the National Theatre Company is operating well, and the Western Australian Ballet is succeeding under the direction of Garth Welch, former principal dancer of the Australian Ballet.

Public buildings for the arts

The changed climate for and attitude towards the arts can perhaps best be seen in the fact that at last the Australian people see public buildings for the arts as an essential part of their welfare.

Right: **Mel Gibson and Noni Hazlehurst in the Sydney Theatre Company production of Bob Herbert's play,** *No Names, No Packdrill.*

Overleaf: **The sculptural purity of the roof shells of the Sydney Opera House which retain the essence of Joern Utzon's design.**

One of the most talked-about buildings in the world is the Sydney Opera House. Its planning and building were marred by a series of disputes, misunderstandings, and changes of direction, so that, sad to say, few of its facilities today discharge the functions for which they were originally designed. The main hall was to have been a lyric theatre, opera house and concert hall, with variable acoustics, and seating 2 700 people, which would make sense as an economical size for an audience for the expensive productions of opera and ballet. However, the building's designer, Utzon, departed over a dispute as to the strength of the structure to hold the acoustic bafflers needed, and the building was then finished by a committee. I am told the 'Yellow River Concerto' was written by a committee. If so, it should become the signature tune for the Sydney Opera House. The Australian Broadcasting Commission insisted that if the Sydney Symphony was to play there, it must have a concert hall, not a theatre with variable acoustics. So the opera theatre became a concert hall and its expensive stage machinery was scrapped. It is a fine concert hall, though somewhat cold and unwelcoming. The opera theatre was then moved to what had been intended as the drama theatre, with disastrous results. The audience size is too small, and constrained by the outside shell, there is no wing space or means of flying scenery. The orchestra pit cannot take a large orchestra without musicians getting caught up in the stage-changing machinery.

The drama theatre has been moved to what was designed as a small cinema theatre, with wide screen. Again it cannot be adapted to scenery brought from another theatre — there is no fly-tower, and the stage is so wide in relation to its height as to present producers with constant problems in staging; it has none of the flexibility required of a modern theatre.

Despite all these problems, it is still a great building, and does provide a constant venue for music, drama, dance, jazz and a community focal point.

Other centres, built or being built in Australia, have learnt from the mistakes made in building the Opera House.

The Adelaide Festival Centre is one of the most successful of performing arts centres built this century. Given the problems in Sydney, its planners insisted that the whole must be planned round internal function — the outside appearance of the building (which is nevertheless beautiful), must be secondary to what was to occur within.

The centre contains a 2 000 seat lyric theatre with a large and flexible stage, which can be converted to concert hall configuration. It also has a 650 seat drama theatre which has a stage available in a variety of forms; an experimental theatre space which can be used in anything from proscenium to thrust to theatre-in-the-round, and seating up to 300, and an open-air auditorium seating 1 200, but with an additional capacity on the steps to the plaza above. The theatres all have very generous foyer space, and the complex contains a small gallery, three restaurants, bars and a convention meeting area. There is enough car and parking space either in the complex or close by, and very comfortable provision for performers, staff and workshops.

It was built in a short time for a modest $22 million — a quarter of the cost of the Sydney Opera House, and is a model which has affected theatre building elsewhere in Australia.

For the building goes on — Perth has built a fine small concert hall. In addition it has commenced a cultural centre, of which the first part, a small modern art gallery, has already been opened, and which will eventually contain as well two theatres to replace the present inadequate Playbox Theatre as a home for the National Theatre Company, and a school of the arts. The State Government has also spent some $9 million on restoring and remodelling His Majesty's Theatre in Perth, now used as a venue for the West Australian Ballet and semi-professional Opera Company which runs three seasons a year. Moreover, a large somewhat barn-like 8 000 seat auditorium, originally built by the Edgley interests and a television station, has now been acquired by the government. The need has become clear in Australia for centres where large audiences can be accommodated — and Sydney is now building such a centre in the Pyrmont area in the inner city.

Melbourne has built a beautiful art gallery to house Australia's most prestigious collection, and has now for a long time been building its cultural centre for the

Above: **The Adelaide Festival Centre, home of the South Australian Theatre Company, was built in 1973 to a design by Hassell & Partners. Its fine acoustic design and striking external appearance have merited international acclaim.**

Right: **The National Gallery of Victoria, Melbourne, was opened in 1968 — and is part of a cultural complex (still unfinished) positioned at the gates of the city. It houses Australia's most prestigious collection of paintings.**

performing arts next to it. Unfortunately the site chosen has presented a number of seemingly intractable but unforeseen difficulties, and it is as yet unfinished. It will eventually house the Melbourne Theatre Company, one of the oldest, most successful and prestigious companies in the country, now operating in three separate venues. And the Melbourne theatre scene will be kept lively by the continuance of alternative theatres at the Pram Factory and the Playbox.

Brisbane has commenced the erection of a $50 million cultural centre on the Brisbane River to contain an art gallery, library, concert and theatre facilities. In Sydney, the Seymour bequest to the University of Sydney has provided the Seymour Centre with medium and small theatres, commercial gallery and good foyer, bar and restaurant facilities, used widely by the public.

In the national capital, Canberra, two theatres have been erected in the centre at Civic. Unfortunately, they have real faults in design, but still provide a means for a lively local theatre scene, particularly as a house for the semi-professional Canberra Opera.

But the change in public attitude had not merely borne fruit in the capital cities — smaller provincial cities have now commenced to build centres of their own. Geelong, for instance, has just opened a new cultural complex which has used old buildings combined with new, and not only provides large and small theatres, foyer,

---

GRAEME MURPHY — dancer and choreographer

The early original ballets presented by the Australian Ballet, largely the work of Sir Robert Helpmann (*Corroboree* and *Display* for example) seemed to represent almost inevitably the imposition of European ballet form on an Australian theme on which it sat uncomfortably — they were impressive works but the marriage of theme and form showed disharmonies. But Helpmann and Dame Peggy Van Praagh encouraged dancers in the company to assay choreography and gave opportunities for these early attempts to gain performance. Some of these works were taken into the Australian Ballet's repertoire.

Graeme Murphy, after a graduate course at the Australian Ballet School, joined the national company in 1968 and toured with it. After experience of performance in the United States, he left the company to seek further study and experience, took classes with the Jeffrey Ballet and then joined the Royal Ballet in England. After some months he became acquainted with the Ballets Felix Blaska, based in Grenoble, and spent two years with that contemporary dance company. Returning to Australia as part of International Ballet Caravan in 1974, he decided to remain, creating ballets and dancing with the governing regional companies. Soon he had choreographed *3 Conversations* for the Queensland Ballet, *Pandora* for the Tasmanian Ballet and a full length *Papillon* for the Australian Ballet School's end of year performance.

The freshness and vitality of his work delighted audiences and dancers alike, and he rejoined the Australian Ballet in 1976 as resident choreographer and his *Glimpses* was performed at Ballet 76. Later in 1976 he was appointed Artistic Director of the Sydney Dance Company.

Since that time there has been a stream of work from him — *Poppy* and *Rumours* — full length works, *Viridian* based on the tone poem by Richard Meale, *Daphnis & Chloe, An Evening* and for the Australian Ballet *Beyond Twelve*.

Graeme Murphy refuses to be bound by ballet convention — his work shares a constant nervous vitality which is expressed without the trammels of previously settled form. He is irritated when American critics endeavour to categorise his work as 'classical', 'modern', 'pop' — for he recognises no such categories. His work uses steps and techniques drawn from widely diverse heritages and schools of dance, but does not confine itself to dance. In *An Evening* he not only based a part of the work round the magnificent brassy voice of dancer and chantress Geraldine Turner, but had the whole company of dancers singing chorus as well. His work has none of the old discomfort of incongruity of classical form imposed on Australian theme — the themes find natural expression through his use of techniques which have no pre-conceived boundaries, frequently enlivened by his own dancing which displays fire and verve and elan. He has successfully developed a new era in Australian dance which at last shows a complete and unselfconscious originality — an originality which is nevertheless essentially Australian.

Right: Ballet, both as an art form and as a profession, demands the rigorous training and dedication of the athlete — often to the point of pain and exhaustion.

exhibition and restaurant space, but makes provision for the teaching of art, drama, dance and music in a way which is to be seen in a number of the French provincial *maisons de culture*, but are normally to be found in adult education centres rather than in performing arts complexes in Australia.

And just across the border, in South Australia, at Mt Gambier, a city of some 25 000 people, a beautiful new complex has been opened which has new council chambers, small theatre and public library; the old council chambers nearby have become an art gallery and an old theatre next door incorporated as a large auditorium.

The creative arts

The greater public concern with and interest in the arts has been matched by a vitality and vigour of creative artists.

The success, maturity and style of Patrick White and our other novelists and poets has been repeated in other fields of art.

After Drysdale and Dobell, came Nolan, Albert Tucker, Arthur Boyd, John Perceval, John Olsen, Clifton Pugh, Fred Williams, Leonard French and Ray Crook. All of these show a sureness of touch, an individual but Australian vision, and a constant inspiration which has meant that Australia has avoided the gimmicks and jejune stylism so evident in much of contemporary European art. Their works sell well in Australia and overseas. Three expatriate artists also sell well in Australia — as well as in London, Milan and New York. Jeffrey Smart, a neo-realist whose paintings have a foreboding surreal, quality, was for years a teacher of art to children on the ABC and affected the art education of thousands of today's Aus-

---

BRETT WHITELEY — artist

What would have happened to Rimbaud if, before his break with Verlaine and disappearance to the Middle East, his iconoclasm and rage had been accepted by the bourgeois as being fashionable and to be acknowledged by payment of very large rewards? Who can say — the situation appears so unreal. But in Australia, post-war, iconoclasm at least had become fashionable in the world of the visual arts; indeed it had developed a new conventionality all its own.

The comfortably wealthy in Australia had become buyers of Australian art, and found none of their conservative social values challenged by art which, a generation before, would have been regarded as subversive of all bourgeois society. And upon this world of the fashionable art buyers Brett Whiteley has burst with enormous success. Undoubtedly the most remarkable virtuoso that Australian art has seen, burningly neurotic, painting with a passion fired by instincts of self-destruction, he has not yet become a widely-known artist among the suburbanites who constitute the overwhelming bulk of Australia's population; but he is so regarded by the *cognoscenti* that in 1977 he won all three of the major art competitions in Australia — the Archibald, Wynne and Sulman prizes.

For Whiteley's fierce originality disposes of conventions, new and old. He paints with a ruthlessness of vision, a cruelty to himself and others which is at times reminiscent of Van Gogh (like Rimbaud, another of his sources of inspiration).

Whiteley grew up in a middle-class home in North Sydney, went to boarding school for a period, and at the age of 17 met Wendy Julius, with whom he then started living and who later became his wife. He won a travelling scholarship to Italy, went on to London and had a painting bought by the Tate. In the early sixties, after exhibiting a gruesome series on Christie, the multiple murderer, he became known as the 'boy wonder' and spent time in Sydney, Calcutta, Morocco and London. He won a Commonwealth Arts Advisory Board scholarship, the International Prize at the Paris Biennale des Jeunes, and grants from both the Stuyvesant and Harkness Foundations. He worked in New York for a time, and then returned to Australia where he and his wife bought a house in Lavender Bay near the Sydney Harbour Bridge. He painted furiously, had a number of exhibitions which were described by critics as 'sensationalist', withdrew for a year of isolation during which he experimented with hallucinatory drugs.

Out of it all has come an outpouring of works — painting which has come to dominate the very lively and vigorous art scene Australia can now boast. His enormous success, critically and commercially, has impinged little on his own brutally critical vision of himself and his subjects. Whiteley is as significant to art in world terms as Patrick White to literature.

244

Right: **Brett Whitely, in his Sydney studio.**

tralians. Justin O'Brien, who like Smart lives in Italy, paints pictures with a jewel-like quality which owes much to the Sienese masters, and Donald Friend has taken most of his subjects recently from the years he has lived in Indonesia.

But the painter who has justly become the most admired and whose works are most sought after is Brett Whiteley — his work is brilliant, compelling, exciting — that of the most significant Australian master to date.

In music composition Don Banks, Malcolm Williamson, Peter Sculthorpe, Richard Meale and Nigel Butterley are now amongst the world's best known and regarded contemporary composers. In all of them there is a clear Australian quality — a vitality and originality which draws from Australian and regional resources.

In drama, after a gap of some years from Lawler's success, came work which started out in experimental theatre — and grew to a contemporary school of Australian drama to rival that of the Dublin Abbey Theatre at its peak. David Williamson has turned his unceasing inventiveness, scorn for pretension and humbug, and incisive wit on a number of aspects of Australian society — from the trendy carryings on of his self-deceptive friends to the crass politicking of the management of a football club. He continues to have critical and commercial success, his work has been

Left: **Director Gillian Armstrong observes the filming of *My Brilliant Career*, her first major film success, with first assistant Mark Egerton and crew. One of the first graduates of the Australian Film and Television School, she is part of a nucleus of exciting female talent which has emerged in the Australian film industry.**

Above: **Peter Weir is renowned for the eerie quality of his films, first apparent in *Picnic at Hanging Rock* (which received a British Academy Award for Cinematography) and *The Last Wave*. His most recent film, *Gallipoli*, has enjoyed considerable international acclaim; *The Year of Living Dangerously*, is due for release in 1982-83.**

Above left: **Returning to Australian opera after 15 years abroad, Dame Joan Sutherland stops the show in the 'mad scene' from** *Lucia di Lammermoor* **at the Sydney Opera House. For five minutes the audience shouted and applauded.**

Above right: **Commissioned in 1900,** *Daphnis and Chloe* **took Ravel three years to write. Graham Murphy reproduces the Longus tale of awakened sexuality in modernised form for the Sydney Dance Company. In this scene Bryaxis and his pirates abduct Chloe with the intention of raping her.**

Left: **Classical ballet still maintains a great popularity with Australian audiences, (a response fired perhaps by the visit of the great Anna Pavlova earlier this century); the pas de deux — with its romance and tension — is particularly popular. Sir Robert Helpmann however sought to develop Australian themes.**

Above: **John Bell, appearing in the Nimrod Theatre production of *Volpone,* a Ben Jonson play. With Richard Wherrett and Ken Horler, he founded the theatre in 1971. Their policy of producing 'risky' new Australian plays and alternatives to mainstream theatre has continued to attract audiences.**

Right: **Frank Thring slumps in his chair in the Sydney Theatre Company's drama, *Close of Play.* Mr Thring is one of many Australian actors who have chosen to 'return home' to work, after enjoying international success.**

toured to the London West End, and he is without doubt the country's greatest playwright. Alexander Buzo and Steve Spears are also dramatists of originality whose works display a vitality which seems to pervade the current Australian artistic scene.

And perhaps the most startling of all developments has been the re-creation of the Australian film industry.

Some Australian film makers had struggled on making an occasional film, and Charles Chauvel, the grand old man of the industry, managed three films in a decade. Every so often Australia would be chosen as the location for a film — and crews and stars would be flown into Australia.

The Melbourne film makers succeeded with two films — *Barry McKenzie,* made from the cartoons of Barry Humphries for London's *Private Eye* about a Lil' Abner-type Australian in Earls Court, London, and *Alvin Purple* — a piece of juvenile ribaldry. Both of these acquired distribution in Australia and made a profit.

But apart from work for television, there was not a consistent run of work in Australian film. Tim Burstall, in Melbourne, was Australia's most competent film director.

In the late 1960s the federal government made the first steps towards supporting a film industry and these eventually emerged into today's Australian Film Commission and the Film and Television School in Sydney. But there had been no consistently-financed entrepreneurial breakthrough. This happened in South Australia in the early 1970s — where there had been no film industry at all. The Commonwealth and some of the State governments, up to this time, had had small film units producing tourist and documentary films. South Australia decided to create a State-owned film corporation, with complete entrepreneurial capacity, in commissioning, making and distributing films. The corporation was guaranteed enough government orders to give it a run of work in the initial years, and the government agreed to the recommendations of Gil Brealey, the corporation's first director, to fund a feature film which together with other work would ensure sufficient continuous employment to enable a range of competent technicians to locate in Adelaide, and make it economic for film makers to work there, by reducing the overhead costs of importing technicians.

The first feature film, *Sunday Too Far Away*, was a success, and the corporation made tourist films and documentaries which were soon piling up awards around the world. But the first success was rapidly followed by others — Peter Weir's *Picnic at Hanging Rock* and *The Last Wave*, co-produced by the McElroy brothers, and the corporation's own extraordinarily successful children's film *Storm Boy*.

Other States proceeded to get into the act — not always wisely. It is difficult for Australia, with a population of 14.6 million, to sustain one film industry, let alone seven. The other State film corporations, however, have not been given the full range of entrepreneurial activity available to the South Australian corporation.

But with their funding, private investment, and money from Australian film commissions, numbers of films have been made of great value. *The Chant of Jimmy Blacksmith* from the novel by Thomas Keneally, a brilliant production of *My Brilliant Career*, Michael Pate's production of *The Mango Tree, Newsfront, Mad Max*, have all won critical acclaim.

There is a danger, however, that Australia is now making more films than the Australian market can bear, and experience shows that unless a film covers its costs from Australian takings, it is hard put to do so from overseas sales.

The South Australian film corporation has continued its success, and in 1980 hit the jackpot both with critics and at the box office with *Breaker Morant* which deservedly won for Jack Thompson the award for the best supporting actor at Cannes. The corporation has now acquired the best and most extensive studio complex in Australia, and will continue to provide a home and a solid basis for the industry. The high point of overseas acclaim, as well as local excitement, was

Right: **Although photography has long had a place in the art galleries of Europe and America, only recently has it gained a wider audience in Australia.**

With the honourable exception of a tiny handful of anthropologists and ethnologists, white Australians ignored Aboriginal tribal art for almost 200 years. Now, almost overnight, more people are appreciating its value as one of the few keys available for unlocking the mysteries of past tribal cultures.

Above right: These relatively recent mouth-blown ochre stencils at Carnarvon National Park, Queensland, are similar to the wall art of European cavemen 30 000 years ago.

Right: Totemic funerary sculpture of the Melville Island and Bathurst Island Aborigines.

Far right: Sacred Churinga or Tjurunga stones, like this one from central Australia, are normally seen only by male tribal elders.

Opposite: Marita Narjic of Port Keats, a Roman Catholic mission south-west of Darwin, learns modern copperworking techniques at East Arm Leprosarium settlement.

252

reached with Peter Weir's *Gallipoli,* scripted by David Williamson, which has established the first really widespread showing of an Australian film in the American market.

Australian films were quickly successful in the English market and before long in Italy. It was not until 1979 that any breakthrough was made into the American market. American critics and the professional journalists now acknowledge the vigour, originality and high standards of Australian films, but (apart from *Gallipoli*) these are still only playing in about 30 theatres out of the thousands in the United States. But steadily, the Australian film industry is being acknowledged as contributing more to the development of film today than the Italian or Swedish film industries did at their peak.

To sum up — the arts in Australia are today alive and well. From what was 15 years ago a country where philistinism ruled more often than not, Australia has become a country with a mature, vigorous, artistic life, acknowledging and celebrating a maturity never before evident.

Left: **Winners of three of the nine Australian Film Institute Awards to** *Gallipoli* **— David Williamson who wrote the screen play** *(centre),* **with stars Mel Gibson** *(right)* **and Mark Lee** *(left).* **Williamson has won several awards, an early accolade from Britain the 'Evening Standard Award for Most Promising Playwright'.**

Above: **Stars in their respective countries, Jack Thompson** *(left)* **and Kirk Douglas** *(right)* **in** *The Man From Snowy River,* **based on the poem by A. B. 'Banjo' Paterson. It is no longer believed that the presence of an overseas 'star' is essential in securing overseas distribution of an Australian film.**

SCIENCE

Dr Peter Pockley

'...stronger in basic research than in applied development.'

After three or four decades of brilliant achievement by a few individuals in disparate fields, Australian science still seeks a coherent identity.

Until the early seventies, science had enjoyed two decades of increasing political support — slow, steady, and essentially *ad hoc*, but at least it increased and gave rise to expectations of a bright future for science and scientists alike. Much of the political patronage for science had come from the skilful lobbying of a federal government largely illiterate in scientific matters. This quiet effort was mounted by a handful of outstanding men at the helm of the nation's scientific institutions — the Commonwealth Scientific and Industrial Research Organisation (CSIRO) and the universities. Few were public figures. Those who were gained attention more from their strident views on controversial matters such as nuclear power than from solid achievements in their own fields of research.

In the mid-seventies, however, the financial advances of the fifties and sixties were partly offset by some disenchantment with the role of science and more specifically with its technological applications and, in turn, with technology's effects on the environment and employment. Science became tarred with the brush of technology and many scientists found themselves on the defensive or imagined themselves to be so. This attitude was not improved by less generous funding of research by government.

The Australian scientific effort is notably sensitive to the ebb and flow of government support. Over three-quarters of the research performed in Australia is supported by federal funds — whether performed in government-run outfits such as CSIRO or in autonomous institutions heavily dependent on government largesse such as the universities. This proportion is uniquely high among developed nations.

It has been suggested that this long-standing dependence on handouts from Canberra is one of the reasons behind the virtual invisibility of scientists in the lobbying and publicity stakes for which other self-interest groups play so hard. In this writer's experience of nearly two decades of following the science scene, there have been only three occasions when scientists have effectively mobilised their latent power on a broad scale to change the government's mind. Two concerned threatened cuts in research funds to universities (one from a Labor Government in 1975 and one from a Liberal/Country Party Government in 1980). The other event concerned

Left: **The CSIRO's radio telescope at Parkes, N.S.W., grand old man of radioastronomy.**

the threatened removal from CSIRO of energy-related research — the Labor Government's plans for this in 1974 were foiled by a concerted public campaign.

In these three isolated cases, scientists were spurred into battle by threats close to their interests. In each instance, once the victory was won the temporary groupings evaporated and lobbying was left to the few scientist-bureaucrats currently running the scientific institutions.

The pervasive influence of government-dominated patronage has led also to a strong institutionalisation of science in Australia. The vast bulk of research scientists are on the public payroll and are subject to the generally conservative influence of organisational priorities and rules. University scientists in Australia, though theoretically freer to express themselves, also display a degree of timidity in communicating their views to the public and the government with a useful degree of continuity.

Though adequate funding is a necessary prerequisite, successful lobbying for political support does not necessarily indicate a healthy and productive research climate.

Good scientists, like forests, grow slowly. They need experience to be effective and they cannot afford to be wrong. They can be exasperatingly slow in producing answers to questions which politicians and other laymen may think simple and necessary of solution for the national well-being — Make rain! Stop bush-fires! Farm the oceans! Defeat cancer! Politicians have been supported to a considerable extent by the scientifically ignorant commercial media intent on headlining so-called 'breakthroughs' while genuine but more gradual progress has been significant but unreported.

Given such pressures it is surprising that, for so long, Australian science has remained stronger in basic research than in applied development. The achievements of Australian-based technology are relatively meagre. Far more significant are the contributions of scientists investigating fundamental problems with no practical applications in sight.

These contributions are themselves scattered geographically and over several specialisations. Concentrated attention, the stuff of national reputation, has been hard to achieve. While we have achieved international prestige in areas like chemistry, medical research, earth sciences and astronomy and we are developing a sound understanding of our own flora, fauna and environment, these remain isolated pinnacles of excellence.

A few stories of individual advances by Australians in science will serve to illustrate the general point and to chart, albeit with little accuracy, the courses our scientists may take in the future.

Viruses, nerves and Nobels

That medical research has received popular support in Australia unmatched by the other sciences is shown by the press coverage of often minor medical advances in Australia and by the existence of private foundations for the financing of medical research. Regular public appeals for medical research funds are reasonably successful (though puny by American standards); the National Heart Foundation leads the field, but is by no means alone in attracting public support.

The government gives funds for medical research, notably through the National Health and Medical Research Council which granted $18 million in the 1980-81 budget, and also indirectly supports academic medical research through the financing of universities where most of this research is done. Drug companies also support some research, although it is difficult to estimate their contributions because many of their grants include consultancies and overseas travel for researchers.

The faith implied by such support has, in the past, been amply justified, for Australian medical science has produced three Nobel Prize winners. The first Nobel Prize awarded to an Australian-born person went to the late Lord Florey for work he did in Britain on penicillin; the first fully indigenous Nobel Prize was won by Professor Sir Macfarlane Burnet; and the second went to Sir John Eccles. It is no coincidence that Burnet and Eccles earned their laureates for research at centres

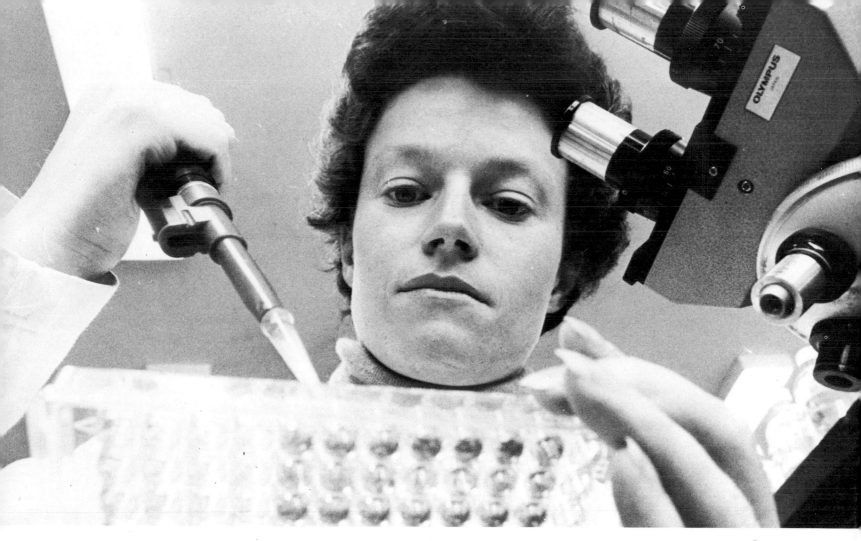

Dr Heather Schagl made news when she received her doctorate from the University of Melbourne for her work in isolating the blood cells which interact to cause the rejection of transplanted tissue. Increasing numbers of women are gaining first degrees in science-based courses at universities and colleges, but fewer go on to higher degrees and only a small fraction of the senior research scientists and tenured academics of Australia are women.

internationally recognised as housing the nation's two leading groups of medical scientists: the Walter and Eliza Hall Institute for Medical Research (associated with the University of Melbourne) and the John Curtin School of Medical Research (an integral part of the Australian National University in Canberra).

When he received his award in 1960, Burnet was Director of the Hall Institute, a post he held for 22 years to 1965. Although lionised by the media, he is a shy, almost introspective person — yet 'Mac' Burnet became the most honoured Australian scientist with a knighthood and the rare Order of Merit, and a four year Presidency of the Australian Academy of Science as further recognition of his standing among fellow scientists.

Even in retirement, while writing erudite books about biological theory he retained his long-held status as the guru of science to the nation. Well into his eighties, he has developed a refreshingly direct approach to the problem of ageing, including his own. For many people, Sir Macfarlane Burnet still *is* Australian science.

Burnet was unashamedly a scholarly scientist. He tackled major problems with a simplicity and tenacity of approach which would tie him to his laboratory bench until the solution was found, long after lesser scientists would have lost heart. He did not work with elaborate apparatus, but spent much of his time in the outwardly boring business of inoculating hundreds and thousands of chicken eggs to discover the rules of tolerance to infection by viruses, notably the elusive influenza strains. Myxomatosis in rabbits and Murray Valley encephalitis in man were two of the diseases whose fundamental patterns of transmission he helped to unravel. This work involved a famous demonstration of faith in his own experiments and theories when he and his colleagues injected themselves with myxomatosis virus to prove it was harmless to humans.

Burnet described himself then as a virologist, but while doing his pioneering work

259

in this field he became fascinated by the broader problems of immunology — how the body builds up antibody and triggers immune reactions to fight infections. In probably his biggest discovery, he showed how the body acquires immunological tolerance to tissue transplants.

Australia's second Nobel Laureate, Sir John Eccles, has, since leaving Australia for the United States on reaching retiring age at the ANU, become known in his adopted country as plain Dr J. C. Eccles. He held a chair at the John Curtin School, a highly prized position because it does not carry the undergraduate teaching responsibilities which make other professorships only part-time research positions. There Eccles achieved scientific fame for his physiological studies on the way nerves work. With great patience and experimental skill he elucidated the intricate mechanism by which nerve impulses act across the membranes separating adjacent nerve cells. After going to America, he expanded his scale of research from the single nerve to the massive problems of understanding the whole brain.

It would be ungenerous and incorrect to give the impression that brilliant individual researchers like Burnet and Eccles were alone in their excellence. High standards of research in immunology and physiology have become a tradition in the past two decades, and these fields are probably among the frontrunners to produce Australia's next Nobel Laureate in science — but because of the large number of expatriate and mainly British scientists in Australia, *he* may not be native-born. 'He' is used advisedly, for women are notably absent from the middle and top echelons of scientists in Australia; there are, for instance, only two female Fellows in the nearly 190-strong Australian Academy of Science.

With the ever-increasing subdivisions of a subject like physiology into smaller specialisations, it is impossible to nominate one branch as the 'key area', but some can be mentioned briefly. At the relatively new Howard Florey Institute for Experimental Medicine at Melbourne University, headed by the enthusiastic Professor Derek Denton, big efforts are being made to understand the mechanisms by which animals adjust and become habituated to levels of salt. Most medical researchers stick to the traditional mouse or, if they can afford it, the monkey, but Denton and his team have made another contribution to uniquely Australian science through pioneering work in the use of the sheep as an experimental animal.

Neurophysiology, the study of the functioning of nerves, is an exciting field of research at various universities — ANU (the Australian National University), Sydney and NSW (University of New South Wales) in particular. One example was the work of English-born (but, unusually, Australian-naturalised) Professor Geoffrey Burnstock at Melbourne University in the 1960s and early 1970s. His remarkable discoveries about the structure and function of nerves led him to propose a hitherto unrecognised nervous system in the body. He termed this third nervous system the 'purinergic system' to distinguish it from the well-recognised 'adrenergic system' and 'cholinergic system' (the names are derived from chemicals of which minute traces are crucial in the functioning of each system of nerves).

Burnstock's work generated much excitement and some scepticism — it requires further confirmation because of the virtual invisibility of the nerves he believes to have discovered — but his colleagues recognise it as a broad-ranging achievement. At the same time it is the kind of result which generates irresistible offers, tempting talented scientists to go overseas. Burnstock now holds a prestigious chair at the University of London.

Another fascinating line of physiological research in Australia is truly home-based in that it involves the study of nerves and the cardiovascular system through the unique, lethal venoms found in our native fauna. The blue-ringed octopus, the funnel-web spider, the sea wasp and the tiger snake secrete compounds which are ferociously toxic when injected into the bloodstreams of their victims. Not only are they among the most lethally venomous animals in Australia, but their venoms have also been found to have particular importance for physiology because of the way they act on life-supporting functions in the body, notably nervous transmission and respiration. The sea wasp, incidentally, is the only one on this list for which a reasonably effective form of *protective* immunisation has so far been developed.

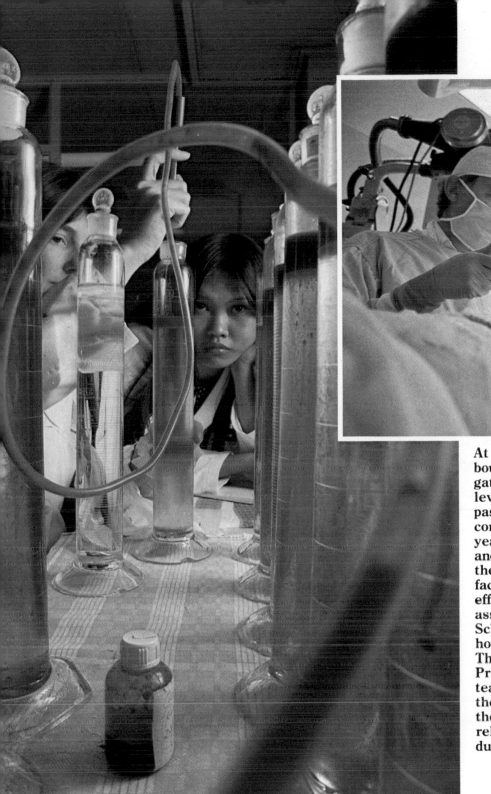

At the Howard Florey Institute, Melbourne, sheep are being used in investigating how animals adjust to dietary salt levels, research which is relevant to the pastoral industry and also to the prevalent condition of high blood pressure. After years of patient effort, researchers here and elsewhere have begun to impress upon the public, politicians and food manufacturers alike, an awareness of the evil effects of salt in food. Graduate research assistants Catherine Oddie and Sabariah Schradrer (*left*) compare levels of steroid hormones in sheep's blood.

The Director of the Florey Institute, Professor Derek Denton (*above*), with his team, operates in their fully equipped theatre. The patient is a sheep. In 1981 the Institute announced the discovery of relaxin, a hormone vital in the reproductive system of mammals.

For tiger snake and funnel-web spider victims, antivenenes are now available — if you can get them in time after the bite!

The School of Physiology and Pharmacology at the University of NSW, led by Professor W. E. ('Darty') Glover and Professor Peter Gage, are among the scientists unravelling the secrets of these venoms and thereby learning more about the basic physiological functions of the body which they affect so drastically. The venoms of the blue-ringed octopus and the funnel-web spider appear to paralyse nerves in a highly specific way: the basic chemical molecules in these venoms, unlike most others, are so small that the body is unable to form antibody, a substance which negates the adverse chemical effect of the venom. The very smallness of the venom molecules makes them difficult to purify for study of their active components. But, when this problem is solved by the chemists, it is not too far-fetched to suggest that these uniquely toxic beasts of Australia might benefit humans through showing the way to produce artificially some highly specific, and therefore much safer, anaesthetics.

261

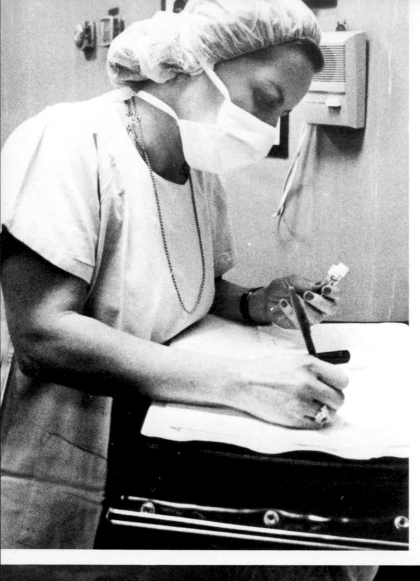

Medical terminology has seldom penetrated the public psyche as rapidly as the string of terms associated with the abbreviation 'IVF', short for 'in vitro fertilisation', the so-called test-tube baby procedure. A British group was the first to successfully produce a full-term baby after fertilising an ovum with sperm of an infertile couple. But a team from Melbourne's Monash University has gone on to be the world's most productive appliers and developers of the technique. Splash headlines greeted the first few IVF babies in Australia, including the world's first IVF twins; but the team led by Professor Carl Wood and John Leeton have worked steadily to improve their techniques through patient research until it is now almost routine in medical terms — to the envy of the British and the Americans. Yet the technique is regarded as far from routine in moral, ethical and legal terms.

Left: Janice Webb, assistant to the team's senior reproductive biologist, Dr Alan Trounson, examines the follicle fluid. Several good eggs were collected from Jan Brennan and placed in a glass dish — to join with sperm donated by her husband, Len — in conditions imitating those prevalent in the Fallopian tubes. Fertilisation was successful and two dividing cells were surgically placed in her uterus. One survived.

Opposite page, above and below: Pippin Jaimee Brennan was born normally on 23 June 1981, the world's thirteenth test-tube baby and the eleventh born in Melbourne.

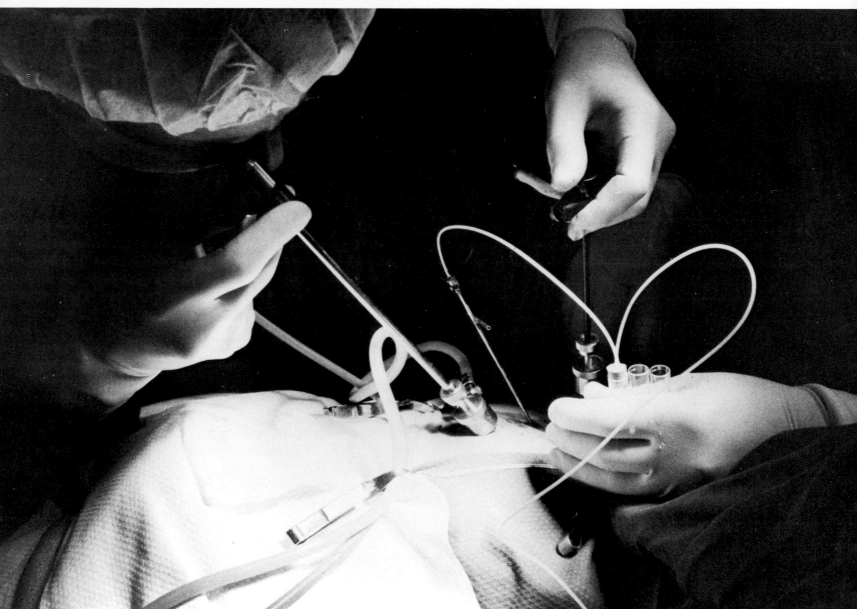

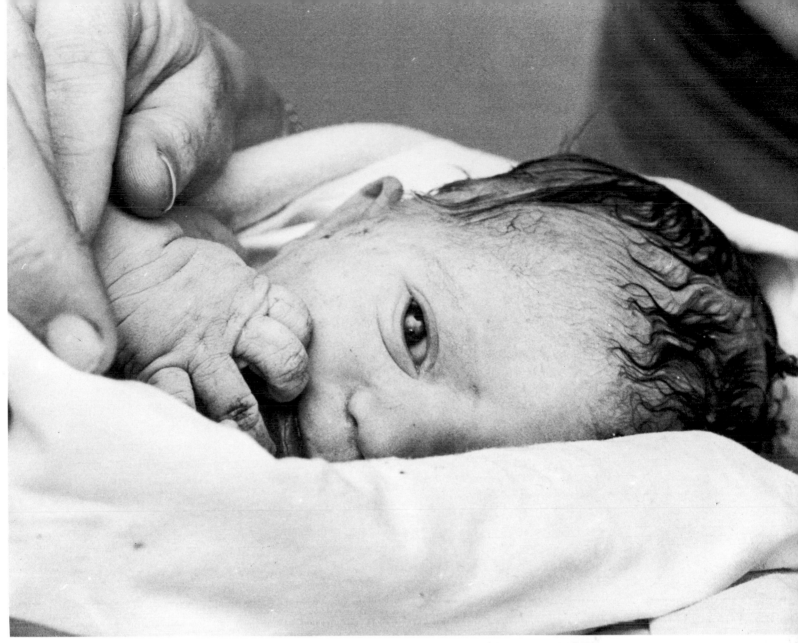

Left: Pippin Jaimee Brennan began not in the bed of her parents, Jan and Len, but in the eye of Professor John Leeton as he peered through his laparascope into the ovary of the anaesthetised mother to be. After a course of hormone drugs to time precisely the production of ripened eggs, Jan Brennan was ready for the procedure which was her only hope of bearing a child. In St Andrews Hospital, the surgeon guides his instruments, including a millimetre-wide needle to remove follicle fluid from the ovary, into the test-tubes held by assistant Dr Nick Lolatgis.

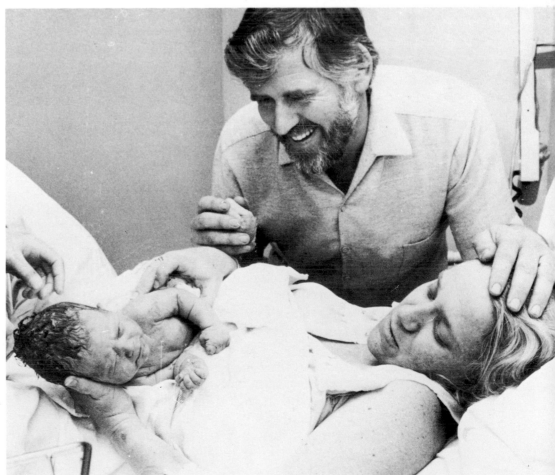

The molecule manipulators

The largest branch of science in Australia, in terms of the number of full-time workers, is almost certainly the least recognised by the public at large. This is the field of chemistry, the study of molecules and atoms and how to manipulate them.

Australian chemists do enjoy international recognition. Several are Fellows of the Royal Society of London, still regarded as the highest honour in the 'British' scientific world; two of them, Professor Arthur Birch (known for some pioneering work leading to the contraceptive pill) and Professor David Craig (a top-class physical chemist) were attracted back to their Australian homeland from excellent jobs in Britain to set up the Australian National University's Research School of Chemistry. But chemists are not only well established in the academic world. Their research and services provide the sinews and growth potential for Australian industries with outputs measured in hundreds of millions of dollars. Yet chemists, in contrast for instance to their colleagues in astronomy, get so little publicity that it would be easy to think they did not exist.

One outstandingly successful line of research must be described to correct the chemists' general failure to project their own achievements. This is spectroscopy, the study of the innermost parts of atoms and molecules as revealed by their tell-tale effects on light or other radiation. Using prisms or diffraction gratings to split light into its composite spectrum, the chemist is also able to identify and estimate the quantity of an element or a compound present in a substance, even if that substance is millions of kilometres away. What goes to make up the sun and stars has been revealed in this way.

While good spectroscopic research is widespread over the nation, the most noted centre until recently was the CSIRO Division of Chemical Physics beside Monash University in Melbourne. The Division's former Chief, the urbane Dr Lloyd Rees, held senior positions for years in the International Union of Pure and Applied Chemistry. The Assistant Chief until 1977 was Sir Alan Walsh, FRS, a Britisher whose jovial, provincial accent shows no sign of more than two decades in Australia; he is now a private consultant.

The remarkable results of Sir Alan's erudite spectroscopic research are now to be found in thousands of laboratories, hospitals and industries throughout the world. No analytical outfit can do without at least one of the instruments derived from his work and patents, and known as atomic absorption spectrophotometers (AAS). These instruments are used to determine how much of an element is present in anything from a drop of blood to a polluted river or a potentially ore-bearing rock. The scientific principle behind AAS cannot be conveyed in two lines. Suffice it to say that Sir Alan solved the very tricky problem of harnessing the enormous potential of an old but crude school science experiment in which the presence of some elements in liquid solution could be detected by introducing drops of the liquid into a flame — a bright yellow flame indicated the presence of sodium, a brick-red flame indicated calcium, and so on.

Sir Alan designed a range of instruments which are quite staggering in their accuracy and sensitivity. As little as one-hundred-millionth part of one gram of some elements can be identified and quantified by the technique. But it is not just its sensitivity which has allowed the AAS method to be described as the most significant advance in chemical analysis of this century. It has also become a commercial winner because it is capable of analysing many different samples for a range of elements with great speed and reliability — and hence cheapness.

Atomic absorption spectroscopy has been described by the CSIRO as 'a long shot that paid off', but it was no shot in the dark. Faced initially by the indifference and scepticism of his colleagues, Sir Alan was nevertheless convinced that the general idea had merit, and with determination he elucidated the basic principles by which the heated *atoms* of an element *absorb* characteristic wavelengths of light emitted separately by the same element — hence 'atomic absorption'. Those principles are now being applied in practice to at least 65 of the 90-odd elements found on earth ('at least', because the list grows annually through continuing refinements). This is one of the signal achievements of Australian science.

Bathed in spectral hues Iain Dawson examines the effect of growing crops under different wavelengths of light in the CSIRO's Phytotron. Plants are grown under controlled conditions to eliminate the varying effects of the weather's vagaries in the field.

The first AAS instruments were built in Melbourne under licence to the CSIRO. The firm's owner became a millionaire. Now the instruments are made all over the world, and the CSIRO has estimated the nett worth of this truly science-based innovation to be $200 million over the 20-odd years for which it is realistic to expect the technique to retain dominance.

The CSIRO has good reason, therefore, to crow over this development, for it is a classic case of how painstaking, fundamental research can lead to profitable and socially useful applications. AAS became one of the basic tools used in the exploration for minerals in Australia, making a significant contribution to the discovery of commercial deposits of nickel, copper, silver, zinc and lead. The detection of traces of harmful elements, and conversely of deficiencies of beneficial elements, in blood samples has led to the saving of lives. The control of purity in food, and newer AAS techniques with solid samples for process control in metal-lurgical operations, are among other daily applications.

One other line of spectroscopic research in Australia led to an unusual alliance between chemists and astronomers, and flourished so fast in the early 1970s that a new branch of chemistry has been born — 'galactochemistry' — which to all intents is the identical twin of the new branch of astronomy, 'molecular astronomy'. While these new studies are not uniquely Australian, our scientists are specially favoured to pursue them through the facilities of the CSIRO Division of Radiophysics and the Monash University Chemistry Department.

The fusion of interests between people like Dr Brian Robinson of the CSIRO Division of Radiophysics and Professor Ron Brown of Monash came about through the astronomers' desire to observe the universe at shorter wavelengths (in the so-called 'microwave' regions) while not knowing how to interpret the signals they received. The chemists, meanwhile, had quite independently been studying the microwave spectrum of simple molecules in the laboratory, and had developed ways of identifying small, life-supporting molecules through 'finger-prints' they imposed on radiation passing through them.

265

It was a short jump for joint teams of radioastronomers and chemists to discover clouds of small molecules in space, many of which contain carbon and have structures like those molecules which are believed to be 'the building blocks of life'. Although structurally unsuited to the millimetre wavelengths involved, the Parkes radio 'dish' nevertheless identified a number of these space molecules, notably methyl formate and vinyl cyanide. The inner 17 metres of the Parkes dish has been refashioned to suit it better for millimetre waves. The CSIRO has also commissioned a small radiotelescope at the Division's headquarters in Epping, Sydney, costing $200 000, which is specifically designed to probe radiations of millimetre wavelengths for signs of organic molecules in the centre of our galaxy. This telescope receives clear signals of molecules in space through the haze of Sydney's atmosphere. Once again, spectroscopy is big business in Australia.

The southern skies

In America and Europe, public debates have raged about how much government funding should be devoted to supporting a few scientists working in so-called 'big science' at the relative impoverishment of larger numbers working on more widely dispersed 'little science'. 'Big science' includes, for example, those huge atom-smashers and nuclear reactor facilities which gave Europe and America the lead in these two capital-intensive fields of research and application.

Astronomy depends for its progress on large, expensive instruments, and is the only field of 'big science' to receive support in Australia. The Australian astronomers who have designed, built and operated their big and spectacular telescopes have been splendidly successful in achieving international and local recognition for the value of their fundamental studies. Now, in an unusual twist for astronomy, basic research in Australia has spun off a highly practical application — the Interscan system for aircraft landing control (see pages 277 and 280).

Australia is superbly positioned for observing the heavens. The Milky Way, the galaxy of which our own solar system forms such a tiny part, passes directly overhead. This provides the richest field for study of the nearest stars which are barely visible, if at all, to telescopes in the northern hemisphere. Southern hemisphere astronomers also revel in the unique availability to them of the two Magellanic Clouds, the nearest galaxies to us outside our own. Such nearness is important, for it allows study of the nature and evolution of stars in detail unobtainable elsewhere. Indeed in 1981, astronomers at ANU announced the first observations of a star actually in the process of formation.

While these advantages of southern hemisphere astronomy were long recognised, Australia's effort in this field of research was minute until after World War II when two significant developments put our star-gazers on the world map. One was the incorporation of the existing, but small observatory at Mount Stromlo near Canberra into the Australian National University; the resulting school of astronomy has expanded its range of instruments and research interests to the point where it has become recognised as a leading centre of optical astronomy. The other was the formation of the CSIRO's radioastronomy group from a number of brilliant men returning from the war with skills in radar; they applied these skills to the study of the then completely mysterious radio signals emanating from space.

By the late 1960s Australian astronomers boasted a dazzling array of devices, some of them outwardly quite eccentric, for unlocking the secrets of the southern skies.

The 'big four' in Australian astronomical organisations are based in New South Wales — the CSIRO Division of Radiophysics, the Department of Astronomy at the ANU, the Anglo-Australian Telescope Board and the School of Physics at Sydney University. Their field stations are spread southward in a gentle arc from northern New South Wales through the west of the state and back in to Canberra. But there have been others too.

Tasmania has a modest but flourishing group of astronomers operating a very nice home-built optical telescope, a radio telescope and a cosmic ray telescope. The

The far north-west town of Carnarvon was one of Australia's early gateways to the world of satellite communications — a revolution highly significant for the geographically isolated continent. Through the earth station of the Overseas Telecommunications Commission, the author of this chapter, Dr Peter Pockley, presented and co-produced in 1966 Australia's first satellite television programme, a 'live' link between migrant families in Carnarvon and their relatives in Britain. From these early beginnings, Australia has become a major user of satellites in communications.

cosmic ray device is operated inside a disused railway tunnel, while the radio telescope beside Hobart airport looks more like a neglected hop field than an array of aerials for detecting very long wavelength radiation from space. The 'father of radioastronomy', a gentle American named Grote Reber who first detected radio signals from space in the 1930s in the United States when few would believe him, has worked quietly in Tasmania in recent years.

Adelaide University also nurtured a small group of astronomically minded physicists. Being the nearest academics to the rocket range at Woomera in South Australia, they naturally sought to take advantage of the high-flying rockets being launched there largely for military purposes. They piggy-backed their experimental packages on British rockets, and on one memorable occasion gained the complete use of an unwanted American Redstone military rocket with which they launched Australia's first and only artificial satellite, called WRESAT after the Weapons Research Establishment (WRE) which ran the Woomera range (now largely mothballed). The Adelaide physicists were among the first X-ray astronomers. With the collaboration of the University of Tasmania and WRE, Dr Ken McCracken (now Chief of CSIRO's Division of Mineral Physics) and his team flew X-ray 'telescopes' in balloons and rockets above the earth's shielding atmosphere to pin-point the sources of intense X-radiation in the universe, such as the emissions from the centre of the well-known supernova remnant, the Crab Nebula.

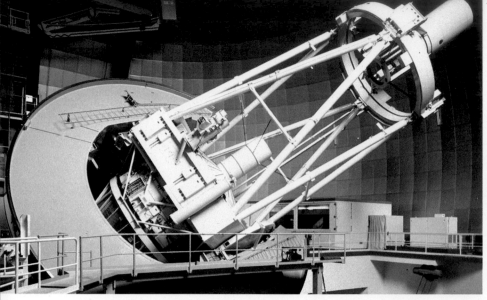

Above: A giant 'light bucket' for catching signals from the faintest of stars, the Anglo-Australian Telescope (AAT) perches on Siding Spring Mountain, north-western N.S.W. Its primary mirror, 3.9 metres across and weighing in at 16 tonnes, is the largest in the southern hemisphere, a superb area for studying the heavens. Its advanced instrumentation makes it one of the best in the world, irrespective of size.

Right: Astronomical photographer superb, David Malin rides in the cage at the prime focus at the top end of the AAT. Malin, who took the pioneering photographs in this spread, has developed world-leading techniques for making colour photographs of the universe — weirdly beautiful to the untrained eye but packed with precious information for the expert.

Left: The 50-metre high dome of the AAT on a dark moonless night. The 10½-hour exposure records star trails of astonishingly different hues, creating the illusion of stars arcing across the sky, whereas it is the earth's rotation which produces the effect.

Above: An exuberant splash of celestial colour, the Cone Nebula is part of an enormous cloud of gas and dust. This cloud contains many recently formed stars, some completely hidden by interstellar matter.

Above right: Looking uncannily like a dividing embryo, the Trifid Nebula (an unimaginably vast cloud of gas) is the birth environment of stars like our sun. The red glow indicates hydrogen gas excited by a number of young hot stars already formed from the cloud.

Right: A cosmic burp, the Sunflower (or Helix) Nebula is the nearest planetary nebula to us — a test of the sensitivity to faint detail of Malin's technique. The light, which took 400 years to reach earth, tells the elemental story of matter ejected from the central star.

The work of the X-ray astronomers typified the exciting expansion in the 1960s of astronomy into entirely new areas of the radiation spectrum. Until radio-astronomy became respectable in the late 1940s and early 1950s, knowledge of the universe had been restricted to the information contained within the comparatively narrow band of radiation which we are biologically capable of detecting as light. Optical astronomers built bigger and bigger reflectors, almost exclusively in the northern hemisphere, to collect and analyse fainter and fainter pin-points of light from deepest space. A bewildering catalogue of facts was assembled — but their interpretation caused a degree of indigestion. As leaders in extending astronomical observations into other non-optical areas of the spectrum, Australians made substantial contributions in solving some of the puzzles posed by the optical astronomers; at the same time, the southern hemisphere astronomers — almost exclusively Australian — helped to pose a whole new set of problems through their extensive observations of hitherto unexplained and unobserved objects, such as the quasars, pulsars, X-ray stars and so-called 'black-holes', which the theoretical astronomers were called upon to explain.

Since the early 1960s, the symbol of Australian astronomy — indeed, almost a symbol of modern Australia — has been the giant 'dish' operated by the CSIRO at Parkes in western New South Wales. This 64-metre diameter, tiltable and rotatable telescope and its 18-metre companion, which moves on railway tracks, also symbolises man's search into the deepest parts of space for evidence of the origin of the universe. Soon after the Parkes main dish was commissioned it featured in the dramatic identification of the first 'quasar' (short for quasi-stellar object), an intense source of radio emission in the sky, known simply by its catalogue number 3C 273. In August 1962, the Parkes team, led by Mr John Bolton, discovered the position and structure of 3C 273 by observing its signals as it was eclipsed and revealed by the moon passing across it. The hundreds of quasars and other radio objects in the universe identified since then by the Parkes instrument have helped to refine our understanding of the way in which the universe began. Quasars were shown by John Bolton and others to be rushing away from the centre of the universe at incredible speeds, the higher speeds being associated with the farther objects, giving support to the so-called 'big bang' theory of the evolution of the universe.

The Parkes telescope wins in the aesthetic stakes over the Mills Cross telescope at Molonglo near Canberra, the Radioheliograph at Culgoora and the Stellar Inter-ferometer at Narrabri (the last two are in north-western New South Wales), but these three telescopes are truly original in concept, design and function.

Professor Bernard Mills of the Sydney University School of Physics wanted a telescope which would observe in radio wavelengths, but which would give much finer detail than could possibly be obtained with a 'dish'. His solution was to lay two long trough-shaped aerials on the ground in the shape of a cross — each arm being nearly 1½ kilometres long — and, by ingenious electronics, to combine the two signals to produce the same effect as a single, dish-shaped aerial of a size much larger than engineering and financial limitations would permit in practice. When the famous ticking radio stars or 'pulsars' were first observed in 1968, the Mills Cross proved to be the best radiotelescope in the best position in the world to study them. And it is still finding them — the fast-ticking pulsar in the constellation Vela is one which led to a successful search by optical astronomers at Siding Spring for pulsating light from the same object.

Dr Paul Wild (see profile, page 280) used a broadly similar electronic principle to Mills but settled on a different arrangement of aerials for studying the radio emissions from the sun. At the Culgoora Observatory, 96 small, fixed, dish aerials are laid out in a circle three kilometres across. As each dish follows the sun, all the separate signals are electronically combined to produce a visible, moving picture of the 'radio sun', a feat of instrumentation which has resulted in a rash of dis-coveries about the sun's behaviour — its sunspots, flares and their manifestations as earthly weather patterns, radio communication disturbances and the beautiful aurorae. In 1981, government funding cuts forced a reluctant CSIRO to decide that this world-leading instrument would have to be phased out of operation.

On the other side of the quiet country town of Narrabri, British-born Professor Robert Hanbury Brown of the School of Physics at Sydney University built his weird-looking but revolutionary instrument (known as a Stellar Interferometer) for measuring the precise sizes of stars — a daunting technical task, equivalent to measuring the size of a coin in Perth from the distance of Sydney. Its two large mirrors mounted on a circular track collected the light from a star, like any optical telescope, but then analysed the phases of the light by techniques derived from Hanbury Brown's experience with radioastronomy at the world's first giant radio dish at Jodrell Bank in Britain. For opening up a new window on the universe, Professor Hanbury Brown's work has been hailed as a 'classic' experiment in astronomy. The Stellar Interferometer has now been closed, having done its job, and Hanbury Brown is nearing retirement. In the tough lobbying needed for financing large instruments, Hanbury Brown came close, but eventually did not receive support for an enlarged version of his Narrabri instrument.

As further evidence of the standing of Australia's astronomers on the world scene, it should be recorded that Bolton, Mills, Wild and Hanbury Brown have all been elected Fellows of the Royal Society of London.

Mount Stromlo was once a pleasant hill near Canberra — close enough to the capital for good communications, but far enough away for the seclusion that telescopes demand. Under the successive leadership of Sir Richard Woolley (later Astronomer Royal of Britain) and Professor Bart Bok, Mount Stromlo became the pre-eminent observatory in the southern hemisphere, boasting the largest telescope south of the equator, a 1.88 metre reflector. But, with the rapid expansion of the public service in Canberra, Mount Stromlo became engulfed in suburbia, the lights of which at night all but ruined much of the observing programme. Under the energetic Bart Bok, the ANU decided to establish a field station for further expansion of its facilities and chose Siding Spring Mountain in the spectacular Warrumbungle Range near Coonabarabran in north-western New South Wales. Reflectors of 1.02 metre, 61 centimetre and 41 centimetre diameter were established and the success of the site in terms of weather and clarity of view made further expansion inevitable. In 1980, Professor Don Mathewson was appointed to head the ANU stellar and galactic effort.

Siding Spring Mountain now boasts one of the giants of optical astronomy — the 3.9 metre reflector of the bi-national Anglo Australian Telescope Board. Formally commissioned late in 1974, the AAT was at that time the largest mirror in the southern hemisphere, but such is the popularity among astronomers of observing the southern skies that at least two other telescopes of similar size were hot on its heels in South America. The AAT's Director is an American, Dr Don Morton. The telescope cost $16 million to build, and its annual operating costs, split equally between Australia and Britain to pay for the strictly equal observing times allotted to each nation, amount to close on $3 million annually. This is Big Science.

The southern seas

While astronomy has arrived and will continue to flourish in Australia, marine science is a comparative newcomer which could outstrip its rivals in its rate of growth and popular appeal. For years now, a few leading and vocal scientists have pleaded the case for a proper attack on the research problems posed by the marine environment of Australia. Our continental island has one of the longest and least understood coastlines in the world, yet it is clearly one of the richest and most diverse habitats of marine life for purposes both of scientific study and of controlled exploitation for commercial and touristic use.

Two problems on the Great Barrier Reef, oil drilling and infestation by the Crown-of-Thorns starfish, have been debated publicly with a mixture of emotionalism and sound scientific sense. The public fuss has shown dramatically how little we really know about the complex environment of the Reef, not to mention the other thousands of kilometres of Australia's coastline and continental shelf regions. There is little basic data to support conservation programmes or to give reliable guidelines to the fishing industry at a time when controlled exploitation of the sea's food potential is an urgent necessity.

The message seems to have penetrated. Australian government money is at last beginning to flow into marine research in significant chunks, the largest investment being in the Australian Institute of Marine Science (AIMS). Distressingly long in gestation, AIMS was initiated politically by the then Prime Minister John Gorton in a Senate election campaign in 1969, but not until 1973-74 was AIMS put on its feet with its first staff and a guaranteed $8 million for its first five years. The Institute built its laboratories on a site near Townsville, chosen for the study of the tropical and sub-tropical waters of Australia. Lately it has appeared that the remoteness of AIMS from the mainstream of Australian science is hindering its development as a true centre of excellence.

AIMS is not now destined to be completely dominant in marine research. Under some pressure from the Labor Government of 1972–75, the Australian Research Grants Committee, which gives money to individuals and small groups largely in

PROFESSOR SIR GUSTAV NOSSAL — medical man of affairs

It was not easy to follow Australia's first Nobel Laureate as Director of the nation's largest medical research institute, but the young Professor Gus Nossal showed no lack of confidence in making a success of it when he took over Melbourne's Walter and Eliza Hall Institute in 1965. He is the television and radio man's ideal scientist. Blessed with a striking, expressive face and an articulate confidence in interview, Nossal early became a familiar subject for media 'profiles'.

It is a mark of his basic talent and resilience in the public arena that, 16 years later, he is still regularly 'profiled'. Looking back over files of press clippings and transcripts of radio and television programmes Nossal presents an astonishingly consistent image — a scientific achiever, a researcher mobile in many worlds at home and abroad, a man involved in more medical scientific and public affairs than would fill the lives of several lesser people. And, in the early 1980s he still appears the epitome of the bright young man.

Nossal has been a constant champion of the pressing need for scientists and public to get to know each other better. Equally, he has been concerned to promote the cause of fundamental science. It is disappointing to him, though, that so few of his scientific colleagues put as much thought and effort into the popularising and promotional tasks.

Born in Vienna in 1931, Nossal came to Australia at the age of eight when his parents escaped from the Nazis. His father was of Jewish extraction, but not religious association; his mother came from one of Austria's most prominent Catholic families; as Nossal himself says, 'Hitler was not one to bother with the fine points'. The religious influence went deep. Educated at the big Catholic school of St Aloysius in Sydney, he has been putting his four children through similar education. He has frequently debated subjects of Catholic ethics, notably in relation to such medical matters as contraception and abortion, where he has found himself moving increasingly to a liberal view.

Nossal is a busy man. He gives the impression of organising his time into strict packages: so much for research, so much for administration, so much for public relations, so much for keeping up contacts overseas.

Although he has to be an administrator and fund-raiser (a successful one, too), Nossal is still a working scientist — he would probably be pretty miserable if he could not keep his hands on the apparatus, his eyes on the microscope and his mind on the complex problems of biological theory.

He recalls that his first big excitement came in the late 1950s and early 1960s while collaborating with the American Professor Joshua Lederberg who later went on to score a Nobel Prize. They showed that one cell makes only one antibody, the substance with which it can fight marauding antigens. This finding was important in providing one of the first pieces of experimental evidence to support Sir Macfarlane Burnet's 'clonal selection theory'. From then on, Nossal has been fascinated by the prospects which the fundamental study of immunology throw up for the conquest of disease.

With over 200 scientific publications to his name, he is a scientific optimist. He has not hesitated to differ in mood from his mentor and former boss, Burnet, who is basically pessimistic about medical science ever conquering cancer. Nossal believes that the latest findings of leading immunologists, himself and his staff at the Hall Institute included, allow hope that certain types of cancer will be controlled within their lifetimes.

In 1977 Nossal was knighted — at 46 probably the youngest Australian scientist to receive the accolade. He was also appointed to a directorship of the mining house CRA Ltd, a most unusual appointment for an academic researcher but one which gave him whatever few credentials he may have lacked in the Melbourne 'establishment'. Rather than settling back on his laurels, Sir Gustav Nossal has added strength to his voice in the government of science through, for instance, his active membership of the Australian Science and Technology Council and fellowship of the Academy of Science. Few areas have not felt the keen edge of this sharp mind.

universities, departed from its previous practice of treating all research equally by earmarking some $900 000 for marine science for the three years 1973-75. Continuance of this support was ensured by the establishment under the Liberal-Country Party Government of an advisory committee on marine sciences and technologies.

There are only three modest research stations on the Barrier Reef itself. The oldest is on Heron Island, off Gladstone, on the south of the Reef. Nearby is the small station of One Tree Island established by the Australian Museum in Sydney, and now run by the University of Sydney. In 1973 the same Museum opened a permanent station on Lizard Island on the far north of the Reef.

Most of the early alarm about, and resulting effort on, tracking the Crown-of-Thorns starfish was mounted from the University of Queensland, while the Queensland State Department of Primary Industry organised surveys which gave a more optimistic view in the medium-term because of the observed rate of regeneration of coral reefs eaten out by the 'wave' of starfish. Early in 1981 signs of another puzzling starfish plague were reported.

The Barrier Reef, though, is not the only place to do valuable marine research. There is a demand for much more study of the temperate waters where commercial fishermen reap their main harvests. This is one of the areas now delineated for the CSIRO's Division of Fisheries and Oceanography, based at Cronulla in Sydney. Plans have been announced to move the Division to Hobart — ostensibly to strengthen Australia's knowledge of its more southerly waters, but worthy though this aim is, it appears that politicians wooing the volatile Tasmanian vote had a strong non-scientific say in the disputed decision to move.

Physically-oriented marine research in Australia has been as slow to put to sea as has biological study of the ocean, but at last a 67 metre research vessel is being built for CSIRO's work; the lack of a decent sized boat greatly retarded Australian marine research.

The commercial potential of Australia's marine life is not limited to fish meat. Scientists believe there is a very real prospect of finding useful drugs among the complex chemicals of the sea, such as the specialised venoms of the animals living on the Barrier Reef. Only a tiny fraction of our marine species have been screened or studied in any detail, for their drug potential. To exploit this possibility, the giant Roche company poured millions into their Institute of Marine Pharmacology at Dee Why in Sydney. Early in 1981, the Swiss-based company shocked the Australian science scene by announcing, without warning, that it was closing the Institute as having proved of little value in its few years of operation.

The marine science boys (as in other research areas in Australia, there are precious few girls in the game, more's the pity) will still have to work hard on their image with the public and politicians — and first of all among themselves — if they are to sustain their growth at an adequate rate. They have plenty going for them — a unique environment, some adventurous spirits, athletic and sometimes hazardous ways of collecting information (it is difficult to avoid becoming a diver), and problems of global importance. Yet, there are not too many marine scientists in Australia, and the 1980s will show whether marine science will sink or swim in Australian waters.

A crusty story

The relatively featureless terrain of Australia has long been attributed to the great age of the continent. Yet, it is only in the past decade or so that we have realised just how old the crust of Australia really is — the tough, metamorphosed rocks of Australia's Pre-Cambrian 'shield' are at least 2 500 million years old, more than half way back in time to the currently accepted date of the formation of the earth itself, 4 500 million years ago.

Because they are so old, the rocks of the Pre-Cambrian shield contain few fossilised remains of living things, the markers used by geologists to determine relative ages of younger rocks. But these old rocks are not entirely devoid of fossils. There was much excitement internationally when some minute and indistinct marks in the hard rocks of South Australia were identified positively as the remains of

Above: **Deep underground at the Mt Isa mine in Queensland, CSIRO scientists Mr Alex Spathis (bearded) and Mr Trevor Nettle monitor the effects of blasting on rock walls alongside the stopes of the mine. By detecting changes in the rock mass before any critical deformation occurs, they are contributing to increased safety in an inherently dangerous industry.**

Left: **High pressures and temperatures and geochemical know-how are used by Professor Ted Ringwood of the Australian National University to produce Synroc, a promising new method for safely encapsulating the radioactive products of nuclear power stations (which are such a concern to the public and a major barrier to the introduction of nuclear power). The hydraulic press produces the synthetic rock by compressing the constituents to pressures of 5 000 atmospheres and heating them up to 1 400°C. When buried, Synroc is impervious to the action of ground water, allowing radioactivity levels to die away safely over hundred of years. The process is being developed to commercial level in collaboration with the Australian Atomic Energy Commission.**

primitive forms of life at least 600-650 million years old — then the oldest known fossils on earth.

But, this paled into insignificance when in 1980, the fossilised record of life on earth was dramatically extended by the discovery of simple bacterial organisms at the remote North Pole in the north of Western Australia. The astonishing aspect of this find was that the rocks preserving the minute remains were positively shown to be 3 500 million years old — an extension of our knowledge of life by astronomical dimensions.

With such a vast tract of old rocks containing few distinguishing marks, the geologist faces serious problems in working out the age relationships of rocks in the field. An accurate idea of these relationships allows him to draw up a history of the rocks in a given region — when they were formed, how they were altered by heat and pressure, when they were uplifted, tilted and fractured, when they were penetrated by volcanic magmas and mineral-containing fluids. Without such precise information, the geologist works only by inspired guesswork, and he is unable to use his knowledge of one area to predict with any accuracy the situation in other, less well-known areas — and accurate predictions are vital in economic geology, the search for minerals.

Unable to determine the absolute ages of Pre-Cambrian rocks, Australian geology was hampered until some very bright geologists in Perth and Canberra began to apply the precise techniques of chemistry and physics. Their quantitative methods were little short of revolutionary in a science as highly generalised and qualitative as geology, and from the mid-1950s to early 1960s Australian geophysicists-cum-geochemists played an important role in making geology both a field study *and* a laboratory science.

Although largely unsung at home, the writings of geological scientists like Professor Ted Ringwood, Dr Bill Compston, Professor John Green, Dr John Richards, Professor John Lovering, Dr Ross Taylor and Professor Richard Stanton became essential reading all over the geological world. Most of these scientists have worked at the Australian National University in Canberra. They developed and refined laboratory techniques for determining the ages of rocks by measuring the long-lasting radioactive decay of elements like uranium, potassium and rubidium. They presented fresh ideas about how igneous rocks are formed within the earth, and how minerals crystallise from volcanic and watery fluids — particularly complex problems to unravel. On even larger scales, their understandings of how the earth and planets were formed have successfully challenged many older theories.

It was no surprise, then, that the American space agency NASA included Australian geological scientists among the select few to receive precious samples of the rocks brought back from the moon by the Apollo astronauts. Australians working in Canberra, Melbourne and Houston, Texas, analysed the chemical and mineral components of these samples to deduce the ages and likely genesis of lunar rocks.

Even though he is a physicist rather than a geologist, we should also credit Dr Brian O'Brien — one of Australia's few space scientists — who later had a period as Director of Environmental Protection in Western Australia. Dr O'Brien built instruments which were flown to the moon's surface for experiments in every one of the six Apollo missions to land there — a rare record in space science.

Professor Ted Ringwood, a bundle of intellectual energy, is probably the world's most adventurous thinker about the complex processes which formed the earth, the moon and the solar system. Previous theorists have been hampered by lack of certain knowledge of what goes on inside the earth at any depth greater than the few thousand metres from which the longest drilling cores can be extracted. Using ultra-high pressure-and-temperature gear at Canberra, Ted Ringwood has managed to subject rocks, and artificial mixtures simulating rock components, to squeezing so massive that their chemical and crystalline characteristics change dramatically, thus reproducing the conditions at depths of thousands of kilometres.

Armed with this information, he has drawn up detailed scenarios of the earth's formation and evolution in a geological sense. His theories about the moon were considered by most as interesting ideas, but too way out. However, the chemical, mineralogical and radioactive information stored in the rocks brought back by the Apollo astronauts has swung opinion in Ringwood's favour, and his theory that the moon was largely formed by the accretion of small solid particles trapped in space near the earth has won wide acceptance. A practical spin-off by Ringwood from his basic research has been his development of the highly innovative Synroc process for safe storage of dangerously radioactive waste from nuclear power stations. Synroc is an artificial rock of natural composition which locks into its crystalline lattice the radioactive atoms. An industrially feasible process is being developed by the Australian Atomic Energy Commission.

The application of science

One of the most regular criticisms of Australian science has been the comparatively low level of applied research and development. Much of the scientific work underpinning Australian industry has been done overseas, and local scientists function more as adapters and quality controllers than as innovators. There is, of course, a problem of scale. In some industries, a research and development effort is unlikely to pay off without a major financial commitment being maintained over decades. Only the very biggest firms maintain research laboratories in the million dollar class: BHP, ICI, CSR, AWA, ACI and APM stand out in this regard. In the mid-seventies about 70 per cent of the money spent by Australian industry on research and development (R & D) was spent by only six per cent of the firms devoting any money to R & D.

The research effort in smaller companies and in firms controlled by overseas financial interests is frequently fragile. When commercial operations get tight, research is one of the first casualties. The closure of the Roche Institute of Marine Pharmacology, already mentioned, exemplifies this problem.

As the so-called 'silicon chip revolution' gathers pace in the United States, Japan and Europe, Australia has few firms engaged in high technology to compete with the overseas products. Investment in such operations is treated by business and government alike as a risky business requiring a different form of 'venture capital' to that which underpins, for instance, the giant mining firms.

Some tentative moves by the government and a handful of adventurous computer people are pointing Australia towards a modestly sized but profitable small-computer industry. Electronic packages which meet specialised needs and are cheaply transported could form the basis of a competitive export trade. The worry is that this potential has been understood too late.

The principal source of expert advice to the federal government on science and technology, the Australian Science and Technology Council (ASTEC), has consistently and publicly pressed for more effort in industrial R & D by government and industrial laboratories alike. ASTEC's advocacy is beginning to bear fruit in the form of increased government funding (in bigger chunks) in this long-neglected field ($53 million in 1980-81).

Indigenous technology is also gaining recognition through the recent formation of the Australian Academy of Technological Sciences, a body of peer-elected Fellows who are actively promoting the utilisation of new ideas in industry. A select list of innovations published by the Academy demonstrates the steady growth in home-grown technology — for 1976-77 the Academy considered 173 innovations worthy of mention; for 1978-79 the figure had grown to 233.

The largest co-ordinated effort in applied research comes from the government's own organisations, the most notable being the CSIRO, the Australian Atomic Energy Commission (while still languishing for lack of a power reactor after years of anxious waiting the AAEC is getting a new lease of life by directing its effort to energy research in general), the defence science effort and the Bureau of Mineral Resources.

Of these, because of its size and stated purpose, the CSIRO is the most productive (CSIRO stands for the Commonwealth Scientific *and Industrial* Research Organisation). Much of its work is directed towards applied objectives in supporting the rural, mining, food and textile industries. Each of these industries has a group of CSIRO laboratories, some of which are heavily dependent on funds provided by the industries themselves; the CSIRO wool laboratories would wither without direct levies from the wool industry. The CSIRO also has some credits for innovations successfully applied in secondary industry.

The multi-million dollar scientific instrument industry based on Sir Alan Walsh's atomic absorption spectrophotometer has been mentioned. The story of the Interscan system for aircraft landing control is also one in which a direct lineage is traced from years of disinterested, 'pure' research (in astronomy in this case, by Dr Paul Wild — see page 280) to the foundation of a specialised industry on an international basis.

Other developments in the same money class are the Self-Twist (Selfil) Spinning

Machines conceived and designed in the Geelong laboratories of the Division of Textile Industry. Traditional spinning is a century old, but the new machine is based on a fresh principle: roll two separate threads between rollers, put them in contact with each other, and they 'self-twist' together. Once the bugs had been removed from successive prototype machines, the CSIRO technologists patented a machine which is quieter, more compact, more reliable and some 15 times faster than the old type. Unlike many other Australian innovations, this one was successfully manufactured here by a locally owned firm, Repco Ltd, which is exporting machines at a great rate. The CSIRO innovators at Geelong and Repco know-how combined again in 1980-81 to launch another world-beating spinning device, simple in concept and highly cost-efficient. The Sirospun process spins and twists yarn in a single stage, thereby eliminating a separate twisting machine.

Government-sponsored R & D is not, however, wholly dominant. From the fertile mind of a single inventor in the romantic 'backyard workshop', for instance, has come the 'orbital engine'. Mr Ralph Sarich is a Perth toolmaker with a flair for finding simple solutions to complex mechanical problems. His compact, economic engine with its few moving parts has great promise; its development to the commercial

Left: Eery quiet pervades this anechoic chamber in Melbourne, one of the most noiseless rooms in Australia. Bill Davern of the CSIRO tests the acoustic requirements of building industry materials. Sound is absorbed by 4000 wedges of polyurethane ether set in a massive concrete chamber weighing 250 tonnes and resting on rubber pads.

Above: Dwarfed by insulators in a building the size of a jumbo jet hangar, a scientist prepares for an investigation of electrical discharges and high voltage insulation. The CSIRO Division of Applied Physics also performs tests for industry such as simulating lightning strikes to see how equipment withstands such stresses.

Right: The geometric beauty of sugar crystals is displayed on a projection microscope for Rod Steindl at the Sugar Research Institute in Mackay, Queensland. Regularity of size and shape are important factors in the crystallisation process for which Institute and CSIRO staff are developing direct control through digital techniques.

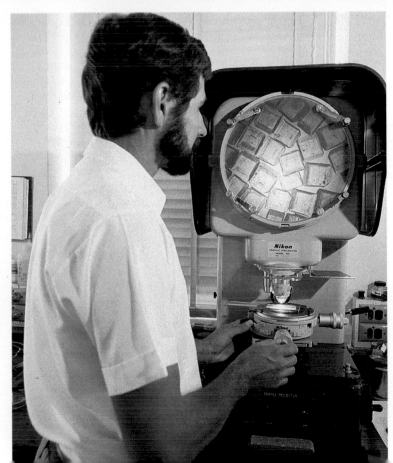

stage has been backed over several years by the BHP research effort. In terms of size, power-to-weight ratio, economy of operation and low exhaust emissions, the Sarich engine and the even newer Sarich fuel injection system are poised to win a world market.

Universities are beginning to see the need for (and potential returns from) patenting and marketing some of the applied developments within their campuses. The most technologically oriented (and the largest) university in Australia, the University of New South Wales, pioneered this trend with the establishment of its own R & D company, Unisearch Ltd. Unisearch contracts the expertise of academics as consultants to industry and also patents and licences University inventions. Some of these in the energy field and in electronics look very promising.

DR PAUL WILD — man in the sun

If anyone had asked the young Paul Wild, when he left Cambridge University in 1943, how he would end up using his physics degree, it is odds-on he would not even have dreamed of astronomy. After all, astronomy was then largely a matter of studying the light from stars through optical paraphernalia. Wild, on the other hand, was a whizz at electronics, a skill which led him straight into the Royal Navy — where he became a radar officer.

Fate brought him, in his ship HMS *King George V*, to the Pacific station. He liked the look of Australia, and he later applied with his eventual lifelong colleague and fellow Yorkshireman, John Bolton, for the same job at the Radiophysics Laboratory of the then CSIR in Sydney. Bolton got the job, but Wild was invited to take up another post immediately afterwards. They were at the beginning of a romantic story of scientific discovery about the universe through the radio 'eyes' of the new breed of electronic astronomers, a story all the more remarkable because of the persistence, over four decades, of its spate of new insights into the heavens.

Paul Wild became fascinated by the nearest star to us, our own sun. The sun's radio emissions were first identified in 1942 by a British scientist who was puzzled by some apparent jamming of radar sets scanning the skies for German raiders. The intensity of the interfering radiation, which varied irregularly, was shown to be related to the violent activity on the sun's surface known as sunspots. By 1952, Wild had so refined such observations that, on a dairy farm at Dapto, south of Sydney, he had constructed a 'radio spectograph' which could study the radio emissions from the sun across a range of wavelengths, that is, across a spectrum.

This approach, a pioneering one in the world, was so revealing of the sun's behaviour that within ten years Wild had persuaded his CSIRO bosses and the American Ford Foundation to invest $500 000 in an even more remarkable instrument to study the sun, the Culgoora Radioheliograph, described briefly on page 270. By taking detailed radio 'movies' of solar flares at different wavelengths, Wild and his team added a whole new dimension to the understanding of the sun.

A truly modest man, Paul Wild has had a heap of scientific honours piled on him which could go to the heads of lesser people, and in 1971 he was appointed from within his own Division of Radiophysics as Chief. Before and during his chieftaincy he applied his otherwise abstruse knowledge in radiotelescope design and operation to a highly practical problem — the development of a new internationally standard system for aircraft traffic control. Interscan, as the brilliant and elegant system came to be known, won an international competition against opposition from the high technology and high finance bases of the United States, the United Kingdom and Europe. Paul Wild was not only the brains behind the system, he led the complex negotiations which ensured Australia's share of the commercial plums which are now beginning to germinate.

It was thus no surprise that Paul Wild was appointed to be the new Chairman of CSIRO when the vacancy arose in 1978. He has probably the highest reputation *as a research and applied scientist* of any to hold this powerful post. His name is now becoming better known in the public arena as the leader of this, Australia's largest scientific enterprise. He has overseen a major re-organisation of CSIRO with remarkably little blood on the laboratory floors.

Apart from fathering three children, Paul Wild's other accomplishments give some insight into the private man — a knowledgeable music lover, a deft impersonator, an expert at *The Times* crossword puzzles and chess, a social cricketer, a walking encyclopaedia on everything that has ever happened in a century of cricket (he has a complete collection of *Wisden*), and a railway enthusiast of forbidding memory (he is reputed to be able to recite every railway station, in correct order, on the old British systems GWR, LMS and LNER). Paul Wild is the antithesis of the archetypal, narrow scientist.

Perhaps the only pity of his elevation to a post where he has to be bureaucrat and politician is that he now seldom gets the chance to put across the excitement of his research into the sun with the simplicity and insight characteristic of his earlier years.

and size of universities, all with portions of their total finance supporting research by academic staff. Three major schemes for making grants to individual researchers or firms were established: the Australian Research Grants Committee, the National Health and Medical Research Council, and the Industrial Research and Development Grants scheme.

None of these handouts happened by accident. All were the result of successful lobbying of one sort or another. That this was so little appreciated by younger scientists of the time reflected the lack both of scientific writing in the popular press and of the incorporation of any *Australian* scientific history in educational courses, omissions which have resulted in such a low level of knowledge about *local* science (even within the scientific community) that outsiders are amazed. This perhaps helps to explain why the Liberal-Country Party politicians were so reticent about scientific successes which had been achieved through direct government support — it is reasonable to assume that they just did not notice, and in the process gave no encouragement to the development of a self-aware identity for Australian science.

The scene changed at the start of the seventies. Following as usual in the train of American and British movements, some scientists began to express publicly their concern about the directions science had been taking (note that their concern about funding was less noticeable — most of those concerned were reasonably secure under direct or indirect government support). The Social Responsibility in Science movement got under way; this had strong personal and emotional ties to the simultaneous environment-conservation-ecology movement. Both movements scored well in the popular press in the two years leading to the watershed election of December 1972, when Labor came into power. Science in the service of man, and not of profits or death, was the catch-cry. The SRS people were, despite their effective publicity, pretty thin among the ranks of scientists, but the environmental angle of the general movement built up a big head of popular steam.

Meanwhile, the leaders of the scientific establishment and a minute handful of people truly expert in science policy matters were pressing the Liberal and Labor Parties alike to define, for the first time in Australia, a co-ordinated and rational policy for science. The Liberals had made the token gesture of adding a 'Science' wing to the existing Department of Education, but their Ministers for Education and Science consistently failed to take science policy seriously, most of them dismissing such a notion as indefinable. However, Labor, in Opposition, formally adopted science into its platform of policies and committed itself to establish a Ministry for Science and Technology. In the event, all we got in December 1972 was a Minister for Science; technology, as before, remained dispersed through other portfolios. This had the unintentioned effect of diminishing the political fallout of the 'anti-science movement', the main thrust of which was really directed against the technological aspects of science.

The new Labor Government also established a Ministry for Environment and Conservation. Both new Ministers, Mr Bill Morrison and Dr Moss Cass, appointed some of the more outspoken radicals to their personal staffs. The teeth of the SRS movement were drawn and the environmentalists gave the government an armchair ride for its first 18 months before again voicing concern about the actions and inactions of government and industry.

The Science Minister was 27th out of 27 in the Caucus ballot for Labor's first Cabinet. Partly because of a resulting low priority in Cabinet, partly because he saw little political advantage in his portfolio ('There are no votes in science,' he had said) and partly because the party platform gave little guidance on administrative and legislative action, it took Mr Morrison over two years to get a long-promised policy advisory body off the ground. The Australian Science and Technology Council (ASTEC) was formed in May 1975 in an interim form under the chairmanship of Sir Louis Matheson, then Vice-Chancellor of Monash University. Those two years of marking time were crucial to the medium-term development of science in Australia. For, while the government made massive commitments to other areas of public funding, such as social security and urban development, science was nudged into a billabong almost without the scientists realising it. The very modest increases in research funds which the government did grant were more than offset by the sharp inflation rate which struck the nation in 1974 and has continued ever since.

The 'anti-scientists' could be well pleased that, though numerically small, their views appeared to have put the brakes on science, although the deceleration acted indiscriminately across most aspects of research. Only some areas favoured politically by Labor, such as analytical work in support of the consumer movement, more food research, and marine science managed to move ahead against the trend. The Labor Government rationalised its position in the introduction of the White Paper launching ASTEC by prefacing its plan of action with talk of 'the growth of public disenchantment with the role of science and technology' and by stating categorically that 'the Australian Government is acutely aware of, and in large measure in sympathy with, public disappointment, disquiet and disillusion associated with many of the products and effects of science and technology'. While it could be said that the scientific evidence for such strong assertions in a formal document about science was so scanty as to be unworthy of a government and to display little understanding of the nature of scientific inquiry (even about opinions), the effect was to jolt some of the more socially aware scientists into a more open political stance.

During one of the volcanic upheavals within the Labor Government in mid-1975, Mr Morrison was promoted from the Science to the Defence portfolio, which was much closer to his real and political interests. His place was taken by Mr Clyde Cameron, who had been demoted by Mr Whitlam from the powerful Labour portfolio, much to Mr Cameron's disgust which he aired volubly and publicly. However, responsibility for the new area of Consumer Affairs was added to Mr Cameron's department and, after his reluctant start, he picked up a good head of steam, although little effective action had occurred by November 1975 when the Governor-General dismissed the government.

After the December election, Australian scientists found themselves under the political wing of a then virtually unknown National Country Party Senator from Victoria, Jim Webster. As Minister for Science ('Consumer Affairs' were bundled off to the new Business ministry), Senator Webster kept things quiet with considerable success. However, his department had to weather six months of intense pressure for its abolition.

When that storm had passed, the Department of Science retained direct influence over only part of the Australian science effort. In the all-important policy stakes, the Prime Minister, Mr Malcolm Fraser, himself a former Minister for Education and Science, kept his hand firmly on the whip. In April 1977, he established ASTEC under his direct responsibility and as a permanent, statutory body. The Chairman of ASTEC was Professor Sir Geoffrey Badger, of the University of Adelaide, who thereby gained influence as the *de facto* pilot for the nation's scientific effort. During his second term of office, Mr Fraser added Environment to the Science portfolio but Senator Webster kept the environmental issues at a low profile publicly and politically. In 1979, he resigned to take up a diplomatic post and was replaced by another unknown National Country Party man, former brigadier Mr David Thomson.

The third Fraser election win in November 1980 saw a subtle but remarkable turn in the affairs of science. Mr Thomson, reappointed Minister, gained responsibility for Science *and Technology* (poor old Environment was shunted around again — to Home Affairs of all places). Eight years after the Liberal/Country Party coalition had rejected the idea of a coherent science policy and ministry, the conservative parties had adopted the basic policies and framework advocated by the Labor Party in 1972.

A Department of Science and Technology makes a sensible — and potentially powerful — combination. But, as usual, such matters went un-noticed in the parliament and the media.

Institutional and political re-arrangements neither make a science policy nor encourage the identity of purpose which drives scientists to greater achievements. Effective communications are the key — communication between scientists themselves and between scientists and an increasingly critical public. These are necessary pre-requisites for a coherent attack on the problems science can solve.

EDUCATION

Dr David Cohen

'Three million kids into 9 700 schools won't go'

The last decade has inevitably been stimulating for anyone involved directly in Australian education. For the first time in Australia's 200 years, educational policies and priorities have become the spotlight of public debate in the press and on radio and television. Political parties at Commonwealth and State levels in the mid-1970s had perceived a political pay-off for providing financial subsidies to implement new educational policies. During the decade too, community views have been canvassed both by Committees of Enquiry and through seeking public submissions to State Departments of Education on such matters as school discipline, particular curricula (e.g. handwriting), and on certification and public examinations. In the mid-1950s, fewer than ten per cent of the 17-year-olds remained at school. In 1978, the figure had peaked at 32 per cent, but has since declined again by nearly ten per cent. In New South Wales (the most populous State), secondary school enrolments grew by more than 50 per cent between 1965 and 1976; but by 1980, there was emerging evidence of a decline.

The flavour from the earlier statistics had generated optimistic hopes for the future. But by 1980, disenchantment with education had started to develop. As in the United States and the United Kingdom, politicians were finding that tough-looking, national cost-reducing economies had become politically popular. With no immediately visible ill-effects, education was a most vulnerable target for cuts. In a period of less than the year of 1980, political intrusions into the education scene began to transform the optimism into a traumatic and seemingly irrational turmoil. In many cases, politicians established 'expert' committees to produce reports to help make the severity of their actions appear legitimate. These validating committees provided politicians with ammunition against outraged and demoralised parents and educators. For example, data from the Commonwealth Government's Report on Education, Training and Employment (Williams Report) indicated that, contrasted with figures of 24 per cent of Japanese and 28 per cent of American 15 to 19-year-olds, 60 per cent of Australian 15 to 19-year-olds are in the labour force. As Parliamentarian Barry Jones commented, 'We have the paradoxical situation of the highest youth unemployment in the advanced world and also the highest youth employment.'

Meanwhile, despite increased percentage retention within schools, the number of schools remained fairly constant at around 9 700, of which 7 300 (77 per cent) were government schools. In fact, by the end of 1980, the first school closures since World

Left: **A stimulating environment helps to develop positive attitudes towards education.**

War II were announced, as a consequence of declining school enrolments. A downturn in reproduction rates (i.e. the average number of children borne by women by the completion of their childbearing) had occurred, dropping from 3.55 in 1961, to 1.98 in 1978. This change was attributed to a complexity of economic and other factors, including marked increases in participation of married women in the workforce (e.g. 35 to 44-year-old married women constituted 29 per cent, 45 per cent and 53 per cent of the workforce successively in 1954, 1971 and 1976), changed attitudes to family living and childbearing, as well as to Australian's highest use in the world of the contraceptive pill, delaying of pregnancies after marriage, and increased acceptance and legalisation of abortion. Immigration has fluctuated (150 000 in 1969, 21 000 in 1976, and 55 000 in 1979), and a variety of factors have influenced governmental migration policy unpredictably (e.g. Italian earthquakes, Asian 'boat' refugees). Steeply escalating house prices have caused some changes in population distributions, and have reinforced the tendencies to move from inner city school areas. Even allowing for such factors, it is predicted that moderate school growth will continue at least until the year 2000, partly as adults seek educational upgrading denied them in their earlier years, and partly as trends towards diversification make educational offerings more attractive to a wider spectrum of the population.

Given such a context, how adequate is education in Australia today? This question may be considered in relation to the organisation of education, financing of education, curricula, teachers and educational research.

Organisation of Australian education

Within the State capital cities (and in Darwin and Canberra for the Northern Territory and the Australian Capital Territory respectively) lie the key educational authorities of Australia. For historical, economic and geographical reasons, responsibility for providing free and universal education for school age children was bequeathed to the State governments after Federation in 1901. To rationalise the vast personnel and economic resources required to support education, each State established a centralised State Education Department, responsible through its Minister to the State Parliament. Centralised control was intended to provide equal opportunities for and access to education for children attending even geographically remote schools. From the outset, 'Head Office' was intended to provide on a State-wide basis uniformly good buildings, uniformly good teachers, and controlled curricula. Standards could be regularly checked (indeed, policed) by departmental inspectors visiting all schools in the State annually, with teacher promotions and salaries dependent upon their inspectors' reports and assessments. The unfortunate side-effects of centralisation, including lack of communication between senior officers and their teachers and students, were often neglected or unrecognised.

As a means of harnessing the seemingly unbridled powers of education departments — to allocate teachers, land, buildings and their maintenance, furniture, equipment, even curricula and examinations — huge superstructures developed. Bureaucratic processes evolved to handle the logistics of each vast State enterprise. The processes, in turn, tended to stifle sensitivity for the major purported function of education departments, which is the right of every child to have the best possible educational experiences. A continuing educational problem which looms large in Australia in the 1980s is: how do you provide three million kids attending 9 700 schools with the best education possible?

State control of the educational systems met the austere expectations both of parents and of the majority of teachers at least until the 1950s. Planning did not lag too far behind evolving needs in education, and the centralised organisations then coped adequately.

A slow growth rate tended to conceal the inadequacies in educational quality. Over the years, the States inherited a legacy of selectivity, over-centralisation, apathy and shoe-string budgets. Even so, States were reluctant to surrender any of their educational powers to the taxing authority, the Commonwealth. By 1975, just three-quarters of a century after Federation, the States jealously guarded education as one of the last bastions of State rights. But meanwhile, the accelerated

Inspection time for pupils at the Tibooburra Hostel. During school terms children from outlying stations live in temporary foster homes provided by a system of children's Bush Hostels.

growth in education of the 1950s had highlighted weaknesses. The huge, unwieldy superstructures often complemented conservative, unimaginative, and even inept decision-making by senior officers. State education departments had been geared to respond to management by crisis. Responses came too late, with too little. Forward planning was inadequate or non-existent.

Personnel selection was based almost solely upon length of service (seniority). Many bright, young and imaginative educators with superstar qualifications were thus overlooked and they soon fled the unrewarding and inhibitive environment for greener pastures.

The State education departments had developed a reputation for rigidity, but by the start of the seventies, the situation was brightening. One State Director of Primary Education, addressing a conference of school principals a decade ago, confirmed this. 'It is true,' he said, 'that our system is viewed as one of rigidity, one so inflexible that individual schools do not have the opportunity for developing initiative. Many of us have been able to deny this by example. But the fact is that the image is that of a system which is very rigid.' Change was needed. 'Already, I have indicated to inspectors that we should be more concerned with the outcome of education, and less concerned with procedures.' The roles and titles of inspectors began changing in the seventies from supervisory to advisory. Such changing ideas spread across State boundaries. Within the State educational systems, a number of factors have helped to overcome Australia's educational inadequacies. Despite the apparently impersonal nature of the huge bureaucracies, changes of all types can often be traced to the influences of perceptive and sensitive individuals in senior education department administrative posts.

Increased postgraduate opportunities overseas, coupled with easier and cheaper air travel, encouraged increasing numbers of top-level Australian educators to widen their horizons by looking at thriving educational alternatives overseas. This helped to produce a new breed of administrators to take up senior positions. For some senior educational appointments, higher qualifications have tended to replace the less relevant criteria of seniority or senior military service.

Determined to tackle the problem being experienced throughout Australia of providing a more effective and valid preparation for its educational leaders, the Victorian Government in 1977 established the Institute of Educational Administration as a statutory body under Director Dr Colin Moyle. It conducts intensive fully residential four-week courses at Geelong for about 40 participants and has attracted leaders from all Australian States and territories.

Perhaps coincidentally, a revival of energy and administrative humaneness has seeped back into most State systems. The new breed has developed a greater depth of understanding of the educational processes. Unlike many of their predecessors, this group can feel confident and secure while increasingly delegating their authority.

This in part explained the changing climate in educational organisation in Australia, towards the devolution of authority which has markedly accelerated for a decade until 1980. In fact, a highlight of recent and crucial educational significance has been the marked increase in levels of *participation*. This was promoted by regionalisation in several States and by moves during the seventies towards 'school-based decision-making' in all States. In most Australian States, not only administrators (principals and inspectors) but also teachers (often as the whole-school staff), and sometimes parents and other community members, and occasionally even students, have increasingly in recent years shared more decisions about a wider range of educational concerns.

These moves have been accompanied more recently by some nervous reactions. These have heralded an increase in some States of political control in education. In Victoria, in a move which took educators by shock, the Minister decided upon a radical transformation of the 110-year-old Education Department. The reforms involved restructuring of the administration, and increased regionalisation, as well as the replacement of its top administrators by a group considered by observers as educationally more conservative. In South Australia, the progressive leadership of Director-General John Steinle and his Assistant Jim Giles is likely to be constrained if the 140 recommendations of Minister Allison's Committee (chaired by Dr John Keeves) concerning curriculum, resource allocation and administration are implemented. Several of its recommendations, for example, are concerned with increasing of school testing and examinations. Imminent changes in key posts in Western Australia and New South Wales are also seen as being likely to cause reversions to more conservative policies. There have been claims that this is 'what the community wants', and that many parents have opted out of government schools to secure this.

Evidence for such claims is provided by recent data from the Australian Bureau of Statistics. This shows that in 1980 about four-fifths of Australian school students (2 320 000) attended the 7 440 government schools for which the State Departments of Education are responsible. The remaining one-fifth (667 000) attended its 2 235

Textbooks and blackboards are beginning to lose ground to audio-visual aids and group work in many schools.

290

It has long been an unquestioned ritual to isolate children into groups, based upon a single aspect of their educational diagnosis. However in recent times, more enlightened thinking has recognised the limitations of the diagnostic tools used. It also recognises that handicaps can be perpetuated through the use of labelling and by separation of students into groups, (often deprived of full social and educational programmes).

This new awareness has led to the adoption of what is known as 'mainstreaming' — educating *all* children in regular classrooms — and providing within the classroom a full curriculum, tailored to the needs of each learner.

The Macquarie University Down's Syndrome Programme has been devised to promote significant development in young intellectually handicapped children. Children from infancy to five years attend the programme for individualised instruction and group sessions. Parents are trained to teach their children at home.

Left: A four-year-old practising his puzzle-solving skills.

Above and right: Graduates of the programme who now attend their normal local schools. Integration is a major concern of the Macquarie Programme.

non-government (including 1 706 Roman Catholic) schools. The 'drift' of students to non-government schools is shown by their enrolments, which rose by 21 500 in 1980 while government school enrolments fell by 18 200. In fact, non-government schools in 1981 enrolled 23 per cent of students compared with 21 per cent in 1976. Of course, there are many possible explanations of such shifts. One explanation concerns relative availability of resources to the two types of school.

Educational financing

By the mid-1960s, the available human and physical resources had been allowed to atrophy to unacceptably deficient levels.

Critics and pressure groups claimed that an education crisis existed. Australian education in the mid-1960s was regularly described by such words as 'shambles', 'crisis' and 'chaos'. Although shown to be the seventh 'richest' of 97 countries surveyed in 1969 by the United States National Aeronautics and Space Administration, it was an unlucky thirteenth in terms of expenditure per student. The spending rate in Australia of $(US) 123 per student, compared with a typical expenditure of $(US) 259 per student by developed countries, could hardly be explained by international differences in arriving at the figures! Yet, expenditure on education had risen astronomically. Total annual Australian expenditure on education was estimated to rise from $74 million in 1950 to $424 million by 1960, and then successively (in the year to June in each case) to $1 480 million in 1970, to $3 696 million for 1975, $5 714 million in 1978, $6 174 million in 1979 and $6 725 million in 1980. The large increase in public expenditure on education caused the percentage of expenditure of the gross domestic product on education to rise from 4.5 per cent in 1950 to 6.0 per cent by 1975, peaking at 6.4 per cent in 1977, and falling to 5.9 per cent by 1980. This reflects the emergence of education as a crucial vote-winning platform for the major political parties, alongside a concern to avoid educational extravagance and the mood to effect cost savings.

Meanwhile, authors such as Illich were arguing that a basic problem preventing educational improvement was the continuing existence of schools as the basic organisational units. Yet, perhaps more in terms of their societal convenience and credentialling qualities than as demonstrably effective broadly educational agencies, Australian schools persisted, affected only by cosmetic change.

True, the figures showed that funding for education had seemingly been increased substantially. In the sixties, there had been token 'ad hoc' funding by the Commonwealth for the provision of science laboratories and apparatus, and for school libraries and library books. In the seventies, there was massive injection of federal funds to the States earmarked for building grants to government and independent schools, for the extension of the school library programme, for the initiation of pre-school and child-care facilities, and for the funding of colleges of advanced education and universities. Large increases were also directed towards the education of geographically isolated children, migrants and Aboriginal education.

The Australian Schools Commission, established in 1972 within one week of the election of the ALP (Whitlam) Government, had highlighted deficiencies of human and material resources, major socio-economically based inequalities, inadequacies of teacher education, and the low quality of education, including the academic narrowness of curriculum objectives. The report called for the development of the 'needs' concept upon which to base the allocation of government funds. This concept included areas of recurrent resources, buildings, libraries, disadvantaged schools and handicapped students, teacher redevelopment (in-service education), and innovation and experimentation.

A controversial recommendation was the reconsideration of State aid to non-government schools, also to be based upon need. Determined that all Australian schools should reach minimum acceptable standards by the end of the seventies, the Commission recommended the policy of supporting schools financially according to their needs. These needs were to be estimated from data provided by every school in Australia. To avoid charges of discrimination, and to provide a strategy for rapid and 'objective' decision-making, the Commission developed a quantitative 'needs index' based upon school-reported operating expenses, adjusted for State differences. Urgency precluded the use of detailed case studies of schools, or of consideration of individual or qualitative criteria.

Estimated average salaries for full-time teachers and auxiliary staff in relation to school enrolments provided the basis for classifying schools into eight categories, labelled A to H Schools spending half (or less) of the annual $511 national average per pupil were classified as Category H, and were recommended to receive maximum Australian government subsidy. Schools spending twice the average were classified as Category A, and it was recommended that no further State aid be provided to them.

However, very few schools were rated so as to receive no funds. An Appeals Committee was constituted to remedy individual injustices. For example, some 'parent co-operative' schools had established deliberate smaller-classes policies, and expenditure per pupil was thus inflated despite general economic stresses in these schools. The Committee's target was to raise expenditure per pupil in Australian schools to 140 per cent of the national average within six years.

The implementation of the 'needs' policy, a substantial cutback in income tax concessions for educational expenses resulting in decreased student enrolments, and mounting educational costs (resulting from rising teacher salaries, increased cost of equipment and apparatus), combined to create financial stresses for the wealthier independent schools. Until 1972, the rich schools had become richer. Many of the older established independent schools were handsomely endowed, and also owned large and valuable tracts of prime land, but they were absolved from paying rates and taxes. These 'snob-and-job-appeal' schools (as influential author and education-

Right: **Sports carnival, Birdsville. Physical and social development are not overlooked, nor is community involvement, even in the more remote areas where schools are located for Australia's more isolated students.**

alist, the late Henry Schoenheimer, described them) progressively increased their fees. By 1976, four such schools had annual fees exceeding $1 500 for day enrolments, while, in addition, 78 schools had boarding fees exceeding $1 000 per year. In 1981, Ascham School in Sydney charged $2 600 per year for Years 11–12 girls (plus $2 300 extra for boarders), fees which were fairly similar to several other private schools. By contrast, Currambena Alternative School (a co-educational parent co-operative — of which I am co-founder) pegged its fees below $1 200 per year in an effort to reduce socio-economic discrimination.

Yet, many such schools remained 'independent' in name alone. They were often ultra-conservative, meticulously preserving the century-old traditions of their ex-students. Their curricula were generally not innovative. Examination achievement upon narrowly academic objectives, sporting excellence (for those who can excel in football, cricket and rowing), religious observance, character-building, neatness of dress, and military precision in the cadet corps, were the key values in many independent boys' schools. And there were corresponding values in many independent girls' schools. However, some independent schools could certainly not be identified with such stereotypes. For example, Ascham introduced individualised assignments in the mid-1960s in a modified 'Dalton Plan', a unit approach to learning. Frensham had diversified its curriculum offerings and students could undertake a programme with emphasis upon art and craft. Under Betty Archdale's earlier leadership, Abbotsleigh placed greater emphasis upon the development of attitudes and values, as had also Melbourne C.E.G.G.S. (Merton Hall). The Kings School introduced 'public service' as an alternative to cadets.

Although often regarded as 'extra-curricula' rather than as part of the curriculum for all independent school students, music, art, drama and debating were more consistently available than in government schools. Greater stability of staffing, with a far higher proportion of teachers staying for ten years or more at the same school, and smaller class size, were other claimed positive benefits of independent schooling.

Recently, several independent schools have adopted co-education. This liberalisation of policy has occurred, for example, by combining boys' and girls' specialist science classes from neighbouring schools, initially because of economic pressures.

Left: **'Take a pair of sparkling eyes.'** Importantly, the curriculum continues *outside* the classroom as students, without inhibition, informally exchange their ideas and views.

Right: **A class for the gifted — who can also benefit within the regular classroom environment. The stimulation of participating in decisions about their own curriculum while working in small groups — with the teacher available as an additional resource person — is an important aspect of intellectual and social development of all students.**

Half a dozen schools have become co-educational, despite the pressure of 'old boys' or 'old girls' who recall their own school days with strong sentimental feelings and who want their offspring to carry on the tradition. The pertinent educational and social evidence about co-education was barely considered.

As the rich schools became richer, deprived schools became poorer. A concerned school principal's plea to a State education department requested special consideration for his school 'situated in a depressed area where interest in education is confined to a small minority of parents'. Income from donations and Parents and Citizens Association activities was barely sufficient to pay bills, 'let alone supply much-needed equipment, some of which is expensive and beyond the scope of annual departmental requisitions'. Slide projectors or tape recorders would be specially helpful to the children 'who have many disadvantages to overcome, and need the best our education system can offer'. Despite favourable endorsement by the district and staff inspectors concerned, the response from upper echelons was, 'Alas, we have no funds!'

Redirection of funding to lessen the imbalance between the richer and the more disadvantaged schools was a major objective of the Schools Commission during the 1970s. However, the Commonwealth Government (in a process described by some as 'de-Whitlamisation') has been steadily shifting resources from government to non-government schools. 'Current grants' to government schools rose from $187 million in 1976 to $264 million in 1980, while in non-government schools, the corresponding rise was from $124 million in 1976 to $264 million in 1980 (remember that non-government school enrolments rose only from 21 per cent to 23 per cent of total enrolments from 1976 to 1981). In 1982, total Commonwealth allocation of funds for 688 000 students in Australian *non-government* schools was $415.3 million, whereas for 2 300 000 students in Australian *government* schools, Commonwealth funding totalled $416.1 million. Pressure groups polarised around the issues of State

297

Aid are certain to continue their debates and challenges concerning resource allocation during the 1980s.

The Schools Commission had a significant influence upon encouraging initiatives (4 400 projects) of individual teachers and schools through its Innovation Grants, generating a large number of educational alternatives (affecting about one-third of all Australian schools) at relatively low cost. However, in 1980, this programme was eliminated by economic policies of the Commonwealth Government.

Increased attention has been paid to the education of minority groups — the geographically isolated, the handicapped, the migrant, and the Aborigine. The merging of activities of Correspondence Schools and Schools of the Air (which employ two-way radio contact) gives promise of further improvements in these fascinating provisions for Australia's isolated children. Compensation for social isolation remains a challenging problem.

Qualitative questions addressed in the 1970s also included a newly articulated concern for various groups designated as disadvantaged students. One such important development related to children with learning handicaps. Although the data are not totally reliable, due partly to different methods used for identifying handicaps, the development of improved methods of diagnosis and treatment for children with learning handicaps has assisted with earlier identification, and has thus improved the possibilities for earlier remediation. This has assisted to increase the trend towards mainstreaming (i.e., maintaining handicapped children in regular classrooms). In broad terms, reports from the Schools Commission suggested that about 25 000 students (about one per cent of the total) attend special schools for the handicapped and an additional one to two per cent of students in ordinary schools suffer physical or mental handicap; 70 per cent of this latter group suffer mild mental handicap. An active lobby was also promoting claims for talented and gifted children as a disadvantaged group.

Another form of handicap was that based upon economic factors. Poverty has been found to be related to early school learning and to failure to learn. An 'Index of Disadvantage' developed by the Schools Commission has been used to identify schools (1 216 schools in 1978) to receive supplementary funding from the Commonwealth under the 'Disadvantaged Schools Program'.

The 1970s heralded changes in Australia's immigration policies and resulted in increased school enrolments by migrants with diverse language backgrounds. For the period 1974–77, the total number of migrant children below the age of 17 years approximated 36 000. The 1976 Census indicated that 20 per cent of Australia's population were born overseas. A further 22 per cent of the population were born in Australia of foreign-born parents.

To assist in meeting the special educational needs of migrant children, since 1976 the Commonwealth Government has injected special funds into the States through the Schools Commission 'Migrant Education Program'. In 1979, the sum provided was $29 million, mostly used to provide salaries of specialist teachers.

In 1976, 48 000 (30 per cent) of the 161 000 Aborigines and Torres Strait Islanders were in the compulsory schooling age range. The percentage participation in schools and retention into higher secondary years and tertiary education for this group, however, remained very low. To encourage more of the group to remain for secondary school, the Aboriginal Secondary Grants Scheme was introduced in 1974, and by 1978 was providing financial assistance to 140 000 students.

Wider and deeper levels of community involvement have also represented an extremely significant step in achieving more relevant curricula. The history of centralised education in Australia had carried with it, loudly and clearly, the message that the views of the general public about education were unsought and unwanted. In fact, virtually the only time parents were able to enter the schools was in 'Education Week', an annual five-day festival to display what didn't happen for most of the year. The opening of schools and provisions for community representation on curriculum and other committees, are a product of the foresight of leaders of the calibre of Ron Reed, Henry Schoenheimer, Bill Hannan and Doug White in Victoria, Doug Swan in New South Wales, and of people like David Schapper, Gerry Tickell and Tony Delves (secondary school principals in Victoria), who translated ideals into action at the local level. Debates about the nature and extent of parental

Acceptance by Australian schools of their curriculum autonomy has been largely constrained by the continued existence of the traumatic ritual of the 'do or die' terminal examination — mostly in the heat of summer.

involvement — whether curriculum, financial and organisational aspects should be included — went on in the seventies as more and more parents asserted their rights to be heard. Despite the anxiety and even opposition of some teacher organisations, the arrival of the 1980s has already heralded much closer relationships between educators, parents and local communities.

The trend towards diversity has been reflected in educational publishing. The now outmoded concept of 'textbook' assumed pre-determined content, identical for all teachers and students alike. In place of the textbook, small self-contained problem-raising units are being developed by the more progressive publishers. Known as modules, they embrace printed and audio-visual items in what is called a multi-media approach. They can be developed to treat each learner as a unique individual, by allowing the student to select the content, sequence and pace of learning.

Another aspect of the curriculum scene has been the methods developed for reporting upon student progress. Before the seventies, a succession of visiting educational critics deplored the apparent lack of purpose of Australian education. The bureaucracies were efficiently maintaining the machine, but why? Lists of high-sounding educational ideals were mouthed as educational objectives; for example, 'To develop each individual fully to optimal ability'. But really it was something else which preoccupied the practising teacher when the classroom door closed. The maintenance of a neat and tidy set of classroom records about a quiet, neat, tidy group of children, with neat and tidy books and minds, was the cynic's all-too-accurate description for primary school teachers wishing to make a favourable impression or gain promotion. What parents knew about their offspring was conveyed via the Report Book or Report Sheet, with comments often limited to one sentence, summarising student performances, attitudes, conduct and attendance. These reports were sent home to parents two to three times a year. In the past, they were occasionally used to provide a basis for initiating discussion between teacher, parent and child, but more often were fuel for neighbourly discussions about the relative merits of various offspring or of the offending teachers.

Many schools have introduced regularly scheduled discussion opportunities for teachers with parents of each student to replace these inadequate and often gravely inaccurate summaries. Diverse and innovative approaches to reporting are among the fruitful results as curriculum autonomy gradually diffuses through Australian schools.

Change has been slower reaching the upper levels of secondary schools. The dreaded hurdles of external examinations, historically conducted at the end of Years 10 and 12, had completely distorted what happened in the schools for at least the last two of the 10 or 12 years. The trauma of a 'do or die' terminal examination lasting two or three hours on each subject was coupled with preparation that included memorising facts to conquer the often re-phrased examination questions from the previous five years.

This academic gamesmanship of teachers outwitting examiners was rivalled by examiners using new techniques to stump the teachers and students. Whatever the strategies used, their effects were to ensure a 'safe' approach to exam preparation, rather than an education concerned with broader objectives. Exams were prepared by a group of anonymous examiners outside schools. The examiners were selected for academic expertise, and were generally unqualified in educational evaluation. The papers were then scored by an anonymous group of markers (enticed by the 'honour' and/or financial incentives offered for each paper marked). Publication of such external examination results of secondary school students has boosted newspaper circulations, as students anxiously pored through the lists of alphabetically arranged or numerically coded sets of results. External examinations continue in Year 12 in most States to strangle any autonomy of curriculum which schools purportedly have gained. The 'best' teachers in the vicious circle were those whose students performed best. Frequently, this merely identified the school with the best parrots and the teacher with the best crystal ball for predicting questions. Under such circumstances, the consideration of educational ideals could only make a teacher less congruent with 'the system' and less happy in the teaching profession.

External examinations at the end of Year 10 have now been abandoned. The external matriculation examination at the end of secondary school, traditionally used both for terminal certification and for university selection, has changed. Many States are moving from the short answer, objectively-scored retention items of the mid-1960s, to essay answers which emphasise comparisons, comprehension and in-

After a day's work in school, teachers assemble centrally (560 of them in this case) to follow a strict code in scoring and grading the examination booklets completed by Year 12 students, collected on a Statewide basis. After being manipulated by complex statistical formulae, 'adjusted' and then aggregated, these scores become the basis for student selection into (or rejection from) universities and colleges.

terpretation of previously unseen data about current affairs and problems relevant to students. A recent biology exam included questions concerning low-fat diets, prawn yields, another Kon Tiki venture, and Australian racial problems. Such examples suggest that secondary schools of the seventies have been relieved of exam preparation for traditional memorisation items, to concentrate on longer-term and more significant educational objectives. Alternative strategies for providing students graduating from Year 12 with community-recognised credentials remain as a challenge for the 1980s.

As what became the swansong of his seven-year term as Schools Commission Chairman, Dr Ken McKinnon in November 1980 courageously released the report 'Schooling for 15 and 16 Year Olds'. The report provided explosive fuel for the view that schools were alienating many of the half-million Australian students in this age group. According to the report, a majority of students were being denied many of school's potential benefits: they *should* have excitement for their futures sparked, develop confidence in their ability to influence decisions, develop self-confidence and marketable skills, learn healthy scepticism, and get involved; but, according to McKinnon, many of the students of 1980 considered school was largely irrelevant and was an utter waste of time. Also in 1980, McKinnon's predecessor Professor Peter Karmel (who had headed the Interim Committee to establish the Schools Commission and was Chairman of the Tertiary Education Commission) was calling for more flexible opportunities for youth to blend schooling concurrently with short-term or part-time employment.

Meanwhile, a more optimistic outlook was presented by the many Australian

301

The teacher's role has become broader and increasingly stressful — higher percentages of students are staying at school, the school has had to assume many responsibilities abdicated by the community, teacher participation in curriculum development has intensified. Yet the needed fundamental changes for improving teacher education have not been introduced. The phenomenon of 'teacher burnout' is becoming familiar to educators.

secondary schools which had capitalised upon their recently gained school-level autonomy to provide enjoyable, stimulating and challenging activities. Both boys and girls were involved in making joint decisions about planning and preparing meals in a Home Science course in one school; medieval dinners and Indonesian meals were part of the menu. Such festivities enriched experiences of other times and cultures. In some schools, student groups managed and operated the school canteen — ordering the food, planning a healthy balanced diet, and preparing the food. In another school course, students operated as consumer scientists, making judgements about averting an energy crisis or about the truth of advertising claims; students examined global issues such as environmental problems, new patterns of population movements across the city or State, the impact of weather on our living conditions, or the effects of technology upon travel habits and world transport patterns. Art had been diversified to include sculpture, batik, photography, weaving, design, pottery and film-making.

Understandably, there was some industrial backlash (e.g. 'let's impose a moratorium') against the extra time required for the increased levels of teacher and community involvement. However, there was little doubt about the positive benefits created by the increased commitment of those involved to ensure effective curriculum implementation.

Teachers and teaching

But if one battle for improved educational quality was won over autonomy of curriculum, limitations in teacher effectiveness have badly hindered improved quality. Research into teacher effectiveness was confusing and even contradictory in suggesting which characteristics and skills of teachers should be emphasised to improve

302

their effectiveness. Teacher education institutions remain as bastions of conservatism, clutching at a subject approach and dominated by history and philosophy of education, teaching methodology, and academic aspects of educational psychology — with token practice-teaching wedged in between. The Diploma of Education continues in nearly all Australian universities to comprise a diluted one-year course, tacked on to a degree in arts, science or commerce. Teacher education courses were lengthened progressively in the last twenty-five years to courses of two, three and four years' duration, as though duration was the key determinant of graduate quality.

During the 1970s, the teaching force rose from 130 000 to 171 000, of whom nearly 60 per cent were women. This increase was achieved partly by extensive overseas teacher recruitment to compensate for teacher shortages. Overseas recruitment persisted in all Australian States until 1975, and then was gradually curtailed, and abandoned by 1978, as a consequence of increased numbers of graduating teachers from Australian institutions. Indeed, declining school enrolments coupled with the increased supply of teachers resulted in a situation, which by the 1980s, left thousands of teachers unemployed. For example, the New South Wales Teachers' Federation in 1980 reported 8 500 unemployed members. Reduced quotas for intake to teacher education programmes were imposed by the Tertiary Education Commission. However, the scare of potential unemployment created a short-fall beyond those quotas which, coupled with a steady wastage rate, have already resulted in shortages in certain areas (e.g., in secondary schools in N.S.W., shortages exist for teachers of science and mathematics, home science, community languages and industrial arts).

While the numbers problem for teachers had been solved, crucial problems concerning selection, recruitment and programmes remained unsolved. It is incongruous that teacher education programmes continue to provide a platform for teacher educators who preach about the 'whole child', 'integrated programmes', 'relevance', 'individualised curricula'; yet their whole set of practices negates such educational ideals.

In the 1960s and early seventies both Commonwealth and States stepped up financial aid for teacher education. The Martin Report of 1964 extended programmes to a three-year minimum, provided teacher college autonomy, and led to recruitment of teacher educators through open advertisement. A 1979 study of teacher educators revealed fewer than 15 per cent with doctorates and 40 per cent with masters' degrees, but a further 30 per cent seeking higher degrees. The conversion of teachers' colleges into multi-purpose colleges of advanced education has been claimed as one factor in providing extra incentive for attracting better qualified staff.

During the seventies, teacher education was abetted by so-called 'competency-based teacher education' (C.B.T.E.) and the development of microteaching skills. One consequence of this has been the further improvement in teacher education at preservice level in technical skills. But regrettably the humane caring aspects of teaching have not been perceived as amenable to C.B.T.E. 'modules'. Also, with increased opportunity for participation in school-based decision-making, there had developed a growing need to develop decision-making skills, demanding social and organisational experiences during teacher education programmes. From such new professional expectations, glaring deficiencies emerged in existing programmes.

It was therefore not surprising that, by mid-1978, concerns about teacher education had moved from questions about quantity. A National Inquiry into Teacher Education was set up at that time under Chairperson the late Emeritus Professor James Auchmuty, deliberating for more than two years. 'We were simply asked to recommend ways of improving the quality of teachers entering the profession and those already teaching', Auchmuty reported. With widely differing views within the Committee, Auchmuty 'soon realised that it was not possible to come up with a clear definition of quality that every member of the Committee would accept'.

Curricula

At least as important as money for education is improvement of the curricula. Historically, centralised educational administrations made curriculum decisions. State-wide curriculum suggestions were adopted as State-wide prescriptions. These were homogenised offerings of content, meted out in equal doses across the State. This was supported by official textbooks (especially for reading and arithmetic), lesson registers, timetables, schedules, syllabus forms, pupil record cards, all of which supported orderly routines and uniformity. Such homogeneity was heavily reinforced by visits of departmental inspectors.

The selection of what to teach, and in what sequence, had typically been the task of centralised curriculum committees. Such committees reinforced the traditional divisions of the school curriculum into a series of often unco-ordinated subjects such as mathematics, English and social studies. Primary school curricula were usually developed by a select group of teachers and principals (usually nominated by inspectors) chaired by an inspector (often the initiator of the curriculum revision). Meeting irregularly and infrequently, such curriculum committees took four or more years to produce the document to receive the Director-General's imprint for State-wide circulation. Ad hoc decisions were made about the sequence for curriculum revisions, rather than the use of a set of systematic procedures for determining priorities.

Under centralisation, local innovations were stifled and variety was inhibited. Emphasis upon accuracy and 'up-to-dateness' in keeping records surpassed concern for educational experiences and the student. But this has changed rapidly. In fact, the seventies may well be remembered as the decade of curriculum innovation. Major changes in curriculum are the result of a fresh approach introduced by the new breed of educational administrators in the various States, reinforced by reports from committees independently established in all States which critically re-examined the directions of education.

The establishment of the Curriculum Development Centre in 1975 as a national body (with astute and far-sighted Director, Dr Malcolm Skilbeck, at the helm until becoming a victim of the 'brain drain' in 1981) helped in developing a comprehensive statement of priorities nationally while generating local and maintaining State initiatives in curriculum activities.

In its first few years, C.D.C. set up working groups to co-ordinate activities on a variety of important curriculum issues. Paradoxically, in terms of initial fears that it would serve as a centralising agency, C.D.C. stimulated support for school-based activities and provided help for teachers in their localised roles as evaluators. In 1980, it distributed free to all Australian schools a statement 'Core Curriculum for Australian Schools', successfully stirring up debate and enlightened discussions about 'that set of basic and essential learnings and experiences which can be expected of all students who pass through our schools'. C.D.C. has also generated the development of curriculum and learning materials in a diversity of areas which includes environmental education, multi-cultural education (including Greek, Italian and other community language materials), social and cultural education (including legal, religious, consumer and electoral education), Aboriginal education (including both Aboriginal culture materials for non-Aboriginals, and English language materials for Aboriginals), the expressive arts, drug education, and agricultural science.

C.D.C. also assumed responsibility for dissemination and additional developments of materials produced by the first curriculum project funded by the Australian government. Known as the Australian Science Education Project (ASEP), the junior secondary school science materials produced by its staff have been purchased by many schools, but inadequate in-service education provisions initially hampered their effective classroom use. The humanities counterpart, the Social Education Materials Project (SEMP), involved one or two small teams of practising teachers in each State in the development of booklets, charts, slide sets and other teaching aids. Topics included Race and Ethnic Relations, Urbanism, and Social Control and Conflict. SEMP, too, contributed to the range of alternative curriculum materials available to localised decision-makers.

However, resulting from the (Lynch) Committee of Review of Commonwealth Functions handed down to Parliament in April, 1980, following a meeting with me in October 1981, the Minister for Education (Mr Wal Fife) informed me (by letter in December 1981) about the future of the Curriculum Development Centre in the following terms:

'The Government has decided that the Curriculum Development Centre is to be replaced by a unit within my Department. The Committee of Review of Commonwealth Functions recommended in April 1981 that unless the State Governments were prepared to meet half of its operating costs then the C.D.C. should be abolished. The State Governments were not prepared to contribute directly to the Centre's operations.

'Commonwealth curriculum development activities will be maintained for the rest of this financial year subject to expenditure not exceeding the total appropriation, a little in excess of $2 million, provided in the Budget. Some national projects, such as those in the Aboriginal and migrant/multicultural areas, will continue to be undertaken by the Departmental curriculum unit and these ongoing activities will be fully funded by the Commonwealth...'

'While the staff of the C.D.C. will be transferred to the new unit, the C.D.C. Council will continue to discharge its legal obligations under the C.D.C. Act.'

Sceptics have said that the closing down of the C.D.C. *building* (opened only in March 1981) was symbolic of the Commonwealth's desire to close C.D.C. itself. But with the delicately balanced parliament unlikely to agree to repeal the C.D.C. Act, the Fraser Government lacked the numbers — and courage — to dismantle a body widely acknowledged to have made a significant educational contribution in its brief period of existence. In fact, in his 1981 opening speech, Minister Fife himself had referred to C.D.C.'s role in promoting 'a formidable array of projects which have resulted in an enrichment of the fabric of Australian education'. In April 1981 alone, the C.D.C. distributed 11 000 separate curriculum items to improve the quality of learning.

With the curriculum divisions of State Education Departments necessarily responding to localised and generally short-term pressures, the curtailment of the C.D.C.'s role in generating collaborative effort across the States has understandably been the subject of criticism as savage as the government's action itself.

Nevertheless, curriculum prospects emerging from the seventies still appeared bright overall. Just as C.D.C. as a national body had provided material and human support for school-level initiatives, the States had increasingly invested resources so as to decentralise curriculum decision-making. Within broadly framed State policies (at least until Year 10 level), fixed content outlines had been replaced by flexible plans. Sharply delineated subject areas were being reintegrated to relate more closely to reality and the children's areas of interests. Curricula fully developed and specified within 'Head Office' under the direction of inspectors had been replaced by curricula developed regionally or locally, with community representation, and with the help of field curriculum advisers. Concurrently, simultaneous State-wide implementation was being replaced by regional trials, localised adaptations, and gradual rather than traumatic change. This flexibility allowed for differences between neighbouring schools related to teachers, students and the community. The content and sequence of what is being taught today more accurately reflects student interests and community needs.

One outcome of autonomy had been the thrust (encouraged by the Schools Commission) towards choice and diversity. The growing literature on 'open education' reflected this thrust. Initially, there was widespread confusion of architecturally 'open spaces' with open *participation* in educational decisions. Larger classrooms were created by knocking down walls between adjoining rooms. Those who mistakenly believed this was sufficient to create an open classroom were rapidly disillusioned. They discovered only that doubling the room area doubled the noise level and other problems, without changing the basic classroom learning climate. On the other hand, others who really understood the issues introduced the more important psychological aspects of openness. This involved students in decision-making about their own learning, what it should include, what materials should be used, where it should take place, and at what rate.

There was, however, evidence of uncertainty about the maintenance of such directions. There were more than hints in the N.S.W. Department of Education, for example, of *re*-centralisation. Centrally-devised policy statements (e.g. in multicultural education) appeared which lacked the benefit of regional consultation and input from interested groups. A Head Office Curriculum Management Committee was established in 1981 to approve all curriculum activities. In Victoria, a Ministerial statement on 'New Directions in the Administration of Education' was issued by Minister Hunt in 1981. It outlined a major reorganisation of the administrative structure of the Education Department of Victoria based upon the report of a firm of management consultants. Concerning curriculum, it stated:

> 'In particular, regions will manage curriculum policy by deploying resources, ensuring that a balance and range of programmes is available, and determining types of schools and networks to deliver programmes. The concept of education on a continuum from Preparatory Grade to Year 12 will be encouraged ... more precise details (about the curriculum function) now need to be developed through the consultative process.'

Resolving the delicate balance between Ministerial responsibility for curriculum on the one hand, and promoting curriculum autonomy on the other hand, represents a major challenge for this decade.

Recognising that the dramatic decreases in teacher resignations and retirements were creating a more stable teaching force (new graduates are expected to comprise only about five per cent of the 1985 teaching force), the Auchmuty Committee put emphasis on in-service education. A key recommendation was the provision of a term's leave for study for every teacher after seven years of teaching. This was also considered to be an expensive project, requiring a relief group of about 7 000 teachers to replace those on in-service programmes. Recruitment of prospective teachers and of teacher aides from Aboriginal and migrant communities, as well as conversion courses for immigrant graduates, and improved preparation for preschool teachers were other key Auchmuty recommendations.

Meanwhile, there have been moves to experiment with the pre-service 'teaching practice' component of teacher education programmes in an endeavour to strengthen the abilities of beginning teachers. For example, school-based teacher education programmes have been trialled. Such programmes are based on the view that from their contact with students, trainee teachers will identify their own needs for professional self-development. The part-time school responsibility of students of the State College of Victoria in Hawthorn (which prepares teachers for secondary technical schools), provides a springboard for their college courses. The concurrent B.A., Dip.Ed. programme introduced at Macquarie University presents education courses interwoven with cognate degree courses in arts, sciences and other teaching areas — a substantial improvement on the traditional end-on 'Dip.Ed.'.

But the 'practise what you preach' model of teacher education remains strangely elusive. The attainment of such an ideal depends on having the right group of teacher educators working with the right group of prospective teachers. Yet many teacher educators have not kept up with contemporary developments in their fields.

Further, the use of matriculation examinations as the major if not sole determinant for selecting prospective teachers is most inappropriate. There is more to teaching than the academic gamesmanship required for a pass in matriculation. Promising research in the early sixties by Balson, which attempted to predict likely teaching success from the personality characteristics of applicants, was unfortunately short-lived. Criteria with seemingly little relevance continue to be used to screen prospective teachers.

Many young people who lack compassion and love for children are enticed to select teaching careers for a different set of reasons, such as the lure of not only free but well-subsidised tertiary-level courses. Owing no doubt to the tighter job situation with respect to secure alternatives, losses from the teaching profession had declined steadily from 15 per cent in the sixties to 12 per cent in 1974, and by 1980, were halved to six per cent. Abolition of tertiary fees and of the teacher bonding system now make it possible to improve teacher selection methods, and to detect and release potentially unsuitable teachers.

The selection and retention of appropriate teachers represent crucial possibilities for the improvement of education. Selection strategies such as judgements by colleagues have not yet been widely employed, but this represents a possible alternative. Some progressive schools have even used primary school students to assist

The rebuilt Alice Springs School of the Air transmits to more than 40 station homesteads in central Australia. At Phillip Creek station, 600 kilometres north of the Alice, Steven Cadzou spent from 30 to 90 minutes daily in radio contact with the school.

in preliminary screening of potential teachers. Similarly, within the State systems, the improvement of the teaching force depends on the identification and promotion of prospective leaders. This must be based upon more valid techniques than in the past. Pre-service and in-service programmes for developing leadership abilities need substantial improvement. In Victoria, the establishment in 1977 of an independent Institute for Educational Administration was a clear recognition of this need. Better selection, pre-service education and promotion will help to maintain an energetic, enlightened, and enthusiastic teaching service.

What else is needed to help teachers cope? One development in the 1970s was the establishment and operation of education centres for in-service education. These were supported by Schools Commission funding and nearly 100 such centres were established during the seventies. Like the earlier-established British Teacher Centres visited by many travelling Australians, these centres are in many cases governed by a committee containing a majority of practising teachers, and conduct courses for the expressed needs of local teachers.

Lifelong learning

The concept of 'lifelong learning' began to take on new meanings in the 1980s. UNESCO had promoted as an ideal increased access to both formal and informal learning opportunities for all people. *Established* aspects of lifelong learning had included pre-school, school and tertiary education.

At pre-school level, services were provided in three ways. Firstly, 'pre-school kindergartens' generally employ highly-trained staffs, operate on a sessional basis, with some conducted by the Departments of Education (free attendance) and others charging as much as $80 per week. The growth of numbers of women in the workforce had necessitated increased provision of child-minding centres for shiftworkers, especially in the most industrialised areas. Some companies have subsidised on-site centres. These centres, known as 'long day care' pre-schools, were non-profit-making centres costing about $30 to $50 per week. Although some accepted children as young as three months, they mainly catered for the two- to five-year-old range. Typically they open from 7.30 a.m. to 6 p.m. for 48 weeks of the year with plans to extend these hours. The government has subsidised some of these for low income families. The third type of pre-school is the 'family day care' centre which provides care for children at around $35 per week by people without formal qualifications. Since 1972, several Australian governments have provided funding for pre-school centres and promised free pre-schooling for all Australian children. However, responsibilities have vacillated between Commonwealth and State Governments, and between a number of departments, with the most recent suggestions that child care will become means-tested.

Meanwhile, academic debate continues on whether the importance of learning in early childhood would be developed or inhibited by formalising education for the three- to six-year-old. In the longer term, gains in educational achievement from early childhood education projects in the United States were found to be dissipated. Nevertheless, regardless of their educational merits, the provision of child-minding facilities as liberators where both parents need or desire to work has become an important part of the emerging social ethos.

Schools were catering for more students for longer periods. 'Retention rates' in secondary schools (percentage of students commencing schools who stayed on) rose from 78 per cent staying to complete Year 10 in 1969, to 90 per cent in 1980. Concurrently, the retention rates to Year 12 rose from to 28 per cent in 1969 and to 35 per cent in 1980. This latter rise was almost totally due to increased *female* retention (24 per cent in 1969, to 37 per cent in 1980, while the percentage of males remained about 32 per cent), a reflection of positive steps to eliminate one aspect of sexism in education.

At tertiary level, in establishing the Tertiary Education Commission in 1977, the Australian Government defined tertiary education as comprising universities, colleges of advanced education (C.A.E.s) and institutions of technical and further education (TAFE). The establishment of the umbrella body known as the Tertiary Education Commission (T.E.C.) in 1977 arose from the rejection of funding proposals from the three previously-existing sectors. The broad charter of the T.E.C. is to promote balanced development and diversification in tertiary education, but its operation by the Commonwealth Government to date has been largely to reduce costs.

The growing financial role of the Commonwealth since World War II in its support of tertiary education has been accompanied by its growing exercise of power. Whereas in 1954, the Commonwealth met 20 per cent of tertiary funding, by 1980 this had grown to 77 per cent. There has been a series of Commonwealth and State Committees of Inquiries during the last 30 years, with a particular emphasis upon attempts to co-*ordinate* tertiary education. For example, the Martin Report of 1964 created the then new tertiary sector of Colleges of Advanced Education. In the absence of definitive guidelines this sector grew in a largely uncoordinated way as a result of conflicting educational and political objectives between Commonwealth, States and the institutions themselves. The rapid development of new colleges took the total to 84 by 1975. By 1980, there were 68 colleges, with the remainder amalgamating with universities or merging with other colleges. Enrolments in colleges of advanced education rose from 44 850 in 1968 to 159 466 in 1980. In 1980, for the first time, more females commenced as students than males, and enrolments of part-timers were growing while full-timers diminished. Political and economic pressures for amalgamation have resulted in several resignations by senior personnel. One newspaper headline ('Director Resigns as Merger Plans Proceed') was followed by reports of 'frantic, last minute planning as administrators try to sort out the bitter and behind-schedule merger'. Similar reports have been made in half-a-dozen other 'mergers'.

The number of Australian universities, only six in 1945, had increased to 19 in the

The N.S.W. Department of Education has summarised the three crucial educational processes as investigating, communicating and expressing. All three seem encapsulated in the spontaneity and enthusiasm of these children participating in early childhood education at Currambena School. Increased use of experiential learning (with children actively involved) is designed to make learning *fun* as well as meaningfully educational.

1970s and has since remained steady for a decade. Although enrolments in universities increased by 40 per cent to total 182 600 students between 1970 and 1981, the number of males decreased, while the corresponding percentage of females increased from 30 per cent in 1970 to 42 per cent in 1981. Full-time students decreased from 63 per cent to 61 per cent, and students aged 30 years and over increased from 13 per cent to 23 per cent between 1970 and 1980, a trend reflecting the significantly higher tertiary success rate of 'mature age' students. Concurrently, after peaking at 55 per cent in 1974, the percentage of Year 12 students moving *directly* into universities and colleges of advanced education declined to 49 per cent in 1977. Perhaps this decline was due partly to disenchantment with the value of tertiary credentials as job tickets. Perhaps it was due also to a growing view that maturity assists tertiary studies. Certain it was that fewer students seeking tertiary admission were being denied entry. The intake of students was falling off at a rate significantly faster than one would have been led to expect by the imposition of tertiary quotas at the close of the seventies.

Economic pressures were being felt in universities and colleges of advanced education through cutbacks in staffing and research funds. Elimination of some small-group teaching, reduced course offerings, shorter library hours, reduced availability of learning resources were other responses. The long-revered Australian phenomenon of automatic staff 'sabbatical leave' provisions was set aside, and replaced by much-reduced schemes for professional refreshment. From 1950 to 1975, tertiary enrolments had shot up from 30 000 to nearly 300 000; and by 1981 enrolments had passed 360 000 in universities and colleges of advanced education, with enrolments in technical and further education (TAFE) programmes in 1981 reaching 346 900 students. Under Foundation Director Graham Hermann, a TAFE Centre for Research and Development was established in 1980 in Adelaide. The main purposes of this Centre were specified as undertaking job skills analyses and reviewing TAFE curricula.

The Commonwealth Government meanwhile had also committed financial support to States for the period 1980–1984 for 'Transition Education' programmes. Generally, these were to be developed within schools for 'students-at-risk' (of leaving and probably becoming unemployed) in typical academic programmes, and designed to provide skills to assist in transition from school to work. Each State education department was required to develop procedures for accrediting, assisting, and supervising this new breed of courses.

In the wider sphere of lifelong education, Australia needs to give urgent thought to developments which have already occurred in many other countries. The need for re-education of adults for new roles, activities and vocations arises from the rapidly changing world in which we live.

Education outside of formal institutions is arranged through such bodies as Councils of Adult Education and Workers Education Associations, in growing recognition of lifelong education, with opportunities for learning undiminished by age. Brief courses cover a very wide diversity of areas, including leisure activities, vocational skills and general interests. Librarianship, textile sciences, health sciences, technological studies, and institutional administration are some additional examples of post-school enrolment growth areas. Rapid societal and vocational changes, with emergence of several careers in the life span of one person, demand continuing practices providing more flexibility for re-education of people of all ages for new roles, activities and vocations.

Educational research

The seventies had ushered in a new (though modest) commitment to educational research in Australia. There had in fact been at least token research for a half-century, as it was in 1930 that the Australian Council for Educational Research (A.C.E.R.) was established by a grant from the Carnegie Corporation in the United States. Although both Commonwealth and State governments have continued to provide some funding, it has proved to be inadequate to create a national powerhouse of research. Officers of A.C.E.R. have reportedly engaged in a continuing battle with federal Treasury to have its grants increased. Supplementary income has been gained by A.C.E.R. acting as an agent for overseas curriculum materials, books and tests. Unfortunately, this pressure has been inhibitive to its activities, **forcing A.C.E.R. to gear its activities heavily towards promoting tests and the** measurement (and statistical) aspects of research, such as elaborating precision and scaling to the detriment of more balanced and school-oriented research. The Directors-General of Education of the States have maintained a niggling concern about the lack of relevance for government schools of A.C.E.R.'s research.

Most recently, despite what its Director acknowledged in the A.C.E.R. Fiftieth Annual Report as 'in some circles vigorously opposed' and in spite of active opposition of a majority of State Directors-General of Education, the Australian Council for Education Research has remained insensitive to the climate of opposition and doggedly persistent in efforts to introduce statewide and national testing of numeracy and literacy into Australian schools. Opponents of such testing (such as the Curriculum Development Centre) justifiably see such narrow measurement concerns as likely to preclude an appropriate balance in the curriculum, creating undesirable backwash effects to erode even further the important areas of development such as the aesthetic and cultural, social, emotional and physical. Again, the need to examine the impact of research in the broader and school-related context appears to have been overlooked.

In a decade characterised by action (sometimes bandwagons) and reaction (sometimes over-conservatism) to an array of educational innovations — such as the use of behavioural objectives, team teaching, effects of reducing school size, community involvement, multimedia resources, educational voucher schemes, programmed instruction, television teaching — one might have hoped for guidance from Australian research findings. It is a sad commentary on at least 50 years of activities and the expenditure of millions of dollars on research, that findings from research have had such little influence during the formulation by decision-makers of policies about practices upon real kids, classrooms, and schools.

In attempting to mimic the experimental methods of the exact sciences, educational researchers have tried to show that the variation of one closely controlled factor A causes a corresponding change in factor B. The vital questions which differ from the sciences include: for whom, and under what conditions? Unfortunately, in attempting to overcome these pertinent questions, educational researchers have created a reservoir of clinical, sterile, irrelevant and trivial findings. So often, the

Despite the formality of this classroom situation, a leavening humour. Most Australian secondary school teachers persist with traditional whole class, 'chalk and talk', textbook teaching.

averaged data have been extracted in the vain quest for generalisable findings from random and/or stratified samples. This results in travesties of realities, masking the dramatic variations between individuals as well as the quality and power of the study of individual cases.

With such a poor track record for educational research, it was somewhat of a triumph of hope over experience that in 1970 the late Dr Bill Radford was able to identify five 'heartening events' on the research scene: first, Australian government grants to establish the precursor to Educational Research and Development Committee (E.R.D.C.); second, grants to provide for research funds related to colleges of advanced education; third, the significant growth of research units in State Departments of Education and in colleges of advanced education; fourth, the promotion of research into university teaching by the Australian Vice-Chancellor's Committee and finally, establishment of the Australian Association for Research in Education to promote the extension, dissemination and application of high quality research in education.

Since the establishment of E.R.D.C. in 1976, the battle to have its meagre funds increased had been perpetual. For example, the funding provided through E.R.D.C. (Australia's major source of funding for educational research) in 1976 totalled $783 000 across 66 projects, a stark contrast with the research funding of even one American university, often exceeding a million dollars. The first official report of the committee drew attention to the fact that it was convinced that there is much research and development work in Australian education, quite directly related to existing problems of policy and practice, which should be undertaken, but which could not proceed because of lack of funds. Funding to this committee was modestly increased to $893 000 in 1979, and hovered around a mere $1 million for research and $250 000 for operating costs. Even so, E.R.D.C. was able to support nearly 100 research activities nationally. It was to the credit of E.R.D.C. that it had more recently redirected its attention to the needs of schools and policy-makers — perhaps responding to the priorities voiced by State Directors-General of Education. In 1980, E.R.D.C. was abolished as a result of the Fraser Government's 'Committee of Review of Commonwealth Functions' (known also as the 'Razor Gang'). This abolition (at a time when its former Chairman, Syd Dunn, has just entered retirement) represented a national tragedy, without providing substantial cost-saving benefits.

Hopeful educators had expected that some of the Federal Government's ten 'research centres of excellence' may have been geared towards the needs of decision-makers. But awards of six of these centres were announced in 1982 for the dominant biological and medical fields. In common with chemistry, astronomy, geology and the humanities, *educational* research received precisely nothing!

Understandably, growth in research funding requires evidence of the influence of research upon practice. Dissemination of research findings in comprehensible and meaningful terms perceived by practitioners as relevant to their needs is a prerequisite to effecting change in practices. More fundamental changes of educational practices, including major variations in traditional school organisational patterns, the effects of 'de-schooling' and elimination of 'subjects' from curricula, need exploration.

Not only in relation to educational research, but for education in general, funding policies require thoughtful and continuing evaluation. In the United States, $10 billion were poured into State and local educational agencies under the 1965 Elementary and Secondary Education Act, in order to improve education for poor children. This American experience has led many to question the wisdom of redirecting money for compensatory education programmes for disadvantaged children. Educational achievement seems pegged by socio-economic factors. Achievement might be enhanced at least as much by other social policies such as by providing additional subsidies to poorer schools. Paradoxically for the educator, the injection of government funds into subsidies for direct increase in incomes, or lowering the taxes of poor, may have more immediate and direct impact upon the ultimate improvement of educational achievement. There remains a vital need for independently-conducted research about the impact (and relevance) of the accruing reservoir of educational research findings in Australia upon decision-making for our schools.

Conclusion

The 1970s in Australian education were characterised as a period of growth, optimism, and excitement. Demands had expanded, and these were coupled with expectations of more responsive provisions for a greater diversity of talents, ages and interests in our student population. More people wanted to know 'which?', 'how?', and 'why?' certain educational decisions had been taken.

However, politics and politicians had begun to have increasing impact upon edu-

The cause for celebrations? These girls in a single-sex government high school had just success-fully petitioned to have panama hats included as part of their compulsory school uniform, perhaps typifying the more conservative aspects of Australian students. Their jubilation may result from having actually influenced a school decision.

cational decision-making. The declining economic situation had led to tighter purse-strings for education. Competition for a share of the scarcer human and financial resources has created a climate in which new initiatives have been reduced. It is paradoxical that at a time when choice and diversity are among recently-won edu-cational ideals, funding cutbacks are likely to force some reversions to conservatism and less desirable practices. All who participate in educational decision-making must be sure that our choices are directed to our most prized heritage, those whom it is our task and duty to educate.

LEISURE

Ian Moffitt

'A healthy, but not fit, people...'

The pursuit of leisure is a serious business in Australia. We may not care much about complex Asia, but we've sent some good racing ponies to Malaysia and a batch of great greyhounds to Macao. Those of us who couldn't care less about racing (and there are a lot) dig gardens, paint bedrooms, go to the local flicks, do a hundred-and-one other things. But, en masse, we're leisure lovers: a healthy, but not fit, people with a premature paunch as a symbol of our mindless affluence.

Take the surf. The old Australia was a bronzed lifesaver stamping into the future with a flag unfurling above him and a big yellow 'A' on the front of his green costume. He was a young nation marching nobly out of War and Depression, with Right and Manhood still unquestioned, Patriotism unchallenged, Service and Sacrifice realistic ideals.

We were (we imagined) kings of the creaming-lemonade water, idols of the world, and the lifesaver in peace became the Digger in war, the myth-men melting into each other.

Vic Rushby, my club captain when I was a youth, was my first Australian hero: tall and grey as a Digger monument, straight as steel, iced salt water in his veins. He symbolised that tight-lipped old Australia, a silent storm-man with bare toes planted deep in the wet sand, staring bleak-eyed at the endless wastelands of ocean which rolled into the long, empty North Coast beaches of NSW.

He had a shoe shop in town. Sometimes I saw him kneeling amid the polished leather, rustling white tissue paper in boxes, but I knew that the *real* Vic Rushby stood like a Viking in the surf boat as it plunged into a green trough, the white spray hissing into his steel (or granite?) face. Of course we read about Grace Darling at school, and sang our praises, shrilly, to the Fishermen of England, but Vic and his squad were closer models to emulate — until, in the seventies, the wave of affluence began to undermine the movement. As the then-President of the Surf Life Saving Association of Australia, Sir Adrian Curlewis, put it: 'The idea of service has become unfashionable'.

The old enemy had been the shark beyond the breakers; the new enemy was the mobile society.

Once kids could only afford to walk or take a tram down to the crumbling surf club pavilions; now they have cars, money, freedom, boards. Eschewing discipline, they turn their backs on institutions and organisations to pursue personal pleasure,

315

Left: **Balmoral Beach, one of Sydney's many popular bathing spots.**

and they don't have to give back a thing to the system (including lifesaving). This unique volunteer movement will survive — streamlined training methods and new publicity campaigns have helped — but the media and the stores fill kids' minds today with images more exotic than rescue and resuscitation. They park curtained panel vans along the beach-fronts (mobile boudoirs which rock gently as you pass) and scores of them follow the waves up and down the coast. The old surf club push has become a bit passe, and some of the old idealism has submerged with it. Some — but not all: women surfers are boosting the movement in the eighties, with Iron Lady events now winning headlines.

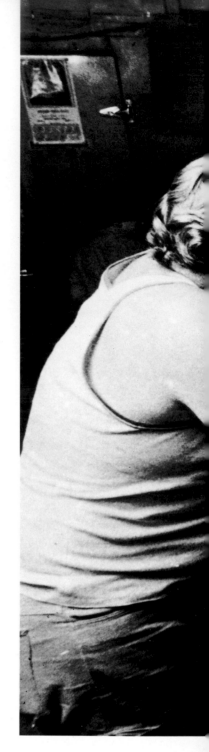

The agricultural show, especially Sydney's famed RAS Easter spectacular, also still survives the past. Every year outside Jimmy Sharman's boxing tent the big drum used to boom like the heart-beat of the 'Easter Show', awakening the primitive in bank-clerks: 'Where are you from, young fella? Tenterfield? Blimey, you're a long way from home, Tenterfield. Well, I'll tell you what we'll do. If you can beat this boy here you get three quid, but if he knocks you out or you squib — what's that? Your mother never had a squib yet? Well, come on up here, Tenterfield . . .'

The tent isn't there any more, but the crowds still stream into the pavilions to see the State's wealth spread before them, and the sideshows are pretty much the same (I once saw an exotic 'French' dancer with MUM tattooed on her arm). Sydney's Easter Show is one of the nation's few old indigenous festivals, and it rekindles chi' .hood memories. 'See death on the French guillotine,' cries a lady in leopard-skin pants, whacking the painted canvas behind her with a sword, 'see the lovely head drop from the lovely shoulders . . .'. And: 'The more you clap, the more she takes off . . . lovely girls, daring girls'. Two youths dig into their jeans and saunter, elaborately casual, towards the ticket box. A man glances tentatively at his wife.

More than a million Australians flock to the Show every year to pick a box, have a shot, throw a ball, have a free chest X-ray, have a headache powder. The sideshows are nostalgic fun: the spruiker addressing the Maori Prince in mock pidgin, 'How you feeling? You good? Plenty good, eh?', and the Prince telling me later as he carefully studies his fingernails, 'Well actually, I was a surveyor'.

But the Show is also a recurring sign, as the old touchstones melt everywhere, that the nation's veins have not quite dried up, its heart calcified. The glossy horses and fat cattle wind out of our pastoral past into the petrol-present to create a celebration of unashamed chauvinism; here, beneath the fairy floss and the kewpie dolls, lies the rich dark humus from which we have sprung; increasingly, we no longer take it for granted.

Indiscriminate nostalgia can be a failing. But thousands of Australians are now beginning to discover the past on holiday trips around the country by car and coach. Their appreciation is often imperfect, but it is, at least, a start.

I take a coach tour into the Hunter Valley on a sunny day when even the husbands in the family groups are grudgingly happy. The lush bowl of the valley is stitched with vineyards, a jet unzips the sky above and we straggle from the coach to inspect a ruined sandstone building: the original homestead of one of the vineyards near Branxton. 'Don't go in there, Kenny,' warns a mother, peering dubiously at the cold fireplaces, the stone strewn floors, the crumbling, empty windows barred against Aborigines and bushrangers. An Alf with a red-brick heart debunks plans to rebuild it, and swigs a can of beer (the rest of us, obediently, sip wine) while his wife murmurs: 'The poor women that lived out here.' Our expectations are much higher these days, and there isn't much of the pioneer spirit left in any of us.

The old and new life-styles don't always mix too well either, as I discover at the Hunter Vintage Festival, the New South Wales answer to the Barossa Festival. Wine novices wander from tasting-tent to tasting-tent with glasses dangling on string hung around their necks, *Don's Party* style, and they try valiantly to absorb vineyard lore at wine lectures as pulsating lines of child mini-bike riders roar around outside. If you're not dazed when you go in you are when you come out: one ear registers the mini-bike announcer ('The riders now go into a horseshoe formation . . .') and the other picks up the lecturer ('In November or so the vine starts growing its fruit . . .').

This pub in the tiny William Creek railway settlement on the southern shores of Lake Eyre, S.A. is typical of many smaller Outback hotels: it dispenses beer, news, and gossip and is the general store.

There's often a difference too in the life-styles of old and new Australians. Some Australian families meet each other once or twice a year in their local Botanic Gardens: elderly sisters dredging snapshots of grandchildren from their handbags before tea in the kiosk, toddlers tossing bread to the ducks amid the mossy-thighed marble nudes. There's a timeless charm in these gatherings (today's toddlers are tomorrow's aging grannies), but New Australians seem to enjoy these family reunions more than Old Australians who mostly don't really *like* children (who reciprocate in later years by shunting the oldies off into institutions and Eventide Homes); the family unit leads a tenuous existence in Australia, where you can't take kids happily into a posh restaurant, or many other places where a shout of childish joy is matched by a glare of anger from older leisure seekers.

Many adults seem immune to the crash and clatter of the poker machines; many are immune to their temptations (in most States they have to be). But for many, the adults-only club is the place to go.

One club is pretty well like another. The compere bounds on stage, flicking the microphone cord as he has seen the top entertainers do a thousand times. 'Good evening, ladies and gentlemen,' he cries. 'Is everybody happy? Getting enough booze down there? No? We'll soon fix that. And now, it gives me very great pleasure to introduce a young lady who is very, very popular at the club. That very sexy

317

Melbourne Cup Day is a moment of national aberration. It is a public holiday in Victoria, and everywhere else in Australia life comes to a standstill as ears and eyes are glued to radio and television screens. At Flemington racecourse, the site of this equine gala, anything goes and generally does, as the social set, the would-be social set and the trendies attempt to outdo or outrage one another.

sausage with the glorious voice . . .' And out she slithers in powder-blue shorts and gold calf-length boots.

The pubs have countered with rock concerts: rock stars are the young's new heroes. (My favourite — I'm coldly detached, of course — is the group *Matt Finish*, with son Matt Moffitt as founder, songwriter, singer and lead guitarist.) Jazz and folk are also winning new audiences among the young. We might produce world champions in the surf and pool, in motor-racing and yachting and squash, but the rock stars are the idols of today's youth: kings of a massive leisure-market.

At a restaurant west of Sydney, Garry Tooth sings 'Wallaby Stew' and then swings into a shearing ballad. He's a nuggety, bushy bearded bloke who looks a

At the Eastern Suburbs Rugby League Club, Sydney, a group of senior citizens settles down to a friendly game of cards. Yet for many of the elderly, confined to their homes through illness or circumstance, the 'box' is the sole source of entertainment and companionship.

little like one of the banksia men out of *Bib and Bub* — horticulture is his hobby, orchids his quiet passion — and he lives in the NSW Blue Mountains though he hails from Queensland. 'I like the transportation songs best,' he says, 'and I always throw in a lot of Irish stuff.' He is a golden bush singer who could make a packet on the American lecture-song circuit, 'but to sing what I like for a living, this is really beaut'. His roots are deeply planted Down Under.

Overseas stars come to grace our stages, and our own home-grown Joan Sutherland, acclaimed around the world, ornaments the Opera House, where she dominates magnificent casts which play to packed houses. Subscription concerts are fully subscribed, home-grown ballet and opera vie with one another in the prestige stakes, and Australian drama surges ahead with perhaps more vitality than any other country. Not all that many people out of 14-odd million actually see these performances; not that many more put aside a Sunday afternoon for the Victorian Arts Centre (though small town museums and folk art centres are popping up like Outback flowers after the rains); and even the outdoor rock festival isn't the drawcard it was, mud or no mud. Mostly it's the 'box' that gets the numbers, and a colour TV set is the current — and expensive — artistic challenge.

We pay for our pleasures, of course. In fact Sydney people, for example, pay among the highest prices in the world for restaurant meals, clothes, household appliances and public transport (such as it is). There is a big shortage of trained staff to help local communities plan and administer leisure facilities, but there is always somewhere to eat. Australians now spend almost $600 million a year on food prepared in commercial kitchens while hoteliers, restaurateurs, clubs and the fast food merchants enjoy the boom. In NSW alone people spend about $200 million a year in restaurants, hotels and club dining rooms and another $50 million on take-away food. Nobody starves. But a cardiologist who surveyed Sydney school children says that 12 per cent of Sydney's teenagers now have so high a cholesterol level that their risk of heart disease might be increased threefold.

The bright lights of the capitals and the bigger towns often blind one to the simple fact that Australia is one of the most beautiful countries on earth. I know scores of unique natural treasures here, and each one is an essay in leisure.

They defy description, these beauties: rainforest and snow country, red desert and mountain streams; Ayers Rock and Katherine Gorge and the Top End where wild buffalo roam and crocodiles still slide into the waterlily lagoons; the apple isle of Tasmania and the bushranger towns and the Indian-Pacific Express, which now spans the continent and is booked out for months ahead (though it lacks the drama of Graham Greene's Stamboul Train: perhaps someone ought to write a light Indian-Pacific TV series starring a fruit-fly inspector); South Australia's Barossa Valley, where the descendants of German settlers grow grapes for Australia's excellent wines; paddle-steamers on the Murray, and the bush race meeting where the punters park light planes, not cars; the opal town of Andamooka, where a fortune lies beneath the red rocks and a .38 pistol lies beneath the miner's pillow. And north Queensland, which thousands of Australians are now discovering.

Tropical north Queensland, and the Great Barrier Reef, are sun-ripe: for me (and

JIM SHARMAN — Brecht, not boxing

Sharman is a magic name in Australia, and it doesn't matter which Sharman you mean: Jimmy, Jimmy or Jim. All three of them — grandfather, father and son — have stamped their images on the national mind, expressing the mood of the nation as it has elevated its pleasures through war and Depression to eighties affluence. Your age dictates which Sharman has impressed you most.

Jim Sharman is Australia's brilliant young stage director and film-maker: his father and grandfather ran the famed Sharman boxing troupe for decades at country and city agricultural shows. His style has certainly soared above theirs; he has swapped the cracked, painted fighter backdrops in bush towns for the world's theatrical capitals. But he is in the entertainment business too, and a brief look at his heritage also tells the nation's story — though he is probably tired of the fight stories themselves, which certainly have little place in his serious investigation of theatre and film.

The elder Jimmy's own grandfather Tom, was an Irish bare-knuckle fighter ('Call that fighting? With chaff-bags on your hands?' he used to snort). Jimmy Sharman I, who died in 1965, was a gravel-voiced fighter-showman who retired in 1911 and took his fight-tent thousands of kilometres around Australia each year. His son Jimmy II carried on, the black and white boxers standing impassively in their silken robes outside the tent as the drum thudded. But Jim Sharman eschewed that role: he attended Randwick High School in Sydney and first attracted attention with magic shows. I asked him once about the boxing tent, and he said: 'Whenever I see those banners I think: "That's the pop culture of Australia".'

He chose a wider stage. It was, for instance, Brecht, not boxing, for him: he took *The Threepenny Opera* into Sydney Opera House during a sizzling display of his varied talents in the seventies. Born in 1945, he has graduated from the reviewers' 'bright young hope' into a brilliant artistic innovator whose work is pleasure, his pleasure work. And he doesn't sit around waiting for pats on the head ('If I took notice of the knockers I'd have put a bullet through my head . . . Australian critics are constantly on the lookout for losers'). Sharman has directed a lot of winners. And, like his father and grandfather, he is a travelling Sharman too — hard to pin down as he jets between Australia, London, North America, directing musicals, operas, plays, feature films.

A sample of his work in the seventies: he directed *Hair* (including Tokyo and Boston), *As You Like It* and *King Lear*, *Jesus Christ Superstar* (concert and stage versions), *The Rocky Horror Show* (London, Sydney, Los Angeles), *The Rocky Horror Picture Show*, and other movies. He also directed David Williamson's play *The Removalists* in London, Benjamin Britten's *Death in Venice* opera in Adelaide and, several Patrick White plays; and, of course, he was Artistic Director of the 1982 Adelaide Festival of the Arts — a truly international cultural event. And so there is no sign of him slowing down the pace in the eighties — another film here, a play there . . . For the Sharman drum now thuds around the globe. . .

for many others) a synthesis of memories of Asia and the Pacific in a beautiful new Australian blend. The mainland is exciting enough. Drive through those forgotten little towns up there, in a tropical downpour when they're burning off the cane, and the spectacle is sheer Cecil B. De Mille. A green surf of sugar-cane and bananas rolls to the coast, and out on the pale green sea, scratched with white wave flecks, the Reef's strings of little palm-thatched islands seem to float just above the horizon.

This is a lush but still dangerous Australia, not wallowing in a tropic torpor, its teeth extracted: beware the deadly stonefish spines, the pretty cone shell which can sting you to death, the box jellyfish which is probably more dangerous than the shark. But it is Paradise too for a quarter of a million visitors each year, with planes, helicopters and cruisers now linking these castaway isles to the world's jet routes.

There are, up north, at least 17 resort isles like Dunk and Green and Magnetic and Hayman, Orpheus and Daydream and Paradise Bay and Lindeman. An English Billy Butlin holiday camp schedule fits awkwardly on some, but for the dreamer escape is easy. Green turtles up to 230 kilograms in weight heave themselves ashore to lay their eggs in the mating season, and underwater observatories are peepholes to a rainbow world of fish and fluted corals.

Above: Not exactly city boys, these three from Alice Springs still enjoy the chance of a headlong gallop across the bed of the out-of-town Todd River. Shayne Johnstone, at all of seven years, gives a no-hands, one-stirrup performance as he challenges 12-year-olds Donald Costello (centre) and David Poots on the grey.

Left: City gimmicks do creep into the Bush. Nine-year-old Aron Fishlock, of Mataranka, N.T. does a minibike slalom through a forest of termite hills on Elsey station. Elsey was the setting for Mrs Aeneas Gunn's 1908 classic, *We of the Never Never.*

Opposite page, above and below: At a Melbourne pop concert, expending somewhat less physical energy, the young nevertheless enter their own world of fantasy.

Dunk Island is an example (it inspired the old book *Confessions of a Beachcomber* by Ted Banfield, who went there for a visit in 1897 and stayed for 25 years). Individual suites nestle beneath umbrellas of palms, and there are 148 species of tropical birds and giant butterflies among the palm groves and in the tropical rainforest. It's easy to understand why some of Australia's 'characters', the true individualists, have fled north from the rat race in the south. The pity of it all is that the Queensland Government has an abysmal attitude towards conservation. Paradise may well become a Paradise lost.

Lazing about on coral sands is one form of pleasantly indolent leisure. Another, observedly popular, is the sometimes not-so-gentle-art of sport watching. Many of us make better spectators than players — though jogging has become as popular here as anywhere. One newspaper survey places tennis as the sport which interests the most Australians, followed by swimming, Australian Rules (Australian National Football is the correct name), Rugby (both codes), cricket, soccer, golf, bowls, squash and athletics. The figures and preferences differ sharply from State to State, but swimming, for the fun of it, enjoys the highest level of participation.

Of the competitive sports (only a handful of swimmers take part in races) golf is probably the most popular, though every sport seems to claim a record of some sort for popularity. Golf has well over 400 000 active players and the advantage that you don't have to be fit. In countries like Japan it's a rich man's game, but here almost anyone can play. We have awesome inland deserts ulcerated by drought where red-dust storms engulf tiny outposts, we have a bigger snow area than Switzerland, and we have 20 000 kilometres of golden beaches — but our Japanese visitors

BRUCE PETTY — cartoonist with a conscience

Bruce Petty always loved drawing: he used to jam the back pages of his State school geography book with Bristol Blenheims and Gloster Gladiators, guns sticking out of every corner. He was living then in his family's yellow weatherboard home on a 12 hectare orchard at Doncaster, Melbourne; they've carved it up now. Bruce lives now in Paddington, Sydney, and he's still drawing.

It is his passion, his obsession, and his job as a weekly cartoonist with *The Age*. He gouges deeply into himself, pushing aside drawings as he spurns easy solutions.

He's always wrestling away at his desk until the last minute, scribbled rejects around him as he tries for a telling statement. A long way from the Box Hill High School and his first passion: Australian Rules.

'We used to bowl along to the Church of Christ every Sunday in a 28 Studebaker with yellow celluloid windows flapping,' he told me. 'I had no ambition, really, except sport . . .' His influences then were pretty standard: the local church, *Catcher in the Rye, Ulysses*, the Goons, a BSA 350, a Standard 12 coupe and girls, and he set out to make his name in Melbourne in 'a Bogart long white waterproof coat, with belt tabs and straps flying about'. He joined a tiny Melbourne firm, and did the lettering for amateur Kodak slides which people sent in, but his spelling was so bad 'they used to lose money over it'.

Well, Topolski and Daumier drawings eventually convinced him that Disney wasn't the ultimate answer, and the beggars in Colombo sparked off his social conscience when he sailed to London in 1953 for a six-year stay. He has drawn many times for *The New Yorker* and *Punch*, made a national reputation in *The Australian* and moved into film as well to project his convoluted insights, and his compassion.

His short animated film, titled *Leisure*, won an Oscar in 1977 ('Leisure's come to be regarded as what's left after work — maybe we should decide on the sort of leisure we want, and then decide on the amount of work necessary to achieve it'). But it's only one of a batch of films he's done — some fully-animated, some blends of drawings and live action — which range over Vietnam, the arts, money . . . This fleshy decade does not distract the patriarch (he's now over 50) of Australian post-war cartooning from dismantling the social machine to spotlight its increasing contradictions.

'The more complex and intelligent the community becomes on these contradictions, the more people want therapy rather than moral messages,' he said. 'I feel the same. But it's a bit of an evasion so I persist in trying to make coherent statements about tricky subjects, like the behaviour which power groups get away with, and the boring old distribution puzzle. You don't stop just because they are out of fashion. We trust the experts to solve these problems, and there's no real evidence that they are. The kids are the bright spots: academically, they mightn't be what we hoped, but they're aware of the system's frailties, and that could be healthy. That's all we have to go on — that they may be sharper than we were. Otherwise, I can't see any big new wave of philosophy sweeping the country . . .'

Left: **Bruce Petty, cartoonist;** *Above:* **Petty, by Petty. His biting cartoons question both the morality and indeed rationality of those who administer power in the major institutions of society — and prick the mass conscience.**

revere our golf courses above all, and always find time in a business trip for a few cheap games.

But golf is not leading by much. Skiers in the Snowy Mountains claim that skiing has risen from seventeenth to fourth in popularity among Australian sports, with at least 300 000 skiing enthusiasts flocking there every winter. Lawn bowls is as popular as it is sedate; almost half the world's bowlers are now Australians. In 1963 we had 150 000 of them; now there are more than 250 000 in more than 2 000 registered clubs. Britain, where Sir Francis Drake put bowls on the map, has only 126 000 bowlers and the United States a mere 6 000.

Organised junior sport has now turned thousands of parents into weekend chauffeurs for their children: football for the boys, netball for the girls. The more aggressive fathers of playing sons sometimes become so involved at games that they spark violence on the sidelines, and it appears that aggression has even permeated netball, with some fathers (and mothers) passing on to daughters rough tactics picked up from watching Rugby League on television.

Delegates at a government sponsored National Seminar on Leisure, held in Canberra, branded Sydney's Rugby League a dirty game and Melbourne's Australian Rules 'a social disease, not a sport ... Gladiators turning out for the weekend' (though, like professional boxing, it is obviously here to stay and is superb spectacle as well).

Boredom is perhaps a natural concomitant of the 'Lucky Country'. A militant pioneer nation, once radical, is now comfortable and fairly conservative, and life for the 'ordinary bloke' is probably more pleasant than in most other countries. In broad terms, the pursuit of leisure in Australia is not especially stimulating intellectually (a Chiko Roll and a cold tube of Resch's on Maroubra Beach are

Left: Long waits at the chairlift at Thredbo Village, one of several ski resorts in the Snowy Mountains. Up to 500 000 skiers a year make their way to the snowfields of New South Wales and Victoria to pursue this popular sport.

Above: This gentleman's paunch is a fine testament to conspicuous consumption. The unabashed pursuit by many Australians of Good Food and Good Drink, and/or 'lots of it', has become something of a cardiologist's nightmare.

Slumped against a parked car, a young girl cools her heels in the main street of Kings Cross, Sydney, on a Saturday night. Increasingly the young are pursuing their leisure activities in such neon-lit 'playgrounds'.

hardly demanding), but neither is it especially harmful. Much leisure time is spent out of doors in what is an essentially healthy climate, and that is all to the good. Blue water mariners abound. They may not all have the steel and whipcord bodies of my old friend Vic Rushby, but they feel good. And a few sets of tennis and 18 holes of golf never did anyone any harm.

But the 19th hole is one of Australia's biggest yet least known problems. Drinking is a popular pastime, and we're good at it (we hate being told that the Belgians drink more than we do). We've learned in recent years to drink and appreciate our own excellent wines, and a few cold beers with a few friends at a weekend out-of-doors barbecue can be the ultimate experience in civilised leisure.

On the other hand, more than 300 000 Australian workers take a 'sickie' every day to recover from hangovers and other effects of alcohol abuse. It's costing industry millions of dollars, and five per cent of the male population and one per cent of the women are on the road to alcoholism.

Australia also breaks world records for road deaths (heedless, aggressive and frequently drunken drivers piloting tomorrow's cars on yesterday's roads), and that is the black underside of leisure which needs massive national attention.

Teenage leisure presents its own problems. The causes are legion, but the generation gap, boredom, the unending quest for 'kicks', and the terrifying prospect of being shunned by one's peers ('Go on, Davo, I dare you...') coupled with the comfort of being 'one of the boys', are often contributing factors. Take Geelong in Victoria, where the co-author of a youth survey, Mr Dennis Challinger, a Melbourne University criminologist, says that one youth in five would resort to stealing 'if he really wanted something and the opportunity came to steal it without being caught'. He adds: 'The survey was designed to assist Geelong in planning facilities

---

TALBOT DUCKMANTON — the business of communicating

Sir Talbot Duckmanton became General Manager of the Australian Broadcasting Commission in the sixties — a solemn man (*too* solemn, radical staff-members were still complaining in the eighties) who puffed his pipe while storms burst around his head. But some employees have seen humour twinkling deep inside him — rather like that pen-picture of Rat peering bright-eyed from his dark burrow in *The Wind in the Willows*. One TV executive saw it when confessing that the staff of the now-defunct 'This Day Tonight' had christened their worm-motif Talbot. 'That's all right,' Sir Talbot said gravely. 'As long as you don't put a pipe in his mouth...'

He is a private man, tightly disciplined, his guard always up — although his life's work has been to channel pleasure (and information) to the masses. A broadcasting professional, he has worked with precision. 'I'm being facetious,' said the ABC's director of sporting broadcasts, Bernard Kerr, 'but I think it's a pity he went into the executive side — we lost a first-class sporting commentator. You have to control your emotions and give maximum concentration — it's a tremendous strain. He was always extremely accurate, and he maintained clarity of diction. He could paint a better picture of a 100 yards race in ten seconds than anyone I've ever heard...'

He drinks sparingly, and has eased the demands of his job — which is a little like walking a tightrope between opposing pressure groups — with Rugby-watching and swimming. Born in Melbourne in 1921, he joined the ABC as a cadet announcer in 1939 after leaving Newington College, Sydney, and then went off to the war, becoming an RAAF pilot. Later he covered many ceremonial occasions, including the Coronation in 1953, and he played a key role in establishing ABC television. A widower with four children, in 1979 he married Janet Strickland (now Lady Duckmanton), Australia's Chief Film Censor. They live in Sydney.

The philosophy of communications concerns him deeply, and he ranges through history for viewpoints — and looks ahead to the home of the future, plugged into a 12-channel cable bearing TV programmes, weather and stock exchange reports; channels on which residents will order the movie they want to see, the page of the library book they want to check. He is all for diversity within a nation, but also has long foreseen an Australia with transmitters linked (and a domestic satellite) so that all Australians can see the same picture at the same time. The prospect does not dismay him, nor does the technological achievement consume him with delight; he quotes G. K. Chesterton to emphasise his confidence in human ability to absorb huge new developments, and force them to fit into a human landscape.

Outwardly austere, he cherishes a special love for radio. 'Radio doesn't deserve to be patronised as a quaint curiosity, because radio didn't merely precede and influence television,' he said once. 'It was and still is a cultural medium in its own right, its somewhat restricted resources making unique demands on the imagination, but at the same time bringing with it unique rewards. No television studio can build sets to equal the wonderful constructions of the human mind.'

Going to the beach is almost a religious ritual for vast numbers of Australians —especially the city dwellers. In Sydney the dedicated beach-goer will drive for 40 kilometres or more, bumper to bumper on a sweltering day, just to 'get away from it all'.

Far left, top: For those who can afford it, Surfers Paradise, 80 kilometres south of Brisbane, is relatively uncrowded and a perfect mecca for jaded southerners intent on escaping the winter cold.

Centre top: The beaches are inhabited primarily by the young — of all ages.

Top: Surf society, Bondi.

Far left: Other fashion fads come and go, but the bikini just gets smaller.

Left: New Year's Day at Bondi Beach, Sydney.

Left: Not-quite-sure-about-it, yet with an expression of pure delight, this woman samples the joys of the giant slide at Sydney's Royal Easter Show.

Above: Like a mirage, this roadhouse appears at Sandfire — on a 650-kilometre stretch of road between Port Hedland and Broome in Western Australia.

for youth, and indicates that for many youths stealing amounts to a leisure time activity'.

There's always been teenage violence. The bodgies and the Teddy Boys fought it out with bicycle chains and razors on the wharves of Woolloomooloo back in the feisty fifties. Today, suburban dances often erupt in a brawl, a bloody clash between locals and 'blow-ins' looking for trouble. It's not endemic, but its worrying.

And what is more worrying than anything else — more worrying than the massive use of booze and drugs among today's young — is the grim fact of permanent youth-unemployment. This is the spectre behind the smiling face of Australian leisure: the thousands of out-of-work kids on the dole who spend their days sitting around; kids who have learned to get by without eating much as they drift on from one year to the next. For many of them, the haven of leisure becomes a prison from which they never escape.

The troubles and the heartbreaks are not peculiarly Australian, but their being symptomatic of a world-wide malaise doesn't make them any the more palatable.

I sit beside a couple of simple old dears in a tea-shop. They are discussing a close friend whose husband has just left her after 40 years of marriage. 'She rang me up,' says one. 'I was expecting her to tell me that God had called her old father home, see. It was the biggest shock of my life. I couldn't believe it — she has to go to work now, of course.' The enticements of modern Australian life had obviously got to the old bloke, but they took it in their stride. 'I don't ever remember better times for young people in the history of Australia — and the older people too,' says her friend. 'They're all catered for . . .'

Perhaps they are. We're eating better, drinking more, working less — fired by no national vision, seized with no corporate purpose other than to take it easy while we can. It isn't an admirable life we lead here, but no cruel destiny has overwhelmed us yet. Retribution burns faintly, far ahead, like a bushfire on the dark horizon. And the wind may change.

SPORT

Jim Shepherd

'... a new, quite discernible air of aggression ...'

M rs Ed Clark, the wife of a former American ambassador, once contributed a neat description of Australia's obsession with competition when she quipped, 'Living in Australia is like living in a gymnasium — there's always somebody practising something'.

Years later, that observation is still valid, but now something of an understatement following some tumultous years in the late seventies which helped change the face of Australian sport.

Commercialism, aggression ... and sport

Australia has entered the eighties still a vigorous sporting nation, but one preoccupied with the perfection of aggression as a necessary means of success and projecting a slightly fragmented image. Part reason for the fragmentation is traceable to the mid to late seventies, when tennis and swimming, traditional national sporting strengths, became so diminished as to be almost non-existent. Administrative revolutions in the same period resulted in the destruction of many traditions and cricket, for more than a century a last refuge from blatant commercialism, was transformed almost overnight into a gaudy circus by the establishment of media baron Kerry Packer's infamous World Series Cricket. Packer, frustrated in his bid to win television rights to Test cricket, did something which would have made his fearsome father, the late Sir Frank Packer, founder of the fabled Packer media and business empire, justly proud. Young Packer simply signed up whole teams of Australian, English and West Indian stars, wrapped them in coloured television tinsel and pitched them together in a semi-meaningless carnival he called 'World Series Cricket' before his National Nine network cameras.

In one costly and audacious move which will forever be justifiably recorded in the history of sports, Packer humbled the world cricket powers in the boardroom and in the courts. When some form of sanity finally prevailed and Packer obligingly allowed his players to return to legitimate Test cricket, he did it on his terms, retaining exclusive Australian television rights to the game and making the administrative bodies of cricket throughout the world appear childlike and foolish.

The Packer brand of aggression somehow spilled into other sports. National football administrators finally dropped the pretence that there would always be room

Left: **Mini rugby players waiting to be called onto the field at Palm Beach, near Sydney.**

for the four codes (Australian Rules, Rugby League, Rugby Union and soccer) and launched themselves into a gloves-off battle for national box-office supremacy. Television networks forgot old understandings and began massive bidding campaigns to obtain exclusive rights to major sports and, with passions unabated, turned to almost any sport that moved or made a noise when the bidding game ran too hot.

Champion Australian sportsmen and women and especially national sporting teams have always been aggressive — after the 1971-72 MCC tour of Australia, former English captain Ted Dexter wrote in *Wisden*, the Bible of cricket, that ... 'Under provocation ... Australians can, and do, quite readily and often in my experience, throw off all their 180 years of civilized nationhood; they gaily revive every prejudice they ever knew, whether to do with accent, class consciousness or even the original convict complex, and sally forth into battle with a dedication which would not disgrace the most committed of the world's political agitators'. And there is certainly nothing new about Australian sporting spectators being ultra biased and aggressive in their support of domestic heroes, a matter of fact probably best summed up by English Test fast bowler John Snow who once described Melbourne spectators as being ... 'like piranha fish when it comes to sport. They will devour anything that will satisfy their appetite for competition'.

But a new, quite discernible, air of aggression crept into sport during the seventies, mounted to towering heights at the beginning of the eighties and spilled from the arenas and playing fields, enveloping spectators and injecting them with a ferocious barracking venom that has no precedence.

Football matches, especially Rugby League in New South Wales and Queensland, plummeted to new troughs of brutality and coaching methods came under intense media scrutiny as the serious injury rate soared to record levels. The new 'killer instinct' aggression even appeared in the comparatively delicate game of soccer when imported German coach Rudi Gutendorf overnight turned the Australian national team from a squad of listless performers into a savage attacking side which literally flattened a long list of top overseas teams, humbled the famous New York Cosmos greats, out-roughed British champions Northern Ireland and gave a near-national British team an unexpected fright.

In so many other team sports, Australia rose to new heights. Even in men's basketball, traditionally the private domain of the United States, Cuba and Russia, the national team slugged their way through dozens of overseas countries and barely missed a bronze medal at the 1980 Moscow Olympics. The field hockey team, which first showed world class at the 1968 Mexico City Olympics, at one stage dominated the game and entered the eighties as the most feared team in the world. In the 'gentlemen's' football game, Rugby Union, Australian sides suddenly dispensed with decorum, out-played and out-fought former world champions Wales and the New Zealand All Blacks. Wales officials and sports writers were appalled at the carnage wreaked by Australia's forwards and described the local tactics as a 'disgrace to the game'. To Australian spectators, the dramatic victory was a monumental tribute to the superior 'manhood' of their heroes.

Australia boasts the best, almost invincible, Rugby League team in the small international sphere that embraces only England, France and New Zealand, some of the best rowing and ocean racing yacht crews in the world, often the best cricket team, world ranking women's softball and cricket sides and such great athletes in the peculiar-to-Australia game called Australian Rules football, that legendary player and coach Ron Barassi once assembled a team which he took to Ireland and beat the locals at their own game of Gaelic football.

Heroes, participants and spectators

Though individual successes in swimming have been sparse since 1974 and only Evonne Cawley has managed to bring any glory to Australian tennis with her win in the 1980 Wimbledon singles final, the new breed of super-psyched, brash and aggressive stars in a wide range of other sports have done the country proud. In 1980, cherubic-looking, grimly determined Melburnian Alan Jones became the first

Evonne Cawley for a time retired from international tennis to raise her two
children with husband Roger. Proudly quarter caste Aboriginal, she has won
many titles, including the French and Wimbledon Singles Championships in
1971, the Australian Singles Championships in 1975, 1976 and 1977; and
Wimbledon again in 1980. Evonne Cawley is returning to the circuit for
a second challenge.

Golf Club, which is strictly for a select group of members, and accommodation expansion at a number of major suburban football grounds. Incredibly, when one considers the population of Sydney and its towering (and inflated) overseas image as a sports centre, the city still does not boast sufficient facilities to stage a Commonwealth Games, let alone the Olympics and does not possess a multi-purpose indoor arena capable of accommodating 10 000-15 000 spectators. During the same period, Melbourne, self-acclaimed leading sports city, developed a contented cow attitude. With the establishment of the vast Football Park complex at Waverley

SIR JOHN BRABHAM – infatuated with mechanical power

The southern Sydney suburb of Hurstville slumbers in neat hectares of red-tiled brick bungalows, each surrounded by the traditional Australian square of neatly-clipped lawn, a haven of concrete garden gnomes, afternoon teas and corner grocers with white aprons.

When one reflects on the Hurstville preoccupation with community responsibility and the moulding of solid citizens, it comes as no real surprise to remember the area spawned Jack Brabham, three times winner of the World Racing Drivers Championship and without question, the suburb's finest sporting son.

There is still, despite years of exposure to the sophistication of the international sporting scene, a great deal of Hurstville respectability about Brabham.

He remains, honours ('Jack' Brabham gave way to Sir John Brabham in the 1979 New Year's Honours lists), wealth and fame notwithstanding, a happily married family man and without a trace of egotism about the feats which made him one of the most successful Australian sportsmen in history.

Brabham's father, Tom, was a Hurstville greengrocer who built up a flourishing business in the 1930s and probably visualised young Jack 'taking over the business' — a powerful parental incentive for hard work in those days. But for reasons young Jack still doesn't understand, the Brabham boy had an early and unquenchable interest in things mechanical.

The Brabhams pandered to this curious childish technical bent, even to the point where Jack was allowed to drive the old family Willys tourer around the spacious backyard when he was barely ten years of age. There was family disappointment — but no objections — when he asked permission to bypass the fruit and vegetable trade and enter an apprenticeship with Harry Ferguson, a local automotive engineer, who later remembered that . . . 'Jack was a good boy, not brilliant, but a good boy. One thing about him, he never gave me any lip . . .'

Brabham, then as now fiercely patriotic, joined the RAAF when he was 18, served almost three years with the ground crew and was discharged at 21 even more infatuated with mechanical power and the idea of owning his own Hurstville corner service station and garage.

And it may have happened, had not

Brabham met an American named Johnny Schonberg, who proposed an adventurous scheme involving a trip to Darwin to purchase two Army trucks, loading them with automotive spare parts and bringing the booty back for sale in a commodity-starved Sydney market. By an incredible fluke of timing, the pair arrived in Brisbane the same day speedway racing was revived at the Exhibition track and Schonberg, who had raced midget cars in the United States before the war, literally dragged a disinterested Brabham along to the circuit.

In his *Jack Brabham Motor Racing Book*, published in 1960, Brabham admits to being mildly terrified of the midget car action: 'Midget drivers, I thought, must be completely nuts!'. But when Schonberg, his old interest in midget racing reborn, decided to re-enter the sport, Brabham agreed to help build a racer, a tiny, shark-nosed creation which Brabham lovingly grafted together from Army disposals bits and pieces and components taken from an old Amilcar, a Morris Cowley, a Harley-Davidson and a speedway J.A.P. motorcycle engine. When Schonberg's brief infatuation waned, Brabham, with a sizeable investment in the $800 creation, decided to try his hand. He was almost 22. His only association with motor sport was the handful of meetings in which Schonberg had competed.

Among the hard-drinking, chain-smoking speedway driver brigade, Brabham looked exactly what he was: a shy and courteous youngster from a moderately well-to-do suburb with more interest in mechanical engineering than in establishing himself as a Saturday night hero at the Sydney Showground speedway.

But Brabham, much to his own astonishment, was a natural speedway driver with reflexes which steered him clear of crash situations and on to a dozen State and national championships between 1948 and 1951.

But speedway was basically an arena for drivers with heavy right feet. Brabham was eager to explore the mechanical intricacies of legitimate racing at Sydney's old Mt Druitt circuit and perhaps even the road racing headquarters — Mt Panorama at Bathurst.

Equipment was hard to obtain, so Brabham tried his hand in the speedway midget, creating a minor controversy by almost immediately winning the Australian Hill Climb Championship at Rob Roy. He fluked the pur-

and the existence of the rather outdated, but practical Melbourne Cricket Ground, surrounded by a brace of well-appointed racecourses and tennis and golf locations, there seemed little point in splurging any more money. Until, that is, Melbourne heard that Sydney was no longer interested in pursuing the 1988 Olympic Games and announced a grandiose series of plans to update that stadium, raze that one and generally tart up the city to prove, as if it were really necessary, that having already staged the 1956 Olympics, it could do so again.

Melbourne is, of course, the unchallenged sports centre of Australia. On a per

chase of a solid little Cooper Mk IV rear-engine racing car, and so impressed the late Reg Shepheard, then Managing Director of the Redex Oil Company, that Shepheard helped him import a brand-new Cooper Bristol racing car in which he became almost unbeatable on local circuits and good enough to lead home many well-known internationals in New Zealand events.

In 1955, Brabham, in formal Hurstville fashion, explained to his wife Betty that he must explore motor racing and either get it out of his system or establish himself overseas. The Cooper Bristol was sold and Brabham flew to England with modest capital and only a dream: he would give himself eight months to succeed in the heady whirl of English and European racing and then make his decision about the future.

The trip was almost a disaster. He could not purchase a competitive car, was unable to attract the interest of works teams and ended the eight months in the workshop run by the small racing car manufacturer John Cooper. He made no money, but he built a car on which much of the future of the Cooper factory was to be based — a revolutionary, rear-engined Cooper Bristol sports car which John Cooper allowed him to bring back to Australia.

Brabham duly won the 1955 Australian Grand Prix at Port Wakefield and returned to England in 1956, this time with his wife. John Cooper put him on the payroll, more as a designer and builder than driver, but with the promise of regular competition.

By 1957, Cooper took him away from drawing boards and put him into the Cooper racing team as No. 2 driver to Roy Salvadori. In 1958, Brabham, known to European motor racing fans as the 'Quiet Australian', was No. 1 Cooper driver. In 1959 he became, almost unobtrusively, World Champion. The brilliant Stirling Moss had to play second fiddle to an Australian who had seen his first road race less than eight years previously.

It was the beginning of everything: his own garage in Chessington, a large house near the Cooper factory, a Cessna 180 to fly to Grand Prix engagements. In 1960 he was World Champion again with an incredible five Grand Prix wins in a row. In 1961, he brought a Sydney engineering associate, Ron Tauranac, to England to help him do something no other driver in history had dared — build and race his own Grand Prix racers.

To add the final miracle touch, Brabham

began to use Australian-made Repco components. The mighty factories of Ferrari, Porsche, Honda, BRM and the substantial works of Lotus and Cooper were more than a little taken aback by the audacity of the Australian teetotaller. And especially in 1966, when Brabham again won the World Championship, this time driving a Brabham F1 powered by an Australian Repco V8 engine.

It was the first time in motor racing history that a driver had won the World Championship in a car he designed and constructed himself. Ferrari especially was shattered — then heart-broken when Brabham's No. 2 driver, Dennis Hulme of New Zealand, won the World Championship in 1967 with boss Brabham finishing runner-up. Two all-Australian cars had whipped the best-known Grand Prix works teams!

In 16 years of Grand Prix racing, Brabham lived with tragedy and incredible strain. Champion drivers like Jim Clark, Peter Collins, Jean Behra, Ivor Bueb, Jochen Rindt, Piers Courage, Ricardo Rodriguez, Count von Trips, the Marquis de Portago and many more, had been killed. Brabham was the oldest Grand Prix driver in the most lethal sport in the world. It was clearly time to quit.

In 1971, in his normal quiet manner, Brabham sold his Brabham construction company and other English business enterprises, returned to Australia and invested in a vast complex of commercial pursuits. The Hurstville boy who entered motor sport by building a backyard speedway midget and graduated to designing a Grand Prix car which for at least two years was the best in the world, had made his mark and his fortune. He could do little more.

Australians will continue to win Olympic gold medals and world championships. Their feats, no matter how brilliant at the time, will remain only passing chapters in international sport. Brabham took on the might and wealth of giant overseas companies — many of them, like Ferrari, heavily backed by government subsidies — and was victorious. There isn't a man in the world capable of emulating his success.

Not even his eldest son, Geoffrey, who began racing in the mid-seventies and who is now a heavily sponsored, full-time professional racer in the United States. Geoffrey, good as he is, will tell you Dad was the greatest.

The former assertion — that Australians are a race of lazy spectators — is a massive untruth. The promotional battle between football codes has resulted in a massive upswing in the number of males from seven years onwards playing football and, with the majority playing soccer, it is little wonder rival codes sometimes fear for their future. More people now play squash, lawn bowls, softball, or surf and sail competitively than any other nation in the world on a per capita basis. The number of men playing cricket in the summer of 1979-80 represented an increase of almost five per cent over the previous season and similar increases apply to basketball and baseball and even swimming, despite the dramatic downturn in Australian performances on the international front. In competitive surfing, Australia is easily the most active nation and marked increases in participation have been recorded in weight lifting, judo and karate, equestrian sports and cycling.

It would hardly be normal if some sports did not suffer. Boom sports such as motor racing and speedway racing, big national attractions in the early seventies, lost pace near the end of the decade, for reasons ranging from sameness of fare to the fact that traditional heavy sponsorship fell away in the period and forced out many competitors. Professional boxing, a television prime time attraction up until the beginning of the seventies, suddenly folded as if felled by a Muhammed Ali right hand. Boxing has been through similar situations many times before and always for the same reasons. When the glamour champions retire or are knocked from their pedestal, the profession always goes into recession. In this case, only one fighter, middleweight and light-heavyweight champion Tony Mundine, remained somewhere near the top after the retirement of world champions Lionel Rose and Johnny Famechon. When Mundine flopped in his quest for a world title, interest in boxing flopped with him and not even the rise of Italian-born Rocky Mattioli of Melbourne could stop the rot, especially when Mattioli left Australia to live overseas. Mattioli finally won the world junior middleweight title, made one defence in Melbourne and drew a sizeable crowd, but then left the country for good. The ups and downs of professional boxing in Australia have little to do with the state of the economy and the need for young men to earn money with their fists. Boxing will return, flooded with hard-fisted young hopefuls as soon as at least two domestic fighters — like Rose and Famechon — put some colour back into the sport and, most important, prove they can mix it with the best in the world.

The lack of class, colour and aggression which helped kill off boxing, at least for the time being, has been completely reversed in horse racing, indisputably the nation's most popular spectator sport. Never, in its long history, has racing been *more* popular, nor populated by as many charismatic and ultra-aggressive jockeys and trainers. Never has there been as much media coverage, sponsorship, prizemoney or high-powered marketing and promotion. All the factors fairly naturally resulted in the betting activities of the population soaring to such heights that it became difficult to remember Australia was suffering unemployment and inflationary problems. And perhaps even more interesting, it resulted in a brand new diversion for the racing enthusiast — becoming involved in the syndicate leasing of thoroughbreds. In 1978, Bob Lilley, the registrar of racehorses, approved names for 12 887. In 1979, the registration figure jumped a massive 34.4 per cent to 17 310, a huge number of the horses leased by as many as five enthusiasts, all hoping they have temporary ownership of a champion like Manikato, sold as a yearling for $3 500 and by early 1980, prince of Australia's stake earners with a record $638 910.

The syndicate leasing plan is unique to Australia. But then, nearly everything that happens in Australian racing is unique. Betting has always been on a scale that is mind-boggling to American, British and French racegoers and there has never been any shortage of bookmakers prepared to accept massive risks. Terry Page, the king of the Sydney rings, proved that in April, 1980 when he became the first bookmaker to reach a turnover of $1 million for a day's racing in Sydney. Page that day accepted a bet of $100 000 from another bookmaker, Mark Read of Melbourne, and gave Read odds of 2/1 about Dark Eclipse, therefore risking a $200 000 loss on a single bet. Dark Eclipse finished second and just to prove he was a man of action, Page tried unsuccessfully to challenge another big punter to place a bet which, if successful, would have lost Page $500 000. To American visitors that day at Randwick would have resulted in some surprises. The only form

Above; **Sydney racing identity, Theo Green — horse trainer, trainer of jockeys and surrogate father to his apprentices — times an early morning run. Once a boxer, he is responsible for the success of such outstanding jockeys as Malcolm Johnston, Sid Spinks and Ron Quinton.**

Right: **Jack Cassidy, bookie, will lay you odds on almost anything, and follows the races from city to country town. His is a familiar face in a game in which the names of top thoroughbreds and jockeys are better known than those of most politicians.**

of betting on American racecourses is with the totalisator. On Australian tracks, the punter has the choice of the tote or the bookmakers. Page and two other book-makers, Bob Blann and Bill Waterhouse, collectively turned over more than $2 400 000 — more than the on-course tote!

There seems no end to the money flow in horse racing. Early in 1980, a Showdown-Vain Queen filly was sold for an Australasian yearling sale record price of $250 000 and the total outlayed at the same three day sale reached a record $4 479 715. With prizemoney for the nation's greatest race, the Melbourne Cup, now well in excess of $300 000 and dozens of other major races carrying in excess of $130 000, little wonder that the racing industry is booming, jockeys becoming mini-millionaires and the successful and luckier trainers and owners joining them in the rush to re-invest in the most buoyant sporting industry the country has known.

With the racing industry still Australia's most publicised sport, it stands to reason that the principal performers, jockeys like Malcolm Johnston, Ron Quinton, Wayne Harris, Peter Cook, Roy Higgins, Johnny Miller, John Duggan and John Letts and glamour trainers such as Bart Cummings, Tommy Smith, Neville Begg and Colin Hayes stand unchallenged as the best-known men in sport. Johnston particularly is the idol of racegoers, a handsome, quick-witted charmer off the course and a courageous daredevil in the saddle. Comparisons to former greats are impossible,

347

but Johnston proved his brilliance in 1979 by out-riding American Steve Cauthen, reputedly the world's greatest rider, at a special international meeting in Perth, Western Australia. Unlike most countries in the world, a popular and successful Australian jockey need not necessarily restrict himself to the industry after retiring from race riding. Many have been invited into a wide variety of commercial business enterprises and one, Melbourne's Peter Bakos, gained nomination to stand for a seat in the 1980 federal elections.

Something which has remained static in an era of massive change, is the fierce rivalry existing between Australia's States. The flames have been fanned by the establishment of Australia's first national soccer league competition in which teams from all States except Tasmania and Western Australia compete, the attempts by the Victorian Football League to establish Australian Rules football in Sydney and the blatant stealing of star cricketers to strengthen State teams involved in the Sheffield Shield competition. Queensland Rugby Union enthusiasts, fired by success of the State side, even resorted to placing newspaper advertising prior to an annual clash with the New South Wales side which openly encouraged home State supporters to help 'bury' the opposition. And such is the home State patriotism in

DAWN FRASER — a swimming legend

If you choose to live in the Sydney suburb of Balmain, you will automatically be required to follow some essential ground rules:

Only one Rugby Leage football team — the Balmain Tigers — is of any real importance. You must appreciate the historical importance of the area (Balmain is steeped in early Sydney history).

Only one of the district's female sports stars, the legendary Dawn Fraser, can be mentioned in the same breath as any of the great male sports heroes spawned by the waterfront suburb.

No accolade for a sports woman could be higher. In Balmain the pub count is higher than in any other square kilometre of Australia, male dominance of household affairs is almost frightening, and the Balmain Tigers are not simply footballers but demigods in what is still largely a commune of dock workers, wharf labourers and steel workers. Women's Liberation has been ignored in Balmain.

But the Balmainites even named the public baths after Dawn Fraser, a towering tribute when one considers that Balmain Tigers superstars like Keith Barnes, Joe Jorgenson, Pat Devery and Billy Marsh have yet to accede to even a humble back lane title.

There is ample reason for the unprecedented recognition of Dawn. She is, after all, as any seasoned Balmain pub drinker will tell you, 'one of the boys', a description which is not in any way a reflection on her femininity but rather the ultimate tribute to her sporting prowess and the manner in which she remained, even when universally recognised as the greatest woman sports star of the century, a true-blue Tiger.

Dawn Fraser is now in her early forties. She has an unsuccessful marriage behind her, a teenage daughter, she's been awarded the MBE for services to swimming and she's been immortalised by having her life story recorded in the feature movie *Dawn!*, released in 1979.

Dawn, true to character, insisted nothing be omitted from the script — even some revealing sides to her past private life.

Ironically, *Dawn!*, warts and all, proved a box office flop. Dawn shrugged off the slight embarrassment. For at long last she's found true happiness.

In 1979, she obtained the lease on her favourite Balmain pub, the Riverview Hotel, where she first acquired the taste for beer. Now, as Mine Host of the tiny, tucked-away Riverview, Dawn has finally found her true niche in Balmain.

It was in this suburb that she learned her first lessons about life as the youngest of eight children, a sickly child hindered by anaemia and chest complaints. Working long hours in a small Balmain tenement after school she helped her parents with cooking, sewing, and making her own clothes. At 14, Dawn admits, she was on the verge of delinquency and even her swimming career, such as it was in those days, started on the wrong basis.

Dawn first swam competitively with the Balmain League Swimming Club, a professional organisation. When local coach Harry Gallagher recognised her undeveloped talent, an official clearance from the Australian Amateur Swimming Union was necessary before Dawn could pursue a course towards Olympic representation.

It is almost inconceivable, when one remembers the sub-teenage trend of modern swimming, that Dawn Fraser did not seriously devote herself to top level training and competition until she was almost 17 — an age which most modern girl champions including the mercurial Shane Gould, believe is the end of the competitive road. A year later, Dawn churned her way into the 1956 Australian Olympic team and into the first stage of her national and, later, international superstar phase.

In Melbourne in 1956, she won the Olym-

Rugby League, that the single most successful promotion in the 1980 winter season was the staging in Brisbane of a unique 'State of Origin' match in which Queensland players attached to Sydney clubs were brought back into the State for the occasion and pitted against a select New South Wales-born team. Queensland won the game, played with frightening vigour, even though many of the ex-Queenslanders were pitted against their own Sydney clubmates.

This match, like all major Rugby League games, was widely televised, amid the usual cries of dismay from parent groups and educationalists who have long deplored the open violence that has become the norm in so many Australian team sports. In the football season, newspapers are usually crammed with letters from irate parents protesting about the dangers of allowing their children to watch the week-end bloodbaths. Their fears are hardly exaggerated. School Rugby and Australian Rules matches have become far more rugged as youngsters aspire to emulate their senior heroes — and every schoolboy cricketer wants to become as fearsome a fast bowler as Dennis Lillee or Jeff Thomson or as aggressive a batsman as Greg Chappell. The defence has long argued that nothing has really changed, that in bygone years, schoolboy cricketers and footballers all strove to be Don Bradman

pic 100 metres freestyle, finished second to Lorraine Crapp in the 400 metres and helped Australia win the relay. Suddenly, Dawn had arrived — a crew-cut, cheeky-faced water urchin who had (all too clearly) far less formal education than her teammates but who carried off the speechmaking with a confident freshness.

Earlier, Dawn had moved into the headlines, but 1956 was the beginning of a swimming era which even the record-breaking span of Shane Gould never really approached. After Melbourne, Dawn broke world records in all sprint distances with monotonous ease, won two gold and two silver medals at the 1958 Cardiff Commonwealth Games, and set herself for the defence of her Olympic 100 metres freestyle title at Rome in 1960.

Although plagued by a stomach upset, she retained her title, became the first woman in history to win two successive gold medals in the same event — and landed in her first real batch of trouble.

The drama started with Dawn bucking authority and wearing her favourite white tracksuit instead of the official team outfit and ended with her refusing to swim in the medley relay (she was ill) and slapping the face of teammate Jan Andrew. She was sent to Coventry by her teammates, omitted from Australian teams touring Japan, South Africa and New Zealand, and became the subject of some extraordinary rumours about other matters alleged to have occurred in Rome.

In 1961, still the best sprinter in the world, she crashed the headlines again — by refusing an invitation to join the Australian Republican Party (she claimed it was anti-Royalist), and by spending an hour in the Adelaide City Watchhouse following a minor traffic offence involving a car in which she was a passenger; police later apologised and no charges were laid.

In 1962 Dawn achieved her prime ambition, becoming the first woman to break a minute for 110 yards (59.9 secs), a feat not loosely described as the greatest sporting achievement of the century.

But more was to come.

In 1962, at the Perth Commonwealth Games she won four gold medals and lowered her 110 yards time to 59.5 secs. Nevertheless, it seemed impossible that Dawn, then aged almost 27, could remain on top and achieve the improbable — a third successive gold medal in the Olympic 100 metres freestyle to be contested at Tokyo in 1964.

A few months before the Olympics, Dawn was involved in a tragic accident: the car she was driving crashed on General Holmes Drive near Sydney Airport, killing her mother and leaving Dawn with a chipped vertebra in her neck. Dawn decided, on recovering, to pursue that third gold.

That she did it — clocking 59.5 secs after a titanic duel with 15-year-old American Sharon Stouder — is history. So, too, is another brush with officialdom.

She defied orders and marched in the opening ceremony, and later took part in a light-hearted but foolish escapade in which a flag was souvenired from the Emperor's Palace.

The ASU suspended her for ten years (the suspension was lifted four years later), but higher powers than the ASU considered her swimming achievements more important and she was awarded the MBE.

Dawn retired from competitive swimming as the greatest woman athlete of her time and (although all her world records have long since been broken) is still the greatest woman swimmer the world has seen.

Out Balmain way, where Dawn is the best-known publican, nobody wants to know about Shane Gould, Michelle Ford or Tracey Wickham. Shane, after all, called it quits before she turned 17 after only one Olympic Games (Munich, 1972). Dawn went to three Olympics, came home with four gold medals and that never-to-be-bettered record of three successive wins in the 100 metres freestyle.

or Ray Lindwall, Clive Churchill or John Coleman, completely overlooking the fact that television did not exist in that era. There is, sadly, an unmistakable air of youthful over-aggression creeping into far too many sports and an increasing number of schools dropping Rugby football codes from their sports programmes in favour of soccer.

The television entrepreneurs have never bothered to argue that they prefer 'tough' sports. The top-rating sports have always been Australian Rules and Rugby League football, cricket — interestingly, ratings invariably jump when Australia is *bowling* and Messrs Lillee, Pascoe, Walker or Thomson hurling down their thunderbolts, as distinct to Australia batting — boxing and motor racing. Soccer, far less a body contact game than Rugby, has yet to make noticeable inroads on the ratings system; snooker, after a brief burst of popularity, has waned; golf, no matter who is playing, has never set any ratings records and tennis, though a huge rating attraction during the annual Australian Open championship, has too short a television season to be seriously stacked against football and cricket.

The future

What does the future hold for Australian sport?

Undoubtedly success in new areas such as basketball, dramatic international strides in long-established sports like soccer and continued success in the other three football codes and cricket. Doubtless there will be a continuing stream of golfers reaching the heights and, now that Alan Jones has exploded the myth of European supremacy in Grand Prix motor racing, more Australians will follow in his wake. The aggression kick doubtless will spread even further and though the purists will mumble, it could possibly be a rewarding long-term theme within the national sporting framework. For a heavy injection of good old fashioned Aussie 'aggro' might well be the antidote for the crippling malaise affecting tennis, track and field, and swimming. All these sports are playgrounds for talented performers lacking killer instinct and, in far too many cases, the necessary dedication.

If the miracle occurs and Australia claws its way back to the top in tennis and swimming and at least improves in track and field, the little country Down Under will be back where it was in the mid-1950s — the greatest per capita sporting nation on earth.

Left: **No holds are barred in this Rugby League match between Eastern Suburbs and St George.**

Right: **Each year, on the first weekend in August, up to 25 000 people assemble at Sydney's Town Hall to participate in a 14 kilometres run — the 'Sun City to Surf'.**

FOREIGN RELATIONS

Alan Renouf

'...foreign policy has been dominated by a perceived need for assurance about security...'

T he relations of one country with another are the product of the interplay of the respective foreign policies. For almost the first 40 years of its independence, Australia did not have a foreign policy of its own, being largely content to follow the leadership of the mother country, Britain. By 1939, circumstances beyond Australia's control had led to the realisation that the long and comfortable period of following Britain had come to an end and that Australia had to devise a separate foreign policy.

The task, it was then found, was by no means easy and even now, 40 years later, Australia gropes uncertainly towards its relations abroad. For one thing, it proved hard to break the habit of reliance upon another. More importantly, the formulation of Australian foreign policy is difficult, probably uniquely difficult. A number of circumstances explain this, notably, the indefensibility of Australia by purely national means.

The conclusion of indefensibility arises mainly from a number of factors which are either immutable or mutable only over a lengthy time. The country is a continent, the sole continent which contains only one sovereign state. While Australia is the smallest of the continents, it is a large country, almost as big as the United States less Alaska. It has some 28 900 kilometres of coastline providing easy access for an invader. It has very few mountains, being extraordinarily flat. Rivers are rare. True, the continent has distance as a defence-aid. However, as distinct from the classic example of Russia, where distance has been used for defence against invasion, the more one penetrates into Australia, the less one finds and before long, there is desert. Distance as a defence is therefore not of much use in Australia's case.

The population of this old and grey continent is very small (absolutely and in relation to size) with 14.6 million people (less than one half of the kangaroo inhabitants), and a current rate of growth close to zero. Moreover, the great mass of the population is clustered in six cities, with about 40 per cent in only two of them. Contrary to popular myth overseas of a country of farmers, Australia is highly

353

Left: **Defending the harbour in play, from derelict defences at Darwin.**

urbanised. All of its major cities are on the coastline, very vulnerable to attack from without. What is more, the national industrial base is centred around these same cities.

To make matters worse, Australia is isolated from its natural friends, the Western democracies of Europe and North America, with whom it has deep ties flowing from history, culture and economic interests and upon whom Australia largely depends for trade, investment and technology. To these countries, Australia is the other end of the earth. Australia has no real military tradition, although it has often been involved in war. Its people have never known war within their own continent (Darwin was heavily bombed in World War II but for most Australians, Darwin is very far away). Those who have had the first hand experience of war are scant. Except in time of world war, the national defence forces have never been strong. Even if they were much stronger, they alone could not ensure the defence of the continent.

Quest for security

Australia is a rich country, replete with natural resources and enjoying a high standard of living. Given this, given its indefensibility, given its isolation, Australia has nearly always felt insecure. In the past, the source of fear was usually, but not constantly, Asia, the 'Yellow Peril', that is, the hordes from Asia who would descend upon the continent. This led to the iniquitous 'White Australia' policy, thankfully now buried. However, even if the fear of invasion from Asia has receded, the feeling of insecurity is still endemic in Australia, Russia being the latest in the succession of those countries which since the 1890s have been regarded as having designs upon Australia.

In these circumstances, it is not surprising that throughout its existence as an independent country, the foreign policy of Australia has been dominated by a perceived need for assurance about security. Such a need must be the predominant objective of any country's foreign policy but in Australia's case, it has become, in most times, almost an obsession. This near-obsession explains Australia's relations with other countries in nearly all the past; it explains those relations today, in major degree.

Australia has consistently sought to ensure its security in three complementary ways, with each government in turn varying the degree of emphasis placed upon one or the other. The first way, the internationalist, has been to behave in its foreign relations in the fashion that Australians believe a democratic and responsible country should behave. This is to join in and support, by arms if necessary, concerted efforts to preserve peace throughout the world, including efforts in the economic and social fields designed to remove the causes of war. Hence, Australia made major contributions in the two world wars and fought in both the Korean and Vietnam Wars, in the latter as the only ally of America, apart from New Zealand, which paid its own way. Hence, too, Australia has been a firm supporter of arrangements to preserve the peace in Asia and the Pacific, such as the ANZUS Pact. Hence, also, Australia has been, at most times, a serious participant in the United Nations and its multiplicity of organisations (dealing for example with health, education, labour conditions) and has invariably been keen upon maintaining its membership of the British Commonwealth of Nations. Hence, finally, Australia has been a leading donor of aid to developing countries, especially those in its region.

The second method of foreign policy is the lingering pattern of being a follower. With the post-1945 progressive decline of Britain's power, Australia turned naturally to the other major Anglo-Saxon nation, the United States, which had been its great protector in World War II. Thereafter, upon Australia's initiative, ties with the United States were gradually built up to a pitch of intimacy, so much so that Australia has become one of the staunchest allies of America. In seeking to develop its relations with the United States, Australia had a motive additional to that of protection. This flowed from the fact that a great deal of the capital needed for economic development could not be found nationally, nor could the modern technology. The United States was the best source for both. Accordingly, Australia has followed successfully, for most of the period 1950-82, a policy of wooing the American investor.

Traditional diplomacy is the third way in which Australia has sought to build up its connections. This is the cultivation of contacts, and, hopefully, friendship with others, the normal first step being the setting up of diplomatic relations. Until 1939, with reliance upon Britain, Australia saw little need for this kind of activity, as shown by the fact that until then, it had representation abroad in only one place, London. However, from that year, Australia embarked upon a programme, which is still continuing, of beginning official ties with other countries. As of 1981, there were few countries with which Australia did not have representation of one kind or another. A priority area for this activity in the aftermath of World War II was Asia. Prior to 1939, Australia saw no need to take much notice of Asia (except Japan), as the part of the region closest to Australia consisted mostly of the colonies of friends. The end of the war quickly saw the transformation of the whole area into one of independent states with whom friendly relations were, for Australia, a requirement. An intense policy in this direction was then commenced and while political and economic fragility was common in South-East Asia, this was especially effective. Further to the north, it did not take Australia long to cast off the bitterness with which its people had regarded Japan's conduct in the war. From 1954, Australia set about building up relations with Japan and this effort paid handsome dividends.

Over the span of 40 years in which Australia has used these three methods in its foreign relations, internationalism, reliance upon another and broad bilateralism, there are four distinct periods. The first, 1941–49, was that in which the adolescent habit of following Britain was abandoned and Australia became assertive, even combative, in making its voice heard. This was the time when a purely indigenous foreign policy was first formulated; it was also the time when Australia was most internationalist. While the new approach occasionally caused displeasure in Britain and the United States (and greater displeasure in Russia after 1945), it won applause elsewhere and put Australia for the first time on the international map. In view of Australia's past quiescence, in view of its outstanding effort in World War II, the assertiveness was not unnatural, even if the manner of assertion was sometimes less than polite.

The second period, 1950–72, was featured more strongly by fear about security than at any previous time of peace. The fear was of Communism, as represented by the alliance between Russia and China formed in 1949; Australia was apprehensive that these Communist allies were determined to sweep down through Asia and ultimately to conquer Australia itself (the Domino Theory). To meet this assumed menace, Australia sought the protection of the United States, this being the principal reason for the development of relations with that country at the time. The policy of 'Forward Defence' was also invented, the notion being that the threat from the north should be met and countered in the north, as far away from Australia as possible. Accordingly, Australia joined the South-East Asia Treaty Organization (SEATO), entered, with Britain and New Zealand, into arrangements to help defend Malaysia and Singapore and fought in the Vietnam War. Concurrently, Australia set about establishing and improving its ties with Asian countries and extending to them economic and some military assistance.

The problem with the foreign policy of this long stretch of 23 years was that whereas on its initiation, the start of the Cold War, and while the Cold War continued, there was a plausible case in its favour, Australia gradually grew more and more unable to appreciate the great changes that were occurring in the world and therefore failed to effect the necessary changes in policy. Indeed, from 1954, Australia's conduct of its foreign relations was remarkably rigid and the crowning criterion became simply to back the United States loyally, that is, unquestioningly. It was believed in those days that this slavish following of the United States lead was the best way to ensure that that country would defend Australia should Australia in the future need defending. Such thinking was seriously flawed, for what causes one country to defend another is not professed friendship but what the protector assesses as the requirements of its own national interests. Furthermore, there were great costs for Australia in this policy of unswerving fealty. For one thing,

Prime Minister Malcolm Fraser calls on the British Prime Minister, Margaret Thatcher, for talks on the Russian invasion of Afghanistan in 1980.

the national reputation suffered, Australia coming to be regarded in some quarters as simply a client-state of the United States. For another, Australia unconsciously abandoned the capacity to think and plan policy independently in the pursuit of its own distinctive national interests. Finally, Australia relegated itself to the position where it was not informed properly (let alone consulted properly) by the United States. One result was that when the United States decided to establish relations with China, Australia, which had faithfully since 1951 simply echoed America's China 'line', was left in the dark. It is fair to say that at the end of this period of 23 years, Australia's foreign policy was bankrupt.

Towards an independent stance

There ensued a brief phase of long overdue enlightenment, 1972–75. In these years, the shackles of the past were cast off and foreign policy was thoroughly overhauled and brought into line with realities in the world. Shades of the wide internationalism of 1941–49 were then seen again; for example, much more importance was attached to the United Nations. But the principal thrust was to reduce the degree of reliance upon the United States (while preserving close ties with it), to attenuate the ideological (the non-Communist) content of policy and both to extend the range of relations abroad and deepen those already in existence. A few of the many illustrations were the opening of diplomatic relations with China, with the German

---

DR HERBERT VERE EVATT — Foreign Minister 1941-1949

Of all Australia's Prime Ministers and Foreign Ministers, no one has done more to establish Australia as a distinctive member of the international community than Dr H.V. Evatt (1894–1965). Even now, 30 years after the end of his control of foreign relations, it is Evatt whom foreigners most readily recall when they think of Australia's place in the world. Evatt is not always remembered by them with favour for he was, at times, abrasive and given to larrikinism, but there are few who would not agree that it was he who first made other countries take notice of Australia, most of them respectfully.

Evatt did this in two ways. First, while he was Foreign Minister (1941–1949), Australia asserted a much greater independence than before in its conduct of foreign relations. This is not to say that Australia then abandoned its historical association with Britain or turned its back upon its other major ally, the United States, for Evatt was strongly attached both to the British Commonwealth of Nations and to the United States. It is to say rather that Australia became more conscious that it had national interests which might be uniquely distinctive and which might sometimes suggest directions different from those taken by friends, and that power did not have a monopoly of wisdom and even a smaller country, like Australia, was capable of views worthy of consideration.

The other way in which Evatt made a notable impact for Australia was his insistence upon justice. Always a great fighter for the underdog in Australia, once Evatt turned his attention to foreign affairs, he became a great fighter for justice internationally, not only for Australia, but also for all countries and peoples. Evatt believed that principle, not power, should be the main regulator of affairs between nations. Some have criticised him on this score, contending that had Evatt had a better knowledge of history, he would have realised his approach was Utopian. To such critics, Evatt would have replied that he knew the role of power but he did not accept that power should be primordial; mankind had to try to do better.

Evatt was such a complex personality that he remains to this day a figure of controversy within Australia; it is a measure of the man that he aroused, and continues to arouse, either marked affection or marked distaste. Christened 'the Red Judge' when upon the High Court, so too when Foreign Minister he was accused by his opponents of being sympathetic to Communists. Yet the record shows that of all Western leaders of the period 1945–1949 when the Cold War started, none resisted the U.S.S.R. more strongly than Evatt whenever that country behaved badly. In fact, Evatt detested political extremism of left or right, being at heart simply a liberal democrat.

The pinnacle of Evatt's success as Foreign Minister was his work at the 1945 San Francisco Conference which finalised the Charter of the United Nations. This was a constitutional convention and at it, Evatt, the brilliant lawyer out for justice, shone. But the sheer virtuoso character of his performance then misled him later. Evatt revealed thereafter an unshakeable faith in the United Nations, a faith which, with the passage of time, became less and less warranted and increasingly unreal. Appropriately, Evatt's last foreign affairs speech in the Commonwealth Parliament in October, 1959, consisted of a plaintive plea that the West, with Australia's help, was destroying the United Nations Charter. Legally, Evatt was right, politically, he was wrong. But, after all, justice was always what Evatt had been all about.

Democratic Republic and with Vietnam, the official termination of the 'White Australia' policy and the beginning of a more intense involvement in South Pacific affairs. More generally, Australia at the time shrugged off the fear-syndrome and became more adult and self-assured. In so doing, it recognised that the emergence of four great centres of power in North Asia (the United States, Russia, China and Japan), in the place of the former bipolarity, enhanced Australia's security prospects and that these were further improved by the fact that the countries of South-East Asia, had, individually and collectively, become stronger.

The fourth and current period of Australia's foreign relations began in 1976. The pattern of the period is strange for there is a mixture of elements of the phases of the past, of novel elements as well as inconsistencies. As in the period 1941–49, Australia is now quite often aggressively, even offensively, assertive, with its closest friends, Western European countries and the United States, being the targets. The play of the internationalist factor is again evident but the emphasis has shifted back to co-operation with great friends rather than with the international community as represented by the United Nations. A lot of the policies initiated in the years 1972–75 have been carried on unchanged, a good example being the relationship with China. Major emphasis has been put upon cultivating the friendship of developing countries around the world yet Australia has done nothing more for them than talk and criticise those whom the developing countries see as their opponents, namely, the more well-to-do. These are also Australia's closest friends! Paradoxically, Australia criticises them trenchantly for maintaining an over-degree of protection of their markets while itself being the most protectionist of the developed countries, except New Zealand. In a marked throw-back to the past, Australia's traditional worry about its security has returned to fashion, with Russia now presenting the threat, or so it is thought. In familiar fashion, Australia has turned once again to the United States for protection, thereby resuming the risk, made so credible by former experience, of over-reliance and of over-identification of Australia's interests with those of America.

Before reviewing, in more detail, the state of Australia's relations with the world today, mention is necessary of the methods by which Australia has advanced its economic, as distinct from its political and defence interests. The promotion of economic interests is, for any country, especially difficult because the results are very meaningful for the material existence of its people and hence, in democratic countries, electorally. And, of course, the smaller a country, the harder it is for that country to defend and advance its interests. Notwithstanding, Australia has, over the many years since 1950, acquired an international reputation of being an awkward country in matters economic. It is a great trading nation and has therefore a very important stake in international economic co-operation. However, in this field, Australia has often shown a higher degree of selfishness than that required to achieve reasonable satisfaction, and has consistently revealed some inability to understand that others have interests which may be just as legitimate to them as Australia's interests are to it. Moreover, while Australia has, in words, been a principal supporter of free trade, it has, in actions, been an arch-practitioner of protectionism; outsiders would be quite entitled to feel that for Australia, free trade applies only to its exports, not its imports.

Relations with the superpowers

The predominant external influence upon Australia's foreign relationships today, as has been the case since World War II, is the United States. Most Australians want to maintain the intimate ties with America which exist in all fields; a lot of them would like to see the ties intensified. Official relations are very close, as witness the fact that the ANZUS Pact is the only security alliance which has never been called into question in the United States Congress. There are a number of highly important defence-related facilities on Australian soil which are operated jointly. There is much co-operation between the respective Armed Services and a major part of the equipment of the Australian Services comes from the United States. On the business front, there is a great deal of American investment in Australia, which has brought with it the technology required by Australian industry. Australia's enormous energy resources are of substantial value to the Western world as a whole. As communications across the Pacific have improved and become cheaper, contacts between the peoples of the two countries have grown. All in all, Australian-American relations are in good shape.

The danger is that into which Australia has fallen before, namely, that apprehension about security may lead once more to over-dependence upon the United States and hence a further interruption of the growth towards maturity as an independent country. There is also the danger of resurrection of the thinking which in the past has been shown as erroneous, namely, that the way to guarantee the protection of the United States is to follow unquestioningly. It is by no means clear that Australia is as yet fully aware of these pitfalls and while maintaining the closest links with the United States, is consciously prepared to avoid them. The best evidence lies in the offers made to the United States at the start of 1980 to establish a naval base in Western Australia and to use airfields in northern Australia for flights by strategic bombers, the latter of which was accepted. These offers indicated a readiness on Australia's part to accept in advance United States policies (in regard to politics and defence in regions and problem areas where the respective national interests could well be different), while the return, the defence of Australia, was not made any more sure.

If Australia's relations with the United States are very satisfactory, those with the other superpower, Russia, are bad. Since 1945, such relations have never been better than cordial and for most of the time, they have been hostile. By 1982, they had descended to the lowest point in 27 years. The cause was Russia's aggression in Afghanistan, which Australia, simplistically, regarded as the latest and most serious crime by Russia in the pursuit of world-wide, imperialistic ambitions. Like the United States and Britain, Australia saw that aggression as a move towards seeking control over the Persian Gulf region and its oil supplies. Apart from becoming one of Russia's most vociferous critics, Australia therefore decided to increase its expenditure upon defence by seven per cent in real terms (the highest increase in the West), joined enthusiastically in a programme of sanctions against Russia and came close to not sending a team to the Olympic Games at Moscow.

It is difficult to make out what, if anything, in the national interests required

---

ANDREW PEACOCK — Foreign Minister of panache

Australia has been fortunate in usually having over what is now a long period of time Foreign Ministers of calibre. Andrew Peacock held the portfolio from 1975 to 1980 and did the job with distinction.

Born in 1939, Peacock has crammed a lot of political life into a relatively short span. Educated as a lawyer, he is more a professional politician than anything else. Entering the Federal Parliament in 1966, he became Minister for the Army in 1969 and Minister for External Territories in 1972 (there playing his part in advancing Papua New Guinea to independence).

Peacock's chief assets are quickness of mind, energy, gregariousness, charm and a good sense of humour. He has also a highly developed public relations skill. Peacock cannot resist enjoying life, as some of his colleagues do, and this has earned him, unfairly, something of a reputation as a playboy. Certainly, Peacock likes the company of intelligent and beautiful people and makes no bones about this, but the propensity is sometimes exploited by his political opponents and rivals.

Peacock's great contribution to Australian foreign policy while Minister for Foreign Affairs was to make the policy of conservative governments more humane, more fair and less ideological. He revealed, and had Australia reveal, a marked sympathy for the plight of the Third World. Peacock was especially effective in developing Australia's relations with the United States where the pleasantness of his personality combined with his ability created for him a lot of useful, influential friends.

Clearly, Peacock has Prime Ministerial ambitions and this is normal. His promotion to the portfolio of Minister for Industrial Relations late in 1980 is evidence of progress towards his goal. Further evidence lies in the fact that shortly afterwards, he chose to quit the Government and to retire to the back bench in Parliament the better to make himself known as a potential leader. In pursuing this quest, Peacock will have to overcome what is a handicap in the national politics of Australia. That is, that he is a decent and honest person operating in an area where there is no premium for such qualities.

the adoption by Australia of such an extremely anti-Russian stance, particularly as it flowed from an assessment of Russia's motives which was never accepted fully by most Western nations and which was quickly and quietly abandoned by most of its advocates abroad. Certainly, strong condemnation of Russia by a responsible country like Australia was required but the impetuous rush into a range of sanctions, sanctions never having been effective in peace-time, was ill-advised. However, there was undoubtedly a perceived need to follow the United States, right or wrong as in the past, and there was the fear-syndrome, now seen not to have been dead, merely dormant. And, of course, anti-Communist stances had been very useful politically in the past and 1980 was an election year. Strange to relate, Australia, without fanfare, continued throughout 1980 to trade lucratively with Russia, even in one of the main areas subject to embargo, grains.

While, after 1945, Australia was obliged to turn away from Western Europe and embark upon a great expansion of relationships elsewhere, as with the United States and Asian countries, the traditional ties with Europe have remained strong. Although the part which Britain plays in the Australian economy has largely declined, affection and respect for the mother country linger on, at the same time as the decrease of Britain's economic stake has been somewhat offset by the growing stake of Britain's partners in the European Economic Community (the E.E.C.), such as France and West Germany. This, together with the migration from Europe which has continued since the end of World War II, although, in recent years, at a slackened pace, has tended to keep up Australia's closeness with the cradle of Western civilisation. It is true that intermittently there have been quite bitter, public arguments about agricultural protectionism within the E.E.C. (Britain having once been a secure market for a lot of Australia's primary products). However, there has always been something unreal about Australia's protestations, both because of Australia's own attachment to protectionism and because after Britain had entered the E.E.C., alternative markets to the British were found. Moreover, Australia was better able to stand the strain imposed upon its economy when Britain entered the E.E.C. by the arrival of its mineral boom. Overall, while leaders in Canberra right up to 1955 were fond of saying that Australia could not contract out of Europe, Australia has, in the intervening years, gone a long way in that direction, not because of any conscious wish to do so but because of the enormous changes in the world scene, such as the advent of the 'Pax America' (which may prove to be the shortest of such Pax in history), the rise of Japan as an economic giant, the emergence of China as a world power, the birth of the independent states of South-East Asia, and so on.

As a whole, such developments meant that for Australia, Europe came quite suddenly not to have the same degree of significance that historically it had had. Washington first supplanted London as the most important centre in the world in the eyes of leaders in Canberra but before long these same leaders came to appreciate that account had also to be taken of the outlook from a considerable number of other centres. One such centre was Tokyo. By dint of mutual effort aided by the way in which the economies complemented each other, Australia's relations with Japan were progressively built up after the conclusion of the Japanese Peace Treaty, this providing that rare phenomenon in Australian politics, an issue upon which all political parties agreed. Today, the relationship has reached a closeness inconceivable at the end of World War II. And whereas previously it had occasionally been punctuated by blazing commercial rows, these are no longer apparent. The absence of them testifies that the relationship has become mature.

Forging new relationships with Asian neighbours

Simultaneous with the *rapprochement* with Japan ran the establishment by Australia of connections with the newly independent countries of South-East Asia. While these countries, Indonesia, Malaysia, the Philippines and Singapore, as well as the long-independent Thailand, were experiencing political and economic fragility as the aftermath of war, Australia's friendship and assistance was appreciated. Later, as these countries entered into a period of unusual political stability and economic prosperity and as at the same time they drew closer together in the Association of South-East Asian Nations (ASEAN), Australia became of less significance to them. By 1980, its relations with the ASEAN countries had become quite cool. Australia was unwilling or unable to do anything effective to prevent the drift. In fact, it seemed indifferent, preferring a world rather than a regional role, especially as a virulent opponent of Russia. Insofar as Australia was not indifferent to the ASEAN countries, it chose to offend them by not affording adequate access to the Australian market for ASEAN manufactures. Then, also, Australia's relations with the most powerful member of the group, Indonesia, had long been troubled. Although Australia had, much earlier, played a major part in the establishment of Indonesia as an independent state, it thereafter came into conflict (on one occasion, armed conflict) with the country in three instances, each being a case of Indonesian aggression (West New Guinea, confrontation of Malaysia and East Timor). Each such episode left a mutual legacy of ill-feeling and unease.

Further to the north, Australia's relations with another very significant country of its region, Vietnam, had by 1980 become nothing more than a diplomatic formality. This was an abrupt change from 1973, when the relationship was begun in an atmosphere which suggested that the Vietnam War, at least as regards Australia and Vietnam, had been forgiven. The honeymoon was short-lived. When, in

---

SIR PAUL HASLUCK — the great servant of the State

Paul Meernaa Caedwalla Hasluck is one of the most outstanding personalities closely associated with the formulation and conduct of Australia's foreign relations in modern times. His is an extraordinary career, encompassing an unusual number of professions. In the autobiography of his early life, *Mucking About*, Hasluck claims that he was always something of a dabbler in what he was about at any time. This is not so; the secret of Hasluck's success in many fields was always to give to what he was doing the full measure of his talents.

A Western Australian, who has remained one to the core, born in 1905, Hasluck's first profession, in a succession of professions, was journalism. This was followed by a University appointment in history. The Second World War brought Hasluck into the Department of External Affairs in Canberra, temporarily, and he there became the principal adviser to Dr H. V. Evatt in post-war planning. As such, Hasluck went to the 1945 San Francisco Conference, which approved the United Nations Charter, and then went on to represent Australia with distinction at the United Nations until 1947. Resigning at that time from the diplomatic service, Hasluck returned home to become Reader in History at the University of Western Australia. In 1949, he was elected to the Commonwealth Parliament, there becoming Minister for Territories from 1951 to 1963 (his work in the portfolio entitles him to the reputation of the father of Papua New Guinea) and then, after a brief stint as Minister for Defence, Minister for External Affairs from 1964 to 1969. Subsequently, Hasluck rose to be Governor-General, at a time when many thought that had he chosen to play his cards differently, he would, before long, have been chosen as Prime Minister. Intermittently, since 1938,

Hasluck has been an author and he is one of the official war historians of Australia during the Second World War.

Hasluck's is a complex character. Not a gregarious person by nature, preferring reading and sports of a solitary kind, such as swimming and horse-riding, he yet has a lot of charm to display, is very supportive of friends and can be a fascinating companion. Despite what might be described as shyness, nearly all of Hasluck's chosen professions were those requiring much contact with people. Hasluck's tastes are catholic — literature, music, antiquity, sport, good food and wine, art and, of course, history. He has always been extremely hard-working.

The clue to Hasluck's career is duty, service to the people. A person not having any great interest in money or what money can buy, or in glory, not being particularly ambitious, Hasluck's dominating motive has been to serve the nation. And what is distinctive of Hasluck is that whereas other Australians in public life usually seek to promote their prospects of serving, Hasluck's approach was to await the call to serve; if it never came, so be it.

The principal foreign policy issue of Hasluck's time as Foreign Minister was the Vietnam War. It is hard to conceive that a person of his intelligence and background believed as deeply in Australian policy as his implementation of the policy suggested. As Hasluck is such a private person, as well as so responsible, one may never know Hasluck's real feelings about the war. He probably did not completely agree with Australia's approach but he felt that his task was not to question but to carry out to the best of his ability what had been laid down before he left the junior portfolio of Minister for Territories.

December, 1978, Vietnam invaded Kampuchea, Australia, discounting the provocation that Vietnam had earlier suffered, denounced the aggression roundly and terminated its aid programme, thereby ending the relationship for all practical purposes. Subsequently, Australia branded Vietnam as a 'surrogate' of Russia. Ironically, whatever be the truth in this judgment (and the lesson of history is that Vietnam is a fiercely independent country), if Australia's view was correct, Australia, by ostracising Vietnam, had helped to produce it. There was very little sense in Australia's policy. Clearly, Vietnam had not been forgiven for having won the Vietnam War; it had later compounded this crime by forming an alliance with Russia.

A consideration which influenced policy towards Vietnam was the friendship which Australia commenced in 1973 with China. Because of the subordination of policy to that of the United States and because of a failure to foresee the course of American policy under President Nixon, Australia was a latecomer in recognising and establishing relations with China. Nevertheless, once the step had been taken, the relationship flourished, being substantially aided after 1975 by the shared antipathy to Russia. This has brought considerable material benefits to Australia, notably, in the form of wheat sales. Perhaps, leaders in Canberra attach over-much importance to such dividends for, as often happens in the case of Australian ties with a much more powerful country, there is a perceptible tendency to be keen about everything that China does. For example, Australia gave implicit approval to China's testing in 1980 of intercontinental missiles in the Pacific Ocean, being the sole country to do so. Earlier, when in 1979 China made its punitive raid into Vietnam, Australia's rebuke was so mild as to be almost negligible yet the raid was just as much a case of aggression as that which caused it, namely, Vietnam's invasion of Kampuchea which had brought forth ringing denunciation from Canberra.

An area which has acquired more significance in Australia's eyes in recent years is the South Pacific. After World War II, Australia, with New Zealand, was very active in the region, being instrumental in having the South Pacific Commission (the S.P.C.) set up to provide technical assistance to the island territories. Later, intent upon the development of its relations with the United States and with the building up of the network of ties in Asia, Australia neglected the South Pacific, being helped to do so by the tranquillity which prevailed there. It was not to be long, however, before this tranquillity was disturbed by demands on the part of the leading island communities for independence, demands which led gradually to the transformation of the region into a collection mainly of small or 'mini', independent states. It has become the lot of Australia, alongside New Zealand, to provide guidance and aid to these fledgling countries, as and when requested, if for no other reason than that in 1976, for the first time, Russia displayed an interest in getting a toe-hold in the area (whereupon Australia quadrupled its aid programme). The provision of guidance and aid by Australia is not always easy as the new South Pacific states, being youthful, are jealous of their prerogatives, and being small, are wary of a much bigger country like Australia, and in at least one of them, Fiji, there are memories of what may be called, with some reason, Australian economic exploitation.

Australia takes pride, rightfully, in the record of its trusteeship over Papua New Guinea which, after 55 years, ended in 1975 when the territory became independent. Papua New Guinea must be the sole example of a colony which was granted independence without seeking it and which when offered independence, was reluctant to accept. The first seven years of Papua New Guinea's independence have shown that the decision was correct. Contrary to the many examples in recent history of rancorous relations between the former coloniser and the former colonised, Australia's ties with Papua New Guinea as an independent country have been harmonious. It is gratifying also for Australia that Papua New Guinea, a large state in South Pacific terms, is assuming a leading and responsible role in the region.

No account of Australia's foreign relations would be complete without treatment of the British Commonwealth of Nations. Time was when many Australians thought that once the Commonwealth expanded beyond the 'White Man's Club' of old, the institution would soon wither away. Yet, as the Commonwealth has, with each accretion in membership, grown less and less 'white', it has remained a force to be reckoned with in world affairs. For some time now, it has been regarded by Australia as having unique advantage in providing a bridge between a significant group of countries with widely different circumstances and interests, particularly those economic. An illustration of the enhanced value of the Commonwealth is that whereas Australia towards the end of World War II proposed the establishment of a Commonwealth Secretariat and received no support at all, the Secretariat was set up some time ago and has proved its usefulness. For its part, Australia has always been a staunch supporter of the Commonwealth, no matter what the political complexion of the government. Over the seven years leading up to 1982, this support has been especially evident, with Australia introducing in 1977 the concept of regional Commonwealth meetings. The results of the first two of such meetings cannot be said to have warranted the effort involved but Australia's initiative was proof of an even deeper belief by that country in the Commonwealth that it had evinced in the past. Further evidence of that deeper belief was also afforded in 1981, when for the first time in its history, Australia hosted a Commonwealth Heads of Government meeting (CHOGM).

Maturity still to be achieved

The overall state of Australia's foreign relations today, over 40 years after the quest for an indigenous approach was begun, shows that maturity in policy and in the conduct of it is still to be achieved. While Australia has in the time acquired a solid reputation as a responsible, principled member of the international community and one prepared to do its fair share in concerted efforts to maintain the peace and to improve the condition of human-kind, signs persist of a less than completely adult outlook upon the world. For one thing, the fear-syndrome deeply colours Australian thinking, as it has nearly always done, yet Australia is now stronger and wealthier than ever before and has a wide set of usually friendly relations covering the various regions. Having, in 1972–75, thrown off the consequence of fear — over-reliance upon the United States for protection — the same over-reliance has re-appeared by reason of an act of aggression by Russia far removed from Australia. For another thing, the national leaders act, as some of them have done in the past, as if Australia were a considerably more important country in world affairs than it is; they have yet to realise, for example, that few Americans, the citizens of Australia's greatest ally, really know anything about Australia. Hence, there is active public Australian involvement in the major issues of world politics, as if the old dictum, 'Peace is indivisible', were still valid, when countries comparable in power usually adopt, in regard to such issues, a lower posture. Australia would be well-advised to do the same and concentrate its attention upon regions and problems which are of special concern to it. Finally, Australia, after the courageous attempt of the years 1972–75, has reverted to the pristine reluctance to think independently and act independently when the national interests so dictate; the tradition of being a great follower lingers on. Only when Australia disposes of this tradition will it find the capacity to conduct its foreign relations in the way that an adult, independent country should. The fact that the task is unusually difficult is no excuse for shirking it.